Cbe New Century Bible

A. R. S. Kennedy

The New-Century Bible

GENERAL EDITOR:
PRINCIPAL WALTER F. ADENEY, M.A., D.D.

Samuel

INTRODUCTION
REVISED VERSION WITH NOTES
INDEX AND MAPS

EDITED BY THE

REV. A. R. S. KENNEDY, M.A., D.D.

PROFESSOR OF HEBREW AND SEMITIC LANGUAGES IN THE
UNIVERSITY OF EDINBURGH

NEW YORK: HENRY FROWDE

OXFORD UNIVERSITY PRESS, AMERICAN BRANCH

EDINBURGH: T. C. & E. C. JACK

1905

CONTENTS

THE BOOK OF SAMUEL

INTRODUCTION

I AND II SAMUEL

INTRODUCTION

I. THE PLACE OF SAMUEL IN THE O. T. CANON.

IN the ordinary Bible of English-speaking Protestants the books of the Old Testament will be found to be arranged in three groups, which have been termed, with sufficient accuracy, the *historical* (Genesis—Esther), the *poetical* (Job—Song of Songs[1]), and the *prophetical*[2] (Isaiah—Malachi). This arrangement, which was adopted directly from the Vulgate, the Latin Bible of the mediaeval Church, and ultimately from the Greek Version of the Seventy (LXX, see below, pp. 26 f.), differs considerably from the order in which the O. T. books are found in the manuscripts and printed editions of the Hebrew Bible. In these we also find three groups of books, representing the three stages in the historical growth of the Old Testament Canon, and named respectively the Law (*tôrā*), the Prophets (*nĕbî'îm*), and the Writings or Hagiographa (*kĕtûbîm*). The first division comprises the five books from Genesis to Deuteronomy, now generally termed the Pentateuch. The second is made up of two smaller groups or subdivisions, to which the Jewish authorities have given the names of the 'Former' and the 'Latter Prophets.' The 'Former Prophets' comprise the four books of Joshua, Judges, Samuel, and Kings, while the

---

[1] This is the more accurate title which the 'Song of Solomon' bears in the R. V., being a translation of the heading of the poem in the Hebrew Bible.

[2] The above nomenclature goes back at least to Gregory of Nazianzus (see Swete, *Introduction to the O. T. in Greek*, 205).

'Latter Prophets' are also reckoned to contain four books, viz. Isaiah, Jeremiah, Ezekiel, and the book of the twelve so-called Minor Prophets. The remaining books of the Canon find a place among the Hagiographa.

In this arrangement of its sacred Scriptures adopted by the Jewish Church, therefore, the Book of Samuel ranks among the writings of the Prophets, the significance of which for the proper understanding of the true aim of the Hebrew historians will appear in the sequel. The expression 'Book of Samuel' has been used advisedly in the above context—and also frequently in the following pages—since the present division of the Hebrew text into two books is of comparatively recent origin, having been introduced, along with a similar partition of Kings and Chronicles, by Daniel Bomberg, the famous Venetian printer, in the second edition of his Hebrew Bible (1517). In this Bomberg was simply following the lead of the Greek and Latin Versions, in which the books of Samuel and Kings together are entitled the First, Second, Third and Fourth Books of Kingdoms (LXX) or of Kings (Vulgate). From the Vulgate are derived also the titles which stand at the head of the two Books of Samuel in the Authorized Version (A. V.), 'the First (Second) Book of Samuel, otherwise called the First (Second) Book of the Kings.' The latter designation has now fallen into disuse, and has been rightly dropped in the Revised Version (R.V.).

That a book, which continues to relate the fortunes of Saul and David for nearly forty years after the death of Samuel, should bear his name is clearly not to be explained by the curious opinion of later Judaism that Samuel was its author. Even such a modification of this view as would accept him as the author of the first part of the book has been shown to be untenable by modern research into its literary structure (see sect. iv below). The explanation of the title is rather to be sought in the fact that the birth and call of Samuel form the theme of the opening chapters, or in the prominent part played by the Seer of Ramah in the establishment of the monarchy. The first two kings, it will be remembered, each received consecration at his hands (1 Sam. x. 1, xvi. 13). We have here, in short, the Book of Samuel 'the King-maker.'

II. ARRANGEMENT AND CONTENTS OF SAMUEL.

With the exception of the Psalter, no O. T. book gives such unmistakable evidence of systematic arrangement on the part of its editor or editors as does the Book of Samuel. The presence, at certain well-defined intervals, of three concluding summaries from editorial hands clearly betrays the design of a fourfold division of our book. The summaries in question are (1) 1 Sam. xiv. 47–51, a brief *résumé* of the wars of Saul, with an equally brief family record; (2) 2 Sam. viii, which is entirely occupied with a more extended summary of David's campaigns (1–14) and a list of the chief officers of his court (15–18), with which the family lists now found in 2 Sam. iii. 2–5 and v. 13–16 were in all probability originally associated; (3) 2 Sam. xx. 23–26, which is practically a duplicate of viii. 15 ff. (for the explanation see p. 25). The remaining four chapters of the book are evidently of the nature of an appendix.

As regards the contents, it may be said, briefly, that in the Book of Samuel we have all that the editors of the exilic and early post-exilic periods thought worthy of preservation regarding the greatest of the Hebrew kings, his predecessor, Saul, and the imposing religious personality who forms the connecting link between the monarchy and the period of the Judges.

The following synopsis shows the four divisions of the book just indicated with appropriate subdivisions. For convenience of expository study, the latter have been further subdivided in the body of the commentary into sections, the extent and contents of which are indicated at the proper places in the notes.

First Division. 1 Samuel I—XIV.

Samuel and Saul.

A. i–vii.   The Early Life and Judgeship of Samuel.

B. viii–xii.   The Establishment of the Monarchy.

C. xiii–xiv.   Saul's First Campaign against the Philistines.

Second Division. 1 Samuel XV—2 Samuel VIII.

Saul and David.

A. xv–xx.   The Rejection of Saul and Introduction of David. Saul's Jealousy and its Results.

B. xxi–xxvi.   David's flight from Court and his subsequent Adventures as an Outlaw Captain in the South.

C. xxvii–xxxi.   David as the Vassal of the King of Gath. The Philistine Invasion and Death of Saul and Jonathan.

D. 2 Sam. i–viii.   David installed as King, first of Judah, then of all Israel.

Third Division. 2 Samuel IX—XX.

At the Court of David.

A. ix.   David's Kindness to Meri-baal.

B. x–xii.   David's War with the Ammonites, including the Affair of Bath-sheba.

C. xiii–xiv.   Amnon and Absalom.

D. xv–xix.   The Story of Absalom's Rebellion.

E. xx.   The Revolt of Sheba.

Fourth Division. 2 Samuel XXI—XXIV.

An Appendix of Various Contents.

A. xxi. 1–14.   The Famine and its Consequences for the House of Saul.

B. xxi. 15–22.   A Series of Exploits against the Philistines.

C. xxii.   David's Thanksgiving Hymn.

D. xxiii. 1–7.   David's 'Last Words.'

E. xxiii. 8–39.   David's Two Orders of Knighthood.

F. xxiv.   David's Census and its Consequences.

III. CHARACTERISTICS OF THE OLDER HISTORICAL LITERATURE.

Apart from the five books of the Law, the more strictly historical books of the O. T. form two distinct and, to some extent, parallel groups, an earlier group comprising the books of the 'Former Prophets,' Joshua, Judges, Samuel and Kings, as explained above, and a later group now included among the Hagiographa, and consisting of the two Books of Chronicles, with Ezra and Nehemiah, the four having originally formed a single continuous narrative in the order given. In addition to this difference of position in the Jewish Canon, the two groups are sharply distinguished from each other by the nature of their general interests, and by a marked difference of religious standpoint. The later group, as represented by the Books of Chronicles, is dominated by ecclesiastical interests [1], and reflects throughout the tone and standpoint of the Priestly Code (for which see Bennett's *Genesis* in this series, pp. 34 ff.). The earlier group, to which the Book of Samuel belongs, requires and will repay a more extended study.

(*a*) *The beginnings of historical literature among the Hebrews.* 'The making of history,' writes Professor Moore of Andover [2], 'precedes the writing of history, and it is often found that the impulse to write history is first given by some great achievement, which exalts the self-consciousness of a people and awakens the sense of the memorable character of what it has done.' As illustrative instances Moore cites the struggle of Greece with Persia, the second Punic war and its influence on Rome, and the empire of Charles the Great among the Germans. In

---

[1] 'The Chronicler's work is an ecclesiastical history; the Jewish Church in Jerusalem is its subject' (Moore, *EBi.* ii. 2085).

[2] See his admirable article 'Historical Literature' in the second volume of Cheyne and Black's *Encyclopaedia Biblica* (denoted in these pages by *EBi.*).

the same way, the first impulse to historical writing among the Hebrews was given by the prolonged struggle with the Philistines for the mastery of Palestine, a struggle which seems to have absorbed almost the whole energies of Saul during his comparatively short reign (1 Sam. xiv. 52), and which was carried to a victorious issue by his great successor.

From another but closely connected point of view, it may without hesitation be affirmed that those material conditions, which have everywhere been found to be indispensable for the cultivation of literature, were first secured to the Hebrews in the reigns of David and Solomon. The former was a capable statesman as well as an able general. To David was due not only the consolidation of the tribes of north and south into a united people, but the introduction of a stable government with an administration suited to the needs of the time. Under the more peaceful reign of his son the kingdom of Israël reached a height of material prosperity to which the land had been a stranger for centuries. With so much in that glorious time to re-create and quicken the national consciousness, enfeebled by two centuries of tribal jealousy and dissension—witness the Song of Deborah (Judges v)—and to fire the imaginations of the more thoughtful spirits of the age, it would be surprising if no literature should spring to birth. Doubtless the most of what was sung and written in the 'golden prime' of Solomon has long since perished. But one historical work, at least, has in great part survived, perhaps the finest flower of Hebrew narrative in the O. T. This is the history of David's family and court which now occupies chapters ix–xx of 2 Samuel, and is continued in the first two chapters of the Book of Kings. Whether the other early narrative, which opens with 1 Sam. ix and tells of the institution of the monarchy and of David's relations to Saul, is part of the same document, as some recent scholars maintain, must here be left an open question (see pp. 21 f.). In any case its date can scarcely be later than the reign of Rehoboam (cf. 1 Sam. xxvii. 6). The view to which expression has just been given that the first essays in historical writing among the Hebrews were made soon after the national revival under David, with the great events of the recent past for their theme, and that only afterwards was the history of the remoter past taken in hand, is the view of most recent students of Hebrew historiography (Stade, Kittel, Budde, Moore, Kent, &c.).

(b) *The two main types of ancient history*[1]. In all ancient literatures the oldest type of historical writing is the *narrative* or *descriptive* type. The writer's aim is to set down the incidents he deems worthy of preservation in such a way as to convey to his readers an accurate impression of their nature and sequence. It is no part of his purpose to draw religious or other lessons from the facts he records. The story is left to point its own moral. Of this kind of history 2 Sam. ix–xx, above referred to, is a classical illustration (see further, pp. 20 ff. and note on 2 Sam. xii, p. 244).

In almost all cases the narrative type of history is succeeded, but not superseded, by the *didactic* type. For the didactic or pragmatic historian the story of the past is not the bare record of a series of successive happenings[2], but a storehouse of political, moral, and religious lessons for the men of the present. That the historian's chief end is the education of the race has been firmly held by some of our most eminent English historians. Thus a recent writer, himself an historian, has said of the late S. R. Gardiner: 'In his conception, if history was not

---

[1] With the following paragraphs compare the fuller treatment of this topic by Professor Skinner in the Introduction to his commentary on *Kings* in this (Century Bible) series, pp. 5 ff. and Moore's article cited above.

[2] An expression suggested by Droysen's almost untranslatable distinction between nature as 'das Nebeneinander des Seienden,' and history as 'das Nacheinander des Gewordenen.'

directly didactic, the writing of it is a vain labour;
and the true scientific historian is he who most conscien-
tiously seeks to ascertain and present the lessons which
the past has to offer[1].'

Now, among the Hebrews, it was pre-eminently the
prophets of the eighth century before Christ who first
made this conception of history a feature of their teaching. 'The prophets of the eighth century interpreted
Yahweh's dealings with His people upon a consistent
moral principle; the evils which afflict the nation and the
graver evils which are imminent are Divine judgements
upon it for its sins ... The application of this principle
by the writers of the seventh and sixth centuries makes
an era in Hebrew historiography; narrative history
is succeeded by pragmatic history' (Moore). In 1 Sam.
xv we have a good example of the pragmatic or didactic
treatment of the tradition[2] respecting Saul's rejection by
Samuel at Gilgal. The historical incident is used in the
spirit of the prophets to enforce the moral lesson that
obedience 'is better than sacrifice' (1 Sam. xv. 22).·

(c) *The Deuteronomic school of historians.* The pro-
mulgation of the legislation of Deuteronomy in the eigh-
teenth year of Josiah (622–621 B.C.) gave an immediate
and far-reaching impulse to the didactic method of
historical writing. The quickly following calamity of the
Exile set the seal of the Divine approval upon the prophetic
interpretation of the past, and in the Exile, accordingly,
the didactic treatment of the pre-exilic history reached
its highest development. From the circumstance that
the devout writers and editors of this period (*circa* 620–

---

[1] P. Hume Brown in Chambers' *Encycl. of English Literature*
(1903), vol. iii. 631. Cf. the same writer's judgement on
Carlyle and Froude, ibid. 500.

[2] On 'the popular misconception that the word "tradition"
implies that the literature thus designated is necessarily un-
trustworthy and unhistorical,' see the excellent remarks of
Professor Kent in his *Beginnings of Heb. History* (1904), p. 4.

450 B.C.) drew their inspiration and their ideals mainly from the Book of Deuteronomy, they have appropriately been named the Deuteronomic or Deuteronomistic school of historians. It is to this school that we owe, in the main, the historical books of the O. T. from Joshua to Kings. This is not to be understood as implying that the chief part of the contents of these books was then first committed to writing, but in the sense that the books in question received, if not the precise form in which we now have them (see sect. vi), yet a form not essentially different at the hands of editors of this school.

The principles which guided the Deuteronomic editors in their treatment of the older narrative histories have been so fully and so ably expounded by Professor Skinner in his Introduction to the Books of Kings (pp. 14 ff.; cf. Thatcher's *Judges*—also in the present series—pp. 5 ff.) [1], that it is unnecessary to enlarge upon them here (but see on 1 Sam. xii. 14), all the more as these principles are but little in evidence in the Book of Samuel compared with their more detailed and systematic application to the Books of Judges and Kings (cf. sect. v below). It must suffice to say, in general terms, that the primary aim of the exilic historians of Israel was not to hand down to posterity a minute and objective history of the chosen people, but *to interpret to their contemporaries God's discipline in history of His people* in the light of the teaching of Deuteronomy, and of the great prophets of whose inspired thoughts Deuteronomy is, in a sense, the literary deposit. This conscious aim determined the selection of their materials from the fuller historical records at their command ; hence the scant treatment which Saul and his reign receive in 1 Samuel ; hence the reduction to bald summaries of David's relations with the

---

[1] See also Moore, *EBi.* ii. 2079, and more fully Wildeboer's chapter on the Deuteronomic conception of history in his *Litteratur des alten Testaments.* 229 ff., esp. 242 f.

Philistines and the other neighbouring states, and of the internal administration of his realm in 2 Samuel; hence, too, the many regrettable omissions in the political history of North Israel in the Book of Kings.

Nevertheless these earnest students and teachers of the Exile were also in their measure prophets, for they were in a very real sense God's 'interpreters' (Isa. xliii. 27 R.V.), men on whom God had put His Spirit (Num. xii. 29) as a spirit of interpretation. The results of their labours have found their proper place in the Hebrew Canon among 'the prophets.' History, in short, as written and compiled by such men is ' prophecy teaching by example[1].' Its lessons, in consequence, are not 'of an age' but for all time.

(d) *The literary methods of Hebrew historians.* Before we pass from the subject of this section a word requires to be said regarding the literary methods of Hebrew historians generally and of the Deuteronomic school in particular. The primary aim of this school, we have just seen, was to impress upon the minds and hearts of their readers the moral and religious lessons which the Divine discipline of Israel was so fitted to teach them. In their pursuit of this aim the method adopted—and it is the method of oriental historiography in general (see Robertson Smith's *Old Testament in the Jewish Church*, 2nd ed., p. 328 ; cf. 113 f.)—presents a striking contrast to the methods of the modern historian of the West. The latter sets himself to master his authorities and original sources, and then seeks to give literary form to the history in his own words and his own style. The Hebrew historian, on the other hand, did this but rarely unless when, as in the case of the earliest of all, he had to draw his materials from oral tradition. As a rule he was content to reproduce, as far as was consistent with his

---

1 The aphorism is Moore's (*EBi.* ii. 2079), and is a happy adaptation of Bolingbroke's dictum (from Dionysius of Halicarnassus) that 'history is philosophy teaching by example.'

purpose, the very words of his documentary sources, weaving his extracts into a connected narrative, while scrupulously preserving their colour and style. It was enough if he supplied the necessary connecting links, harmonized, so far as was deemed advisable or possible, the more glaring discrepancies, and perhaps passed judgement on the actors and the incidents from his higher moral and religious standpoint.

This uniform characteristic of Hebrew historiography explains why modern scholars prefer to speak of the compiler, rather than of the author, of Samuel or Kings or the Pentateuch. Fortunately also, it makes possible, in large measure, the task which lies before us in the next section of this Introduction.

IV. THE SOURCES OF THE BOOK OF SAMUEL

Like the Pentateuch, and like the other books associated with it in the canonical group of the 'Former Prophets,' Samuel has disclosed itself to modern research as a compilation from a number of previously existing historical documents. In the preceding section we have learned something of the aims and methods of the compilers and editors who gave to the historical books what was essentially their present form, and how the fidelity with which they have reproduced these older documents with all their original characteristics of style and representation has enabled modern scholars to separate and study, each by itself, the works of these earliest historians of Israel.

The credit of having first laid down the main lines along which the literary analysis of Samuel must proceed belongs, above all, to Julius Wellhausen [1], with whom the

---

[1] In his edition (the fourth) of Bleek's *Einleitung in das alte Test.* (1878), afterwards in his *Comp. des Hexateuchs*; for these and the other works referred to see the bibliographical list in the Appendix, note B (cf. H. P. Smith, *Samuel*, xxviii f.).

names of Budde and Cornill must be honourably associated. With regard to the results of the critical labours
of these and other recent scholars, details of which will
presently be laid before the reader, it may be said that
there is now a general consensus of opinion among
critical students as to the broad lines of demarcation
between the various 'sources' of the book. On the other
hand, there is still considerable divergence, as will appear
in the sequel, as regards the number, age, and mutual
relations of the documents which the analysis has disclosed, and as to the details of the literary process by
which the Book of Samuel has gradually assumed its
present form. While the general outline of this process
is sufficiently clear as involving three distinct stages of
growth—represented by the original documents circulating
independently, the Deuteronomic edition and the post-
Deuteronomic or present canonical edition respectively
(see below)—there is much of the detail that admits of
more than one plausible explanation, so that Stade's
verdict is not far from the truth that 'the history of the
origin of the Books of Samuel, in spite of the great predominance of the ancient sources, is very complicated'
(article 'Samuel,' *EBi.* iv. 4274). In a popular work
such as the present it would manifestly be out of place to
enter into the minute details of the literary and historical
criticism of Samuel; it will be sufficient to indicate in
broad outline the nature of the critical argument.

(*a*) *Analysis of 1 Sam. i-xiv.* Our study of the sources
may begin with an examination of the structure of the
first of the four divisions of Samuel, in which the composite nature of the present narrative is peculiarly evident. The most promising starting-point is provided by
the second subdivision, 1 Sam. viii-xii[1], which gives a

---

[1] As an illustration of method the study of this section has
been given in more detail than is possible or necessary in the
case of the others.

detailed account of the introduction of the monarchy and of Saul's election as the first king of Israel. The following is a summary of the contents of these five chapters as they now stand. Moved to action by the unworthy character and conduct of his sons, the elders of Israel approach the aged Samuel, as the theocratic representative of Yahweh, with the request that he would appoint a king to rule over Israel, after the manner of the surrounding nations. This request Samuel regards as treason to Yahweh, but is advised by Him to accede to the people's demand (ch. viii). At this juncture Samuel makes the acquaintance, under interesting circumstances, of a Benjamite noble, Saul, the son of Kish, and is divinely informed that this is the man whom Yahweh has appointed to be the deliverer of His people from the Philistine oppression and their future king. Saul is anointed by Samuel (x. 1), and instructed as to certain signs by which Yahweh's gracious purpose with regard to him will be confirmed. The Divine choice is afterwards ratified by the arbitrament of the sacred lot at Mizpah (chapters ix-x). As yet, however, Saul is only king *de iure*, but soon afterwards an opportunity occurs for him to show his capacity for military leadership (xi. 1 ff.)—he had meanwhile returned to his farm—and the people are thereafter summoned by Samuel to Gilgal ' to renew the kingdom there' (xi. 14). At Gilgal Saul is solemnly confirmed in the kingship, and is henceforth king *de facto*. Samuel at the same time takes an impressive farewell of the people, reserving only to himself the office of intercessor with Yahweh in the new and doubtful situation in which his compatriots have placed themselves (xii).

Now it is impossible to read the complete narrative in these chapters without receiving the impression that *the dominant note is one of hostility to the monarchy as an institution*. But a closer examination reveals the fact that this attitude is not maintained throughout, but is confined to certain sections of the narrative. Viewing

chapter viii in the light thrown upon it by the preceding
chapter, of which it is the continuation, we see that Israel
is conceived as living in an ideal state of peace and
security under theocratic government, untroubled by foes
from without or from within (vii. 14).   The request for
a human king, 'to judge us like all the nations' (viii. 5), is an
act of rebellion against Yahweh, their true King (xii. 12),
since the theocracy is the form of government under
which His people were intended by God to fulfil their
mission to the world.

In chapter ix, on the other hand, the condition of
Yahweh's 'people Israel' is one of sore 'affliction' (see
note on ix. 16) at the hands of the Philistines.   Yahweh
has 'heard their cry,' and of His own free will resolves
to give them a king in the person of Saul.   *Here the
monarchy is God's gracious gift to His people.*   In this
chapter, furthermore, the picture of Samuel as the
comparatively unknown seer of a country village (ix. 6 ff.)
offers a striking contrast to that of Samuel the theocratic
judge of all Israel, the all-powerful vicegerent of Yahweh,
as he appears in chapters vii, viii and xii.

Following the clues thus provided (1) by the radically
opposed attitudes to the monarchy, and (2) by the
divergent representations of the then political condition
of Israel and of the person of Samuel, it is not difficult to
analyse chapters viii–xii into two mutually independent
documents.   These, for reasons to be given presently, we
shall denote by the symbols D and M.   We have then :—

D (hostile to the monarchy) : viii. 1–22 [closely connected with ch. vii], x. 17–24, xii. 1–25.

M (favourable to the monarchy) : ix. 1–x. 16, xi. 1–11,
15 [continued xiii. 2–7ª, 15ᵇ–18, 23, xiv. 1–46, 52].

The verses not found in either of the above series are
from the hand of the compiler or redactor (R, see p. 24), and
are due to the necessity of providing, so far as this could be
done, a chronologically and otherwise consistent narrative
from the two documents at his command.   There is good

reason, also, for believing that the compiler has, from the same motive (see in detail, p. 74), been led to rearrange the sections of **D** in an order different from that in which they originally stood. Since the document beginning ix. 1, and continued in chs. xiii–xiv, is so entirely favourable to the institution of the Monarchy, the introduction and early history of which it is clearly its writer's purpose to record, we propose in the following pages to indicate it by the symbol **M**. The other, which, as will immediately appear, betrays an unmistakable affinity with the Book of Deuteronomy, will be denoted by **D**.

As to the relative value of the two documents as authorities for the history of Samuel and Saul, there can be no question that **M** is more in harmony with the actual conditions of the time, as these are reflected in the previous and subsequent course of Hebrew history. In **D** we have rather an illustration of the later idealization of the earlier portions of the history of Israel, such as we find in the ideal representation of the conquest of Canaan in the Book of Joshua as contrasted with the more historical account in the first chapter of Judges (cf. p. 68). The ideal traits in **D**'s treatment of the period of Samuel is still more apparent in ch. vii. Take, for example, the statement that 'the Philistines came no more within the border of Israel . . . all the days of Samuel,' which is directly at variance not only with the equally precise statement in 1 Sam. xiv. 52, but with all that we know of the historical circumstances which gave birth to the monarchy. The numerous resemblances in expression and general standpoint between those chapters of 1 Samuel assigned to **D**, on the one hand, and the Book of Deuteronomy and the characteristically Deuteronomic parts of Judges and Kings on the other, have been convincingly demonstrated by Löhr in his recent edition of Thenius' commentary, pp. xxii ff.[1]

---

[1] That the chapters in question are a product of the Deuteronomic school is also maintained by Wellhausen, Kuenen,

As to the date of **D**, it is impossible to speak with certainty. Its pronounced hostility to the monarchy, to which reference has so frequently been made, implies a long and unhappy experience of monarchical government. This fact, together with certain linguistic features, especially in ch. xii (see p. 91), seems to point to a date in the Exile. If such is indeed the case we have in this document the bitter reflections of a member of the Deuteronomic school, who regarded the defections and excesses of the monarchy as largely responsible for the sins of the people, and the consequent destruction of the state.

Passing now to the opening chapters of the book, we find in chapters i–iii, when freed from the later expansions ii. 1–10 and ii. 27–36 (see pp. 42, 48), a fragment of a biography of Samuel (hence the symbol **S**). Since its representation of the *prophet*, who is held in esteem throughout 'all Israel, from Dan to Beer-sheba' (iii. 20), differs materially both from the *theocratic judge* of ch. vii, and from the *seer of Ramah* in ch. ix, it must be regarded as an independent source. If, as is at least probable, xv. 1—xvi. 13 originally formed part of this biography, its author may have been a contemporary of Jeremiah (see on xv. 22 and xvi. 7).

In chapters iv–vi, finally, we have still another document which, from the antique cast of the religious ideas underlying it, particularly as regards the Ark (hence our symbol **A**), must be of a considerably earlier date than the preceding chapters. It is now a torso, both the commencement and the continuation having been dropped by the compiler (pp. 56, 67). From the fact that no explanation is now given of how the 'affliction' of Israel at the hands of the Philistines (ix. 16) was brought about, some scholars are of opinion that chapters iv–vi (see on vii. 1 ; cf. iv. 9) originally formed part of the document we have termed **M**.

Stade, H. P. Smith, Nowack, and others in opposition to Budde and Cornill, who regard them as, with 1 Sam. i-iii, a continuation of the Hexateuch source E, which has been revised merely by a Deuteronomic hand (see further, p. 22).

As in a similar case which will emerge in the sequel, this view has much to recommend it, but we prefer, here as there (pp. 21 f.), to leave the question an open one.

(b) Analysis of 1 Sam. xv—2 Sam. viii. By the insertion of the concluding summary (xiv. 47–51) the Deuteronomic editor or redactor (R) would indicate that henceforth the central figure of the narrative is to be no longer Saul but another. The way is prepared for the entry of this new character upon the scene by the rejection of Saul (xv), which is followed immediately by the consecration of his successor (xvi. 1–13), both incidents, as has been already indicated (see more fully pp. 110, 116 below), being probably derived from the prophetic biography of Samuel (S).

With the second introduction of David (cf. the introductory note, p. 116) in xvi. 14 ff. the problem of the literary analysis becomes complicated with another involving the question of the original text of the two following chapters. These problems, both literary and textual, will be found discussed in some detail in the notes, where the reasons are set forth for adopting the shorter form presented by the Greek text. The additional matter now found in our Massoretic text has been stamped as a later expansion of the true text by having the symbol Z prefixed. Apart from this post-redactional matter, to which such remarkable sections as xix. 18–24 and xxi. 10–15 fall to be added, the whole of the narrative of this division (more precisely from xvi. 14 to 2 Sam. vi. 23) has, with comparatively few exceptions, been drawn from the early document (M), which gave us the most trustworthy account of the introduction of the monarchy [1]. These exceptions consist for the most part of such inci-

---

[1] Compare the following list of mutually connected passages in this division of Samuel given by Driver (after Wellhausen) in *LOT.* p. 184, footnote : 1 Sam. xviii. 7 and xxix. 5; xviii. 25, 27 (LXX) and 2 Sam. iii. 14 ; 1 Sam. xxii. 20 ff. and xxiii. 9 ff. ; xxiii. 2, xxx. 8 and 2 Sam. ii. 1, v. 19; 1 Sam. xxv. 2 ff. and xxx. 26 ff. ; xxvii. 3 and xxx. 5.

dents of David's chequered life at this period as must have formed the favourite themes of the popular tradition of the time (hence the symbol T, see pp. 135 f.). The most interesting of these is the tale of David's magnanimity to Saul now found in 1 Sam. xxiii. 19—xxiv. 22, which is almost certainly a variant of the older, and, in some respects, more trustworthy form of the same incident as related in ch. xxvi[1]. To the documentary source or sources from which the compiler derived these popular traditions we have no clue.

The promise of the permanence of David's dynasty recorded in 2 Sam. vii—a passage of cardinal importance for the study of the evolution of Israel's Messianic Hope —is recognized on all hands as at once a document apart, and as a product of the Deuteronomic school. Since a descendant of David is still evidently on the throne of Judah, its date may with some confidence be assigned to the period *circa* 600 B. C.

Chapter viii, finally, is the editorial summary, not merely closing this division of the book, but, as we shall see reason to believe (see next section), originally forming the conclusion to the first or Deuteronomic edition of Samuel. The literary feature of 1 Sam. xv—2 Sam. viii is thus the predominance of one leading authority (M), which has been supplemented by the Deuteronomic editor from other sources (S, D, T), the whole having, in the course of transmission, received a number of post-redactional expansions (Z), for which see section vi.

(c) *The unity of 2 Sam. ix-xx.* The third division of Samuel is to all intents and purposes a literary unit[2]. In virtue of their perfect style and their life-like portraiture, the amount of picturesque detail and the often dramatic intensity of the action, these twelve chapters constitute

---

[1] For numerous other duplicate narratives in Samuel, see under 'doublets' in the Index.

[2] See Driver, *LOT.*[6] 183, for the mutual connexion of the incidents, and cf. the introductory note p. 250 below.

the finest, as they are the earliest, specimen of continuous prose narrative in the O. T. The writer's interest is centred throughout in the person of David and in the members of his family and court (hence the symbol C). With the same impartiality are recorded David's loyalty to the memory of his dearest friend (ix), his own great sin and the sins of his family, which brought scandal on his court and sorrow on his old age. The original commencement has been dropped (see on ix. 1), but the continuation and probable close are still found in 1 Kings i-ii. The freshness and vividness of the narrative and the abundance of minute personal detail compel us to see in the author one who either himself played a part in the events he so graphically records, or has derived his information, at first hand, from those whose names are for ever enshrined in his pages[1].

The abruptness with which C now opens at 2 Sam. ix. 1 has been already mentioned. Are Budde and Cornill right in their contention that C is simply the continuation of the other early document which we have termed M? There is undoubtedly much to be said for this view. Few readers would venture to say that such admirably conceived chapters as 1 Sam. xiv, xxii, xxv and xxvi are unworthy to be compared with the best chapters of C. And yet in other cases it is difficult to escape the conclusion that the incidents recorded reflect rather the plastic mould of popular tradition, and a greater distance from the events than we find in C. On the whole, therefore, it is better to leave the question open. In any case M is also a source of undoubted antiquity, and, equally with C, may confidently be assigned to the tenth century.

---

[1] See Klostermann, *Die Bücher Samuelis und Könige*, p. xxii f., for the interesting suggestion that the author is no other than Ahimaaz, the son of Zadok who figures repeatedly in the story of Absalom's rebellion. Duhm, on the other hand, regards the family of Abiathar (see on 1 Sam. xxii. 20) as the source of these chapters, an alternative preferred by Budde to the other (see Duhm, *Das Buch Jeremia*, p. 3).

Allusion has just been made to the view of Budde and Cornill that M and C (in large part A also) are one and the same document. This is perhaps the proper place for a reference to the literary theory of Samuel associated with the names of these eminent scholars. · It is, in brief, that the contents of Samuel have been drawn in the main from two earlier historical works which practically cover the same ground, after the manner of the J and E narratives of the Pentateuch[1]. Indeed the scholars above named go so far as, if not absolutely to identify the sources of Samuel with the J and E sources of the Hexateuch, at least to maintain that they are the continuation of the latter[2] (roughly, Budde's J = our A, M, C ; his E = our S, D, T).

(d) *The appendix, 2 Sam. xxi–xxiv.* Of the six parts or sections of this appendix (for the contents, see page 6), the first and sixth, the story of the three years' famine

---

[1] The same view, practically, is advocated by H. P. Smith in his *Commentary on Samuel.* The two parallel sources he denotes by Sl and Sm. Budde has also secured the adherence of Driver in his *Introduction* and of Stenning in his article 'Samuel' in Hastings' *DB.* iv. 383 ff.

[2] This theory of the mutual relation of the various sources which the critical analysis has brought to light thus stands in somewhat sharp contrast to the position adopted in the foregoing pages, which in its essential features is that of Wellhausen, Kuenen, Stade, and Löhr. But not only Budde but also the other critics just named seem to the present writer to base a large part of their analysis from 1 Sam. xv onwards on a mistaken view of the relation between xvi. 14 ff. and xvii. 1 ff. In the former passage, it is asserted, David is a man of mature age and already a warrior of distinction, while in the latter he is but a shepherd-boy, fresh from his father's flocks. Consequently the two passages and their continuations must belong to different sources. It will be our endeavour in the notes (see especially pp. 119-122) to show on how insecure a foundation this supposed distinction rests, and that in what appears to us to be the original form of the text no such 'irreconcilable' difference is to be found. For the further question of the presence of J and E in Samuel see the unfavourable verdicts of Kittel (*Studien und Kritiken,* 1892, 61 ff.) and Smith (*Journ. of Bib. Literature,* xv (1896), 1 ff.

and that of the three days' pestilence, are closely connected both in style and contents (see the notes on each).
The incidents of both, moreover, must be assigned to the
early part of David's reign, but for various reasons it is
unlikely that they form part of either of our two earliest
sources. In the commentary they are grouped among the
other miscellaneous additions (Z), the question of their
date being left undetermined.

Between these two cognate sections there seems to
have been driven, first of all, a wedge in the shape of a
list of David's heroes with some achievements of the
more celebrated. This list, in its turn, was rent in two
by the further insertion of the much later poetical pieces
(xxii and xxiii. 1–7). The two lists thus created, now
found in xxi. 15–22 and xxiii. 8–39, are generally admitted
to contain ancient and genuine historical material (see
e. g. the note on xxi. 19). Inasmuch as the exploits recorded seem to belong almost exclusively to the period
of David's early struggles with the Philistines, of which
M has preserved a fragmentary record in 2 Sam. v. 17–25,
it is highly probable that the lists in question stood originally in that early source (see further on 2 Sam. v. 17).

All that is necessary to be said on the subject of
David's Thanksgiving Hymn and his 'Last Words' will
be found in the notes.

V. THE DEUTERONOMIC EDITION OF SAMUEL[1].

It remains now to present a broad constructive view,
omitting all details, of the process by which the Book of
Samuel took shape at the hands of its Deuteronomic
editor, as this may be inferred from the internal evidence
of the book itself. Among the most precious of the literary
treasures which the Exiles carried with them to their new
homes 'by the rivers of Babylon' were two historical

[1] Cf. what has been said under section iii of the aims and
methods of this school.

works dating from the first century of the monarchy (**C** and **M**), each of which had David for its theme. Or it may be that these had long since been joined together, if indeed they had not been one from the outset. The first-fruits of the new school of historians had already appeared. This was the first edition of Kings, giving the history of the kingdoms of Judah and Israel from the accession of Solomon (see Skinner, *Kings*, 18 ff.), for which its editor had appropriated, as a suitable introduction, the original close of the court memoirs of David (1 Kings i-ii, from **C**). For a whole generation, if the date above suggested (p. 18) for 1 Sam. vii and xii be accepted, men were content, as well they might, with the history of the early monarchy as told by **M** and **C**. But towards the close of the Exile a Deuteronomic writer, imbued with the theocratic ideas of the time, worked up the still floating traditions of Samuel's age into a new treatise (our **D**) on the introduction of the monarchy, representing it as a breach of the divinely-ordained plan of a permanent theocracy for Israel[1].

This apology for the theocracy a redactor (**R**), dominated like all his school by a high religious purpose, set himself to work into the older history, prefixing the introductory sections (1 Sam. i-vi) from **S** and **A**[2]. But just as the Deuteronomic editor of Judges is understood to have omitted from his work such unsuitable or unedifying portions as Judges ix, xvi, and xvii-xxi[3], so our editor seems to have omitted from his edition 1 Sam. xxviii. 3 ff., and the whole of 2 Sam. ix-xx, as from the nature of their contents less suitable for the religious and moral edification of his readers. In place of the latter he substituted the summary of David's reign now appearing

---

[1] For the contents and original order of **D** see above, p. 16 f., and below, p. 74.

[2] This, however, may have been already done.

[3] See the writer's *Joshua and Judges* (*Temple Bible*), p. xxii.

as ch. viii, with which his work concluded[1] (for the kindred sections, iii. 2-5, v. 13-16, see p. 5 and the note, p. 229). A briefer summary (1 Sam. xiv. 17-51), in the same way, took the place of a fuller record of Saul's campaigns which **M** may have once contained. In addition to such larger insertions as 1 Sam. ii. 27-36 and 2 Sam. vii, a number of smaller additions likewise betray the hand of the Deuteronomic editor, such as the brief chronological notices, 1 Sam. iv. 18, 2 Sam. v. 4 f. These minor additions have been pointed out in the notes.

VI. The Post-Deuteronomic Redaction and Later Additions.

The Book of Judges once more affords a parallel to the literary history of Samuel. There a later and more liberal editor restored the parts omitted by his predecessor and gave to the Book of Judges its present form. In the same way the precious court memoirs were restored, and the close of the new and enlarged Samuel indicated by the *repetition of the last verses of the Deuteronomic edition* (xx. 23-26 = viii. 16-18)[2]. The dates at which the appendix gradually took shape cannot be determined. This applies also to the various late insertions in the style of the Jewish Midrash (edifying expansions or alterations of the older text such as 1 Sam. xix. 18-24, xxi. 10-15), the Song of Hannah (1 Sam. ii. 1-10), and the other passages denoted throughout by **Z**. Latest of all must be put the extensive additions in 1 Sam. xvii and xviii which had not yet found a place in the Hebrew text that lay before the Greek translators *circa* 200 B.C.

Three stages, therefore, are distinctly traceable in the literary history of the canonical Book of Samuel—a pre-Deuteronomic stage, in which the sources circulated as independent documents, a Deuteronomic edition, pre-

---

[1] This was first advanced and made probable by Budde.

[2] So Budde, whose theory of the two editions and their mutual relation is now generally accepted.

pared towards the close of the Exile, and the final or post-Deuteronomic edition, which for perhaps two centuries continued to receive minor additions to its contents [1].

VII. THE TEXT OF SAMUEL AND THE VALUE OF THE GREEK VERSION.

The text of Samuel is considered by competent authorities to be the worst preserved in the O. T. with the possible exception of the text of Ezekiel. Nor is this surprising when one considers the great age of its main sources, and the popularity which they must have enjoyed, both while circulating as independent works and as combined into one whole. The more frequently a work is copied the more numerous the mistakes in the later copies are sure to be. Now, as our O. T. Revisers have reminded us in their preface, 'the Received, or, as it is commonly called, the Massoretic Text of the O. T. Scriptures, has come down to us in manuscripts which are of no very great antiquity, and which all belong to the same family or recension [2].' Indeed most modern Hebraists are of opinion that all existing MSS. of the O. T. have been derived from a single MS. of a date not earlier than the first or second century of our era. In these circumstances it is matter for congratulation that we have in the Greek Version of 'the Seventy' or Septuagint (LXX) [3] an independent witness to the text of Samuel as it circulated about the year 200 B. C. By its aid it has been found possible in almost every chapter of Samuel to restore, or at least improve, passages that are unintelligible or confused in the Hebrew, a fact of which illustrations in abundance

---

[1] Three similar stages may be traced for Joshua and Judges (see the *Temple Bible*, pp. ix ff., xix ff.).

[2] 'The earliest MS. of which the age is certainly known bears date A. D. 916' (Revisers' footnote).

[3] For the fullest information regarding the LXX and the principles which should regulate its use in the criticism of the Hebrew Text, see Swete's *Introduction to the O. T. in Greek*; Driver's *Notes*, xxxvi ff.; H. P. Smith, *Samuel*, 395 ff.

will be found in the following pages.   In this work of
textual emendation, by the help of the LXX in particular,
Thenius, Wellhausen, Klostermann, and Driver—the last
named in his invaluable *Notes on the Hebrew Text of the
Books of Samuel*—have rendered conspicuous service.

In several instances it can be shown from the LXX
that the obscurity of the received text has arisen from
what is technically known as *homoeoteleuton* (Gk. ὁμοιοτέ-
λευτον).   When a particular word or phrase stood in two
consecutive lines, particularly if at or near the end,
the eye of the copyist sometimes wandered from the one
occurrence of the word to the other, omitting all that
stood between.   In this way one or even two lines have
disappeared from the MSS. of the Massoretic text.
Examples will be found in 1 Sam. x. 1, 21, xiv. 41
(a case of double *homoeoteleuton*), 2 Sam. xiii. 27, 34, and
elsewhere[1].   The most interesting of all the textual problems raised by the divergent witness of the LXX in the
Book of Samuel will be found stated and discussed in the
notes on 1 Sam. xvii. 1—xviii. 5 (pp. 120 ff.).

The texts to which reference is most frequently made
in the notes are those of the Codex Vaticanus, cited as
LXX (B), as printed in Swete's standard edition of the
Septuagint, and of Lucian's recension[2], cited as Lucian
or as LXX (L), edited by Lagarde in his *Librorum Vet.
Test. Pars Prior Graece* (1883).

VIII.   THE HISTORICAL VALUE OF THE BOOK OF SAMUEL.

The historical value of the Book of Samuel, as of every
other ancient historical work, must be measured by the

---

[1] It will be found, when the omitted lines are re-translated
into Hebrew, that 'the roll of the book' from which the oldest
Greek translation was made can be proved to have been
written in columns, each line of which contained from 21-23
letters.

[2] For which see Swete's *Introduction*, pp. 81 ff.

age and trustworthiness of the sources from which its
material is derived. In the case before us, it has been
repeatedly shown that the oldest parts of Samuel are but
little younger than the events they record. The court
memoirs of David, in particular, have been subjected to
the test of the most searching criticism and have emerged
as a document of the first rank in the historical literature
of antiquity. In both C and M, at least, the student of
Hebrew history may rest assured that he possesses
a trustworthy record of the early monarchy and of the
circumstances that gave it birth. In the later prophetic
biography of Samuel (S) we have also historical material,
although not in so pure a form as in the older sources.
Even as regards the theocratic sections, the student who
has a true sense of the deeper significance of Israel's
history will not fail to do justice to the philosophy of
history which underlies them (cf. on 1 Sam. xii. 14).

In Samuel, further, the student has access to an
incomparable gallery of historical portraits. One thinks,
first of all, of David, whom a consummate literary artist
has painted to the life. Where in the whole range of
ancient literature is there a character whom we know as
intimately as we know 'the darling of the songs of Israel'
(2 Sam. xxiii. 1)? Here is a man alike distinguished in
the arts of peace and of war, a man who knew, as scarcely
another in history, the secret of winning the selfless devotion of his friends. While utterly loyal in his friendships, David extended to his personal enemies a forbearance all too rare in those early days. As in all great
men, the elemental human passions were strong in the
son of Jesse, and have left at least one dark stain on his
memory. Nor can his culpable remissness as a parent
be excused. Yet all this is forgotten in the recollection
of the other and better David, who at every turn asked
to know the will of Yahweh and strove to do it, and
whose serene trust in his God even in the darkest hour is
here for all to read.

How skilfully, again, does the artist portray the gradual deterioration in the character of the vain and ambitious Absalom! We still can see the scowl that rested on that fair but sullen face for 'two full years' as he waited for the hour of his revenge (2 Sam. xiii. 23, 32, emended text). And what shall we say of Saul the patriot and victim of a mind diseased, of the brave unselfish Jonathan, of the masterful Joab and the impulsive Abishai, of Hushai and Ahithophel, not to speak of the pious Hannah, the prudent Abigail, the devoted Rizpah, and the other immortal figures that pass before us? One's chief regret must ever be that the cross-lights of Hebrew tradition have made it difficult to fix the portrait of Samuel himself. But is not this variety of tradition itself a tribute to the greatness of the man and his life-work?

For the student of early Hebrew religion the Book of Samuel is of paramount importance. It is not too much to say that the study of this book has contributed more than anything else to the more accurate views of the historical development of religious thought in O. T. times, which are characteristic of the present day. The subject is too large for adequate treatment here. Only one or two outstanding points can be mentioned, and that briefly.

In the first place we see how firmly established in Israel was the central thought of the Mosaic teaching, that Yahweh was the God of Israel and Israel the people of Yahweh. So literally, indeed, is this belief reflected in our oldest sources, that David can conceive of no greater calamity than to be driven forth from the fellowship of Israel, 'the inheritance of Yahweh,' to 'serve other gods' (1 Sam. xxvi. 19). Beyond the limits of Canaan, Yahweh's land, other deities held sway, who claimed the allegiance and worship of all who dwelt within their territory. Between this primitive particularism and the attitude to the gods of the heathen reflected in 1 Sam. xii. 21 lie many centuries of the progress of revelation.

Similar primitive traits are discernible in the character
of Yahweh, whose actions are often inscrutable and even
arbitrary (see on 2 Sam. xxiv. 1).   Yet the God of even
our oldest sources is a God of justice and righteousness,
the Guardian of morality (2 Sam. xi. 27 ff.) and the Avenger
of a broken covenant (xxi. 1 ff.).

In this connexion one recalls the light which is thrown
by the narratives of Samuel on such important adjuncts
of worship as the Ark, the ephod-oracle of Urim and
Thummim and the Teraphim.   To these may be added,
in the sphere of social life, the institution of the ban, the
abstinence from blood, the war-taboos, and many more.

A mere reference must suffice for such subjects of surpassing importance for the study of the O. T. as the
emergence for the first time into the light of history of the
prophetic order (1 Sam. x. 5), the consecration of the site
of the future temple, the illustrations of the Messianic
Hope and of the ideas of the after-life among the
shadows of Sheol, or even, it may be, a hint of a future
resurrection (see on 1 Sam. ii. 6)[1].

IX. The Chronology of the Book.

Samuel differs in a marked degree from Judges and
Kings in the absence of a regular chronological scheme.
It is evident, however, that the period covered by the
book is practically equivalent to the long life of Samuel
(cf. 1 Sam. xxviii. 14), with David's reign of forty
years in addition, in all rather more than a hundred
years.   This is confirmed by the repeated references to
the descendants of Eli, of whom we can trace no fewer
than five generations, ending with the youthful Jonathan,
the son of Abiathar (1 Sam. xiv. 3, xxii. 18, 2 Sam. xv. 27).[2]

---

[1] See the Index for references to the foregoing.
[2] This argument that five generations represent a period of
over a century is based on the fact that, in the 350 years from
Rehoboam to the Exile, seventeen monarchs in direct descent

For the later part of this period we have the trustworthy editorial note, 2 Sam. v. 4 f. (which see), and several invaluable data in 2 Sam. xiii ff. Assuming that Solomon reigned from 970 B. C. (cf. Skinner's tables in his *Kings*), David ascended the throne of Judah in 1010, and that of all Israel 1003-02. Since Amnon and Absalom, both born before 1003 (see 2 Sam. iii. 2), are grown up in ch. xiii, we may place the episode of this chapter *circa* 985. Between this point and Absalom's rebellion eleven years elapsed (xiii. 23, 38, xiv. 28, xv. 27 marg.), bringing us down to *circa* 974. In the following four years will fall the incidents of the Great Rebellion, Sheba's abortive insurrection (ch. xx), and the events of 1 Kings i, a period of time by no means too large (note the change in David, 1 Kings i. 1).

As regards the reign of Saul we are less fortunate. The chronological scheme in 1 Sam. xiii. 1 has unfortunately been left a blank (see p. 96). Since the estimate of David's forty years' reign (2 Sam v. 4 f.) has just proved itself correct[1], the accompanying statement that he was thirty years of age at his accession must also be accepted. Now if we assume that Jonathan was approximately of the same age—he must have been, by a few years, the elder of the two—and bear in mind that he was at least from eighteen to twenty years of age at the beginning of his father's reign (1 Sam. xiii. 2), we are compelled to limit that reign to some fifteen years at most, from ± 1025-1010 [2].

For the preceding period the materials for a trustworthy estimate are entirely wanting (see on iii. 1, iv. 15, 18, vii. 2). It can only be said that the birth of Samuel must fall somewhere in the neighbourhood of 1080-75 B. C.

---

occupied the throne of Judah (*c.* 933-586). This gives 21 years as the average age of the father at the birth of his eldest son.

[1] Kautzsch (*Literature of the O. T.*, 172 ff.), followed by Driver (article 'Chronology (Biblical),' *Encycl. Brit.*[10], xxvii. 10), allows David a reign of only 30 years (*c.* 1000-970), but this the data above given clearly prove to be some years too short.

[2] Contrast the forty years of Acts xiii. 21, and Josephus *Antiq.* vi. 14. 9, a period, for many reasons, much too long.

NOTATION OF THE SOURCES AND ABBREVIATIONS OF
THE TITLES OF WORKS FREQUENTLY CITED.

C The Memoirs of David's Court (see pp. 20 ff.).

M The History of the Introduction of the *M*onarchy and of
Saul and David to the establishment of Jerusalem as the
civil and religious centre of the kingdom (pp. 16 ff.).

A A fragment of a History of the *A*rk, or, it may be, of the
Philistine oppression (p. 18). These three may well
date from the latter half of the tenth century B. C.—
C from *circa* 950 B. C., M, *c.* 920—if they did not originally
form parts of a single work (in this case 1 Sam. xxvii.
6^b will be a later gloss).

S A Biography of *S*amuel the Prophet, pre-Deuteronomic
(i. e. before 620), but perhaps not earlier than 630 (see
p. 18 and the ref. there).

T Various *T*raditional elements, mostly variants of incidents
recorded in **M** (p. 20).

D Various contributions from writers of the *D*euteronomic
school (sect. iii), notably the apology for the theocracy
(1 Sam. vii ff.), from the latter half of the Exile (pp. 16 ff.,
24 f.).

P 1 Sam. xiii. 7^b-15^a (see p. 98), a passage of uncertain
affinities and date.

Z A symbol for passages of the most various origins and
dates, which there is reason to believe formed no part of
the first edition of Samuel (pp. 19, 23, 25).

R denotes the hand of a Compiler or *R*edactor (pp. 19, 24 ff.).

DB. Hastings' *Dictionary of the Bible.*

EBi. Cheyne and Black's *Encyclopaedia Biblica.*

BDB. Hebrew and English Lexicon, edited by Brown,
Driver and Briggs.

LOT⁶. Driver's *Introduction,* 6th edition (see p. 326).

OTJC². and *Rel. Sem².* W. Robertson Smith's *Old Test.
in the Jewish Church* and *Religion of the Semites,* 2nd editions.

KAT³. Die Keilinschriften und das Alte Testament, 3rd edition
(edited by Winckler and Zimmern).

PEFQSt. The Palestine Exploration Fund Quarterly Statements.

LXX (B), LXX (L), the Vatican Codex and Lucian's recension of the Septuagint (see p. 27).

M. T. The Massoretic or Received Hebrew Text (see p. 26).

THE BOOK OF SAMUEL

REVISED VERSION WITH ANNOTATIONS

THE
FIRST BOOK OF SAMUEL

[S] Now there was a certain man of Ramathaim- **1**
zophim, of the hill country of Ephraim, and his name

First Division. 1 SAMUEL I—XIV.

SAMUEL AND SAUL.

A. i-vii. *The Early Life and Judgeship of Samuel.*

THE contents of the Books of Samuel fall into three parts or
divisions, followed by an appendix (see the Introduction to this
Commentary, section ii). The first of these parts or divisions,
1 Sam. i-xiv, comprises three subdivisions, the extent and contents of which have already been given. The first subdivision,
embracing chapters i-vii, may, in its turn, be conveniently divided
into three sections :—(*a*) i. 1-iv. 1ᵃ, the birth, dedication, and call
of Samuel ; (*b*) iv. 1ᵇ-vii. 1, the invasion of the Philistines, followed
by the capture and return of the Ark ; (*c*) vii. 2-17, Samuel, as
judge, delivers Israel from the Philistines.

(*a*) i. 1-iv. 1ᵃ. *The birth, dedication, and call of Samuel.*
The prayer of Hannah, the childless wife of Elkanah, for a son
is answered. He is named Samuel, and while still a child is dedicated to the service of Yahweh, and placed in charge of Eli, the
chief priest of the sanctuary at Shiloh. When on the verge of
adolescence Samuel receives the Divine call to the prophetic
office. As later additions (see below) to this idyllic narrative are
included the Song of Hannah (ii. 1-10) and the first announcement by an anonymous prophet of the impending fate of Eli and
his house (ii. 27-36).

1. Ramathaim-zophim: as a place-name this form is inde-
fensible. Elsewhere the name of Samuel's birthplace and later
home is Ramah (i. 19, ii. 11, &c.). We must therefore read
either : 'a certain man of Ramah, a Zuphite,' or 'a certain man
of the Ramathites, a Zuphite.' That Ramah lay in 'the land of
Zuph' is evident from ix. 5. Samuel is here clearly an Ephraimite
by descent. Later genealogists, for dogmatic reasons, made him
a member of the tribe of Levi (1 Chron. vi. 33-35 ; cf. 26-28).
The situation of Ramah—*lit.* 'the high (place)'—is uncertain.

was Elkanah, the son of Jeioham, the son of Elihu, the
2 son of Tohu, the son of Zuph, an Ephraimite : and he
had two wives; the name of the one was Hannah, and
the name of the other Peninnah : and Peninnah had
3 children, but Hannah had no children.   And this man
went up out of his city from year to year to worship and
to sacrifice unto the LORD of hosts in Shiloh.   And the

By most recent authorities it is identified with the modern *Beit
Rima*, which lies on a hill about thirteen miles north-east of
Lydda, and twelve miles west of *Seilun*, the ancient Shiloh.   In
this case Ramah will have lain near the western edge of the
central highlands of Palestine, which are termed in the O.T. 'the
hill country of Ephraim.'

2. For a well-to-do citizen to have two wives of equal status
was evidently not uncommon in early times (cf. Gen. xxix. 28 ff.,
and especially the law of Deut. xxi. 15 ff.), more particularly if
the first was childless.   The incidents here recorded (verses 6 ff.)
were only too often paralleled, we may be sure, in other house-
holds.

Hannah . . . Peninnah: the former signifies Grace, the
latter Coral, less probably Pearl.

3. the LORD of hosts: this, the most majestic of the Divine
titles, and here first met with in the canonical books, is specially
frequent in the prophetical writings of the O.T.—not, however, in
all—and occurs eleven times in the Books of Samuel.   In A.V. and
R.V. LORD in small capitals is used to represent the personal
name of the covenant God of Israel.   Owing on the one hand to
Hebrew having been originally written with consonants only, and
on the other to the fact that in the post-exilic period the Jews,
from motives of reverence, ceased to pronounce the 'ineffable
name,' the original pronunciation of the latter has been lost.
Wherever it occured, with certain exceptions, they substituted
the word *Adonai*, Lord.   Influenced by the same motives, the
Greek translators (*c.* 250 B.C.) set the example of inserting the
rendering of Adonai, viz. *Kurios*, hence the Latin *Dominus*,
and the English LORD.   The consonants of the tetragrammaton
(four-letter word), as it is called, may be represented by YHWH
(otherwise IHVH), which a variety of evidence leads us to con-
clude was pronounced YaHWeH.   The familiar pronunciation
Jehovah (IeHoVaH), which is not older than the sixteenth century, is due to an unfortunate attempt to combine the original
consonants with the vowels of Adonai.   As to the signification
of Yahweh, modern scholars are mostly divided between 'He that

two sons of Eli, Hophni and Phinehas, priests unto the

---

is,' i.e. 'the self-existent One' (see Exod. iii. 14), and 'He that causes to be,' the Life-giver, Creator.

With regard to the original meaning of the compound title, 'LORD of hosts' or armies, in Heb. *Yahweh Ṣĕbā'ôth*—admittedly a contraction of the fuller 'Yahweh, the God of hosts' (Amos vi. 14; Hos. xii. 5)—a similar divergence of opinion still prevails. Most probably this title had its origin in the association of Yahweh with the early conquests of His people, by whom Yahweh was regarded as peculiarly a God of war (note especially 1 Sam. xvii. 45, where Yahweh Ṣebaoth is defined as 'the God of the armies of Israel,' and cf. Num. xxi. 14, 'the book of the wars of Yahweh'). Those who advocate this view also point to the frequent association, in the Books of Samuel especially (1 Sam. iv. 4; 2 Sam. vi. 2, &c.), of this title with the sacred Ark, which in early times often —originally, perhaps, on all occasions—accompanied the armies of Israel to battle (cf. the early passages Num. x. 35 f.; Josh. vi. 4 f.; 1 Sam. iv. 3 ff.; 2 Sam. xi. 11).

In later and more peaceful times the title would suggest rather the hosts or armies of heaven, both angels and stars; and even if the explanation just given be regarded as giving the historical genesis of the title, it must be admitted that the reference to the hosts of heaven, which some authorities regard as the earlier and original, is that which dominates the prophetic usage of the title. Even in the earliest of the prophets, Amos and Hosea, Yahweh Ṣebaoth has become practically a proper name, denoting Yahweh as the supreme controller of the spiritual and material forces of the universe, a signification aptly brought out by one of the Greek renderings of the title, *Kurios Pantokratōr*, 'the Lord All-sovereign.'   In the N. T. it occurs in the form *Kurios Sabaôth*, E. VV., 'the Lord of Sabaoth,' Rom. ix. 29 (a quotation from the LXX), Jas. v. 4. See further *Encyclopaedia Biblica* (*EBi.*), article, 'Names,' § 123; Driver in Hastings' *Dicty. of the Bible* (*DB.*), iii. 137 f.; and Kautzsch, *ibid.*, extra volume, 636 ff.

Shiloh: now *Seilun*, about nine and a half miles north-east of *Beitin* the ancient Beth-el (see Judges xxi. 19). At this period Shiloh derived its importance as the principal sanctuary of Central Palestine, at least, from the presence of the Ark, which was housed, as shown in the sequel, not in a tent or tabernacle, but in a substantial structure, here called a 'temple' (i. 9, iii. 3), the 'house of Yahweh' (i. 7, 24), with doors (iii. 15) and door-posts (i. 9). This sanctuary appears to have been destroyed by the Philistines after their victory (iv. 10 f.), as the successors of Eli in the priesthood are found later at Nob (xxi. 1 ff.; cf. also Jer. vii. 12). The representation of the later priestly historians that the gorgeous tabernacle of the Priests' Code (Exod. xxv ff.)

4 LORD, were there.   And when the day came that
Elkanah sacrificed, he gave to Peninnah his wife, and to
5 all her sons and her daughters, portions : but unto
Hannah he gave a double portion : for he loved Hannah,
6 but the LORD had shut up her womb.   And her rival
provoked her sore, for to make her fret, because the
7 LORD had shut up her womb.   And *as* he did so year
by year, when she went up to the house of the LORD,
so she provoked her ; therefore she wept, and did not
8 eat.   And Elkanah her husband said unto her, Hannah,
why weepest thou ? and why eatest thou not ? and why

---

was set up at Shiloh (see note on ii. 22), and afterwards removed
to Gibeon (2 Chron. i. 3), is now regarded as unhistorical.

The occasion of Elkanah's yearly visit was doubtless the great
autumn festival known as 'the Feast of Ingathering,' and later as
'the Feast of Booths (Tabernacles),' the feast or pilgrimage *par
excellence* (1 Kings viii. 2), which was held 'at the turn of the
year' (Exod xxxiv. 22), i. e. after the grape and olive harvests had
been gathered in and the cycle of the year's agricultural operations
completed (cf. v. 20, and Judges xxi. 19-22).

In 3ᵇ we expect · 'Eli and his two sons ' (so LXX).

4-7. The main statement in these verses runs thus : 'And it
fell on a day when Elkanah sacrificed (4ᵃ) . . . that she (Hannah)
wept and did not eat (7ᵇ) '   The intervening sentences form
a long parenthesis describing what had regularly taken place in
former years.   According to early Hebrew custom, after Yahweh's
portion had been burned on the altar (ii. 15 f.) and the priests had
received their share, the worshippers, if of one family, used the
flesh of the victim to provide a family meal within the sanctuary
precincts, or a whole village community might similarly unite in
the sacrificial meal (ix. 12 ff.).   On the presence of women on
such occasions, see Peritz, 'Woman in the Ancient Hebrew Cult,'
Journ. of Bibl. Lit. xvii. (1898) 111 ff.

5. a double portion :   a token of special honour and affection
(cf. Benjamin's fivefold portion, Gen. xliii. 34), A. V. ' a worthy
portion,' but the Hebrew text will not bear either meaning.
A slight change of text (see R. V. marg.) gives : ' To Hannah he
was wont to give a single portion ;   howbeit he loved Hannah,
although Yahweh had,' &c.

7. Render with change of one letter : 'And so she (Peninnah)
did year by year.'

is thy heart grieved? am not I better to thee than ten sons? So Hannah rose up after they had eaten in 9 Shiloh, and after they had drunk. Now Eli the priest sat upon his seat by the door post of the temple of the LORD. And she was in bitterness of soul, and prayed 10 unto the LORD, and wept sore. And she vowed a vow, 11 and said, O LORD of hosts, if thou wilt indeed look on the affliction of thine handmaid, and remember me, and not forget thine handmaid, but wilt give unto thine handmaid a man child, then I will give him unto the LORD all the days of his life, and there shall no razor come upon his head. And it came to pass, as she 12 continued praying before the LORD, that Eli marked her mouth. Now Hannah, she spake in her heart; only her 13 lips moved, but her voice was not heard: therefore Eli

---

9ᵃ. Read, as suggested by the LXX: 'So Hannah rose up after they had eaten, and presented herself before Yahweh' (for the expression, see x. 19; Joshua xxiv. 1). She goes to cast her heavy burden upon the Lord and to seek solace in prayer. 'The most general, the most constant, and therefore the most important element in worship is prayer' (Tiele, Gifford Lectures, ii. 133), frequently in the O. T. associated, as here, with a preceding sacrifice. Of the favourite attitudes in prayer, standing (Gen. xviii. 22; 1 Kings viii. 22, &c.; cf. Matt. vi. 5; Luke xviii. 11), kneeling (1 Kings viii. 54; Dan. vi. 10; Luke xxii. 41), and the characteristic oriental attitude of prostration (Gen. xxiv. 26; 1 Kings xviii. 42; Neh. viii. 6), Hannah chose the first, standing (verse 26) with her face towards the sacred Ark, the visible symbol of the presence of Yahweh. So David in his distress went into the tent which he had prepared for the Ark (see note on 2 Sam. vii. 18), and Daniel, at a later time, turned towards Jerusalem and its temple (Dan. vi. 10; cf. 1 Kings viii. 38). From verse 13 below we must infer that it was customary at this period to pray aloud.

11. Like Jacob (Gen. xxviii. 20 ff.) and Absalom (2 Sam. xv. 8), Hannah combines a vow with her prayer. It has been too hastily assumed that the child was to be a Nazirite or devotee from his birth in the sense of Num. vi, which belongs to the later legislation.

13. That these sacrificial feasts were often accompanied by excess is plain from Isa. xxviii. 7; cf. Amos ii. 8.

14 thought she had been drunken. And Eli said unto her,
How long wilt thou be drunken? put away thy wine
15 from thee. And Hannah answered and said, No, my
lord, I am a woman of a sorrowful spirit : I have drunk
neither wine nor strong drink, but I poured out my soul
16 before the LORD. Count not thine handmaid for a
daughter of Belial : for out of the abundance of my
complaint and my provocation have I spoken hitherto.
17 Then Eli answered and said, Go in peace : and the God
of Israel grant thy petition that thou hast asked of him.
18 And she said, Let thy servant find grace in thy sight.
So the woman went her way, and did eat, and her
19 countenance was no more *sad*. And they rose up in
the morning early, and worshipped before the LORD, and
returned, and came to their house to Ramah : and
Elkanah knew Hannah his wife ; and the LORD re-
20 membered her. And it came to pass, when the time
was come about, that Hannah conceived, and bare
a son ; and she called his name Samuel, *saying*, Because

---

16. a daughter of Belial : a disreputable woman (cf. R. V.
marg.) ; only here, but 'sons of Belial' and 'men of Belial' are
frequently used in the historical books for 'disreputable characters'
such as the sons of Eli (ii. 12). The etymology underlying the
supposed meaning, 'worthlessness' (R. V. marg.), is not free from
difficulty. In the O. T. Belial is never a proper name, but in
post-biblical Jewish literature it often occurs as a name for Satan
(so 2 Cor. vi. 15). See further *EBi.* i. col. 525 ff.

19. remembered her : implying that she conceived (so expressly LXX here ; cf. Gen. xxx. 22 f. of Rachel). The mention
of her conception in the next verse is due to a copyist's slip.

20. Render : 'And it came to pass at the turn of the year that
she bore a son.' The date intended is the autumn or fall, shortly
before the return of the Feast of Ingathering (see note on verse 3).

Samuel : in Heb. *Shĕmū'ēl* , here associated by the historian
with the verb *shā'al*, to ask, by which he 'means to express (as
often in the O. T.) an assonance, not an etymology' (Driver, *Notes
on the Hebrew Text of Samuel*, in loc.). Of the numerous attempts
at a more scientific etymology, the two most plausible agree in

I have asked him of the LORD.   And the man Elkanah, 21 and all his house, went up to offer unto the LORD the yearly sacrifice, and his vow.   But Hannah went not up; 22 for she said unto her husband, *I will not go up* until the child be weaned, and then I will bring him, that he may appear before the LORD, and there abide for ever.   And 23 Elkanah her husband said unto her, Do what seemeth thee good; tarry until thou have weaned him; only the LORD establish his word.   So the woman tarried and gave her son suck, until she weaned him.   And when 24 she had weaned him, she took him up with her, with three bullocks, and one ephah of meal, and a bottle of wine, and brought him unto the house of the LORD in

---

connecting the first part of the word with the Semitic root for 'name.'   Thus many scholars take *Shemuel* to mean 'Name of God,' with which they compare names like Penuel ('face of God'), Reuel, &c.   More recently it has been suggested, on the analogy of some early Babylonian and South Arabian names, that the first element denotes 'His name' as a periphrasis for Yahweh—'His name is God' = 'Yahweh is God.'   Samuel would thus be identical in meaning with the name Joel (see Hommel, *The Ancient Hebrew Tradition*, 100, and index under Samuel).

21. A full year has now elapsed since the events of the earlier part of the chapter.

23. his word: read with LXX 'thy word,' meaning 'may Yahweh permit thee to carry out thy intention,' as expressed in verse 22^b.

24. The child's age at this point is not stated.   Hebrew mothers usually nursed their children for two to three years (2 Macc. vii. 27), but a period of five to six years is not unknown in Palestine at the present time.   The longer period is suggested here by the fact that Samuel was able from the first to minister at Shiloh (ii. 11).

   three bullocks. The ancient law required that at the redemption of the firstborn none should appear 'before Yahweh empty' (Exod. xxxiv. 20), but the first part of Hannah's offering in the Hebrew text is not only out of proportion to the rest, but is inconsistent with verse 25^a; read therefore, by dividing the words differently, 'with a bullock of three years old' (see R. V. marg.).

   An **ephah** was about equal to an imperial bushel (see the

25 Shiloh: and the child was young. And they slew the
26 bullock, and brought the child to Eli. And she said,
Oh my lord, as thy soul liveth, my lord, I am the woman
27 that stood by thee here, praying unto the LORD. For
this child I prayed; and the LORD hath given me my
28 petition which I asked of him: therefore I also have
granted him to the LORD; as long as he liveth he is
granted to the LORD. And he worshipped the LORD
there.

2   [Z] And Hannah prayed, and said:
      My heart exulteth in the LORD,

---

writer's article 'Weights and Measures,' Hastings' *DB.* iv. 912),
and was of the same capacity as the corresponding 'bath' for
liquids. The last clause of the verse is corrupt.

25. Since it is stated so circumstantially in the narrative that
Hannah alone went up to Shiloh with her child — Elkanah
appearing only in ii. 11, where the name is a later intrusion,
unsupported by the LXX—we should render: 'And after they
(the temple officials) had slain the bullock, the mother of the child
(so LXX with change of one letter) came to Eli, and said,' &c.

28. Samuel is solemnly **granted, i. e.** dedicated to the lifelong
service of the LORD. The last clause must be taken in connexion
with ii. 11, and the original text may be thus restored with the
help of the LXX: 'And she left him there before Yahweh, and
went to Ramah to her house. And the child continued to minister
unto Yahweh before Eli the priest.' The insertion of the song
by a later editor (see below) led to the disruption of the original
context. With the position of Samuel as Eli's *famulus* compare Joshua's relation to Moses at the Tent of Meeting (Exod.
xxxiii. 11).

ii. 1–10. Hannah's prayer is really a psalm (cf. Ps lxxii. 20,
'the prayers of David'). The reference to the king in verse 10
—no matter whether an actual or an ideal sovereign is intended—
alone shows that this beautiful sacred lyric cannot have been
sung by Hannah in the circumstances described. To Hannah's
special circumstances, indeed, there is no *explicit* reference whatever. The words of 5° alone approach her situation, and
doubtless led to the insertion of the psalm in its present context;
scarcely, however, by the original compiler of Samuel (see
Introduction), but by a later hand. The original, which has
suffered in some places in the course of transmission, consists of

Mine horn is exalted in the LORD :
My mouth is enlarged over mine enemies ;
Because I rejoice in thy salvation.
There is none holy as the LORD ;   2
For there is none beside thee :
Neither is there any rock like our God.
Talk no more so exceeding proudly ;   3
Let not arrogancy come out of your mouth :
For the LORD is a God of knowledge,
And by him actions are weighed.
The bows of the mighty men are broken,   4
And they that stumbled are girded with strength.

---

a number of distichs, or short double lines, each marked by the parallelism of thought and expression which is characteristic of Hebrew poetry. The Magnificat (Luke i. 46-55) is largely modelled on the Song of Hannah. The main theme of the Song is the sovereignty of God as the supreme disposer of the destinies of men (verses 4-8), which is preceded by a note of jubilant praise (1 f.) and a note of warning (3), and followed by a reference to the Messianic future (9 f.).

1. mine horn is exalted (cf. verse 10^d) : a familiar figure, drawn from animal life, for abounding vitality and somewhat self-conscious strength. The widening of the **mouth** was a gesture of contempt (Ps. xxxv. 21 ; Isa. lvii. 4).

2. The original distich is probably to be restored by omitting the second line of our text, which interrupts the parallelism. The figurative designation of God as a **rock**, that is, as the steadfast support and refuge of His people, is frequent in Hebrew poetry (2 Sam. xxii. 3, 47, xxiii. 3 ; Deut. xxxii. 4, &c., and often in Pss.).

3. by him (to be preferred to R.V. marg.) **actions are weighed:** with this figure of the balance as the means of testing human worth (so Prov. xvi. 2 ; Dan. v. 27) we may compare the familiar illustration from the Egyptian *Book of the Dead*, representing the heart of the deceased in one scale being weighed against the symbol of Truth and Right in the other before being admitted to the realm of Osiris. The test to which the Hebrew poet refers, however, is applied in this life, and the changes in the fortunes of men and women adduced in the following verses are to be regarded as the ensuing rewards and punishments, and not as due to the caprice of an arbitrary sovereign.

5   They that were full have hired out themselves for
         bread ;
     And they that were hungry have ceased :
     Yea, the barren hath borne seven ;
     And she that hath many children languisheth.
6   The LORD killeth, and maketh alive :
     He bringeth down to the grave, and bringeth up.
7   The LORD maketh poor, and maketh rich :
     He bringeth low, he also lifteth up.
8   He raiseth up the poor out of the dust,
     He lifteth up the needy from the dunghill,
     To make them sit with princes,
     And inherit the throne of glory :
     For the pillars of the earth are the LORD's,
     And he hath set the world upon them.
9   He will keep the feet of his holy ones,

---

5. have ceased (to be hungry) : better with R.V. marg., 'have rest' from toil.   The rest of the verse seems to be an expansion of Jer. xv. 9ᵃ.   **seven** here has the sense of 'a numerous family' ; note the parallelism.

6. the grave : Heb. *shĕ"ôl,* corresponding to the Greek *Hades,* the abode of departed spirits, good and bad alike.   It was thought of as lying beneath the earth, where the so-called 'shades' passed a shadowy existence, scarcely worthy to be called life.   In the A.V. Sheol is variously rendered by 'the grave,' 'hell,' and sometimes 'the pit' ; for these the R.V. has substituted 'Sheol' in about half the passages (e.g. 2 Sam. xxii. 6 for 'hell,' which with its modern associations is a peculiarly unhappy rendering). In the light of the parallelism in 6ᵃ it is difficult to avoid the conclusion that in 6ᵇ the poet declares his belief in a resurrection from the dead.   If this be so, the date of the poem must be sought well on in the post-exilic period (cf. Isa. xxvi. 19 ; Dan. xii. 1 ff.). By most commentators, however, Sheol is here understood as a figurative expression for the extreme of distress and peril, as in Ps. lxxxvi. 13.

8. Cf. the parallel Ps. cxiii. 7 ff.   The terms used are not to be explained as mere oriental figures (see W. R. Smith, *Religion of the Semites,* 2nd ed., 235 n. 1).

In verses 9 f. the poet turns from the present to the future ; the

But the wicked shall be put to silence in darkness;
For by strength shall no man prevail.
They that strive with the LORD shall be broken to 10
    pieces;
Against them shall he thunder in heaven:
The LORD shall judge the ends of the earth;
And he shall give strength unto his king,
And exalt the horn of his anointed.

[S] And Elkanah went to Ramah to his house. And 11
the child did minister unto the LORD before Eli the priest.

Now the sons of Eli were sons of Belial; they knew 12
not the LORD. And the custom of the priests with the 13
people was, that, when any man offered sacrifice, the
priest's servant came, while the flesh was in seething,

---

destruction of the wicked, the preservation of the pious Israelites—
the 'holy' or 'godly ones' of verse 9—and the judgement of the
world preceding the advent of the Messiah are all characteristic
features of the later Jewish eschatology. Verse 10^b should probably read, with a slight change: 'The Most High in heaven
shall shatter them' (cf. Ps. ii. 9), which improves the parallelism.

    And he shall give strength: rather 'in order to give... and
to exalt,' &c., both being final clauses.

    his king . . . his anointed: these terms are best taken
as referring to the Messianic King, the same who is the theme of
the second Psalm. For the origin and significance of the expression 'Yahweh's anointed,' see on x. 1.

    11. The original close of the narrative of ch. i (see on i. 28 above).

    ii. **12-17.** *The misconduct of Eli's sons, Hophni and Phinehas.*

    12. sons of Belial: see on i. 16.

    they knew not the LORD: 'did not acknowledge the LORD'
more nearly reproduces the thought of the original; Eli's sons
lived in open disregard of God's moral requirements. Cf. Hos.
iv. 1, 6, where 'the knowledge of God' is synonymous with
obedience to His moral law. We have here the O.T. parallel to
the faith which 'if it hath not works is dead' (Jas. ii. 17 ff.).

    13-16. In these verses the historian explains the irregularities
of which 'the young men' (verse 17) were guilty. With the
margin, however, we should join the first part of verse 13 to verse
12, and read: 'they regarded neither Yahweh nor what was due

14 with a fleshhook of three teeth in his hand; and he
struck it into the pan, or kettle, or caldron, or pot; all
that the fleshhook brought up the priest took therewith.
So they did in Shiloh unto all the Israelites that came
15 thither.   Yea, before they burnt the fat, the priest's
servant came, and said to the man that sacrificed, Give
flesh to roast for the priest; for he will not have sodden
16 flesh of thee, but raw.   And if the man said unto him,
They will surely burn the fat presently, and then take
as much as thy soul desireth; then he would say, Nay,
but thou shalt give it me now: and if not, I will take it
17 by force.   And the sin of the young men was very great
before the LORD: for men abhorred the offering of the
LORD.

---

to the priest from the people.'   At this early period the priests'
dues were not yet a matter of written prescription (see Deut.
xviii. 3 for a later period), but were apparently left to the free will
of the worshipper.   The sons of Eli were not satisfied with this
arrangement, but 'whenever a man offered a sacrifice' they sent
a servant with the demand of the text.   In this way they sinned
against the use and wont of the sanctuary of Shiloh.

14. the priest took therewith: read with the Versions and
R.V. marg.: 'took for himself.'

15 f. record a serious aggravation of the breach of hallowed
custom just mentioned.   Hophni and Phinehas were guilty not
only of high-handed conduct towards the worshippers, but of
sacrilege, in that they were wont to demand their share of the
sacrificial flesh before Yahweh had received His portion by the
burning of the fat upon the altar.   This, next to the solemn shedding
of the blood of the victim at the foot of the altar, was of the
essence of the rite.

16. presently: better, as margin, 'first' (let them burn the
fat).   Only after the blood and the fat had been duly offered could
priest and worshipper partake of the sacrificial meal that followed
(cf. i. 4 ff.).

17. for men abhorred the offering of the LORD: grammatical
usage requires us to render as in the margin: 'for the men (i. e.
the sons of Eli) despised, showed contempt for, the LORD's
offering.'   Probably, however, the original was simply 'for they
despised,' &c. (so LXX).

But Samuel ministered before the LORD, being a child, 18 girded with a linen ephod. Moreover his mother made 19 him a little robe, and brought it to him from year to year, when she came up with her husband to offer the yearly sacrifice. And Eli blessed Elkanah and his wife, 20 and said, The LORD give thee seed of this woman for the loan which was lent to the LORD. And they went unto their own home. And the LORD visited Hannah, 21 and she conceived, and bare three sons and two daughters. And the child Samuel grew before the LORD.

Now Eli was very old; and he heard all that his sons 22 did unto all Israel, and how that they lay with the women

---

ii. 18-21. *Samuel the boy-priest.* This charming picture of Samuel in the serene innocence of childhood, clothed in priestly dress and the object of a pious mother's care, is skilfully introduced between 12-17 and 22-25 in order to heighten the contrast between him and the unworthy sons of Eli, who, scorning all parental restraint, had brought the priestly office into contempt.

18. girded with a linen ephod (Heb. *'ēphōd bad*): so David when he danced before the Ark (2 Sam. vi. 14). From the sequel to the latter incident (*ibid.* 20 ff.) we learn that the 'linen ephod' must have been a short skirt girt about the waist, and a distinctive part of the priests' dress. It was as a boy-priest that Samuel 'ministered before the LORD.' Elsewhere in the Books of Samuel, with one apparent exception, where our versions speak of 'wearing an (*or* the) ephod,' an entirely different object is intended. See note on verse 28 below, and for the exception referred to see on xxii. 18.

20. The LORD give thee seed, &c.: the text is difficult and doubtless corrupt. We should probably read: 'The LORD repay thee with offspring (*or* seed) from this woman, in return for the loan which she hath lent to the LORD.' The terms 'loan' and 'lend' are used with reference to i. 28.

ii. 22-26. *Eli makes an ineffectual attempt to restrain his sons.*

22 f. The original text seems to have run thus: 'Now Eli was very old, and when he heard all . . . Israel, he said unto them,' &c. The second half of verse 22, which is wanting in the LXX (B), is rejected by all modern critics as an interpolation from Exod. xxxviii. 8, with a view to heighten the iniquity of the priests. The introduction here of 'the tent of meeting' is altogether

23 that did service at the door of the tent of meeting. And
he said unto them, Why do ye such things? for I heai
24 of your evil dealings from all this people. Nay, my sons;
for it is no good report that I hear: ye make the LORD's
25 people to transgress. If one man sin against another,
God shall judge him: but if a man sin against the
LORD, who shall intreat for him? Notwithstanding they
hearkened not unto the voice of their father, because the
26 LORD would slay them. And the child Samuel grew on,
and was in favour both with the LORD, and also with men.

---

at variance with the picture of the temple of Shiloh in ch. i (see
note on Shiloh, i. 3).

23 f. Read : 'Why do ye these things that I hear from all the
people ; nay, my sons, for evil (*lit.* 'not good') is the report
which I hear the LORD's people do spread abroad' (see marg.).
For the text here, see Driver, *Notes* in loc.

25. God shall judge him : rather, 'doth act as arbiter.' In
cases of wrongdoing between man and man, God arbitrates or
mediates between them, either through His representative, the
judge (cf. marg.), or through an oracle, or otherwise ; but in the
case of sins directly affecting God, such as the sacrilege of Eli's
sons, there is no third party to act as mediator. The sinner in
consequence cannot hope to escape the punishment incurred.

26. Imitated by Luke in his description of the boyhood of
Jesus (ii. 52).

ii. 27-36. *The doom of Eli's house foretold.* There is a consensus of opinion among scholars that this section in its present
form is of later date than the main body of the narrative of
chs. i–iii, and consequently from a different hand. The main
arguments in favour of this view are (1) the absence of all
reference to Samuel, who is the centre of interest in the main
narrative ; and (2) the acquaintance which the section betrays
with the long subsequent history of the Israelite priesthood, down
apparently to the reformation under Josiah (see below). It is not
so clear whether the passage is entirely to be referred to a writer
of the Deuteronomic school, or whether the latter has merely
expanded a shorter passage of more general import by the original
narrator. If iii. 12 is to be retained (see there), the latter is the
more plausible view (cf. Driver, *LOT.*⁶, 174). Unfortunately the
text is in several places corrupt, and the exegesis in consequence
uncertain.

[D] And there came a man of God unto Eli, and said 27
unto him, Thus saith the LORD, Did I reveal myself unto
the house of thy father, when they were in Egypt *in
bondage* to Pharaoh's house? And did I choose him 28
out of all the tribes of Israel to be my priest, to go up
unto mine altar, to burn incense, to wear an ephod before
me? and did I give unto the house of thy father all the

---

27. a man of God: one of the oldest and most frequent designations of a prophet (as of Samuel himself, ix. 6 ff.), emphasizing the prophet's close connexion with God as His confidant (Amos iii. 7) and messenger. In the historical books anonymous prophets are, as a rule, characteristic of later passages, and in almost every case they are messengers of threatening and doom. The questions following (verses 27, 28) imply in each case an affirmative answer.

the house of thy father : the genealogy of Eli is nowhere given in the O. T. By the Chronicler, however, one of his descendants is described as 'of the sons of Ithamar' (1 Chron. xxiv. 3), the fourth son of Aaron. The name of Eli's son, Phinehas, is another link connecting him with the family of Aaron (see Exod. vi. 23, 25). The reference here is manifestly to the Divine choice of the tribe of Levi for the priestly office (cf. the parallel passage, Deut. xxxiii. 8-11).

28. Note here the threefold division of the priestly duties, with which should be compared another threefold division in Deut. x. 8 f.

to wear an ephod before me : in view of the fact that the verb (*nāsā*) here rendered 'to wear' is nowhere else found in the sense of wearing an article of dress, we must here, and in the other passages where the expression occurs, render 'to bear an ephod before me.' The precise nature of the ephod, of which mention is so frequently made in the Books of Samuel, is still undetermined. That it was an object made, in whole or in part, of precious metal (Judges viii. 27), that it stood free like an image or idol (1 Sam. xxi. 9), that it was carried on occasion by a priest (xiv. 3, xxiii. 6 'in his hand'), and that it was chiefly used in connexion with divination, especially for ascertaining the will of Yahweh by means of the sacred lot (xiv. 18, where see note ; xxiii. 6, 9, xxx. 7, &c.), are conclusions now generally accepted by scholars. See the articles 'Ephod' in *DB*. i (Driver), and *EBi*. ii (Moore), and Kautzsch in Hastings' *DB.*, extra vol. 641 f. The connexion between the ephod as an image or such like and the *ephod bad* or linen ephod of verse 18 is still matter of conjecture (see the authorities just cited).

E

29 offerings of the children of Israel made by fire? Wherefore kick ye at my sacrifice and at mine offering, which
I have commanded in *my* habitation; and honourest thy
sons above me, to make yourselves fat with the chiefest
30 of all the offerings of Israel my people? Therefore the
LORD, the God of Israel, saith, I said indeed that thy
house, and the house of thy father, should walk before
me for ever: but now the LORD saith, Be it far from
me; for them that honour me I will honour, and they
31 that despise me shall be lightly esteemed. Behold, the
days come, that I will cut off thine arm, and the arm of
thy father's house, that there shall not be an old man in
32 thine house. And thou shalt behold the affliction of
my habitation, in all the wealth which *God* shall give

---

all the offerings: for the priests' share in the various
offerings as determined by the Deuteronomic and Priestly legisla-
tions, see Deut. xviii. 1 ff.; Num. xviii. 8 ff., and elsewhere.
Contrast verses 13 ff. above (with note).

29. which I have commanded in my habitation: the text is
here, by universal consent, admitted to be corrupt, and no
convincing restoration has as yet been proposed. The plural
pronouns show that Eli is involved in the iniquity of his sons, in
that he shared with them the meat which they secured by
sacrilegious means.

30. Yahweh revokes His intention with regard to the house of
Eli, with whose descendants the highest offices of the priesthood
would have remained had they proved themselves worthy of so
great an honour.

and the house of thy father: these words, and the corresponding reference in verse 31, must be deleted as a mistaken
addition, suggested by 27 ff. (so Löhr and others), since the doom
about to be pronounced affects only the descendants of Eli; the
honour of the priesthood is about to be transferred to another
branch of the house of Levi (see on verse 35).

31 f. The text of these two verses is extremely uncertain, the
best Greek version, LXX (B), omitting the latter half of verse 31
and the first half of 32. In particular, the words rendered 'the
affliction of my habitation' are hopelessly corrupt. The general
sense appears to be that the strength and vitality of the house of
Eli, symbolized by the expression 'arm,' will be so undermined

Israel: and there shall not be an old man in thine house for ever. And the man of thine, *whom* I shall not cut 33 off from mine altar, *shall be* to consume thine eyes, and to grieve thine heart: and all the increase of thine house shall die in the flower of their age. And this shall be 34 the sign unto thee, that shall come upon thy two sons, on Hophni and Phinehas; in one day they shall die both of them. And I will raise me up a faithful priest, that shall 35 do according to that which is in mine heart and in my mind: and I will build him a sure house; and he shall

---

that no member thereof will ever reach old age. 'Premature death is a sign of the Divine displeasure' (H. P. Smith).

33. And the man of thine: i. e. of thy family, the reference being to Abiathar, the son of Ahimelech and great-grandson of Eli, who alone escaped from the massacre of the priests of Nob (xxii. 20). The whole may be rendered thus: 'Yet (one) man belonging to thee I will not cut off from mine altar, that he may consume his eyes and cause his soul (reading 'his' for 'thy,' with LXX) to pine away.' For the last expression see Lev. xxvi. 16 R. V. This reading brings out more clearly the reference to Abiathar's loss of his office, and banishment by Solomon. So, at least, the passage was understood by the author of 1 Kings ii. 27 (see Skinner's Commentary in this series).

in the flower of their age: a more than doubtful rendering of the text. The Greek reading, 'by the sword of men,' is generally preferred (see R. V. marg.).

34. The death of Eli's two sons in one day (iv. 11) is to be at once the beginning of the threatened doom and the earnest of all that is to follow.

35. The opening words might lead us to identify the 'faithful priest' with Samuel, but this identification is ruled out by the following clauses, which point unmistakably to Zadok, the future head and ancestor of the Jerusalem priesthood.

I will build him a sure house: that is, I will establish his descendants permanently in the priesthood, as explained in the following clause. 'House' as a figure for 'family,' descendants, is a common figure in the O. T. from Gen. xviii. 19 (Abraham) onwards; for 'building a house' in the modern sense of 'founding a family' see Deut. xxv. 9; Ruth iv. 11. The exact counterpart of this promise of the permanence of the Zadokite priesthood is the assurance of a similar permanency for the dynasty of David (2 Sam. vii. 11 ff., also from the pen of a Deuteronomic historian).

36 walk before mine anointed for ever.   And it shall come
to pass, that every one that is left in thine house shall
come and bow down to him for a piece of silver and
a loaf of bread, and shall say, Put me, I pray thee, into
one of the priests' offices, that I may eat a morsel of
bread.

3   [S] And the child Samuel ministered unto the LORD

---

before mine anointed: see on x. 1 for the origin of this
frequent designation of a Hebrew king.   Here, however, and
in 2 Sam. xxii. 51, the expression is used in a collective sense of
the Davidic dynasty (see on xii. 3, where the various occurrences
are cited).

36. Most moderns find in this verse a picture of the straits to
which the priests of the local sanctuaries were reduced, when the
latter were abolished by the reformation of Josiah.   It seems to
have been found impossible to carry out the injunctions of Deut.
xviii. 6–8, which provided for the due support of the dispossessed
priests (cf. 2 Kings xxiii. 8 f.) at the temple of Jerusalem, henceforth the sole legitimate sanctuary.   On this view, which is
that now generally adopted by O. T. scholars, we have a clear
indication of the date of the section (ii. 27–36), as already noted.
The intention of the writer to whom its present form is due is
clearly betrayed in verses 33–36.   He wishes by the expansion
of an earlier prophecy to give Divine sanction to the supersession
of the priestly family of Eli by Zadok and his descendants,
a measure which in reality was carried through by Solomon on
grounds of public policy.   This, as has been already indicated,
is the interpretation put upon it by the Deuteronomic author of
1 Kings ii. 27.

iii. 1–iv. 1ª.   *The call of Samuel and second announcement of*
the fate of Eli's House.
The boy-priest is called to a higher office as the prophet of
Yahweh.   In simple but graphic style the narrator tells the story
of Samuel's first direct intercourse with God.   In the end
Samuel is found established as 'a prophet of the LORD,' and
sought after as such throughout the length and breadth of the
land.

1. the child Samuel: the term *na'ar* here applied to Samuel
gives no indication of his age at this important crisis, since it is
found applied to any age, from a new-born infant (iv. 21) to a man
of forty (2 Chron. xiii. 7, cf. xii. 13).   From the statement, ii. 21,
however, we may infer that he had now reached the age of at

before Eli. And the word of the LORD was precious in those days; there was no open vision. And it came to 2 pass at that time, when Eli was laid down in his place, (now his eyes had begun to wax dim, that he could not see,) and the lamp of God was not yet gone out, and 3 Samuel was laid down *to sleep*, in the temple of the LORD, where the ark of God was; that the LORD called Samuel: 4 and he said, Here am I. And he ran unto Eli, and said, 5 Here am I; for thou calledst me. And he said, I called not; lie down again. And he went and lay down. And the LORD called yet again, Samuel. And 6 Samuel arose and went to Eli, and said, Here am I; for thou calledst me. And he answered, I called not, my son; lie down again. Now Samuel did not yet 7 know the LORD, neither was the word of the LORD yet revealed unto him. And the LORD called Samuel again 8

---

least thirteen to fifteen years (see on i. 24), an age at which a greater than he was already busy with 'the things of His Father' (Luke ii. 49).

the word of the LORD was precious: rather, as in the margin, 'rare,' a sense which the word has in Isa. xiii. 12 (R.V.), and which requires us to render the following clause: 'there was no frequent vision' (so R. V. marg.).

2 ff. The main statement runs: 'and it came to pass . . . that the LORD called Samuel' (verse 4), all between being explanatory details (cf. on i. 4-7).

3. the lamp of God was not yet gone out: the time indicated is towards morning; the lamp which burned in the temple during the hours of darkness was evidently supplied with oil sufficient for one night only. The custom, here vouched for, of the *aedituus* or temple guardian sleeping within the sanctuary has its parallel in the early notice of Joshua. Samuel's predecessor in the guardianship of the Ark, who 'departed not out of the Tent' of Meeting (Exod. xxxiii. 11). Eli apparently slept in an adjoining chamber.

4. The Greek text is here generally preferred, as more in keeping with the graphic character of the narrative: 'and it came to pass (verse 2) . . . that the LORD called, Samuel, Samuel.' Cf. verse 10, 'as at other times.' In verse 6, also, the LXX repeats the name.

the third time.   And he arose and went to Eli, and said,
Here am I; for thou calledst me.   And Eli perceived
9 that the LORD had called the child.   Therefore Eli said
unto Samuel, Go, lie down: and it shall be, if he call
thee, that thou shalt say, Speak, LORD; for thy servant
heareth.   So Samuel went and lay down in his place.
10 And the LORD came, and stood, and called as at other
times, Samuel, Samuel.   Then Samuel said, Speak; for
11 thy servant heareth.   And the LORD said to Samuel,
Behold, I will do a thing in Israel, at which both the
12 ears of every one that heareth it shall tingle.   In that
day I will perform against Eli all that I have spoken
concerning his house, from the beginning even unto the
13 end.   For I have told him that I will judge his house

10. the LORD came, and stood: the Deity is now, for the
first time, visible as well as audible.   The whole passage is of
importance for the writer's conception of the mode of revelation
in early times.

iii. 11-14. *Announcement of the impending punishment of Eli and
his house.*   Render: 'Behold, I am about to do a thing in Israel,'
&c.; the Hebrew idiom emphasizes the fact that the punishment
is on the eve of execution.   The figure of the tingling ears is also
found 2 Kings xxi. 12; Jer. xix. 3.

12. The reference is clearly to the contents of ii. 27-36.   Those
who hold the latter section to be entirely Deuteronomistic are
obliged to regard this verse as a harmonistic addition (see
above on ii. 27 ff.).

from the beginning even unto the end: *lit.* 'beginning and
ending'; the Divine purpose with regard to Eli will be completely
and thoroughly carried out.

13. For I have told him: the Massoretic pointing continues
the backward reference to the message of the 'man of God,' but
the object of the vision to Samuel is only made apparent, and the
latter's fear (verse 15) fully justified, if we read with Klostermann
and most others: 'and thou shalt tell him that I am about to judge
(i.e. punish) his house for ever'; the Divine judgement is
irrevocable.   The text of the following clauses has been altered
from religious motives, and is to be restored, following the LXX,
somewhat as follows: 'because he knew that his sons were
blaspheming God (see R.V. marg.), and he restrained them not.'

for ever, for the iniquity which he knew, because his sons did bring a curse upon themselves, and he restrained them not. And therefore I have sworn unto the house 14 of Eli, that the iniquity of Eli's house shall not be purged with sacrifice nor offering for ever. And Samuel 15 lay until the morning, and opened the doors of the house of the LORD. And Samuel feared to shew Eli the vision. Then Eli called Samuel, and said, Samuel, my 16 son. And he said, Here am I. And he said, What is 17 the thing that *the LORD* hath spoken unto thee? I pray thee hide it not from me: God do so to thee, and more also, if thou hide any thing from me of all the things that he spake unto thee. And Samuel told him every whit, 18 and hid nothing from him. And he said, It is the LORD: let him do what seemeth him good. And Samuel grew, 19 and the LORD was with him, and did let none of his words fall to the ground. And all Israel from Dan even 20 to Beer-sheba knew that Samuel was established to be

---

17. God do so to thee, and more also: this form of oath is especially common in the Books of Samuel (xiv. 44; xx. 13; xxv. 22, &c.), although most frequently the punishment is invoked by the speaker upon himself, 'God do so to me,' &c. The formula is to be explained as 'an imprecation originally connected with the ceremony of slaying an animal at the taking of an oath. The parties pray that the fate of the victim may be theirs' (H. P. Smith).

18. Eli's pious resignation may be compared with David's in less distressful circumstances (2 Sam. xv. 26).

iii. 19–iv. 1ᵃ. From this time onwards Samuel takes his place as the leader of the religious life of Israel. The reality of his call to be Yahweh's prophet was confirmed by the fact that Yahweh 'did let none of his words fall to the ground,' i. e. become ineffectual or unfulfilled.

20. from Dan (in the furthest north) **even to Beer-sheba** (in the extreme south): the oft-recurring expression for the whole extent of Canaan. From verse 20 to iv. 1 inclusive (see next section), the Greek text of Samuel differs considerably from the Hebrew. The latter, especially in iii. 21 and iv. 1ᵃ, is clearly in

21 a prophet of the LORD. And the LORD appeared again
in Shiloh : for the LORD revealed himself to Samuel in
4 Shiloh by the word of the LORD. And the word of
Samuel came to all Israel.

[A] Now Israel went out against the Philistines to

---

some disorder, but it is scarcely possible now to determine the
precise contents and order of the original.

(b) iv. 1ᵇ–vii. 1. *An invasion of the Philistines is followed by the
capture and subsequent return of the Ark.*

In their present connexion these three chapters form the
historical continuation of chs. i–iii. That the two sections,
however, are not from the same hand is now universally
admitted by O T. scholars, chiefly on the following grounds : (1)
the centre of interest now shifts from the person of Samuel, *who
is not once mentioned in* iv–vi, to the fortunes of the Ark ; (2) the
fate of the house of Eli, which the preceding narrative has led us
to expect as the main subject of the chapters before us, proves to
be but an incident in the story of a greater disaster ; and (3) the
religious standpoint of this section is much less advanced than
that of the previous chapters. In particular, the ideas here
associated with the Ark are of a more antique cast than those
reflected in almost any other O. T. references thereto. For these
and other reasons critics generally are agreed in detecting in this
section one of the earliest strata in the Books of Samuel. The
editor, however, has given us but an excerpt from a fuller
narrative (see on iv. 1, vi. 1), which must originally have
contained some account of the further success of the Philistine
invasion, including the destruction of the sanctuary of Shiloh (see
on xxi. 1) and the conquest of Central Palestine (see on xiii. 3,
a Philistine resident in Geba). As it now stands we have (1) the
defeat of the Israelites by the Philistines, involving the capture of
the Ark of Yahweh and the subsequent death of Eli (ch. iv) ; (2) the
fortunes of the Ark in the country of the Philistines, by which
the superiority of Yahweh to the native deities is vindicated (v) ;
and (3) the restoration of the Ark to Israelite territory (vi).

iv. 1–5. *A Philistine invasion and victory lead the Israelites to
fetch the Ark of Yahweh from Shiloh.*

1. The fuller LXX text is to be preferred : ' And it came to pass
in those days that the Philistines were gathered together to battle
against Israel, and Israel went out against them to battle,' &c.
This is the first mention in Samuel of these powerful enemies of
Israel, who were destined to play so large a part in the establish-

battle, and pitched beside Eben-ezer : and the Philistines
pitched in Aphek.   And the Philistines put themselves 2
in array against Israel : and when they joined battle,
Israel was smitten before the Philistines : and they slew
of the army in the field about four thousand men.   And 3
when the people were come into the camp, the elders of
Israel said, Wherefore hath the LORD smitten us to-day
before the Philistines?   Let us fetch the ark of the

---

ment of the Hebrew monarchy. The Hebrews knew that the
Philistines (*Pĕlishtîm*), like themselves, were foreign invaders,
whose original home is given as Caphtor (Amos ix. 7 ; Jer. xlvii. 4,
&c.).   The older identification of Caphtor with the Delta of the
Nile is now abandoned in favour of Crete or, on better grounds,
the southern coast of Asia Minor.   The *Pĕlishtîm* are undoubtedly
the *Pulusati* of the Egyptian monuments, the leading tribe among
a number that invaded Palestine by land and sea early in the reign
of Ramses III. *circa* 1200 B.C.   In the time of the Judges they are
already in possession of the great maritime plain from Joppa
southwards, the Philistia of the R.V. (so uniformly for Palestina
of A.V.), a name which in its later Graeco Latin form, Palestina,
was extended to the whole country west of the Jordan.   As
a race of Aryan extraction, the Philistines did not practise the
Semitic rite of circumcision, hence the opprobrious epithet 'the
uncircumcised' so often applied to them by the Hebrews.
Politically they formed a confederacy under the control of five
'lords,' whose seats of government were the cities of Ashdod,
Ekron, Ashkelon, Gaza, and Gath.   Owing largely to their superior
political and military organization, they successfully contested, for
at least a century, the hegemony of Central and Southern Palestine
with the Israelites until their power was finally broken by David.
According to 1 Sam. xiv. 52, 'there was sore war against the
Philistines all the days of Saul.'   See further Moore's article
'Philistines' in *EBi.*, vol. iii.

   Eben-ezer: 'stone of help,' is not to be identified off-hand
with the Ebenezer of vii. 12 (which see), but must be placed in
the neighbourhood of **Aphek**, which is probably located at some
spot in the plain of Sharon commanding the entrance to the plain
of Dothan, the natural line of march for an attack on Central
Palestine.

   2. in the field: in the open country where the Philistines
could use their famous war-chariots (xiii. 5 ; 2 Sam. i. 6).

   3. For the significance of the Ark and the fuller designations
employed here and in verse 4, see note A in the Appendix.

covenant of the LORD out of Shiloh unto us, that it may
come among us, and save us out of the hand of our
4 enemies.   So the people sent to Shiloh, and they
brought from thence the ark of the covenant of the LORD
of hosts, which sitteth upon the cherubim : and the two
sons of Eli, Hophni and Phinehas, were there with the
5 ark of the covenant of God.   And when the ark of the
covenant of the LORD came into the camp, all Israel
shouted with a great shout, so that the earth rang again.
6 And when the Philistines heard the noise of the shout,
they said, What meaneth the noise of this great shout in
the camp of the Hebrews ? And they understood that
7 the ark of the LORD was come into the camp.   And the
Philistines were afraid, for they said, God is come into
the camp.   And they said, Woe unto us ! for there hath
8 not been such a thing heretofore.   Woe unto us ! who
shall deliver us out of the hand of these mighty gods ?
these are the gods that smote the Egyptians with all
9 manner of plagues in the wilderness.   Be strong, and
quit yourselves like men, O ye Philistines, that ye be not
servants unto the Hebrews, as they have been to you :

---

4. Omit 'there' with LXX.   The two sons of Eli accompany
the Ark to the camp as its bearers (cf. 2 Sam. xv. 29).

iv. 6-11. *Consternation of the Philistines. Israel is again
defeated, and the Ark captured.*

6. the Hebrews : the name by which the children of Israel
were known to the surrounding nations (xiv. 11 ; xxix. 3). 6[b]
should be taken along with verse 7 : ' and when they understood
. . . the Philistines were afraid,' &c.

7. God (*Elohim*) **is come :** Hebrew writers carefully avoid
putting the sacred name Yahweh into the mouth of a non-Israelite.
But such an unqualified confession is strange in the present connexion, and we should read, as suggested by LXX (B) : ' these are
their gods (cf. 8 f.), they have come to them to the camp.'

8. in the wilderness : either an excusable inaccuracy, or
a copyist's slip for the word signifying ' and with pestilence '
(Wellhausen).

quit yourselves like men, and fight.   And the Philistines 10
fought, and Israel was smitten, and they fled every man
to his tent : and there was a very great slaughter ; for there
fell of Israel thirty thousand footmen.   And the ark of 11
God was taken ; and the two sons of Eli, Hophni and
Phinehas, were slain.   And there ran a man of Benjamin 12
out of the army, and came to Shiloh the same day with
his clothes rent, and with earth upon his head.   And 13
when he came, lo, Eli sat upon his seat by the way side
watching : for his heart trembled for the ark of God.
And when the man came into the city, and told it, all
the city cried out.   And when Eli heard the noise of the 14
crying, he said, What meaneth the noise of this tumult ?
And the man hasted, and came and told Eli.   Now Eli 15
was ninety and eight years old ; and his eyes were set,
that he could not see.   And the man said unto Eli, 16
I am he that came out of the army, and I fled to-day out
of the army.   And he said, How went the matter, my
son ?   And he that brought the tidings answered and 17
said, Israel is fled before the Philistines, and there hath

---

iv. 12-18.   *How the tidings reached Shiloh and how they affected
Eli.*

12. To rend one's clothes and to put earth or ashes on one's
head were the universal signs of mourning for the dead (2 Sam.
i. 2), or for a national calamity (Joshua vii. 6 ; 2 Sam. xv. 32).

13. The M.T. is here in some disorder, otherwise Eli, if he sat
by the way side watching, would have been the first to receive
the fugitive's report.   The LXX text gives a better reading : 'Lo,
Eli sat upon his seat beside the gate [probably the gate of the
temple at Shiloh, as in i. 9], watching the way,' a reading confirmed by verse 18.

15. This verse interrupts the narrative, and is probably a later
insertion based, in part, on iii. 2.   The fact that Eli was an old
man is stated by the original author in verse 18.

17. The elements of the fourfold disaster are skilfully arranged
—defeat, loss of life, personal bereavement, and finally, the
climax of all, the capture of the Ark.

been also a great slaughter among the people, and thy
two sons also, Hophni and Phinehas, are dead, and the
18 ark of God is taken.   And it came to pass, when he
made mention of the ark of God, that he fell from off
his seat backward by the side of the gate, and his neck
brake, and he died: for he was an old man, and heavy.
19 And he had judged Israel forty years.   And his daughter
in law, Phinehas' wife, was with child, near to be delivered: and when she heard the tidings that the ark of
God was taken, and that her father in law and her husband were dead, she bowed herself and brought forth;
20 for her pains came upon her.   And about the time of
her death the women that stood by her said unto her,
Fear not; for thou hast brought forth a son.   But she
21 answered not, neither did she regard it.   And she
named the child Ichabod, saying, The glory is departed
from Israel: because the ark of God was taken, and
22 because of her father in law and her husband.   And she
said, The glory is departed from Israel; for the ark of
God is taken.
5   Now the Philistines had taken the ark of God, and they

---

18. forty years: LXX twenty.   In chs. i–iii Eli is represented
solely as a priest, not as a 'judge'; the clause is editorial.

iv. 19–22. *The effect of the tidings, now aggravated by the death
of her father-in-law, on the wife of Phinehas.*

21. Ichabod: Heb. *I-kābōd* = No-Glory, the reference being, as
explained in the text, primarily to the capture of the Ark, but including also the loss of those who were its appointed priests.

22. Added as a corrective to 21[b] by an editor or reader acquainted with the character of Eli's sons as depicted in the
younger narrative, chs. i–iii.

v. 1–5. *The Ark and the image of Dagon.* The underlying
idea in chs. v–vi is the superiority of the God of the Hebrews,
who throughout this section is so inseparably associated with the
Ark as to be almost identified with it (see Appendix, note A), and
whose greater power is manifested by the misfortunes of which
the chief deity and the whole race of the Philistines are victims.

brought it from Eben-ezer unto Ashdod. And the 2
Philistines took the ark of God, and brought it into the
house of Dagon, and set it by Dagon. And when they 3
of Ashdod arose early on the morrow, behold, Dagon
was fallen upon his face to the ground before the ark of
the LORD. And they took Dagon, and set him in his
place again. And when they arose early on the morrow 4
morning, behold, Dagon was fallen upon his face to the
ground before the ark of the LORD; and the head of
Dagon and both the palms of his hands *lay* cut off upon
the threshold; only *the stump of* Dagon was left to him.
Therefore neither the priests of Dagon, nor any that 5

---

1. Ashdod: the modern *Esdud*, halfway between Joppa and
Gaza, and about three miles from the coast, was at this period
apparently the chief of the five cities of the Philistine confederation
(Pentapolis), a position for which its central situation marked
it out.

2. The Ark is deposited beside the statue of Dagon, in the *cella*
or *adytum* of the latter's temple. According as the name Dagon
is to be connected with *dag*, 'fish,' or with *dagan*, 'corn,' this
deity will have been originally a god of the sea, or a god of
agriculture. The fairly numerous place-names in Palestine
into which the name enters render it probable that Dagon was
originally a Canaanite deity, a conclusion in favour of the second
of the alternative etymologies just given. Temples were dedicated
to Dagon in Gaza (Judges xvi. 21 ff.) and Ashdod—the latter being
still in existence in the time of the Maccabees (1 Macc. x. 71 ff.)—
and doubtless in the other cities as well. Hebrews and Philistines
alike deposited military trophies in temples (cf. xxi. 9 with xxxi.
10, 1 Chron. x. 10).

3. Dagon was fallen: note the identification of the god with his
stone image. The latter is found prostrate, but as yet intact,
before the Ark of Yahweh, as if in acknowledgement of Yahweh's
superiority, of which verse 4 brings still more convincing evidence.

4. A word signifying 'trunk' or **stump** has dropped out of the
last clause of the Hebrew, as the Versions attest.

5. A note tracing the custom of leaping over the threshold of
the *cella* of Dagon to this *contretemps*. The custom, however, is
found in many ancient cults (cf. Zeph. i. 9, and see Trumbull,
The Threshold Covenant, 116 f.).

come into Dagon's house, tread on the threshold of
Dagon in Ashdod, unto this day.

6 But the hand of the LORD was heavy upon them of
Ashdod, and he destroyed them, and smote them with
7 tumours, even Ashdod and the borders thereof. And
when the men of Ashdod saw that it was so, they said,
The ark of the God of Israel shall not abide with us : for
his hand is sore upon us, and upon Dagon our god.
8 They sent therefore and gathered all the lords of the
Philistines unto them, and said, What shall we do with
the ark of the God of Israel? And they answered, Let
the ark of the God of Israel be carried about unto Gath.
And they carried the ark of the God of Israel about
9 *thither*. And it was so, that, after they had carried it
about, the hand of the LORD was against the city with a
very great discomfiture : and he smote the men of the
city, both small and great, and tumours brake out upon
10 them. So they sent the ark of God to Ekron. And it
came to pass, as the ark of God came to Ekron, that the
Ekronites cried out, saying, They have brought about
the ark of the God of Israel to us, to slay us and our
11 people. They sent therefore and gathered together all

---

v. 6-12. *Further evidence of the displeasure and power of Yahweh
in the outbreak of plague.*

6. Sickness and disease are referred by the O.T. writers to the
direct action of God without the intervention of secondary or
contributory causes. In this case it is now agreed that some
variety of bubonic plague is intended. The Hebrew word for
'tumours' does not signify 'haemorrhoids,' the 'emerods' of A.V.,
but, as in R.V. marg., 'plague boils' or buboes.

8. The site of Gath has not yet been recovered. It is usually
identified with the modern *Tel-es-Safi*, the Blanche Garde of the
Crusaders, about sixteen miles east of Ashdod. See R.V. marg.
for the LXX addition to this verse, and to vi. 1, also the note
on vi. 4.

10. Ekron: the most northerly member of the Pentapolis, the
modern *Tel-Akir*.

the lords of the Philistines, and they said, Send away the
ark of the God of Israel, and let it go again to its own
place, that it slay us not, and our people : for there was
a deadly discomfiture throughout all the city ; the hand
of God was very heavy there. .And the men that died 12
not were smitten with the tumours : and the cry of the
city went up to heaven.

And the ark of the LORD was in the country of the 6
Philistines seven months. And the Philistines called for 2
the priests and the diviners, saying, What shall we do
with the ark of the LORD? shew us wherewith we shall
send it to its place. And they said, If ye send away 3
the ark of the God of Israel, send it not empty ; but in
any wise return him a guilt offering : then ye shall be
healed, and it shall be known to you why his hand is not
removed from you. Then said they, What shall be the 4
guilt offering which we shall return to him? And they
said, Five golden tumours, and five golden mice, *accord-*

---

11. Here the source of their misfortunes is ascribed by the
Philistines indifferently to the Ark and to the 'hand of God.'

vi. 1–18. *The restoration of the Ark.* The original narrative
appears to have been somewhat curtailed by the editor, for verses
1 ff. do not seem a natural continuation of v. 12.

3. a guilt offering (Heb. *'āshām*): R.V. marg. 'trespass
offering,'.reversing the position of these terms in A.V. The word
occurs only here and in 2 Kings xii. 16 outside of the Priests' Code,
and denotes primarily compensation or reparation 'for the infringe-
ment of the rights of another, or for misappropriation of his
property,' as in the present case.

4 f. Five golden tumours: for the conception underlying this
form of offering, see Frazer's *Golden Bough*, 2nd edition, ii. 426 f.
Cf. the analogous case of the brazen serpent (Num. xxi. 4 ff.).

five golden mice: the first indication in the M.T. of what,
at first sight, seems an additional plague of mice, as expressly
stated in the Greek text of verse 6, vi. 1 (see R.V. marg.). This
view of the meaning of the golden mice, however, is at variance
with the words that follow : 'for one plague was on you all.' The
Hebrew word for 'mouse,' moreover, is a comprehensive term

ing to the number of the lords of the Philistines : for one
5 plague was on you all, and on your lords. Wherefore
ye shall make images of your tumours, and images of
your mice that mar the land; and ye shall give glory
unto the God of Israel: peradventure he will lighten his
hand from off you, and from off your gods, and from off
6 your land. Wherefore then do ye harden your hearts,
as the Egyptians and Pharaoh hardened their hearts?
when he had wrought wonderfully among them, did they
7 not let the people go, and they departed? Now therefore take and prepare you a new cart, and two milch
kine, on which there hath come no yoke, and tie the
kine to the cart, and bring their calves home from them:
8 and take the ark of the LORD, and lay it upon the cart;
and put the jewels of gold, which ye return him for a
guilt offering, in a coffer by the side thereof; and send
9 it away, that it may go. And see, if it goeth up by the
way of its own border to Beth-shemesh, then he hath
done us this great evil: but if not, then we shall know

---

for numerous small rodents, and the introduction of the 'mice
that destroy, or spread destruction through, the country'—not
'that destroy the crops'—is to be explained by the well-established
fact that rats and similar house vermin 'are at once the earliest
victims and the most dangerous propagators of the bubonic plague'
(see Dr. Gibson in *Expository Times*, xii. 378-380; cf. *ibid*. xv.
(1904) 476).

6. The margin 'when he had made a mock [or made sport] of
them' is preferable, cf. xxxi. 4; Num. xxii. 29. The reference is
to Exod. x. 2 (J).

7-9. The procedure here recommended is entirely in the
spirit of antiquity, which found omens in so many ways that appear
strange to the modern mind. For other omens see xiv. 9 f.;
2 Sam. v. 24. The two milch kine, like the new cart, are to be
such as had never been used for ordinary purposes, as in the
parallel cases Num. xix 2; Deut. xxi. 3. All are 'virgin' in the
sense in which we speak of 'virgin soil.'

9. he hath done, &c. : the meaning is that if the mother-kine,
instead of making direct for their calves, took the road to Beth-

that it is not his hand that smote us; it was a chance
that happened to us. And the men did so; and took 10
two milch kine, and tied them to the cart, and shut up ·
their calves at home: and they put the ark of the LORD 11
upon the cart, and the coffer with the mice of gold and
the images of their tumours. And the kine took the 12
straight way by the way to Beth-shemesh; they went
along the high way, lowing as they went, and turned not
aside to the right hand or to the left; and the lords of
the Philistines went after them unto the border of Beth-
shemesh.   And they of Beth-shemesh were reaping their 13
wheat harvest in the valley: and they lifted up their eyes,
and saw the ark, and rejoiced to see it.   And the cart came 14
into the field of Joshua the Beth-shemite, and stood there,
where there was a great stone: and they clave the wood
of the cart, and offered up the kine for a burnt offering
unto the LORD. And the Levites took down the ark of 15
the LORD, and the coffer that was with it, wherein the
jewels of gold were, and put them on the great stone:
and the men of Beth-shemesh offered burnt offerings and
sacrificed sacrifices the same day unto the LORD.   And 16

shemesh—the nearest point across the frontier—it would be clear
that a course so entirely contrary to their natural instincts could
only be due to a special impulse from the God of the Hebrews.
The source of the present distress would then be evident. Beth-
shemesh, 'house (or temple), of the sun,' is the modern *Ain Shams*,
'fountain of the sun,' at the mouth of the *Wadi Sarar*, the ancient
'Valley of Sorek' (Judges xvi. 4).

13. rejoiced to see it: read by a slight change: 'came rejoic-
ing to meet it' (LXX).

14. a great stone: cf. xiv. 33, in both cases clearly 'an altar-
stone.' The idea appears to be that the kine spontaneously
offered themselves as a sacrifice (*Rel. Sem.*² 309).

15. A post-exilic addition by some one who missed the services
of the Levites, the proper ministers of the Ark according to the
Priests' Code. The details are impossible after verse 14, which
has its proper continuation in verse 16.

when the five lords of the Philistines had seen it, they returned to Ekron the same day.

17 And these are the golden tumours which the Philistines returned for a guilt offering unto the LORD ; for Ashdod one, for Gaza one, for Ashkelon one, for Gath 18 one, for Ekron one ; and the golden mice, according to the number of all the cities of the Philistines belonging to the five lords, both of fenced cities and of country villages : even unto the great stone, whereon they set down the ark of the LORD, *which stone remaineth* unto this day 19 in the field of Joshua the Beth-shemite. And he smote of the men of Beth-shemesh, because they had looked into the ark of the LORD, even he smote of the people seventy men, *and* fifty thousand men : and the people mourned, because the LORD had smitten the people with 20 a great slaughter. And the men of Beth-shemesh said, Who is able to stand before the LORD, this holy God ? 21 and to whom shall he go up from us ? And they sent

---

17-18ᵃ (to 'villages'), another addition in the 'repetitious' style of late writers. The large number of mice here implied is at variance with verse 4 (*five* mice).

18ᵇ : read, with a slight emendation : 'and the great stone upon which . . . is a witness unto this day in the field,' &c.

19. The M.T. is again in disorder. The text from which the Greek translators worked seems to have run thus (see R.V. marg.): 'Now the sons of Jeconiah rejoiced not among (with) the men of Beth-shemesh when they beheld (with joy) the ark of Yahweh.' This gives at least an intelligible motive, indifference to the honour of Yahweh, for the punishment that follows· 'and he (Yahweh) slew of them seventy men.' The absurd exaggeration 'and fifty thousand men' is an evident gloss.

20. this holy God : different aspects of the Divine character are expressed by the term 'holy' in different contexts. See Davidson, *Theology of the O. T.*, 144 ff., 'the Holiness of God.' Here the majesty and might of Yahweh, and His zeal for His own honour are implied. The incident is a striking illustration of Deut. iv. 24 : 'Yahweh, thy God, is a devouring fire,' bringing death to those who do Him dishonour. Cf. Joshua xxiv. 19, 'he is an holy God ; he is a jealous God.'

messengers to the inhabitants of Kiriath-jearim, saying,
The Philistines have brought again the ark of the LORD ;
come ye down, and fetch it up to you.   And the men of 7
Kiriath-jearim came, and fetched up the ark of the LORD,
and brought it into the house of Abinadab in the hill,
and sanctified Eleazar his son to keep the ark of the
LORD.

[D] And it came to pass, from the day that the ark abode 2

---

21. Kiriath-jearim: 'the city of thickets,' usually identified
with *Kiryat-el-Enab*, nine miles west of Jerusalem, and about the
same distance north-east of Beth-shemesh.   It was a Canaanite
city, one of four which formed the Gibeonite league (Josh. ix. 17),
and now almost certainly under Philistine suzerainty.   For the
bearing of this on the subsequent history of the Ark see on 2 Sam.
vi. 1, and more fully in the Appendix.

vii. 1. **sanctified**: the form of the verb here used signifies to
set apart persons, things, or places for a sacred use ; the person
thus set apart became ' holy,' and therefore qualified to perform
the necessary rites, and even to handle the Ark with impunity
(see Davidson, *Theology*, 145).

As indicated in the introduction to this section, the original
narrative doubtless contained further details of the invasion.   In
the present text of Samuel we have no explanation of the Philistine
ascendancy over Israel, such as is implied by the presence of
a Philistine officer with the necessary garrison at Gibeah (xiii. 19 ff.)
and at Beth-lehem (2 Sam. xxiii. 14).   One result of the present
campaign, at all events, was almost certainly the destruction of
the sanctuary at Shiloh, to which Jeremiah makes repeated
allusion (vii. 14, xxvi. 6 ; cf. Ps. lxxviii 60, and the note on
ch. xxi. 1 below).

(c) vii. 2-17. *Samuel the theocratic Judge.*

The interest of the narrative once more centres in Samuel, who
appears in this remarkable chapter as the theocratic ruler or judge
of all Israel.   After prevailing upon his contemporaries to abandon
the worship of the heathen deities of the Canaanites, Samuel summons the tribes to a great religious assembly at Mizpah.   Here
a national fast is held accompanied by a public sacrifice and confession of the nation's sins.   While the sacrifice is proceeding,
the Philistines suddenly attack the assembled worshippers, but
are miraculously repulsed.   So complete, indeed, is their defeat that

in Kiriath-jearim, that the time was long; for it was
twenty years : and all the house of Israel lamented after
3 the LORD.   And Samuel spake unto all the house of
Israel, saying, If ye do return unto the LORD with all

---

they cease from further attacks during the remainder of Samuel's
lifetime, while a large part, at least, of the Philistine territory is
ceded to Israel.   During Samuel's judgeship, also, there is peace
between Israel and the former inhabitants of the country, and an
ideal state of society generally prevails.   How far this highly
coloured picture of Israel in the period preceding the institution of
the monarchy is removed from the true historical situation as
reflected in our oldest sources will appear in due course.   We have
here rather a conspicuous illustration of that idealization of the
early history of Israel which is a characteristic mark of what is
known as the Deuteronomic school of Hebrew historians.   The
nearest parallel is found in the 'framework' of the Book of Judges
(see Thatcher, *Judges*, pp. 5 ff.), a product of the same school.
The 'almost rhythmic alternation' of apostasy and oppression,
penitence and deliverance which characterizes the schematic setting
of the narratives of the greater judges is evident in the present
narrative.   Samuel, indeed, is here represented as the last and
greatest of the judges, God having wrought through his intercession a more marvellous deliverance than any preceding judge had
achieved.   (See further, Introduction, sect. iv.)

2. for it was twenty years : it is doubtful if much reliance can
be placed on this note of time.   The sentence in the original is
awkwardly constructed, and perhaps had no such note originally,
the writer having pictured the reformation under Samuel as following immediately on the return of the Ark.   This view is at
least in harmony with the Deuteronomistic chronology of Judges
xiii. 1, according to which the Philistine oppression lasted forty
years, of which twenty were passed under Samson (Judges xv.
20, xvi. 31) and twenty under Eli (1 Sam. iv. 18, LXX).

lamented after the LORD : the verb thus rendered denotes
elsewhere 'to lament for the dead,' a meaning hardly suitable here.
A slight change gives 'and Israel turned after Yahweh' (cf. 'return,'
verse 3).   Samuel, it will be noted, is throughout brought into
relation with 'all the house of Israel,' just as in the framework of
Judges the local or tribal heroes of the older narratives are trans-
formed into theocratic rulers of all Israel.

3. The call to repentance. Any good reference Bible will show
the resemblance in phraseology between verses 3, 4, Deuteronomy
and the Deuteronomic parts of Judges (cf. especially Judges x.
10-16 with the present passage).

your heart, then put away the strange gods and the Ashtaroth from among you, and prepare your hearts unto the LORD, and serve him only : and he will deliver you out of the hand of the Philistines. Then the chil- 4 dren of Israel did put away the Baalim and the Ashtaroth, and served the LORD only.

And Samuel said, Gather all Israel to Mizpah, and I 5 will pray for you unto the LORD. And they gathered 6

the strange gods: foreign, non-Israelite deities, such as were worshipped by the native races of Canaan—the Baalim of verse 4.

the Ashtaroth: the Hebrew plural of Ashtoreth, the goddess whom the Babylonians called Ishtar and the Greeks Astarte (cf. xxxi. 10), one of the oldest and most widely distributed of Semitic deities. Among the Western Semites she was the goddess of fertility and the sexual relations ; hence rites of a most licentious character were associated with her worship. The name of the goddess was most probably pronounced Ashtart in Palestine (hence the Greek form), the traditional form Ashtoreth being an intentional deformation, as in the case of Molech and the personal names Ishbosheth and Mephibosheth (see on 2 Sam. ii. 8). The plural form here used refers to the various local Astartes (cf. the localization of the Virgin in Roman Catholic countries).

4. the Baalim: each locality, in the same way, had its *ba'al* (*lit.* 'owner,' 'proprietor'), the guardian *genius loci*, and bearing its name, Baal Hermon, Baal Peor, &c. The more important local Baals had proper names ; that of Tyre, for example, was known as Melkarth, the Baal of 1 Kings xvi. ff. 'The Baalim and the Ashtaroth,' therefore, may be paraphrased 'the gods and goddesses of Canaan.'

vii. 5-9. *The national religious convention at Mizpah.* Amendment has been promised for the future, but the guilt of past unfaithfulness has yet to be taken away.

5. Mizpah: sometimes also 'Mizpeh' (watch-tower), the modern *Nebi Samwil*, on a lofty height five miles north-west of Jerusalem. It was the rallying place of the tribes in the story of Judges xx. 1 ff., and at a later period the residence of Gedaliah, the governor appointed by Nebuchadnezzar (2 Kings xxv. 23). Still later it was selected by Judas Maccabaeus to be the scene of another great day of national humiliation, ' for in Mizpah was there a place of prayer aforetime in Israel' (1 Macc. iii. 44).

I will pray for you: Samuel was both the child of prayer and a man of prayer (viii. 6, xii. 19, 23). In Jer. xv. 1 Moses and Samuel are cited as men of prevailing prayer.

together to Mizpah, and drew water, and poured it out
before the LORD, and fasted on that day, and said there,
We have sinned against the LORD.   And Samuel judged
7 the children of Israel in Mizpah.   And when the Philistines heard that the children of Israel were gathered together to Mizpah, the lords of the Philistines went up
against Israel.   And when the children of Israel heard
8 it, they were afraid of the Philistines.   And the children
of Israel said to Samuel, Cease not to cry unto the LORD
our God for us, that he will save us out of the hand of
9 the Philistines.   And Samuel took a sucking lamb, and
offered it for a whole burnt offering unto the LORD : and
Samuel cried unto the LORD for Israel ; and the LORD
10 answered him.   And as Samuel was offering up the
burnt offering, the Philistines drew near to battle against

6. drew water, &c. : we have here a ritual survival from the
nomad period of Hebrew history.   After the change to the
peasant life of Canaan, water, the most precious of desert offerings,
was supplanted by the fruit of the vine.   On the present occasion
the pouring out of the water 'before the LORD' is probably intended also to symbolize the outpouring of the heart in penitent
confession.

vii. 7-12.   *The attack and miraculous defeat of the Philistines.*
7 f. The Philistines are naturally suspicious of this national
gathering, and prepare to nip in the bud any attempt to throw off
their yoke.   An attack is made while Samuel is in the act of
sacrificing.   The closing words of verse 8 occur again in the
much older narrative (ix. 16), in a setting which illustrates the
different theological standpoints of the two writers.   Here God
works by direct intervention, there through a chosen human
instrument.
9. The offering of the sucking lamb (Lev. xxii. 27) is to be
regarded as part of the ceremony of expiation following upon
confession, rather than as the sacrifice usual at the beginning of
a campaign (see on xiii. 9 ff.).
10 f. The discomfiture of the Philistines is represented as
having been accomplished by Yahweh alone, without even such
co-operation as is implied in the similar incidents, Joshua x. 10 f.,

Israel : but the LORD thundered with a great thunder on that day upon the Philistines, and discomfited them ; and they were smitten down before Israel. And the 11 men of Israel went out of Mizpah, and pursued the Philistines, and smote them, until they came under Beth-car. Then Samuel took a stone, and set it between 12 Mizpah and Shen, and called the name of it Eben-ezer, saying, Hitherto hath the LORD helped us. So the 13 Philistines were subdued, and they came no more within the border of Israel : and the hand of the LORD was 14 against the Philistines all the days of Samuel. And the cities which the Philistines had taken from Israel were restored to Israel, from Ekron even unto Gath ; and the border thereof did Israel deliver out of the hand of the Philistines. And there was peace between Israel and the Amorites. And Samuel judged Israel all the days 15

Judges v 20. 'The men of Israel,' in verse 11, merely complete the rout which Yahweh had begun. The site of Beth-car is unknown.

12. Shen: *lit.* 'tooth' or crag, but the LXX apparently read Jeshanah (2 Chron. xiii. 19), which is here generally preferred.

Eben-ezer; see R.V. marg., also note on iv. 1b.

Hitherto: of time, 'until now,' not of space, 'thus far.'

vii. 13 f. *The extraordinary result of the Philistine defeat.* The statement that the Philistines 'came no more within the borders of Israel' cannot be reconciled with the facts of history. There cannot be the least doubt that our oldest source is correct in representing the continued oppression of the Philistines as the historical motive of the introduction of the monarchy (see ix. 15-17). The true state of the relations between the Hebrews and their powerful enemies is accurately depicted in the same early source as a state of continual warfare 'all the days of Saul' (xiv. 52). The two verses before us are full of the characteristic phraseology of the Deuteronomic edition of Judges.

14. the Amorites: a general name for the native races of Canaan, specially in the Pentateuch documents E and D ; the corresponding term in J is Canaanites.

15 ff. The theocratic ideal has been realized. Under Yahweh, his true king, Israel is at peace from all his enemies within and

16 of his life.   And he went from year to year in circuit to
Beth-el, and Gilgal, and Mizpah ; and he judged Israel
17 in all those places.   And his return was to Ramah, for
there was his house ; and there he judged Israel : and he
built there an altar unto the LORD.

8   And it came to pass, when Samuel was old, that he

without   Samuel is Yahweh's earthly representative, dispensing
justice to a united Israel as did Moses in the birth-time of the nation
(Exod. xviii. 13 ff.).

16. Beth-el, the modern *Beitin*, ten miles north of Jerusalem,
was one of the oldest sanctuaries in the country.   This applies
also to **Gilgal**, if the famous sanctuary near Jericho is the locality
intended, but there were many Gilgals—Gilgal signifies a stone
circle—in Palestine (see the Bible dictionaries).   For the probable
site of **Ramah**, see on i. 1.

B. viii–xii.   *The Establishment of the Monarchy.*

The contents of these chapters in their present form, the result
of compilation from at least two originally independent documents,
may be divided into four sections : (1) viii. 1–22, the demand for
a king and ' the manner ' of the same ; (2) ix. 1—x. 27, Saul the son
of Kish anointed by Samuel and chosen at Mizpah ; (3) xi. 1–15,
Saul delivers Jabesh-gilead from the Ammonites, the kingdom
renewed at Gilgal ; (4) xii. 1–25, Samuel's farewell address.

These five chapters, recording the election of Saul to be the first
king of Israel, have already (see Introduction, sect. iv) been the
subject of detailed investigation, as throwing a flood of light upon
the literary methods of the Hebrew historians in general and upon
the compilation of the Books of Samuel in particular.   It will
suffice to note here, by way of recapitulation, that, as now
arranged, the whole section (chs. viii–xii) gives the impression that
the introduction of the monarchy was an act of disloyalty to
Yahweh, Israel's true and only King, the theocratic form of
government being that under which Israel was intended by God
to work out his destiny in the world.   On closer inspection,
however, it was found that the narrative is not homogeneous, that
alongside of certain sections which are hostile to the monarchy are
found others in which it is represented as the gift of God and the
destined instrument of the deliverance of His people from the
oppression of the Philistines.   The latter view is reflected in
ix. 1—x. 16, xi. 1–11, 15, derived from an early source, M (a history
of the introduction of the monarchy), the former in viii. 1–22,
x. 17–27, which betray the peculiar standpoint of ch. vii, and may
be assumed to belong to the same Deuteronomistic source, D.

made his sons judges over Israel. Now the name of 2
his firstborn was Joel; and the name of his second,
Abijah: they were judges in Beer-sheba. And his sons 3
walked not in his ways, but turned aside after lucre, and
took bribes, and perverted judgement.

Then all the elders of Israel gathered themselves to- 4
gether, and came to Samuel unto Ramah: and they said
unto him, Behold, thou art old, and thy sons walk not 5
in thy ways: now make us a king to judge us like all
the nations. But the thing displeased Samuel, when 6
they said, Give us a king to judge us. And Samuel
prayed unto the LORD. And the LORD said unto Sam- 7
uel, Hearken unto the voice of the people in all that
they say unto thee: for they have not rejected thee, but
they have rejected me, that I should not be king over

For further exposition of the numerous points of divergence
between the two original narratives, see the Introduction, and
the notes below.

(a) viii. 1-22. *The demand for a king and the 'manner' of the
same.*

1. Israel has continued under theocratic government until the
old age of Samuel. As the representative of Yahweh, Samuel
delegates part of his judicial functions to his sons, who are installed
as judges in the remote south.

2. **Joel . . . Abijah:** both names contain, as the first and
second component respectively, the Divine name Yahweh.
Delitzsch in his *Babel and Bible* (English edition by Johns,
pp. 71 f., 133 ff.) claims that Joel is found in its full form *Ya-ve-ilu*
in Canaanite names as early as *circa* 2200 B. C., a fact of far-reaching
significance were it capable of proof. Delitzsch's reading, however,
has been vigorously contested (see *inter alia*, *ZATW.*, xxiii (1903),
pp. 355 ff.).

viii. 4-9 *The elders of Israel request Samuel to give them a king.*
The motives alleged for this request are (1) the unfitness of
Samuel's sons to succeed him as the executive of the theocracy,
and (2) the popular—and, for the writer, sinful (cf. xii. 17-19)—
desire to copy a heathen institution. A third motive is introduced
at the end of verse 20.

7. they have rejected me, that I should not be king over

8 them.   According to all the works which they have
done since the day that I brought them up out of
Egypt even unto this day, in that they have forsaken me,
9 and served other gods, so do they also unto thee.   Now
therefore hearken unto their voice : howbeit thou shalt
protest solemnly unto them, and shalt shew them the
manner of the king that shall reign over them.

10   [R] And Samuel told all the words of the LORD unto
11 the people that asked of him a king.   [D] And he said,

---

them: a definite expression of the writer's contention that the
theocracy was the form of government under which God had
willed that Israel should continue to the end, a position still more
definitely formulated in xii. 12ᵇ (cf. Judges viii. 23) : 'Yahweh,
your God, was your king.'

8. The people's conduct in this matter is of a piece with their
ingratitude to Yahweh in the past.   The comparison expressed in
the last clause is more clearly brought out by reading with LXX
'to me' after 'have done' in the first clause.   This view of the
period of the judges as a continuous declension from the worship
of Yahweh finds its classical expression in the kindred introduction
to the Deuteronomic edition of Judges (ii. 11—iii. 16 ; cf. with this
verse especially ii. 12 f. and iii. 11 ff.).

9. the manner (*mishpāṭ*) **of the king** : i. e. his constitutional
rights as enumerated verses 11–17, not those usurped by him.
Cf. 2 Kings xvii. 26, 'the manner of the God of the land,' the
proper rites and ceremonies pertaining to His worship.

10. unto the people that asked, &c.: by themselves these
words might be interpreted as in verses 7, 9 above, but the contents
of the following address, and especially verses 19 ff., show that
Samuel is here addressing a popular assembly as in chs. vii and xii.
Löhr in his commentary (see above, p. 31), improving on a suggestion by Cornill, has made it very probable that the editor of
this section, in combining the two narratives, M and D, has been
obliged to alter the original sequence of the latter in order to avoid
relating the election of Saul at Mizpah before he had given us the
contents of ch. ix.   The original arrangement in D, according to
Löhr, whom Nowack follows, was as follows : (1) viii. 1–9, the
elders approach Samuel at Ramah; (2) x. 17–19 (to 'over us'),
viii. 11–22 (to 'Israel'), the people summoned to Mizpah, exposition
of the 'manner of the king'; (3) x. 19ᵇ–24, election of Saul by
the sacred lot, followed immediately by (4) xii. 1–25, the farewell
address delivered at Mizpah, not at Gilgal, the whole concluded

This will be the manner of the king that shall reign over
you : he will take your sons, and appoint them unto him,
for his chariots, and to be his horsemen ; and they shall .
run before his chariots : and he will appoint them unto 12
him for captains of thousands, and captains of fifties ;
and *he will set some* to plow his ground, and to reap his
harvest, and to make his instruments of war, and the
instruments of his chariots.   And he will take your 13
daughters to be confectionaries, and to be cooks, and to

---

by (5) x. 25–27, the dismissal of the assembly and Saul's return to
Gibeah.   The verse viii. 10, the last words of viii. 22, and xi. 12–
14, which refers back to x. 27, are all due to the harmonizing
necessities of the editor, and are here indicated by R.   By this
arrangement D's narrative unquestionably gains in clearness and
consistency.

viii. 11–22.   *The King's Right.*
As implied in verse 9, Samuel has convened a national assembly
at Mizpah (x. 17. cf. vii. 5), and after accusing the people of their
ingratitude and disloyalty to their true King (x. 18 f., cf. viii. 8),
proceeds, as instructed (viii. 9), to show them ' the manner of the
king.'   First among the constitutional rights of the latter is placed
his demand for military service—here regarded very differently from
xxii. 7—and forced labour (*corvée*) on crown lands and in the royal
arsenal (verses 11 f.) ; then follow the needs of the royal kitchen,
and the appropriation of lands to reward the king's favourites
(13 f.) ; the throne, further, has to be supported by taxation, and
a numerous retinue of slaves is required to uphold the royal
dignity (15 f.).

11. they shall run before his chariots: as a bodyguard of
' runners ' for the sovereign ; hence adopted by ambitious aspirants
like Absalom (2 Sam. xv. 1) and Adonijah (1 Kings i. 5).

12. captains of thousands . . . of fifties: cf. ' captains of
hundreds ' (xxii. 7, 2 Sam. xviii. 1), all graded units in the organization of the national militia under the monarchy.   As this organization
was on a territorial basis, a district was known as the ' thousand ' (cf.
the ' hundreds ' of English constitutional history), which also became
synonymous with ' clan,' the unit of population which occupied the
district (see x. 19, 21).   Each tribe consisted of a varying number
of clans (R. V. ' families,' ix. 21, &c.), each clan of a number of
septs, technically called ' fathers' houses ' (ii. 27 f., xvii. 25, and
often). .

13. confectionaries: compounders of aromatic ointments and

14 be bakers.   And he will take your fields, and your vineyards, and your oliveyards, even the best of them, and
15 give them to his servants.   And he will take the tenth of
   your seed, and of your vineyards, and give to his officers,
16 and to his servants.   And he will take your menservants,
   and your maidservants, and your goodliest young men,
17 and your asses, and put them to his work.   He will take
   the tenth of your flocks : and ye shall be his servants.
18 And ye shall cry out in that day because of your king
   which ye shall have chosen you ; and the LORD will not
19 answer you in that day.   But the people refused to
   hearken unto the voice of Samuel ; and they said, Nay ;
20 but we will have a king over us ; that we also may be
   like all the nations ; and that our king may judge us,
21 and go out before us, and fight our battles.   And Samuel heard all the words of the people, and he rehearsed
22 them in the ears of the LORD.   And the LORD said to

---

spices (Exod. xxx. 25 ; cf. 1 Chron. ix. 30 R.V.), hence R.V. marg.
'perfumers.'

15. the tenth: the royal tithe levied on the annual produce of
corn-land and vineyard ; a third source of tithe is added in verse 17.

16. your goodliest young men: read, with LXX, 'your goodliest cattle'; the royal claim on the freemen has been already
stated in verses 11 f.

The tone of this remarkable passage is decidedly hostile to the
monarchy as an institution, far exceeding in its condemnation the
parallel passage, Deut. xvii. 14-20, in which the king is warned
merely against multiplying horses, wives, and wealth.   With the
rest of the document (D) of which it forms a part, it implies a long
and unhappy experience of monarchical government, suggesting
a date in the Exile, and the bitter reflections of a school which
regarded the defections and excesses of the monarchy as largely
responsible for the destruction of the state.

viii. 19-22.   *The people persist in their demand.*

20. Note the twofold function of an Eastern monarch—to act
as the supreme judge in internal affairs, and to lead his people in
battle against external foes.

Samuel, Hearken unto their voice, and make them a king. And Samuel said unto the men of Israel, [R] Go ye every man unto his city.

[M] Now there was a man of Benjamin, whose name 9 was Kish, the son of Abiel, the son of Zeror, the son of Becorath, the son of Aphiah, the son of a Benjamite, a mighty man of valour. And he had a son, whose name 2 was Saul, a young man and a goodly : and there was not among the children of Israel a goodlier person than he : from his shoulders and upward he was higher than any

---

22. Go ye every man, &c. : in the present arrangement of the text, Samuel's delay in executing the Divine command of 22ª is inexplicable ; by the rearrangement explained above, however, the original continuation of 22ª is to be found in x. 19ᵇ ff. : 'And Samuel said unto the men of Israel, Now, therefore, present yourselves,' &c.

(*b*) ix. 1—x. 27. *Saul the son of Kish anointed by Samuel and chosen at Mizpah.*

The compiler at this point postpones the election of the new king, which was impending in viii. 22, in order to introduce a long and valuable extract (ix. 1—x. 16) from the older historical document at his disposal, our M, in which the introduction of the monarchy is presented in a very different light from the marked antagonism of D (see for details the Introduction to this commentary, sect. iv).

ix. 1-14. *Saul sent in search of his father's asses.*

1. The analogy of i. 1 makes it probable that the text originally ran : 'Now there was a man of Gibeah of Benjamin (cf. xiii. 2, 15, xiv. 16) whose name was Kish' (so Wellhausen and others). This Gibeah was also known afterwards as Gibeah of Saul (xi. 4), and since Robinson's day has been generally identified with the modern *Tell-el-Fûl*, about four miles due north of Jerusalem.

a mighty man of valour: rather, 'a man of wealth' (see R. V. marg. and 2 Kings xv. 20) or substance, the owner of a large estate.

2. Saul : in Hebrew *Shā'ûl*, one 'asked' (from God), cf. i. 20.

a young man: the original denotes a man 'in the prime of manhood' (*BDB, Heb. Lex.*). Not Saul's age but his physical fitness for kinghood is the point here. Saul was 'every inch a king.' The last clause of the verse, however, looks like an explanatory gloss borrowed from x. 23. where it is more in place. The

3 of the people.   And the asses of Kish Saul's father were
lost. · And Kish said to Saul his son, Take now one of
4 the servants with thee, and arise, go seek the asses.. And
he passed through the hill country of Ephraim, and passed
through the land of Shalishah, but they found them not :
then they passed through the land of Shaalim, and there
they were not : and he passed through the land of the
5 Benjamites, but they found them not.   When they were
come to the land of Zuph, Saul said to his servant that
was with him, Come and let us return ; lest my father
6 leave caring for the asses, and take thought for us.   And
he said unto him, Behold now, there is in this city a man
of God, and he is a man that is held in honour ; all that
he saith cometh surely to pass : now let us go thither ;
peradventure he can tell us concerning our journey
7 whereon we go.   Then said Saul to his servant, But, behold, if we go, what shall we bring the man ? for the
bread is spent in our vessels, and there is not a present

grounds on which some scholars have detected a discrepancy—
implying a difference of sources—as to the age of Saul at his
election between this chapter and xiii. 2 ff., where he is the father
of a grown-up son, are illusory.

4. The verbs should be read in the plural throughout. The
route followed is uncertain. If **Shaalim**, as is probable, is a
corruption of Shaalbim (Judges i. 35, 1 Kings iv. 9), which was
near Ajalon, the travellers appear to have crossed the hills to the
west of Gibeah, descended the valley of Ajalon, and then turned
northwards through the western end of Benjamin to the land of
Zuph, in which lay Ramah (see i. 1), the home of Samuel.

6. a man of God : the first of three names in this chapter for
a prophet, emphasizing the latter's close relation to God. The
mark of a true prophet (cf. Deut. xviii. 21 f.) was the fulfilment
of his predictions, as illustrated in x. 2 ff. The contrast is here
very striking between Samuel, the little-known seer of an
Ephraimite village, and Samuel the theocratic ruler of all Israel
in chs. vii and viii (D).

7 f. afford an interesting glimpse of early Hebrew custom.   It
was usual to fee the professional seer either in money or in kind.

to bring to the man of God : what have we?   And the 8
servant answered Saul again, and said, Behold, I have in
my hand the fourth part of a shekel of silver :. that will I
give to the man of God, to tell us our way.   (Beforetime 9
in Israel, when a man went to inquire of God, thus he
said, Come and let us go to the seer : for he that is now
called a Prophet was beforetime called a Seer.)   Then 10
said Saul to his servant, Well said ; come, let us go.   So
they went unto the city where the man of God was.   As 11
they went up the ascent to the city, they found young
maidens going out to draw water, and said unto them,
Is the seer here? And they answered them, and said, 12
He is ; behold, *he is* before thee : make haste now, for
he is come to-day into the city ; for the people have a
sacrifice to-day in the high place : as soon as ye be come 13

---

8. the fourth part of a shekel: not a stamped coin—true
coins were a much later invention—but a piece of silver of any
shape weighing a quarter of a shekel, *cir.* 56 Troy grains, and
worth intrinsically about 8*d.* of our money, but of course of much
greater purchasing power.   See the writer's article 'Money' in
Hastings' *DB.*, iii. 420.

that will I give: better, with LXX, 'that wilt thou give.'

9. A gloss by a later hand, originally written in the margin
opposite verse 11, where the word 'seer' first occurs. 'Seer' is
the rendering of two distinct Hebrew participles, *rō'eh* and *ḥōzeh* ;
the former is applied only to Samuel and one other (2 Chron. xvi.
7, 10), which is due to the fact that but a small part of the O.T.
can be older than the present narrative, the bulk of our extant
literature dating from a period when *rō'eh* had been superseded by
nābi, 'prophet' (see on x. 5).   The later date of ch. iii, compared
with ch. ix, is shown by the use there of the latter term (iii. 20).

11. going out to draw water: indicating ''the time of
evening,' see Gen. xxiv. 11.

12. before thee, &c. : read, with a slight change of text : 'lo,
he is before you (plur.) ; now, at this moment (as verse 13), he is
come into the city' (Wellh., Driver, &c.).   See below on verse 14.

in the high place: Hebrew *bāmā*, the standing term for the
local sanctuaries at which the sacrificial worship of Yahweh was
lawfully celebrated until the reformation of Josiah.   Ramah lay

into the city, ye shall straightway find him, before he go
up to the high place to eat : for the people will not eat
until he come, because he doth bless the sacrifice ; *and*
afterwards they eat that be bidden. Now therefore get you
14 up ; for at this time ye shall find him. And they went up to
the city, *and* as they came within the city, behold, Samuel
came out against them, for to go up to the high place.

15   Now the LORD had revealed unto Samuel a day before
16 Saul came, saying, To-morrow about this time I will send
thee a man out of the land of Benjamin, and thou shalt
anoint him to be prince over my people Israel, and he
shall save my people out of the hand of the Philistines :
for I have looked upon my people, because their cry is

---

on the slope of the hill, the village well was at its foot, and the
sanctuary, as elsewhere, on the hill-top (note the verbs in verses
11-14). The precision of the topographical vocabulary of the
Hebrew historians is a noteworthy feature of their style.

14. as they came within the city : read, with most modern
editors, as in verse 18, 'within the gate,' or better 'the gatehouse'
(see on 2 Sam. xviii. 24). Samuel seems to have come down from
presiding at the sacrifice, as is required by verse 23, with the
express object of finding his unknown but expected visitor (see
verse 16). After inquiring at the gate if a stranger had entered,
he is now on the point of returning for the deferred sacrificial
meal at the high place.

ix. 15-26.   *The meeting of Samuel and Saul.*

15. the LORD had revealed unto Samuel : *lit.* 'had uncovered
Samuel's ear' (as R. V. marg.) ; the Divine message had come as
a ' word ' (see verse 17, and cf. the familiar phrase, ' the word of the
LORD came unto . . .'), not as a ' vision ' (Isa. i. 1, and often).
The uncovering of the ear is also used in this document of
ordinary communications (xx. 2, 12 f., xxii. 8, 17).

16. I have looked upon : add, ' the affliction (so LXX) of my
people,' as Exod. iii. 7. In nothing is the contrast between the
historical presuppositions of the earlier and later narratives more
conspicuous than in the picture they respectively present of the
condition of the Hebrew tribes at this particular crisis of their
history. Here the Philistine oppression is at its height, and the
' cry ' of God's people ' is come unto ' Him, as aforetime in Egypt
(Exod. iii. 7). According to the representation of the later

come unto me.   And when Samuel saw Saul, the LORD 17
said unto him, Behold the man of whom I spake to thee!
this same shall have authority over my people.   Then 18
Saul drew near to Samuel in the gate, and said, Tell me,
I pray thee, where the seer's house is.   And Samuel 19
answered Saul, and said, I am the seer; go up before me
unto the high place, for ye shall eat with me to-day: and
in the morning I will let thee go, and will tell thee all
that is in thine heart.   And as for thine asses that were 20
lost three days ago, set not thy mind on them; for they
are found.   And for whom is all that is desirable in
Israel? Is it not for thee, and for all thy father's house?
And Saul answered and said, Am not I a Benjamite, of 21
the smallest of the tribes of Israel? and my family the
least of all the families of the tribe of Benjamin? wherefore then speakest thou to me after this manner?   And 22
Samuel took Saul and his servant, and brought them into

document, on the other hand, the Philistines were completely
crushed at the beginning of Samuel's judgeship, and 'came no
more within the border of Israel' (vii. 13). The initiative, further,
is here taken by Yahweh Himself without the slightest hint of the
incidents recorded in the previous chapter. The monarchy is
God's free gift to His people; the future 'prince,' in the might of
God's own spirit, is destined to be the instrument of their
deliverance from the Philistine yoke. The single fact—and it is an
important one—in which both narratives agree is the leading part
taken by Samuel in the appointment of Saul.

17. Behold the man: the rendering given in R. V. marg. to
the rest of this clause is preferable to that of the text, 'Behold the
man of whom I said unto thee, This same,' &c.

19. all that is in thine heart: as a 'man of God,' Samuel
'knoweth the secrets of the heart' (Ps. xliv. 21). In the light of
Saul's character as revealed in the sequel, we can hardly go
wrong in understanding these words as an indication that Saul
had brooded in secret over the tyranny of the Philistines, and
was perhaps already forming plans for ending it.

20. all that is desirable in Israel: the honour and material
advantages of royalty. Cf. Hag. ii. 7 (Driver).

the guest-chamber, and made them sit in the chiefest
place among them that were bidden, which were about
23 thirty persons.   And Samuel said unto the cook, Bring
the portion which I gave thee, of which I said unto thee,
24 Set it by thee.. And the cook took up the thigh, and
that which was upon it, and set it before Saul. And
Samuel said, Behold that which hath been reserved! set
it before thee and eat; because unto the appointed time
hath it been kept for thee, for I said, I have invited the
25 people.: So Saul did eat with Samuel that day. And
when they were come down from the high place into the
26 city, he communed with Saul upon the housetop. And
they arose early : and it came to pass about the spring of
the day, that Samuel called to Saul on the housetop,
saying, Up, that I may send thee away. And Saul arose,
and they went out both of them, he and Samuel, abroad.
27 As they were going down at the end of the city, Samuel
said to Saul, Bid the servant pass on before us, (and he
passed on,) but stand thou still at this time, that I may

---

22. the guest-chamber : rather, 'the dining-hall,' in which the
sacrificial meal was eaten, an adjunct doubtless of every important
sanctuary. The Greek translators seem to have found a similar
hall at Shiloh in their text of i. 18.

24. and that which was upon it: a tautology due to textual
corruption. Almost all recent commentators, by a slight emendation, read 'and the fat tail,' a delicacy much esteemed in
Syria at the present day. In later times, however, it had to be
burned on the altar (Exod. xxix. 22 ; Lev. iii. 9, both as R.V.).
The rest of this verse is admittedly corrupt. H. P. Smith's
conjectural restoration is accepted in the main by Budde and
Nowack: 'Behold the meal is served! Eat! for to the appointed
time we have waited for thee to eat with the guests' (*Intern. Crit.
Comm., in loc.*).

25 f. Here also the text is in some disorder. The opening clause
of verse 26 comes too soon. We must read with LXX (see R.V.
marg.) : 'And they spread a couch for Saul on the housetop, and
he lay down to sleep. And it came to pass,' &c.

cause thee to hear the word of God. Then Samuel took 10
the vial of oil, and poured it upon his head, and kissed
him, and said, Is it not that the LORD hath anointed
thee to be prince over his inheritance? When thou art 2
departed from me to-day, then thou shalt find two men by
Rachel's sepulchre, in the border of Benjamin at Zelzah;

ix. 27—x. 1. *Saul anointed by Samuel.*

1. The Greek and Latin versions have a much fuller text in the
second half of this verse : ' Hath not Yahweh anointed thee [to be
prince over his people Israel? And thou shalt have authority over
the people of Yahweh, and shalt save them out of the hand of their
enemies (cf. ix. 16), and this shall be to thee the sign that Yahweh
hath anointed thee] to be prince over his inheritance.' This
repetition of the words of a Divine message is entirely after the
Hebrew manner, and the reference to the 'sign' is necessary to
explain verse 7. The copyist's eye has simply passed from the
first occurrence of 'Yahweh hath anointed thee' to the second,
as indicated by the square brackets.

the LORD hath anointed thee: the earliest recorded instance
in the O. T. of this almost universal method of consecration to the
kingly office. The custom was doubtless one habitually observed
by the native princes of Canaan, as may be inferred from the
reference to it in the very early passage Judges ix. 8, 15, and
from the actual instance of the prince of Nuḥashshe, anointed by
Thothmes III (*c.* 1500), as mentioned by his grandson in one of
the Tell-el-Amarna letters (see Winckler's edition, No. 37). The
origin of the ceremony must be sought in Egypt rather than in
Babylonia, where it appears to have been unknown (*KAT.*³, p. 602).
At the outset it clearly signified the transference to the person
anointed of part of the mysterious holiness or virtue of the deity
in whose name and by whose representative it was performed.
By the Hebrews the anointing was believed to impart a special
endowment of the spirit of Yahweh (x. 6, 10, and especially xvi.
13 ; cf. Isa. lxi. 1). The kingship is the only office thus consecrated
in our oldest sources, hence the king is frequently in the Books of
Samuel termed 'Yahweh's anointed,' whose sacrosanct and inviolate character is well illustrated by such passages as xxiv. 6, 10
and parallels. See for the whole subject Weinel's elaborate study
in *ZATW.* xviii (1898), 1 ff., especially 20-27, also Kautzsch in
Hastings' *DB.*, extra vol., 659 f.

x. 2-13 *Saul's destiny to be confirmed by three signs.*
2. Rachel's sepulchre: 'but a little way' from Beth-el (Gen.
xxxv. 16). The present reputed site, a little to the north of

and they will say unto thee, The asses which thou wentest
to seek are found : and, lo, thy father hath left the care
of the asses, and taketh thought for you, saying, What
3 shall I do for my son? Then shalt thou go on forward
from thence, and thou shalt come to the oak of Tabor,
and there shall meet thee there three men going up to
God to Beth-el, one carrying three kids, and another
carrying three loaves of bread, and another carrying
4 a bottle of wine : and they will salute thee, and give thee
two loaves of bread; which thou shalt receive of their
5 hand.   After that thou shalt come to the hill of God,
where is the garrison of the Philistines : and it shall come
to pass, when thou art come thither to the city, that thou
shalt meet a band of prophets coming down from the

Beth-lehem, is due to a late gloss (Gen. xxxv. 19, xlviii. 7) which
wrongly identifies Ephrath with Beth-lehem.

Zelzah is unknown, and appears corrupt.

3. going up to God : a striking expression for going to worship
at the sanctuary, viz. of Beth-el.   The kids, the loaves, and the wine
were destined for the sacrificial meal (i. 24).   The future king is
to receive at the hands of the travellers his first tribute of royalty
(contrast verse 27).

5. the garrison of the Philistines : the true meaning of the
word rendered ' garrison ' here and xiii. 3 f., 2 Sam. viii. 6, 14 is
uncertain.   Since this is evidently the correct rendering of a
cognate noun in xiii. 23, xiv. 1, &c., the alternative 'officer' (so
1 Kings iv. 19) or 'resident' is on the whole to be preferred (Smith,
Budde, Nowack).   Either rendering, however, attests the fact that
Central Palestine was then in the hands of the Philistines.   For
the hill of God we should probably substitute the marginal
rendering 'Gibeah of God' (see on xiii. 3).

a band of prophets : this passage with its sequel, verses
10-13, is important for the evolution of the prophetic order in Israel.
As here met with for the first time in Hebrew history, the
'prophets' closely resemble the bands of excited dervishes of the
modern Orient.   Under the influence of music (cf. 2 Kings iii. 15)
they worked themselves into a condition of religious ecstasy, which
on occasion might pass into a wild, convulsive (xix. 24), and even
dangerous frenzy (xviii. 10), akin to madness (2 Kings ix. 11).
While first of all zealots for Yahweh and His worship, these

high place with a psaltery, and a timbrel, and a pipe, and a harp, before them; and they shall be prophesying: and 6 the spirit of the LORD will come mightily upon thee, and thou shalt prophesy with them, and shalt be turned into another man.   And let it be, when these signs are 7 come unto thee, that thou do as occasion serve thee; for God is with thee.   [R] And thou shalt go down before me 8 to Gilgal; and, behold, I will come down unto thee, to offer burnt offerings, and to sacrifice sacrifices of peace offerings: seven days shalt thou tarry, till I come unto thee, and shew thee what thou shalt do.   [M] And it was 9 so, that when he had turned his back to go from Samuel, God gave him another heart: and all those signs came to pass that day.

And when they came thither to the hill, behold, a band 10 of prophets met him; and the spirit of God came mightily upon him, and he prophesied among them.   And it came 11 to pass, when all that knew him beforetime saw that, behold, he prophesied with the prophets, then the people said one to another, What is this that is come unto the

---

early prophets doubtless worked for their country's deliverance. Patriotism was still inseparable from religion (see Budde, *The Religion of Israel to the Exile*, pp. 97 ff.).

psaltery, &c.: for the instruments here enumerated see the article 'Music' in the Bible dictionaries.

6. the spirit of the LORD: see notes on verse 1 above and on xvi. 14, and for the endowments attributed by the Hebrews to this source, Moore's *Judges* (Intern. Crit. Series), pp. 87 f.

and shalt be turned into another man: otherwise expressed in verse 9: 'God gave (*lit.* turned) him another heart.' Saul's is the first conversion recorded in sacred literature (for the date, tenth century B.C., see the Introduction).

7. Saul, as the future saviour of his country, is instructed to take occasion by the hand (note the literal rendering in the margin).

8. This verse breaks the sequence of the narrative, and is now recognized as a later editorial insertion preparing the way for xiii. 7[b]-15[a], which see.

10. the hill: rather, as margin, 'Gibeah,' see on verse 5.

12 son of Kish? Is Saul also among the prophets? And
one of the same place answered and said, And who is
their father? Therefore it became a proverb, Is Saul
13 also among the prophets? And when he had made an
end of prophesying, he came to the high place.
14   And Saul's uncle said unto him and to his servant,
Whither went ye? And he said, To seek the asses: and
when we saw that they were not found, we came to
15 Samuel. And Saul's uncle said, Tell me, I pray thee,
16 what Samuel said unto you. And Saul said unto his
uncle, He told us plainly that the asses were found. But
concerning the matter of the kingdom, whereof Samuel
spake, he told him not.

17   [D] And Samuel called the people together unto the
18 LORD to Mizpah; and he said unto the children of Israel,
Thus saith the LORD, the God of Israel, I brought up
Israel out of Egypt, and I delivered you out of the hand
of the Egyptians, and out of the hand of all the kingdoms

---

12. And who is their father? A difficult phrase. It probably
expresses the questioner's surprise that the son of a wealthy noble
should associate with a band of fanatics of humble origin, men of
no 'family.' A different explanation of the origin of the proverb
following, taken from a later source, is given xix. 22 ff. —another
of the many indications of the composite origin of the book.

13. he came to the high place: the meeting of Saul and his
uncle—probably Ner, the father of his future general, Abner
(xiv. 50)—which immediately follows, has suggested that we
must read here : 'he came to the house' (so most moderns).

14 ff. In this interview Saul's modesty and prudence are
alike conspicuous.

17-19ª (to **over us**). *The people summoned to Mizpah.* This
passage, which we have seen reason to regard as the original
continuation of viii. 1-9 (D), owes its present position, as
introducing the scene at Mizpah, to the editor's desire to reduce to
a single chronological sequence the two conflicting accounts of
Saul's election which he found in his sources (see above, p. 74 f.).
Its contents are a recapitulation of the Divine message, viii. 7 f.

that oppressed you: but ye have this day rejected your 19
God, who himself saveth you out of all your calamities
and your distresses; and ye have said unto him, *Nay*, but
set a king over us. Now therefore present yourselves
before the LORD by your tribes, and by your thousands.
So Samuel brought all the tribes of Israel near, and the 20
tribe of Benjamin was taken. And he brought the tribe 21
of Benjamin near by their families, and the family of the
Matrites was taken: and Saul the son of Kish was taken;
but when they sought him, he could not ·be found. 22
Therefore they asked of the LORD further, Is there yet
a man to come hither? And the LORD answered, Behold,
he hath hid himself among the stuff. And they ran and 23
fetched him thence; and when he stood among the
people, he was higher than any of the people from his
shoulders and upward. And Samuel said to all the 24
people, See ye him whom the LORD hath chosen, that
there is none like him among all the people? And all
the people shouted, and said, God save the king.
    Then Samuel told the people the manner of the 25

---

x. 19^b-24. *Saul elected by the sacred lot*, the continuation of
viii. 22 (see p. 74 and on viii. 22).
    19. by your thousands: i.e. 'by your clans,' R. V. 'families,'
the subdivisions of the tribe, and in turn subdivided into 'fathers'
houses,' see on viii. 12.
    20. was taken: the technical term for selection by the sacred
lot, for which see on xiv. 41 f. The procedure in the case of
Achan (Joshua vii. 16 ff.) forms a close parallel.
    21. A line has fallen out of the Hebrew MS. after 'was taken,'
see R. V. marg: 'and he brought the family (i e. the clan) of the
Matrites near man by man' (LXX).
    22. Read, again with LXX and R. V. marg: 'Is the man
(i.e. Saul) yet come hither?'
    25 ff. *Saul returns to Gibeah.* Since Samuel has already in the
original sequence of D told the people 'the manner of the king'
(viii. 11 ff.), we now expect the farewell address, but the compiler,
not inappropriately, has removed the latter to the close of the

kingdom, and wrote it in a book, and laid it up before
the LORD. And Samuel sent all the people away, every
26 man to his house. And Saul also went to his house to
Gibeah; and there went with him the host, whose hearts
27 God had touched. But certain sons of Belial said, How
shall this man save us? And they despised him, and
brought him no present. But he held his peace.

11   [M] Then Nahash the Ammonite came up, and encamped against Jabesh-gilead: and all the men of Jabesh

---

whole section, retaining here, with some redactional adjustments
in verse 25, the original close of D's narrative.

26. there went with him the host: read, 'the men of worth,'
men brave and loyal, in marked contrast to the disloyal 'sons of
Belial.' The expressive description of this spontaneous bodyguard
—'whose hearts God had touched'—is unique in the O. T.

27. The last sentence is a corruption of the true opening of the
following chapter (see on xi. 1).

(c) xi. 1–15. *Saul delivers Jabesh-gilead from the Ammonites.
The kingdom renewed at Gilgal.*

The thread of the older source, which was dropped at x. 16, is
now resumed. On his return from his fateful interview with
Samuel, Saul resumed his place on his father's estate and awaited
the 'occasion' foreshadowed by the seer (x. 7). This was supplied,
after the lapse of a month (see on verse 1), by the king of the
Ammonites attacking the Israelite city of Jabesh-gilead. How
Saul, in the expressive words of his later namesake, made market
of his opportunity (Eph. v. 16) is recorded in this chapter. On
no intelligible hypothesis, on the other hand, can the present
narrative be regarded as the continuation of x. 20–27. There
Saul has been formally invested with the royal authority and has
returned to Gibeah in semi-state. A superficial reading of xi. 4 ff.
might suggest that the messengers from Jabesh-gilead had come
to Gibeah expressly to invoke the assistance of the new king, but
this will be seen to be an entire misconception of the plain sense
of the passage (see on verses 4 f.).

1. Nahash the Ammonite: see on 2 Sam. x. 1 f. The Greek
text has preserved the true reading here: 'And it came to pass
after about a month that Nahash, &c.' (so R. V. marg.).

Jabesh-gilead: i.e. Jabesh in Gilead; the name is still
preserved in the *Wadi Yabis* which opens into the Jordan valley
opposite *Ibzik* (Bezek of verse 8), but the precise location of the

said unto Nahash, Make a covenant with us, and we will
serve thee.   And Nahash the Ammonite said unto them, 2
On this condition will I make it with you, that all your
right eyes be put out; and I will lay it for a reproach
upon all Israel.   And the elders of Jabesh said unto 3
him, Give us seven days' respite, that we may send
messengers unto all the borders of Israel: and then, if
there be none to save us, we will come out to thee.
Then came the messengers to Gibeah of Saul, and spake 4
these words in the ears of the people: and all the people
lifted up their voice, and wept.   And, behold, Saul came 5
following the oxen out of the field; and Saul said, What
aileth the people that they weep? And they told him
the words of the men of Jabesh.   And the spirit of God 6
came mightily upon Saul when he heard those words,
and his anger was kindled greatly.   And he took a yoke 7
of oxen, and cut them in pieces, and sent them throughout all the borders of Israel by the hand of messengers,
saying, Whosoever cometh not forth after Saul and after
Samuel, so shall it be done unto his oxen.   And the

city is uncertain; *Ed-deir* and *Miryamin* have been proposed.
Jabesh figures honourably in the later history of Saul (xxxi. 11,
2 Sam. ii. 4 ff.).

4 f. In the course of prosecuting their appeal for help, the
messengers arrive at Gibeah of Saul, where the citizens are
moved to tears. Saul, however, is all the while at work in
the field, and only learns casually, as it were, the urgency of
the situation on his return at nightfall. Clearly, therefore, the
purpose of the messengers' visit to Gibeah was not to invoke the
aid of a man—be he king or commoner—whom it was not even
thought necessary to inform of their arrival.

7. The symbolism adopted by Saul was similar in significance
to that of the fiery cross among the Scottish clans in former times.
So shall it be done unto his oxen is perhaps a toning down of
a more vigorous threat applied to the owners of the latter. Cf.
the action of the Levite, Judges xix. 29, which, however, is not
an exact parallel.

and after Samuel: a later addition by a reader who failed to

dread of the LORD fell on the people, and they came out
8 as one man.   And he numbered them in Bezek; and
the children of Israel were three hundred thousand, and
9 the men of Judah thirty thousand.   And they said unto
the messengers that came, Thus shall ye say unto the
men of Jabesh-gilead, To-morrow, by the time the sun is
hot, ye shall have deliverance.   And the messengers
came and told the men of Jabesh; and they were glad.
10 Therefore the men of Jabesh said, To-morrow we will
come out unto you, and ye shall do with us all that
11 seemeth good unto you.   And it was so on the morrow,
that Saul put the people in three companies; and they
came into the midst of the camp in the morning watch,
and smote the Ammonites until the heat of the day: and
it came to pass, that they which remained were scattered,
12 so that two of them were not left together. ·[R] And the
people said unto Samuel, Who is he that said, Shall Saul
reign over us? bring the men, that we may put them to
13 death.   And Saul said, There shall not a man be put to
death this day: for to-day the LORD hath wrought deliverance in Israel.

note the subordinate rôle played by the seer in this source
compared with the other (D).
   the dread of Yahweh: rather, as margin, 'a terror from
Yahweh'; so Gen. xxxv. 5 'a terror from God,' where however
it paralysed, deterred from, not as here stimulated to, action.
Cf. xiv. 15.
   8. Bezek: represented by the ruins at *Ibzik*, some fourteen
miles south-west of *Beisān*, the ancient Beth-shan, almost due
west of the mouth of the *Wady Yabis*, mentioned above.   The
exaggerated numbers that follow, and the suspicious mention
of Judah at this early stage, suggest a later interpolation.
   11. in the morning watch: the last of the three watches into
which the night was divided (Exod. xiv. 24; Lam. ii. 19; Judges
vii. 19).   The continuation of this narrative is now found in
verse 15. Saul has approved himself worthy of the Divine selection,
and is recognized by the people also as their future king.   In

Then said Samuel to the people, Come and let us 14
go to Gilgal, and renew the kingdom there. [M] And 15
all the people went to Gilgal; and there they made Saul
king before the LORD in Gilgal; and there they sacrificed
sacrifices of peace offerings before the LORD; and there
Saul and all the men of Israel rejoiced greatly.

[D] And Samuel said unto all Israel, Behold, I have 12
hearkened unto your voice in all that ye said unto me,
and have made a king over you. And now, behold, the 2
king walketh before you : and I am old and grayheaded ;
and, behold, my sons are with you : and I have walked
before you from my youth unto this day. Here I am : 3

---

this the *vox populi* is in harmony with the *vox Dei*. The army,
accordingly, repairs to the ancient sanctuary of Gilgal, near Jericho,
and with befitting ceremonial installs its victorious leader as king
of Israel.

12-14 on the other hand, is recognized by all critics' as an
editorial paragraph, the purpose of which is to harmonize, as far
as may be, the two divergent accounts of the manner and place of
Saul's installation. This is so far accomplished by representing
the ceremony at Gilgal as a 'renewing of the kingdom,' that is,
as a repetition of the scene at Mizpah. Saul, as yet, as it were,
merely king *de jure*, now becomes king *de facto*. Verses 12 f. are
clearly based upon the closing verses of the younger narrative
(x. 25-7).

(*d*) xii. 1-25. *Samuel's farewell address.*
Once more Samuel appears as the judge of all Israel, an office
which he now formally abdicates. The whole chapter evidently
belongs to the same source as chs. vii and viii, and forms, as we
have seen, the natural sequel of x. 20-24. The scene, therefore,
of Samuel's farewell has been transferred for harmonistic purposes
from Mizpah to Gilgal. The address is an excellent specimen of
the rhetorical prose of which the discourses of Deuteronomy are
the classical example. Yet, while the style is cast in the characteristic Deuteronomic mould (see notes below), the language shows
undeniable points of contact with Jeremiah, Ezekiel, and the
exilic portions of Isaiah, a statement of which the proof must
be sought in the larger commentaries of Smith, Löhr, and
Nowack.

witness against me before the LORD, and before his
anointed : whose ox have I taken? or whose ass have
I taken? or whom have I defrauded? whom have
I oppressed? or of whose hand have I taken a ransom
to blind mine eyes therewith? and I will restore it you.
4 And they said, Thou hast not defrauded us, nor oppressed us, neither hast thou taken aught of any man's
5 hand. And he said unto them, The LORD is witness
against you, and his anointed is witness this day, that ye
6 have not found aught in my hand. And they said, He
is witness. And Samuel said unto the people, It is the
LORD that appointed Moses and Aaron, and that brought
7 your fathers up out of the land of Egypt. Now therefore
stand still, that I may plead with you before the LORD
concerning all the righteous acts of the LORD, which he
8 did to you and to your fathers. When Jacob was come
into Egypt, and your fathers cried unto the LORD, then

xii. 1-6. *Samuel protests his integrity as judge.*

3. before the LORD, and before his anointed : see on x. 1.
The principal occurrences of this notable phrase in the historical
and prophetical books are, in addition to verses 1, 5 : xxiv. 6, 10,
xxvi. 9, 11, 16, 23, 2 Sam. i. 14, 16, all applied to Saul; 2 Sam.
xix. 21 (cf. xxiii. 1) David; 1 Sam. ii. 35, and 2 Sam. xxii. 51
(= Ps. xviii. 50) with reference to the Davidic dynasty ; Isa. xlv. 1,
to Cyrus; 1 Sam. ii. 10, Ps. ii. 2 and elsewhere, to the Messianic
king, so expressly Dan. ix. 25 f., the only O.T. passage where the
word Messiah occurs in A.V. The R.V. has 'the anointed one.'

a ransom (*kōpher*) **:** the technical term for blood-money paid
to the relatives of a murdered man—the *wergild* of the Germanic
races—which was strictly forbidden by Hebrew law (Num. xxxv.
31 f.). Here, as in Amos v. 12, it denotes the bribe (so R.V.
marg.) offered to a judge to induce him to acquit the murderer.

to blind mine eyes therewith : this reading gives an excellent
sense, although some would prefer the interesting variant offered
by the LXX, see margin.

6. It is the LORD : better, with LXX : 'Witness is the LORD
that,' &c.

xii. 7-15. *The witness of history* (cf. the parallel in Joshua xxiv. 2 ff.).
8. cried unto the LORD (also verse 10, vii. 8 f., viii. 18) : like

the LORD sent Moses and Aaron, who brought forth your fathers out of Egypt, and made them to dwell in this place. But they forgat the LORD their God, and 9 he sold them into the hand of Sisera, captain of the host of Hazor, and into the hand of the Philistines, and into the hand of the king of Moab, and they fought against them. And they cried unto the LORD, and said, We 10 have sinned, because we have forsaken the LORD, and have served the Baalim and the Ashtaroth: but now deliver us out of the hand of our enemies, and we will serve thee. And the LORD sent Jerubbaal, and Bedan, 11 and Jephthah, and Samuel, and delivered you out of the hand of your enemies on every side, and ye dwelled in safety. And when ye saw that Nahash the king of the 12 children of Ammon came against you, ye said unto me,

---

'he sold them into the hand of' (verse 9), one of the standing formulae of the Deuteronomic framework of Judges, the latter phrase, indeed, occurring nowhere else.

and made them to dwell in this place: this 'expresses just what Moses and Aaron did not do' (Driver); read, therefore, with the Versions: 'and he (Yahweh) made them dwell.'

9 ff. With this reading of Israel's history during the period of the judges the exposition of the author of Judges ii. 11 ff. and parallels should be compared. The scheme is the same in both— apostasy and oppression followed by penitent prayer and deliverance. See further on verses 14 ff.

Sisera, captain of the host of [Jabin, king of] **Hazor:** the inserted words are from the LXX; the reference is to Judges iv. 2 ff.

11. Bedan: a corruption of Barak (see marg.).

and Samuel: this unexpected introduction of Samuel in the third person is most easily explained by the assumption that the author of this chapter had before him, or in his recollection, an edition of the Book of Judges in which Samuel appeared as the deliverer from the Philistine oppression. The existence of such an edition has been maintained on other grounds by several recent critics. The remainder of this verse is thoroughly Deuteronomistic in its phraseology.

12. The first half of the verse is almost certainly redactional. It is difficult to credit the author of this source with a statement so

Nay, but a king shall reign over us : when the Lord
13 your God was your king.   Now therefore behold the
king whom ye have chosen, and whom ye have asked for :
14 and, behold, the Lord hath set a king over you.   If ye
will fear the Lord, and serve him, and hearken unto his
voice, and not rebel against the commandment of the
Lord, and both ye and also the king that reigneth over
15 you be followers of the Lord your God, *well* : but if ye
will not hearken unto the voice of the Lord, but rebel
against the commandment of the Lord, then shall the
hand of the Lord be against you, as it was against your
16 fathers.   Now therefore stand still and see this great
17 thing, which the Lord will do before your eyes.   Is it
not wheat harvest to-day ?   I will call unto the Lord,

---

clearly at variance not only with the picture drawn in ch. vii. 13 ff.,
but even with the closing words of verse 11.

when the LORD [Yahweh] **your God was your king** : the
principle of the theocracy in its simplest form, already implied in
viii. 7, x. 19 (cf. Judges viii. 23).

14. This long verse illustrates the rhetorical figure termed
aposiopesis, the apodosis to the ' if' clause being left unexpressed.
The italicized ' *well*' of R.V. gives the sense intended.   Verses
14 f. are full of Deuteronomistic words and phrases, and present
an excellent summary of what may be called the theodicy of the
Deuteronomic school.   Reading the history of their nation in the
light of the ideals and doctrines of the Book of the Deuteronomy, the
historians of this school found the master-key to the vicissitudes of
the past in the conviction that ' fidelity to Yahweh is rewarded
by national prosperity, and unfaithfulness punished by national
misfortune' (see Skinner's *Kings* in this series, 15 ff.).   This re-
tributive pragmatism is the distinguishing mark of the editorial
framework of the Books of Kings.

15. as it was against your fathers : for this read with LXX :
' and against your king,' cf. verses 14, 25.

xii. 16-25. *The people, miraculously convinced of their error,*
make humble confession.

. **17. wheat harvest** : the time was early summer (May-June),
when thunder and rain are almost unknown in Palestine.   The

that he may send thunder and rain ; and ye shall know
and see that your wickedness is great, which ye have
done in the sight of the LORD, in asking you a king.
So Samuel called unto the LORD ; and the LORD sent 18
thunder and rain that day : and all the people greatly
feared the LORD and Samuel.   And all the people said 19
unto Samuel, Pray for thy servants unto the LORD thy
God, that we die not : for we have added unto all our
sins *this* evil, to ask us a king.   And Samuel said unto 20
the people, Fear not : ye have indeed done all this evil :
yet turn not aside from following the LORD, but serve
the LORD with all your heart ; and turn ye not aside : 21
for *then should ye go* after vain things which cannot profit
nor deliver, for they are vain.   For the LORD will not 22
forsake his people for his great name's sake : because it
hath pleased the LORD to make you a people unto himself.   Moreover as for me, God forbid that I should sin 23

---

second half of the verse betrays the author's uncompromising
hostility to the institution of the monarchy.

21. Read as in the margin, after LXX : 'and turn ye not
aside after the vanities which cannot profit,' &c. **Vain things**
(Heb. *tōhū*, a barren waste, Gen. i. 2, hence 'nothingness,'
'vanity')—a favourite word of the 'second' Isaiah, by whom the
epithets 'vanity' and 'profitable for nothing' are both applied to
the idols of the heathen (xliv. 9 f.).   This is also the sense here.
It is difficult to avoid the inference that the writer of this chapter
was, at the earliest, a contemporary of the author of Isaiah xl. ff.
(*c.* 540 B.C.).   See further, Introduction, sect. iv.

**22. it hath pleased the LORD to make you a people unto
himself**: God's free choice of Israel to be His 'peculiar people'
is one of the characteristic ideas of Deuteronomy (See Driver's
Deut., pp. xx f.), but goes back to the classical formulation of the
covenant relation between Yahweh and Israel in Exod. xix. 5 f. (J).

23. Samuel divests himself of his authority as Yahweh's
representative in the theocracy, reserving only the privilege of
being his people's intercessor (see on vii. 5).

The original close of D's narrative is probably to be sought in
x. 25 ff. (see above).

against the LORD in ceasing to pray for you: but I will
24 instruct you in the good and the right way.   Only fear
25 the LORD, and serve him in truth with all your heart:
for consider how great things he hath done for you.
But if ye shall still do wickedly, ye shall be consumed,
both ye and your king.

13 [Z] Saul was [*thirty*] years old when he began to reign;
2 and he reigned two years over Israel.   [M] And Saul
chose him three thousand men of Israel; whereof two

C. xiii–xiv.   *Saul's First Campaign against the Philistines.*

In this subdivision it is not difficult to recognize in its main
portion (xiii. 2–7ª, xiv. 1–46, 52) the hand of the early historian
and friend of the monarchy who has already told us of Saul's
first essay in leadership, and of his subsequent elevation to the
throne of Israel at Gilgal.   Saul's life-work—the work to which
he had been expressly called of God through His prophet—
was now before him.   This was no other than the deliverance
of Israel from the Philistine yoke (ix. 16), and to this Saul now
bends his energies, assisted by his son Jonathan, whose youthful
impetuosity in slaying the Philistine Resident in Gibeah (see on
verse 3) struck the first blow in the cause of Hebrew liberty
and independence.   From a later source we have the account
of Saul's rejection, and other accretions to the main story, as
will appear in the notes.   The present chapter-divisions represent the two sections of the narrative.

(a) xiii.   *The opening of the War of Independence—Saul rejected at
Gilgal.*

1. This verse is an excellent illustration of the way in which
notes of all kinds find their way from the margins of ancient MSS.
into the text.   As it stands it is palpably absurd, since Jonathan
was already of an age to be in command of a division of the Hebrew
troops.   The only plausible explanation is that the verse was
originally a note by a reader on the margin of his MS. in this form:
'Saul was ... years old, &c.; and he reigned ... years over Israel,'
on the model of the editorial note 2 Sam. v. 4.   The blanks were
intended to be filled in later by computation.   For an attempt to
compute approximately the real numbers see Introduction, sect.
ix, the Chronology of Samuel.

2. Of the troops that had accompanied him to Jabesh-gilead and
thence to Gilgal, Saul retains 3,000 picked men, whom he stations

thousand were with Saul in Michmash and in the mount of Beth-el, and a thousand were with Jonathan in Gibeah of Benjamin : and the rest of the people he sent every man to his tent.　And Jonathan smote the garrison of 3 the Philistines that was in Geba, and the Philistines heard of it.　And Saul blew the trumpet throughout all the land, saying, Let the Hebrews hear.　And all Israel 4 heard say that Saul had smitten the garrison of the Philistines, and that Israel also was had in abomination with the Philistines.　And the people were gathered together after Saul to Gilgal.

And the Philistines assembled themselves together to 5 fight with Israel, thirty thousand chariots, and six thousand horsemen, and people as the sand which is on the sea shore in multitude : and they came up, and

---

in three important positions.　The similarity of the place-names Geba and Gibeah (both = 'hill'), of which there were several in Central Palestine, has led to confusion between them, and obscured the real progress of the campaign.　(See notes below.)

Michmash : the modern *Muḥmās*, high up the *Wadi Suweinit* on its northern side, separated by a narrow valley with steep sides, 'the pass of Michmash' (verse 23), from Geba (xiv. 5).

Gibeah of Benjamin : read 'Geba of Benjamin,' as in verse 16, the town just described as lying opposite Michmash.

3. Jonathan smote the garrison : rather, 'the Resident' or political officer of the Philistines, who had his seat at Gibeah of God (see on x. 5), which should be read for **Geba** of the text. The original seems to have continued thus : 'And the Philistines heard say, the Hebrews have revolted (Wellhausen and most moderns after LXX), and Saul blew the trumpet throughout all the land.'

4. to Gilgal : a harmonizing addition to the true text, preparing the way, like x. 8, for the insertion of the later section xiii. 8-15.

5. thirty thousand chariots : the numbers, as so frequently, are absurdly high, and out of proportion to the number of cavalry. The Philistines scored the first success, driving in the advance guard near Beth-el (verse 2), causing Saul to evacuate Michmash. and perhaps inflicting on him a severe defeat, which would explain the panic of verses 6 f.

6 pitched in Michmash, eastward of Beth-aven. When the
men of Israel saw that they were in a strait, (for the
people were distressed,) then the people did hide themselves in caves, and in thickets, and in rocks, and in
7 holds, and in pits.   Now some of the Hebrews had gone
over Jordan to the land of Gad and Gilead ; [?] but as for
Saul, he was yet in Gilgal, and all the people followed
him trembling.
8   And he tarried seven days, according to the set time
that Samuel *had appointed* : but Samuel came not to
9 Gilgal ; and the people were scattered from him.   And
Saul said, Bring hither the burnt offering to me, and the

---

7. the land of Gad and Gilead : the districts respectively south
and north of the Jabbok (*Wadi Zerka*).

xiii. 7^b^-15^a^. *The first rejection of Saul.*
This passage, as to the origin of which we can only conjecture,
must be judged from its author's standpoint, not from ours.   The
compiler of Samuel has already prepared the way for its insertion
at this point (cf. verses 8, 11 with x. 8 and note there).   That it
interrupts the natural sequence of the early narrative of the
Philistine campaign, that it is inferior, to say the least, in historical
probability to its parallel in ch. xv, and that it is the product of
the religious reflection of a later age are points on which most
modern scholars are agreed.   The key to its origin and meaning
seems to be given in verse 13, read in the light of 2 Sam. vii. 11-16.
The reflective piety of an age dominated by the Deuteronomic
doctrine of Divine retribution (see on xii. 14 f.) saw in the fact
that Saul founded no dynasty like David some heinous sin against
the Most High.   Tradition had long been busy with the historical
fact of Samuel's breach with Saul at Gilgal, and here we have one
form of the tradition used to inculcate the truth that the will of
God must reign supreme upon the earth.   Though it is impossible
for the modern reader not to sympathize with Saul in his extremity,
yet many times in the previous history of Israel ' man's extremity '
had been ' God's opportunity.'   So, thought this pious writer, it
would have been again at Gilgal, and he has the argument of
history on his side (see xiv. 6).
7^b^. followed him: read, with LXX (L), 'forsook him trembling.'
9. Bring hither the burnt offering, &c. : the reference is to the
ancient custom of opening a campaign with sacrifices for the con-

peace offerings. And he offered the burnt offering.
And it came to pass that, as soon as he had made an 10
end of offering the burnt offering, behold, Samuel came;
and Saul went out to meet him, that he might salute
him. And Samuel said, What hast thou done? And 11
Saul said, Because I saw that the people were scattered
from me, and that thou camest not within the days
appointed, and that the Philistines assembled themselves
together at Michmash; therefore said I, Now will the 12
Philistines come down upon me to Gilgal, and I have
not intreated the favour of the LORD: I forced myself
therefore, and offered the burnt offering. And Samuel 13
said to Saul, Thou hast done foolishly: thou hast not
kept the commandment of the LORD thy God, which he
commanded thee: for now would the LORD have established thy kingdom upon Israel for ever. But now 14
thy kingdom shall not continue: the LORD hath sought
him a man after his own heart, and the LORD hath
appointed him to be prince over his people, because
thou hast not kept that which the LORD commanded
thee.

---

secration of the warriors. Hence to 'prepare' war (Mic. iii. 5,
Joel iii. 9, &c., R.V. marg.) is literally to 'consecrate' war, and
the 'consecrated ones' of Isa. xiii. 3 (R.V.) and elsewhere are the
soldiers. For effects of the war taboo see xxi. 4 f., 2 Sam. xi. 11 ff.

10. Saul went out to ... salute him: it is significant of the
dogmatic standpoint of this passage that of the two chief officers
of the theocracy the priest is greater than the king.

13. The point of Samuel's remark is better brought out by a
slight change of reading: 'hadst thou kept the commandment...
the LORD would now have established thy kingdom for ever.'
For the bearing of this on the whole passage see introductory
paragraph.

14. a man after his own heart: the idealized David of the
later Hebrew writers. For the form of the expression cf. Jer. iii. 5,
for its substance, 2 Kings xv. 3-5.

15 And Samuel arose, and gat him up from Gilgal unto Gibeah of Benjamin. [M] And Saul numbered the people that were present with him, about six hundred men.

16 And Saul, and Jonathan his son, and the people that were present with them, abode in Geba of Benjamin :

17 but the Philistines encamped in Michmash. And the spoilers came out of the camp of the Philistines in three companies : one company turned unto the way that

18 leadeth to Ophrah, unto the land of Shual : and another company turned the way to Beth-horon : and another company turned the way of the border that looketh down upon the valley of Zeboim toward the wilderness.

19 [Z] Now there was no smith found throughout all the land of Israel : for the Philistines said, Lest the Hebrews

20 make them swords or spears : but all the Israelites went down to the Philistines, to sharpen every man his share,

21 and his coulter, and his axe, and his mattock ; yet they had a file for the mattocks, and for the coulters, and for

---

xiii. 15ᵇ-23. *The Philistines overrun the district.* Verse 15ᵇ continues the early narrative interrupted at verse 7. Saul, as we saw, had been compelled to retire upon Geba, leaving Michmash in the enemy's hands.

17. For the direction of the three raiding parties and identification of the sites, see G. A. Smith, *Hist. Geog.* p. 291, note 1.

18. the way of the border : read, as suggested by the LXX : ' the way of the hill that overhangs the valley of hyenas,' a name still preserved in the neighbourhood.

19-22. Another interpolation inserted into M, giving a legendary exaggeration of the straits to which the Hebrews were reduced. Had it really gone so hard with them, however, as is stated here, one is at a loss to see how Saul could have relieved Jabesh-gilead, and still less how he could have ventured to face the Philistines themselves. The text is much corrupted in parts, as the margin informs us ; the student is referred to Driver's *Notes* and the larger commentaries for suggested emendations. Much light on the nature of the implements mentioned in the text will be found in Dr. Post's illustrated paper on those of the Syrian peasantry of to-day. *PEFQSt.*, 1891, pp. 110 ff.

the forks, and for the axes ; and to set the goads. So 22 it came to pass in the day of battle, that there was neither sword nor spear found in the hand of any of the people that were with Saul and Jonathan : but with Saul and with Jonathan his son was there found. [M] And the 23 garrison of the Philistines went out unto the pass of Michmash.

Now it fell upon a day, that Jonathan the son of Saul 14 said unto the young man that bare his armour, Come and let us go over to the Philistines' garrison, that is on yonder side. But he told not his father. And Saul 2 abode in the uttermost part of Gibeah under the pome-granate tree which is in Migron : and the people that were with him were about six hundred men ; and Ahijah, 3 the son of Ahitub, Ichabod's brother, the son of Phinehas, the son of Eli, the priest of the LORD in Shiloh, wearing an ephod. And the people knew not that Jonathan was gone. And between the passes, by which Jonathan 4 sought to go over unto the Philistines' garrison, there was a rocky crag on the one side, and a rocky crag on the other side : and the name of the one was Bozez, and the name of the other Seneh. The one crag rose up on 5 the north in front of Michmash, and the other on the south in front of Geba. And Jonathan said to the young 6

(*b*) xiv. *Jonathan's exploit and its sequel.*

2. Gibeah : read 'Geba,' as required by xiii. 16 and verse 5 below, and continue : 'under the pomegranate tree which is by the threshing-floor' (so Wellhausen, reading *migrān* for *migrōn*).

3. Ahijah, the son of Ahitub : usually, but unnecessarily identified with Ahimelech, the priest of Nob, see on xxi. 2.

wearing an ephod : a mistaken rendering for 'carrying the ephod,' see on ii. 28. The statement throws into relief the deeply religious character of Saul, who, like David (xxiii. 9, xxx. 7, &c.), took no important step without inquiring of God by means of this sacred object. See further on verses 18. 41 below, and xxviii. 6.

man that bare his armour, Come and let us go over
unto the garrison of these uncircumcised : it may be that
the LORD will work for us : for there is no restraint to
7 the LORD to save by many or by few. · And his armourbearer said unto him, Do all that is in thine heart : turn
thee, behold I am with thee according to thy heart.
8 Then said Jonathan, Behold, we will pass over unto the
9 men, and we will discover ourselves unto them. If they
say thus unto us, Tarry until we come to you ; then we
will stand still in our place, and will not go up unto them.
10 But if they say thus, Come up unto us ; then we will go
up : for the LORD hath delivered them into our hand :
11 and this shall be the sign unto us. And both of them
discovered themselves unto the garrison of the Philistines :
and the Philistines said, Behold, the Hebrews come forth
12 out of the holes where they had hid themselves. And
the men of the garrison answered Jonathan and his
armourbearer, and said, Come up to us, and we will
shew you a thing. And Jonathan said unto his armourbearer, Come up after me : for the LORD hath delivered
13 them into the hand of Israel. And Jonathan climbed
up upon his hands and upon his feet, and his armourbearer after him : and they fell before Jonathan ; and

---

6. there is no restraint to the LORD, &c. : a fine *confessio
fidei* of which Gideon's adventure (Judges vii. 4 ff.) is the classical
embodiment and illustration. It was quoted with effect by another
Hebrew paladin, the hero of a later War of Independence (1 Macc.
iii. 18). Cf. 2 Chron. xiv. 11 R. V.

7. The Greek text of the armourbearer's reply *is more ex*-
pressive : ' Do all to which thine heart inclines ; behold, I am with
thee, as thy heart so is my heart,' a Hebrew idiom for unanimity
of sentiment (2 Kings x. 15).

9. Underneath this, to us somewhat casual, method of ascertaining the Divine will, lies the profound conviction that every
word and act of men is ordered by the Divine governance.
Cf. vi. 7 ff.

his armourbearer slew them after him. And that first 14
slaughter, which Jonathan and his armourbearer made,
was about twenty men, within as it were half a furrow's
length in an acre of land. And there was a trembling 15
in the camp, in the field, and among all the people ; the
garrison, and the spoilers, they also trembled : and the
earth quaked ; so there was an exceeding great trembling.
And the watchmen of Saul in Gibeah of Benjamin 16
looked ; and, behold, the multitude melted away, and
they went *hither* and thither.

Then said Saul unto the people that were with him, 17
Number now, and see who is gone from us. And when
they had numbered, behold, Jonathan and his armourbearer were not there. And Saul said unto Ahijah, 18
Bring hither the ark of God. For the ark of God was

---

14. The last clause is exceedingly corrupt, and no satisfactory
reconstruction has yet been proposed.

15. The first half of the verse seems overloaded. Deleting the
comma after **camp**, we may find four bodies enumerated, (1) the
main body of armed men encamped in the open country (**the
field**), (2) the array of camp-followers (**all the people**) indispensable to an Eastern army, (3) the outpost garrison surprised by
Jonathan, and (4) the foraging parties of xiii. 17 f. An earth-
quake increased the panic, which the historian terms 'a trembling
of—*i.e.* sent by—God' (R. V. marg.). The word panic itself
reminds us that such attacks of fright without apparent cause
were ascribed by the Greeks to the god Pan.

xiv. 16-23. *General rout of the Philistines.*

16. Gibeah of Benjamin: read 'Geba of Benjamin,' as xiii. 16.

18. The verse as it stands cannot be original, for the simple
reason that the Ark was *not* **at that time with the children of
Israel**, but in apparent oblivion at Kiriath-jearim. Read with
the LXX (see R. V. marg.), as required by verse 3. 'Bring
hither the ephod ; for he bore the ephod at that time before
Israel.' The thoughtless alteration in the received text is due to
a scribe who took offence at this ancient method of ascertaining
the will of the deity. Cf. the same change 2 Kings ii. 26, which
refers back to 1 Sam. xxiii. 9. xxx. 7 ; in both these passages the
original reading 'the ephod' is still preserved.

19 *there* at that time with the children of Israel.   And it
came to pass, while Saul talked unto the priest, that the
tumult that was in the camp of the Philistines went on
and increased : and Saul said unto the priest, Withdraw
20 thine hand.   And Saul and all the people that were with
him were gathered together, and came to the battle :
and, behold, every man's sword was against his fellow,
21 *and there was* a very great discomfiture.   Now the
Hebrews that were with the Philistines as beforetime,
which went up with them into the camp *from the country*
round about; even they also *turned* to be with the
22 Israelites that were with Saul and Jonathan.   Likewise
all the men of Israel which had hid themselves in the
hill country of Ephraim, when they heard that the
Philistines fled, even they also followed hard after them
23 in the battle.   So the LORD saved Israel that day : and
24 the battle passed over by Beth-aven.   And the men of
Israel were distressed that day : but Saul adjured the
people, saying, Cursed be the man that eateth any food
until it be evening, and I be avenged on mine enemies.
25 So none of the people tasted food.   And all the people

---

19. Withdraw thine hand : before Ahijah is able to manipulate
the oracle Saul has become convinced that the time for action has
come.

21. into the camp . . . round about: a very slight change
removes the awkwardness of the construction in the original and
gives the following : 'The Hebrews that were with the Philistines
heretofore, and that had come up with them into the camp, they
also turned to be with,' &c. (Greek and Syriac Versions).

23. Beth-aven may be Beth-el ; but the more natural direction
of the flight was westwards (verse 31).   Smith and Budde would
read ' Beth-horon ' with some ancient Versions.

xiv. 24-35. *Jonathan unwittingly violates a food taboo, rashly
ordered by Saul.*

24-26. Saul's action at this point must be interpreted in the
light of the religious ideas of his time.   Yahweh had just shown

came into the forest ; and there was honey upon the
ground.   And when the people were come unto the 26
forest, behold, the honey dropped : but no man put his
hand to his mouth ; for the people feared the oath.
But Jonathan heard not when his father charged the 27
people with the oath : wherefore he put forth the end of
the rod that was in his hand, and dipped it in the honeycomb, and put his hand to his mouth ; and his eyes
were enlightened.   Then answered one of the people, 28
and said, Thy father straitly charged the people with
an oath, saying, Cursed be the man that eateth food
this day.   And the people were faint. . Then said 29
Jonathan, My father hath troubled the land : see, I pray
you, how mine eyes have been enlightened, because
I tasted a little of this honey.   How much more, if haply 30
the people had eaten freely to-day of the spoil of their
enemies which they found? for now hath there been
no great slaughter among the Philistines.   And they 31
smote of the Philistines that day from Michmash to
Aijalon : and the people were very faint.   And the 32
people flew upon the spoil, and took sheep, and oxen,

that He was present with the host, and the motive of the food
taboo or prohibition was, by this act of self-denial, to secure the
continued assistance of the deity.   The Greek text is here fuller
and more intelligible, and by its help the original may be thus
conjecturally restored : 'And all the people were with Saul,
about ten thousand men, and the battle was spread over the hill
country of Ephraim.   And Saul vowed a vow on that day, and
adjured the people, saying, Cursed . . . enemies.   And there was
honeycomb upon the face of the ground, and the people came to
the honeycomb, and the honey overflowed (Klostermann, or 'the
bees had gone,' Wellhausen), but no man,' &c.

29. My father hath troubled the land : this is too feeble for
the 'ominous word' of the original ; rather, 'my father hath brought
disaster upon the land' (Joshua vii. 25 ; Judges xi. 35, &c.).

32 f.   The earliest recorded instance of the abstinence from
blood, which the Jews have rigorously observed to the present

and calves, and slew them on the ground : and the
33 people did eat them with the blood. Then they told
Saul, saying, Behold, the people sin against the LORD,
in that they eat with the blood. And he said, Ye
have dealt treacherously : roll a great stone unto me this
34 day. And Saul said, Disperse yourselves among the
people, and say unto them, Bring me hither every man
his ox, and every man his sheep, and slay them here,
and eat ; and sin not against the LORD in eating with the
blood. And all the people brought every man his ox
35 with him that night, and slew them there. And Saul
built an altar unto the LORD : the same was the first
altar that he built unto the LORD.
36 And Saul said, Let us go down after the Philistines
by night, and spoil them until the morning light, and let
us not leave a man of them. And they said, Do whatsoever seemeth good unto thee. Then said the priest,
37 Let us draw near hither unto God. And Saul asked
counsel of God, Shall I go down after the Philistines ?
wilt thou deliver them into the hand of Israel ? But he
38 answered him not that day. And Saul said, Draw nigh

day. It was formally embodied in the later legislation, Deut.
xii. 6, 23 : Lev. xvii. 10 ff. For the underlying motives see *Rel. Sem.*[2],
pp. 234 f., and the article 'Food' (Kennedy) *EBi*. ii. 1544.

roll a great stone : see on vi. 14. Over and at the base of
this altar-stone the blood was poured out, a gift to the Giver of life.

35. the same was the first altar : implying that others
followed, which shows that we are still at the very beginning
of Saul's reign, and—a fact of much greater significance—that
the Deuteronomic doctrine of the legitimacy of the one central
sanctuary was still in the future. Throughout this early source,
it may be added, Saul appears as a man sincerely zealous for the
worship and honour of God.

xiv. 36-46. *The discovery of Jonathan's guilt by means of the
sacred lot (Urim and Thummim).*

37. he answered him not : the oracle gave no response,
affirmative or negative. As the following verse shows, this silence

hither, all ye chiefs of the people: and know and see
wherein this sin hath been this day. For, as the LORD 39
liveth, which saveth Israel, though it be in Jonathan my
son, he shall surely die. But there was not a man
among all the people that answered him. Then said he 40
unto all Israel, Be ye on one side, and I and Jonathan
my son will be on the other side. And the people said
unto Saul, Do what seemeth good unto thee. Therefore 41
Saul said unto the LORD, the God of Israel, Shew the
right. And Jonathan and Saul were taken *by lot*: but
the people escaped. And Saul said, Cast *lots* between 42
me and Jonathan my son. And Jonathan was taken.
Then Saul said to Jonathan, Tell me what thou hast 43
done. And Jonathan told him, and said, I did certainly

---

was interpreted, in harmony with the ideas of the time, as a sign
of the Divine displeasure. Saul at once concludes that this must
be due to a breach of the food taboo, and proceeds by another
appeal to discover the guilty party.

41. Shew the right (Heb. *tāmīm*): neither this nor the
alternative rendering, 'give a perfect lot' (A.V., R.V. marg.), can
be got from the Hebrew text. Happily the Greek text has
preserved a reading which bears on its face the evidence of its
genuineness: 'And Saul said, O Yahweh, God of *Israel*, why hast
thou not answered thy servant this day? If the iniquity be in me
or in my son Jonathan, Yahweh, God of *Israel, give* Urim; but if
thou sayest thus, the iniquity is in thy people Israel, *give* Thummim.
And Saul and Jonathan were taken,' &c. A careless copyist allowed
his eye to pass first over two lines, then over one line, between the
identical words given in italics above. The passage is of the first
importance for the light which it throws on the nature of the
mysterious Urim and Thummim, and of the manner of manipulating
the sacred lot. Reference may here be made to the writer's discussion of the subject in Hastings' *DB*. iv. 838 ff. (article 'Urim
and Thummim').

42. Here too we have a fuller Greek text, and the presumption
is again in its favour, in view of verse 45: 'And Saul said, Cast
between me and Jonathan, my son, and whomsoever Yahweh
shall take he shall die. And the people said to Saul, It shall not
be so: but Saul prevailed over the people. And they cast between
him and his son Jonathan, and Jonathan was taken.'

taste a little honey with the end of the rod that was in
44 mine hand; and, lo, I must die.   And Saul said, God
do so and more also : for thou shalt surely die, Jonathan.
45 And the people said unto Saul, Shall Jonathan die, who
hath wrought this great salvation in Israel?   God forbid :
as the LORD liveth, there shall not one hair of his head
fall to the ground ; for he hath wrought with God this
day.   So the people rescued Jonathan, that he died not.
46 Then Saul went up from following the Philistines : and
the Philistines went to their own place.

47   [R] Now when Saul had taken the kingdom over
Israel, he fought against all his enemies on every side,
against Moab, and against the children of Ammon, and
against Edom, and against the kings of Zobah, and

---

43. lo, I must die: this rendering is unfair to the heroic
Jonathan ; it should be, ' lo, I am ready to die.'   Cf. Josephus'
rhetorical but truthful expansion, *Antiq.* VI. vi. 5.   To our modern
way of thinking, Jonathan was innocent and Saul doubly blame-
worthy, first because of his rash vow, and secondly, because he
insisted with an oath on the death of an innocent man.   But as
regards the former charge, we have seen how entirely the food
taboo reflected the primitive religious ideas of the time, and as
regards the second, Jonathan himself acknowledged that he had
incurred the death penalty.   It must be remembered, however,
how undeveloped as yet was the inward and moral conception of
sin.   A man was often aware that he had sinned only by the
unpleasant consequences, as in this case and in the case of Balaam
(Num. xxii. 34).   See further W. R. Smith, *The Prophets of Israel*,
lecture iii, ' The Hebrew Conception of Sin.'

xiv. 47-51.   *A summary of Saul's conquests and of his family
connexions*, closing the first division of Samuel.   The occurrence
in this section of certain characteristic expressions of the Deuteronomic school (e. g. 'all his enemies on every side,' Judges ii. 14,
1 Sam. xii. 11, 'them that spoiled them,' Judges ii. 14 ff.) has led
to the conclusion, first suggested by Budde, that we have here
a summary paragraph from the pen of the Deuteronomic editor,
in which he formally takes leave of Saul before introducing his
successor (see further Introduction. sects. iv f. and on 2 Sam. viii).
   47. the kings of Zobah: see on 2 Sam. viii. 3.

against the Philistines: and whithersoever he turned
himself, he vexed *them*.   And he did valiantly, and 48
smote the Amalekites, and delivered Israel out of the
hands of them that spoiled them.

Now the sons of Saul were Jonathan, and Ishvi, and 49
Malchi-shua: and the names of his two daughters were
these; the name of the firstborn Merab, and the name
of the younger Michal: and the name of Saul's wife was 50
Ahinoam the daughter of Ahimaaz: and the name of
the captain of his host was Abner the son of Ner, Saul's
uncle.   And Kish was the father of Saul; and Ner the 51
father of Abner was the son of Abiel.

[M] And there was sore war against the Philistines all the 52
days of Saul: and when Saul saw any mighty man, or
any valiant man, he took him unto him.

[S] And Samuel said unto Saul, The LORD sent me to 15

---

he vexed them: read with LXX, 'he was victorious.'
49. Ishvi: a corruption of Ishyo, a contracted form of Ish-
Yahweh, 'the man of Yahweh,' and a synonym, therefore, of
Ishbaal, see on 2 Sam. ii. 8.
50. Read as in R.V. marg.: 'And Kish the father of Saul and
Ner the father of Abner were the sons of Abiel' (cf. ix. 1).
Abner, therefore, was Saul's cousin, not his uncle as stated
1 Chron. viii. 33, ix. 36.
52. The continuation and close of the extract from the early
narrative of the introduction of the monarchy, which opened with
ix. 1.   The discrepancy between the contents of this verse and the
unhistorical representation of the later source (vii. 13) has been
already commented upon.   The second half of the verse seems
designed to prepare us for the introduction of David, xvi. 14 ff.

Second Division. 1 SAMUEL XV—2 SAMUEL VIII.
SAUL AND DAVID.
A. 1 Sam. xv-xx.   *The rejection of Saul and introduction of David.
Saul's jealousy and its results.*

The second division of the Books of Samuel opens with another
account of Saul's rejection, which prepares the way for the entry
upon the scene of David, the son of Jesse, who from this point

anoint thee to be king over his people, over Israel : now
therefore hearken thou unto the voice of the words of
2 the LORD.   Thus saith the LORD of hosts, I have marked
that which Amalek did to Israel, how he set himself
against him in the way, when he came up out of Egypt.
3 Now go and smite Amalek, and utterly destroy all that

---

onward is the central figure of the story. Four subdivisions may
be recognized, the first embracing chapters xv–xx, the contents
of which may conveniently be distributed among the following
sections : (*a*) xv. 1–35ᵃ, (*b*) xv. 35ᵇ—xvi. 13, (*c*) xvi. 14–23, (*d*) xvii.
1—xviii. 5, (*e*) xviii. 6–30, (*f*) xix. 1—xx. 42. The problems—
literary, historical and textual—presented by these six chapters
are among the most difficult, as they are certainly not the least
interesting, with which the critical student is confronted in the
Books of Samuel.

(*a*) xv. 1–35ᵃ. *Saul's second rejection by Samuel.*
In this section we have an account of the breach between Samuel
and Saul, which betrays no acquaintance with, and must be regarded as entirely independent of, the account already given in
ch. xiii. The absence of the characteristic and readily recognizable
phraseology of the Deuteronomic school shows that it originally
formed no part of the document we have termed D, while its
inculcation of the prophetic doctrine, that 'to obey is better than
sacrifice' (verse 22), betrays a more advanced theological standpoint than the early historical source, M, which we have just left.
The majority of scholars are agreed in assigning it 'an intermediate
position between the two currents of narrative, ix. 1, &c. and
ch. viii, &c. [i. e. between our M and D]; it presupposes the
former (for verse 1 points back to x. 1, and a phrase in verse 19ᵇ
appears to be borrowed from xiv. 32), but approximates in its
prophetic tone to the latter' (Driver, *LOT.*⁶, 178 f.). Inasmuch as
the rôle in which Samuel appears suggests the prophet of iii. 20, we
have assigned it provisionally to the same source as chs. i–iii, viz. S.
   2. I have marked: rather, 'I will visit,' i. e. punish.
   Amalek was a nomad people inhabiting the steppes of the
Sinaitic peninsula. The 'theoretical motive' here suggested for the
expedition—the reference is to Exod. xvii. 8 ff. (cf. Deut. xxv. 17 ff.)
—though itself the product of later reflection, does not invalidate
the general historicity of the narrative. 'There is no occasion to
question the fact that Saul really chastised the Amalekites, and
that Samuel actually offered Agag, as the best of the spoils of war,
to Yahweh at Gilgal' (Wellhausen, *Comp. d. Hexateuchs*³, p. 247).
   3. and utterly destroy, &c.: that is, put to the ban, which is

they have, and spare them not; but slay both man and woman, infant and suckling, ox and sheep, camel and ass.

And Saul summoned the people, and numbered them 4 in Telaim, two hundred thousand footmen, and ten thousand men of Judah. And Saul came to the city of 5 Amalek, and laid wait in the valley. And Saul said 6 unto the Kenites, Go, depart, get you down from among the Amalekites, lest I destroy you with them: for ye shewed kindness to all the children of Israel, when they came up out of Egypt. So the Kenites departed from among the Amalekites. And Saul smote the Amalekites, 7 from Havilah as thou goest to Shur, that is before Egypt. And he took Agag the king of the Amalekites alive, and 8 utterly destroyed all the people with the edge of the sword. But Saul and the people spared Agag, and the 9

the meaning of the marginal note 'devote' (to Yahweh). The institution of the ban (*herem*) is frequently referred to in early Hebrew history. Two degrees of severity are found—the one involving, as in the case before us, the destruction of every living creature together with every vestige of property, the other involving only the death of the human beings, the cattle and the spoil in this case becoming the property of the victors. For the underlying ideas, see article 'Ban' (Bennett), *EBi.*, i. 468 ff., and Kautzsch in Hastings' *DB.*, extra vol., 619 f. 'The religious element,' according to the latter scholar, 'is found in the complete renunciation of any profit from the victory, and this renunciation is an expression of gratitude for the fact that the war-God has delivered the enemy, who is His enemy also, into the hands of the conqueror.'

4. Telaim: rather Telam, as xxvii. 8 (LXX), otherwise Telem, Joshua xv. 24, in the south of Judah.

6. The **Kenites** were also a nomad tribe of the peninsula, with whom Moses was connected by marriage (Judges i. 16, where, according to the true text, they are mentioned as dwelling among the Amalekites).

7. from Havilah, &c.: the original is obscure, perhaps 'from Telam until thou comest to Shur (Exod. xv. 22), eastwards from Egypt.' Cf. xxvii. 8.

9. The obscurity is here still greater, but the R.V. seems to give the sense intended. Only the ban of the second degree was

best of the sheep, and of the oxen, and of the fatlings, and the lambs, and all that was good, and would not utterly destroy them : but every thing that was vile and refuse, that they destroyed utterly.

10 Then came the word of the LORD, unto Samuel, saying,
11 It repenteth me that I have set up Saul to be king : for he is turned back from following me, and hath not performed my commandments.   And Samuel was wroth ;
12 and he cried unto the LORD all night.   And Samuel rose early to meet. Saul in the morning ; and it was told Samuel, saying; Saul came to Carmel, and, behold, he set him up a monument, and is gone about, and .passed
13 on, and gone down to Gilgal.   And Samuel came to Saul : and Saul said unto him, Blessed be thou of the LORD : I have performed the commandment of the
14 LORD.   And Samuel said, What meaneth then this bleating of the sheep in mine ears, and the lowing of the
15 oxen which I hear ? And Saul said, They have brought them from the Amalekites : for the people spared the best of the sheep and of the oxen, to sacrifice unto the LORD thy God ; and the rest we have utterly destroyed.
16 Then Samuel said unto Saul, Stay, and I will tell thee what the LORD hath said to me this night.   And he said

---

carried out, and even that not thoroughly, for Agag was spared. Saul's motive for this clemency is not recorded.

xv. 10-23. *Samuel's rebuke and Saul's excuse.*

12. Carmel : a place seven or eight miles south of Hebron, which figures prominently in the history of David (xxv. 5 ff.). The **monument** (Hebrew ' hand,' as 2 Sam. xviii. 18) was in honour of the victory over Amalek.   The scene of Saul's second rejection, as of the first, is laid at **Gilgal** in the Jordan Valley.

15. Convicted of falsehood, Saul proceeds to lay the blame upon the people, at the same time pointing out that Yahweh will receive His share all the same, only by way of a formal sacrifice. In this way hypocrisy is added to falsehood.

unto him, Say on.   And Samuel said, Though thou wast little in thine own sight, wast thou not made the head of the tribes of Israel?   And the LORD anointed thee king over Israel; and the LORD sent thee on a journey, 18 and said, Go and utterly destroy the sinners the Amalekites, and fight against them until they be consumed.   Wherefore then didst thou not obey the 19 voice of the LORD, but didst fly upon the spoil, and didst that which was evil in the sight of the LORD?   And Saul 20 said unto Samuel, Yea, I have obeyed the voice of the LORD, and have gone the way which the LORD sent me, and have brought Agag the king of Amalek, and have utterly destroyed the Amalekites.   But the people took 21 of the spoil, sheep and oxen, the chief of the devoted things, to sacrifice unto the LORD thy God in Gilgal. And Samuel said, Hath the LORD as great delight in 22 burnt offerings and sacrifices, as in obeying the voice of the LORD?   Behold, to obey is better than sacrifice, and to hearken than the fat of rams.   For rebellion is as the sin 23

---

20 f. Saul repeats his former plea, attempting 'to unite obedience in the general with a trifle of disobedience in the particulars' (Wellhausen).

22. Samuel's reply is couched in the rhythmical form peculiar to Hebrew poetry and the higher prophetic style, and consists of four distichs with the usual parallelism.   In the great words 'to obey is better than sacrifice' the author of this chapter brings to a luminous point the whole ethical teaching of the Hebrew prophets from Amos downwards (see Amos v. 21-24: Isa. i. 10-17; Mic. vi. 6-8 and—the nearest in expression—Hos. vi. 6 and Jer. vii. 22 f.).   The O. T. has no word for 'duty'; its moral ideal is embodied in the words 'as the LORD commanded.'   Samuel's 'obedience,' accordingly, is but another aspect of Hosea's 'mercy' —'I desire mercy (*hesed*, loving deeds), not sacrifice,' a golden truth twice re-affirmed by our Lord Himself (Matt. ix. 13, xii. 7). ' Not all the blood of beasts, On Jewish altars slain' can take the place of clean hands and a pure heart, and the love that fulfils itself in the service of our fellow men.

23. the sin of witchcraft: rather, as margin, 'divination,'

of witchcraft, and stubbornness is as idolatry and teraphim.
Because thou hast rejected the word of the LORD, he
24 hath also rejected thee from being king. And Saul said
unto Samuel, I have sinned : for I have transgressed the
commandment of the LORD, and thy words : because I
25 feared the people, and obeyed their voice. Now therefore, I pray thee, pardon my sin, and turn again with me,
26 that I may worship the LORD. And Samuel said unto
Saul, I will not return with thee : for thou hast rejected
the word of the LORD, and the LORD hath rejected thee
27 from being king over Israel. And as Samuel turned
about to go away, he laid hold upon the skirt of his robe,
28 and it rent. And Samuel said unto him, The LORD hath
rent the kingdom of Israel from thee this day, and hath
given it to a neighbour of thine, that is better than thou.

---

a more general term. The rendering 'arrogance' or 'presumption'
(BDB, *Heb. Lex.*) is more appropriate to Saul's sin than **stubbornness.** It is doubtful, further, if the word in the original can bear
the meaning **idolatry.** The parallelism requires a genitive construction, and one Greek translator read : 'the iniquity of idols.'
The couplet, therefore, will run :

> Rebellion is (as) the sin of divination
> Arrogance is (as) the iniquity of teraphim.

The **teraphim,** it is now agreed, were images of some sort, sometimes, if not always, in human form, or at least with a human
head, as appears from xix. 13 ff. They are associated with
divination, as here, in 2 Kings xxiii. 24, Ezek. xxi. 21, Zech. x. 2,
and with the ephod in Judges xvii f., Hos. iii. 4. By the more
spiritual teachers of Israel, the teraphim were held to be incom-
patible with the religion of Yahweh (Gen. xxxi. 19, 34, xxxv. 2, 4).
This stanza, like the foregoing, presupposes the teaching of the
eighth-century prophets, and requires for the chapter a later date
than that of the document M (see introductory note, p. 110).

24 ff. Saul confesses his sin and begs to be forgiven, but in vain.
'The author means to teach that the most sincere repentance is
of no avail when God has made his final decision' (H. P. Smith).
Saul's rejection is indicated first in express terms (verse 26) and
then symbolically (verse 28).

28. a neighbour of thine, that is better than thou : 'even to

And also the Strength of Israel will not lie nor repent: 29
for he is not a man, that he should repent. Then he 30
said, I have sinned: yet honour me now, I pray thee,
before the elders of my people, and before Israel, and
turn again with me, that I may worship the LORD thy
God. So Samuel turned again after Saul; and Saul 31
worshipped the LORD.

Then said Samuel, Bring ye hither to me Agag the 32
king of the Amalekites. And Agag came unto him
delicately. And Agag said, Surely the bitterness of death
is past. And Samuel said, As thy sword hath made 33
women childless, so shall thy mother be childless among
women. And Samuel hewed Agag in pieces before the
LORD in Gilgal.

Then Samuel went to Ramah; and Saul went up to 34
his house to Gibeah of Saul. And Samuel came no 35
more to see Saul until the day of his death; for Samuel

David' (xxviii. 17, where see notes). Here we have another
of the frequent 'omens' to be found in this book (see p. 64). The
incident is therefore to be distinguished from the premeditated
rending of Ahijah's garment, 1 Kings xi. 30.

29. the Strength of Israel: the precise meaning is uncertain.
The margin gives 'Victory,' or 'Glory.'

32 ff. *Samuel executes the ban upon Agag.*

delicately: the word so rendered has not yet been satisfactorily explained, and may be corrupt. It is almost certain that
neither voluptuousness nor cheerfulness (R.V. marg.) is intended.
The Greek has 'trembling.'

33. before the LORD in Gilgal: i.e. at the altar of Yahweh,
to whom everything included in the ban was 'devoted.'

34. The statement here made that Samuel and Saul never met
again in life, when compared with xix. 23 f., is one of the many
indications of the diversity of the sources from which the material
of the Books of Samuel has been derived. In his grief over Saul's
rejection, Samuel recalls the type of religious zealot—by no means
rare in the Church—who unites the tenderest of hearts with the
sternest of creeds. The latter half of the verse is better taken
with the chapter following.

mourned for Saul : and the LORD repented that he had
made Saul king over Israel.

16   And the LORD said unto Samuel, How long wilt thou
mourn for Saul, seeing I have rejected him from being
king over Israel ? fill thine horn with oil, and go, I will
send thee to Jesse the Beth-lehemite : for I have provided
2   me a king among his sons.   And Samuel said, How can
I go ? if Saul hear it, he will kill me.   And the LORD

(b) xv. 35[b]—xvi. 13.   *David secretly anointed by Samuel.*

In chapters xvi and xvii, as they now appear in our Hebrew
Bibles, David is introduced to the reader in no fewer than three
passages, xvi. 1 ff., xvi. 14 ff., and xvii. 12 ff.   That these passages
are mutually independent is now generally admitted.   The remarkable contradiction between xvi. 21 ff. and xvii. 55 ff. has
long been the subject of comment and of many futile attempts at
harmonizing.   It is further noteworthy that neither of these sections of the narrative betrays the slightest acquaintance with
the contents of xvi. 1 ff. (see especially on xvii. 28), nor does David
anywhere in the sequel betray the least consciousness of the high
destiny marked out for him by this scene at Beth-lehem (note
xviii. 18, and the fact that Saul alone in these chapters is called
'the LORD's anointed').   The more recent critics have all but
unanimously put down the section before us as a late addition to
the original Book of Samuel, derived from such a collection of
edifying expansions of the latter as that cited 2 Chron. xxiv. 27.
'the Midrash of the book of the kings' (for which see Driver,
LOT.[6], 529).   But the easy transition from ch. xv does not suggest
a mere interpolator, and, moreover, we naturally expect the
author of chapter xv to furnish us with something more explicit
and detailed regarding Saul's destined successor than the vague
reference in verse 28.   We prefer therefore, with H. P. Smith
(cf. the arguments of N. Peters, *Beiträge zu . . . Samuel*, 70 ff.),
to regard xvi. 1-13 as a further extract from the same source as
the preceding chapter, that is, from the prophetic biography of
Samuel (S).   It is true that the portrait of Samuel in the two
narratives is not entirely consistent (see on verse 2), but if, as
we believe, the author derived his materials from the popular
traditions of his time, perfect consistency is not to be expected.
The section properly begins with xv. 35[b]; 'And the LORD
repented,' &c.

2.   Samuel's hesitation, as has just been admitted, is scarcely
what we should have expected of the fearless spokesman of
Yahweh in xv. 14 ff.

said, Take an heifer with thee, and say, I am come to
sacrifice to the LORD. And call Jesse to the sacrifice, 3
and I will shew thee what thou shalt do : and thou shalt
anoint unto me him whom I name unto thee. And 4
Samuel did that which the LORD spake, and came to
Beth-lehem. And the elders of the city came to meet
him trembling, and said, Comest thou peaceably? And 5
he said, Peaceably : I am come to sacrifice unto the
LORD : sanctify yourselves, and come with me to the
sacrifice. And he sanctified Jesse and his sons, and
called them to the sacrifice. And it came to pass, when 6
they were come, that he looked on Eliab, and said,
Surely the LORD's anointed is before him. But the 7
LORD said unto Samuel, Look not on his countenance,
or on the height of his stature ; because I have rejected
him : for *the LORD seeth* not as man seeth; for man
looketh on the outward appearance, but the LORD
looketh on the heart. Then Jesse called Abinadab, 8
and made him pass before Samuel. And he said,
Neither hath the LORD chosen this. Then Jesse made 9
Shammah to pass by. And he said, Neither hath the
LORD chosen this. And Jesse made seven of his sons 10
to pass before Samuel. And Samuel said unto Jesse,
The LORD hath not chosen these. And Samuel said 11
unto Jesse, Are here all thy children? And he said,
There remaineth yet the youngest, and, behold, he

5. sanctify yourselves: a frequent expression for preparation
for worship by means of ablutions and abstinence from whatever
might render one ceremonially unclean (Exod. xix. 10, 14 f.,
and often).

7. the LORD seeth: as the italics show, these words have
been supplied (from the LXX); their omission in the Heb. text
is purely accidental. The thought of God as the Searcher of
hearts is a favourite with Jeremiah (xi. 20, xvii. 10, xx. 12), and
is the theme of Ps. cxxxix.

keepeth the sheep.   And Samuel said unto Jesse, Send and fetch him: for we will not sit down till he come
12 hither.   And he sent, and brought him in.   Now he was ruddy, and withal of a beautiful countenance, and goodly to look upon.   And the LORD said, Arise, anoint him:
13 for this is he.   Then Samuel took the horn of oil, and anointed him in the midst of his brethren: and the spirit of the LORD came mightily upon David from that day forward.   So Samuel rose up, and went to Ramah.

14   [M] Now the spirit of the LORD had departed from Saul,
15 and an evil spirit from the LORD troubled him.   And

---

11. we will not sit down: i. e. to the common meal which followed the sacrifice (i. 4 f., ix. 22 ff.).

12. he was ruddy: only of David (also xvii. 42) and Esau (Gen. xxv. 25), and generally taken as referring to the colour of the skin.   Possibly, however, it refers to the colour of the hair. Klostermann, indeed, would add this noun to the text.   It is interesting to think of David as the *red-haired* 'darling of the songs of Israel' (2 Sam. xxiii. 1), or, as Browning has it in his *Saul*, 'God's child with His dew, On thy gracious gold hair.'

and withal: a very dubious rendering.   Read here and xvii. 42, with Graetz and most moderns, by inserting a letter: 'a stripling (so xvii. 56) with beautiful eyes (see marg.) and of a comely person.'

13. For the endowment of the spirit as conveyed by the act of anointing, see on x. 1.   Here we have the first mention of **David**, a name peculiar, in the O. T., to Israel's national hero.   The etymology of the word is uncertain.   It may either be akin to Dodo or Dodai (2 Sam. xxiii. 24), and the fuller form Dodavahu (2 Chron. xx. 37, R. V.), both probably signifying 'Yahweh is a friend' or 'is beloved,' or it may have underlying it, as is suggested by its unique occurrence, the name of some obscure Canaanite deity (cf. the names Dudu, in the Amarna tablets, and Dido of Carthage).   The best recent study of David is perhaps the article by H. A. White in Hastings' *Dictionary of the Bible*.

(*c*) xvi. 14-23.   *David brought to court as the king's minstrel.*
Of the two extant accounts of David's introduction to Saul (cf. xvii. 55 ff.), it is admitted on all hands that the account here given is the older, and the one to which alone an historical value attaches. There need be no hesitation in assigning it to the early source, M.

14. an evil spirit from the LORD: This expression, like so

Saul's servants said unto him, Behold now, an evil spirit
from God troubleth thee.   Let our lord now command 16
thy servants, which are before thee, to seek out a man
who is a cunning player on the harp : and it shall come
to pass, when the evil spirit from God is upon thee, that
he shall play with his hand, and thou shalt be well.
And Saul said unto his servants, Provide me now a man 17
that can play well, and bring him to me.   Then answered 18
one of the young men, and said, Behold, I have seen
a son of Jesse the Beth-lehemite, that is cunning in
playing, and a mighty man of valour, and a man of war,
and prudent in speech, and a comely person, and the

---

many others in this ancient document, must be interpreted in the
light of the ideas of its time.   All antiquity was at one in
ascribing every form of disease, and mind-sickness in particular,
to the agency of evil spirits.   As the presence of such a spirit
was impossible while Saul was still under the influence of the
spirit of Yahweh (x. 10), it was evident to the thought of the time
that this Divine influence had been withdrawn.   And yet, since
Yahweh was supreme in the realm of spirits, the evil spirit could
only come from Him and by His permission.   Saul is usually
believed to have suffered from morbid melancholia.   A recent
authority (Professor Macalister in Hastings' *DB.*, iii. 327), however,
informs us that 'his case is a typical one of recurrent paroxysmal
mania rather than of melancholia.'   The influence of music on
such morbid natures was and is universally recognized.

18. prudent (better, as marg., 'skilful') **in speech** : this must
either refer to the recitative which accompanied the music, or
signify 'of a ready wit,' one of the necessary qualifications of an
Eastern musician (see Lane, *Arabian Society in the Middle Ages*,
176).   David is here described as at once a 'cunning' or expert
harpist and a skilful improvisor or poet.   This enumeration of his
qualifications for the post of the king's minstrel is now cut in two
by the irrelevant description of David as a **mighty man of valour
and a man of war**.   That they are an intrusion, suggested
probably by xiv. 52[b], is further shown by the well-attested youth of
David at this date, (see Introduction, sect. ix), and by his employ-
ment now 'with the sheep' of Jesse (verse 19), and afterwards as
Saul's armour-bearer (verse 21), a post entirely beneath the dignity
of a 'man of war' (see on xvii. 33, and cf. xiv. 13).   The bearing of
all this on the literary analysis will appear presently.

19 LORD is with him. Wherefore Saul sent messengers unto Jesse, and said, Send me David thy son, which is
20 with the sheep. And Jesse took an ass *laden* with bread, and a bottle of wine, and a kid, and sent them by David
21 his son unto Saul. And David came to Saul, and stood before him : and he loved him greatly ; and he became
22 his armourbearer. And Saul sent to Jesse, saying, Let David, I pray thee, stand before me ; for he hath found
23 favour in my sight. And it came to pass, when the *evil* spirit from God was upon Saul, that David took the harp, and played with his hand : so Saul was refreshed, and was well, and the evil spirit departed from him.
17   Now the Philistines gathered together their armies to

---

20. an ass laden with bread : an attempt, as the italics show, to make sense of a corrupt text ; read : 'ten loaves of bread' (cf. xvii. 17).

(*d*) xvii. 1—xviii. 5. *David and the Philistine champion.*

By a strange irony the chapter of 1 Samuel which contains perhaps the most popular incident in the book presents the most complicated of its literary problems to the scholar. For in addition to the ordinary questions of the higher criticism, which deals with the literary sources and their historical value, we have here to reckon with a serious problem in the domain of the lower, or textual, criticism. Of the sixty-three verses contained in the received text of this section, more than thirty are wanting in the original text of the oldest Greek Version (Codex B), viz. xvii. 12–31, 41, 50, 55–58, xviii. 1–5. The question is, which of the two forms, the longer Hebrew, or the shorter Greek form, represents the text as it left the hands of the compiler of Samuel ? At first sight the fact that, in the longer text, David appears as an absolute stranger to Saul (xvii. 55 ff.), when in reality he had been for some time a member of his court (xvi. 20 ff.), naturally suggests that the parts above enumerated have been deliberately omitted by the Greek translators for harmonistic purposes. Such, indeed, is the opinion of many of our foremost critics, Wellhausen, Budde, Cheyne, Driver, and others. On the other hand, not a few scholars of equal eminence maintain that the verses in question are later additions to the original text of Samuel from an independent account of the Goliath episode, and that the part that remains when these are excised is complete in itself. This view,

battle, and they were gathered together at Socoh, which
belongeth to Judah, and pitched between Socoh and
Azekah, in Ephes-dammim.　And Saul and the men of 2
Israel were gathered together, and pitched in the vale of
Elah, and set the battle in array against the Philistines.
And the Philistines stood on the mountain on the one 3
side, and Israel stood on the mountain on the other

---

it is further maintained, is confirmed by the imperfect connexion
between verses 11 and 12 and verses 31 and 32 in our present
text (see notes below).　The case for the originality of the
shorter text has been ably argued by the late Robertson Smith in
his *OTJC.*[2], 120 ff., 431 ff., who has been followed by Stade,
Cornill, H. P. Smith, Löhr, Nowack, Kirkpatrick (*Cambridge
Bible*), and Peters.　Their position seems to the present writer to
afford the best solution of an admittedly difficult problem.

It remains now to inquire how this result will affect the
literary analysis. The additions, as we must regard them, of the
present text at once fall apart as later accretions (Z). The
remaining half of the section, xvii. 1–11, 32–40, 42–54, recent
critics almost without exception assign to a source distinct from,
and younger than, the early source (our M) to which xvi. 14–23 is
now unanimously attributed.　The main and continually recurring
argument in support of this attribution is that in xvii. 1 ff. David
appears as a youth, whereas in xvi. 14 ff. he is represented as
a man of mature years and of wide repute as a man of war, a position
which has been shown above to be entirely due to a later erroneous
insertion in xvi. 18.　Hebrew tradition, we maintain, is consistent
in representing David as a youth of eighteen or twenty (see
Introduction, sect. ix) at his introduction to the court of Saul.
Robertson Smith alone ventured to regard xvii. 1 ff. as the
continuation of xvi. 14–23 (*OTJC.*[2], 435). An attempt will be
made in the notes to follow the hint thrown out by this acute
critic, and to meet the objections that may reasonably be taken to
this attribution.

1 f. For details of the topography of this chapter, see the
dictionaries, G. A. Smith, *Hist. Geog.*, 226 ff., and especially W.
Miller, *The Least of all Lands*, ch. v, with map of the battlefield.
The latter lay in the valley of **Elah**, the modern *Wadi es-Sunt.*
On its southern edge lay **Socoh**, the modern *Shuweikeh;* the name
Socoh has recently been found on jar-handles in this neighbourhood.
The other sites have not been identified.　Saul, as we shall see.
was naturally accompanied to the field of battle by his youthful
armourbearer.

4 side: and there was a valley between them. And there
went out a champion out of the camp of the Philistines,
named Goliath, of Gath, whose height was six cubits and
5 a span. And he had an helmet of brass upon his head,
and he was clad with a coat of mail; and the weight of

---

4. Goliath, of Gath: modern critics are practically unanimous
in regarding the famous encounter related in the sequel as
unhistorical. One of the main arguments—that it formed no part
of the earliest extant source—has been already dealt with. More
serious is the difficulty raised by the statement from an undoubtedly ancient document that the slayer of Goliath was
a Beth-lehemite, Elhanan, the son of Jair (2 Sam. xxi. 19, where
see note for true text), in the reign of David. By the recognized
principles of historical criticism, this early authority is the more
worthy of credit, assigning as it does to an obscure champion
a feat which, as can readily be believed, a later tradition loved to
assign to its favourite hero, David. But we are convinced that
the real relation between these mutually inconsistent statements
has not hitherto been satisfactorily explained. An examination
of the original and shorter form of the narrative before us discloses
the remarkable fact that David's opponent is throughout termed
'the Philistine' or 'this Philistine,' with the single exception of
verse 4. We are driven to the conclusion that in the source M,
which we believe the compiler to be following here, *the Philistine
champion was nameless*. The identification with Goliath of the
later Elhanan episode was rendered all the more easy by the
common description of their respective spears by means of a
popular comparison to a weaver's leash-rod (see on verse 7, and
cf. 2 Sam. xxi. 19). The historicity of the achievement by which
David gained his early renown and aroused the jealousy of Saul
(xviii. 6 ff.) is thus vindicated. The passage last referred to is
unanimously assigned to the same source as xvi. 14-23, and the
critics, by regarding xvii. 1 ff. as a legendary extract from a later
source, are obliged to postulate in its place some other feat of
arms sufficient to account for this sudden access of royal jealousy.
But it is difficult to see the compiler's reason for omitting such
an achievement had he found it in his source.

six cubits and a span: about nine feet six inches. The
span was half the cubit, which was somewhat under eighteen
inches (Hastings' *DB.*, iv. 909).

5. a coat of mail: the original implies that it was composed of
scales of bronze. Its weight, 5,000 shekels of bronze, was probably about 220 lb. avoirdupois, according to the standard termed
by the present writer 'the Syrian or 320 grain unit' (see 'Weights
and Measures,' *ibid.*, iv. 904 ff.).

the coat was five thousand shekels of brass. And he 6
had greaves of brass upon his legs, and a javelin of brass
between his shoulders. And the staff of his spear was 7
like a weaver's beam ; and his spear's head *weighed* six
hundred shekels of iron : and his shield-bearer went
before him. And he stood and cried unto the armies of 8
Israel, and said unto them, Why are ye come out to set
your battle in array? am not I a Philistine, and ye
servants to Saul? choose you a man for you, and let
him come down to me. If he be able to fight with me, 9
and kill me, then will we be your servants : but if
I prevail against him, and kill him, then shall ye be our
servants, and serve us. And the Philistine said, I defy 10
the armies of Israel this day ; give me a man, that we
may fight together. And when Saul and all Israel heard 11
those words of the Philistine, they were dismayed, and
greatly afraid.

[Z] Now David was the son of that Ephrathite of 12
Beth-lehem-judah, whose name was Jesse ; and he had
eight sons : and the man was an old man in the days of
Saul, stricken *in years* among men. And the three 13

7. like a weaver's beam: rather, 'a weaver's shaft' or leash-
rod, for which the curious student is referred to the special investigation of this obscure term in the article 'Weaving' (Kennedy).
EBi., iv. 5285.

11. At this point, according to the original text, David, Saul's
armourbearer, steps forward and accepts the challenge (verse 32).

xvii. 12-31. *Another account of David's appearance on the scene.*
The reasons for regarding these verses as forming no part of the
original text of the compiler of Samuel have been given above.

12. This verse has all the appearance of having once been the
commencement of an independent narrative. W. R. Smith conjectures that it read originally: 'And there was a man, an
Ephrathite of Beth-lehem-judah, whose name was Jesse' (cf. i. 1,
ix. 1)

eldest sons of Jesse had gone after Saul to the battle:
and the names of his three sons that went to the battle
were Eliab the firstborn, and next unto him Abinadab,
14 and the third Shammah.   And David was the youngest:
15 and the three eldest followed Saul.   Now David went to
and fro from Saul to feed his father's sheep at Beth-lehem.
16 And the Philistine drew near morning and evening, and
presented himself forty days.

17   And Jesse said unto David his son, Take now for, thy
brethren an ephah of this parched corn, and these ten
loaves, and carry *them* quickly to the camp to thy
18 brethren; and bring these ten cheeses unto the captain
of their thousand, and look how thy brethren fare, and
19 take their pledge.   Now Saul, and they, and all the men
of Israel, were in the vale of Elah, fighting with the
20 Philistines.   And David rose up early in the morning,
and left the sheep with a keeper, and took, and went, as
Jesse had commanded him; and he came to the place
of the wagons, as the host which was going forth to the
21 fight shouted for the battle.   And Israel and the Philis-
22 tines put the battle in array, army against army.   And
David left his baggage in the hand of the keeper of the
baggage, and ran to the army, and came and saluted his

---

15. We have here clearly the hand of a harmonizer, who
sought to explain the absence of Saul's armourbearer from the
camp by suggesting that David divided his time between the
court and his father's farm.

16. A legendary heightening of the Philistine's truculence of
which the older narrative knows nothing, and which, moreover,
here appears too early in this narrative.

18. captain of their thousand: see on viii. 12.

take their pledge: some token which David could show to
their father as proof that they were alive and well.

20. the place of the wagons: also xxvi. 5, 7; the original
is probably a military term for the camp. R.V. marg. gives 'barri-
cade'; others 'entrenchment' (BDB, *Heb. Lex.*).

brethren. And as he talked with them, behold, .there 23
came up the champion, the Philistine of Gath, Goliath
by name, out of the ranks of the Philistines, and spake
according to the same words : and David heard them.
And all the men of Israel, when they saw the man, fled 24
from him, and were sore afraid. And the men of Israel 25
said, Have ye seen this man that is come up? surely to
defy Israel is he come up : and it shall be, that the man
who killeth him, the king will enrich him with great
riches, and will give him his daughter, and make his
father's house free in Israel. And David spake to the 26
men that stood by him, saying, What shall be done to
the man that killeth this Philistine, and taketh away the
reproach from Israel? for who is this uncircumcised
Philistine, that he should defy the armies of the living
God? And the people answered him after this manner, 27
saying, So shall it be done to the man that killeth him.
And Eliab his eldest brother heard when he spake unto 28
the men ; and Eliab's anger was kindled against David,
and he said, Why art thou come down? and with whom
hast thou left those few sheep in the wilderness? I know
thy pride, and the naughtiness of thine heart ; for thou
art come down that thou mightest see the battle. And 29

---

23. spake according to the same words : the terms of the
challenge have been omitted, as they were already given in 8 ff.
(from M).

25. free in Israel: i.e. from all dues in kind or money, from
unpaid labour (see on 2 Sam. xx. 24), &c.

26. the living God : this Divine name is supposed to belong to
the Deuteronomic age (Deut. v. 25 ; Jer. x. 10, xxiii. 36). Cf.
verse 36 below.

28. I know thy pride, and the naughtiness of thine heart:
the writer of these words cannot have been acquainted with the
scene depicted in xvi. 12 f., the solemn anointing of David ' in the
midst of his brethren.' No Hebrew, least of all a brother, could
thus have spoken to ' the LORD's anointed.'

David said, What have I now done ? Is there not a cause ?
30 And he turned away from him toward another, and spake
after the same manner : and the people answered him
31 again after the former manner.   And when the words
· were heard which David spake, they rehearsed them
32 before Saul; and he sent for him.   [M] And David
said to Saul, Let no man's heart fail because of him;
33 thy servant will go and fight with this Philistine.   And
Saul said to David, Thou art not able to go against this
Philistine to fight with him : for thou art but a youth,
34 and he a man of war from his youth.   And David said
unto Saul, Thy servant kept his father's sheep; and when
there came a lion, or a bear, and took a lamb out of the
35 flock, I went out after him, and smote him, and delivered
it out of his mouth : and when he arose against me,

---

31. and he sent for him: a paraphrase rather than a translation of the original 'and he took him.'   Lucian's recension of the
later Greek text has 'and they took him and brought him to Saul,'
which at least gives sense.   But the fact is that the interpolated
narrative here breaks off abruptly, and we do not know how the
verse really ended.

xvii. 32-54. *David accepts the challenge and slays the champion.*
The original narrative, which was dropped at verse 11, is now
resumed.   David, who was in the camp from the first, where
indeed he had a tent assigned to him (verse 54), hears the Philistine's challenge (verses 8 ff.) and at once—note the contrast in
verse 16—accepts it.   The close connexion between verses ·11
and 32 is self-evident.

33. thou art but a youth: the assumed discrepancy between
this statement and the data of xvi. 18, of which so much has been
made, was there shown to be illusory.   'An armourbearer was not a
full warrior, but a sort of page or apprentice in arms' (*OTJC.*², 431 f.).

34. David had proved his courage in another school.   Common
sense and grammar alike require the rendering of R. V. as compared with A. V.   We have not the record of a single adventure
but of many.   A still closer reproduction of the text would run
thus : 'when a lion—or (it might be) a bear—used to come out,
and take a lamb,' &c.   For the hardships of a shepherd's life, see
Gen. xxxi. 39 ff., and cf. Amos iii. 12.

I caught him by his beard, and smote him, and slew him.
Thy servant smote both the lion and the bear: and this 36
uncircumcised Philistine shall be as one of them, seeing
he hath defied the armies of the living God. And David 37
said, The LORD that delivered me out of the paw of the
lion, and out of the paw of the bear, he will deliver me
out of the hand of this Philistine. And Saul said unto
David, Go, and the LORD shall be with thee. And Saul 38
clad David with his apparel, and he put an helmet of
brass upon his head, and he clad him with a coat of
mail. And David girded his sword upon his apparel, 39
and he assayed to go; for he had not proved it. And
David said unto Saul, I cannot go with these; for I have
not proved them. And David put them off him. And 40
he took his staff in his hand, and chose him five smooth
stones out of the brook, and put them in the shepherd's
bag which he had, even in his scrip; and his sling was
in his hand: and he drew near to the Philistine. And 41

---

36. The last clause is probably an addition from verse 26 (see
there), the verse originally ending with 'one of them.' The LXX
text is still fuller.

37. The author now begins to lead up to the religious lesson
of the story. Saul wishes to give the youthful champion the best
equipment in all the camp, his own. But this only serves to bring
into stronger relief the intention of Him 'who saveth not with
sword and spear' (verse 47).

38. And Saul clad David with his apparel: rather, as A.V.,
'with his armour,' as may be seen from xviii. 4, where the various
items are enumerated. Cf. 2 Sam. xx. 8, Joab's 'apparel of
war.' The last clause, accordingly, is unnecessary and is wanting
in LXX.

39. he assayed to go: i. e. he tried unsuccessfully to go, for
the weight of the unaccustomed armour impeded his movements.

40. his scrip: a better order would be: 'and put them in his
scrip (the shepherd's bag which he had),' the words within parentheses being a gloss on the unique word (*yalkut*) rendered
'scrip.'

41. With verse 50, no part of the true text (see above). The

the Philistine came on and drew near unto David; and
42 the man that bare the shield went before him. And
when the Philistine looked about, and saw David, he
disdained him : for he was but a youth, and ruddy, and
43 withal of a fair countenance. And the Philistine said
unto David, Am I a dog, that thou comest to me with
staves ? And the Philistine cursed David by his gods.
44 And the Philistine said to David, Come to me, and
I will give thy flesh unto the fowls of the air, and to the
45 beasts of the field. Then said David to the Philistine,
Thou comest to me with a sword, and with a spear, and
with a javelin : but I come to thee in the name of the
LORD of hosts, the God of the armies of Israel, which
46 thou hast defied. This day will the LORD deliver thee
into mine hand ; and I will smite thee, and take thine
head from off thee ; and I will give the carcases of the
host of the Philistines this day unto the fowls of the air,
and to the wild beasts of the earth ; that all the earth
47 may know that there is a God in Israel : and that all
this assembly may know that the LORD saveth not with
sword and spear : for the battle is the LORD'S, and he
48 will give you into our hand. And it came to pass, when
the Philistine arose, and came and drew nigh to meet

---

next verse should end with 'youth,' the rest being generally regarded as an irrelevant expansion derived from xvi. 12.

45. the God of the armies of Israel: for the importance of
this definition of Yahweh Ṣebaoth (the LORD of hosts) for the
original significance of this Divine title, see on i. 3. Its occurrence
here seems to tell in favour of the derivation of the main stock of
this chapter from the early source M. From the time of Amos
onwards Yahweh Ṣebaoth had another and higher significance, as
explained above (p. 37).

46 f. Cheyne has rightly seen that these two verses have been
added by a 'later writer of the post-Deuteronomic period to bring
the lesson of the tale into clearer view.'. . Nowhere else outside
of the N.T. does the message of encouragement to the humble and

David, that David hastened, and ran toward the army to meet the Philistine.   And David put his hand in his bag, 49 and took thence a stone, and slang it, and smote the Philistine in his forehead; and the stone sank into his forehead, and he fell upon his face to the earth.   So 50 David prevailed over the Philistine with a sling and with a stone, and smote the Philistine, and slew him; but there was no sword in the hand of David.   Then David 51 ran, and stood over the Philistine, and took his sword, and drew it out of the sheath thereof, and slew him, and cut off his head therewith.   And when the Philistines saw that their champion was dead, they fled.   And the 52 men of Israel and of Judah arose, and shouted, and pursued the Philistines, until thou comest to Gai, and to the gates of Ekron.   And the wounded of the Philistines fell down by the way to Shaaraim, even unto Gath, and unto Ekron.   And the children of Israel returned from 53 chasing after the Philistines, and they spoiled their camp.   And David took the head of the Philistine, and 54 brought it to Jerusalem; but he put his armour in his tent.

---

exhortation to the weak in faith receive so affecting, so inspiring an expression' (see for details his article 'Goliath,' *EBi.* ii. 1755, and *Aids to the devout Study of Criticism*, 116 ff.).

52. Gai: a slip for Gath, for which and for Ekron see on v. 8 ff.   The rest of the verse is corrupt.   Nowack reads: 'And the wounded of the Philistines fell down even in the gateways' (note R. V. marg.).   What follows appears to be a gloss from the preceding sentence.

54. and brought it to Jerusalem: a curious anachronism, since David's future capital was still in the hands of the Jebusites. Cheyne conjectures 'to Saul.'

he put his armour in his tent: a sentence which is fatal to the unity of the chapter, but which affords a striking confirmation of the analysis here advocated, which sees in xvii. 1 ff. the natural sequence of xvi. 14-23 (cf. on 32 ff., p. 126).   Goliath's sword is found somewhat later at Nob (xxi. 9).

55 [Z] And when Saul saw David go forth against the Philistine, he said unto Abner, the captain of the host, Abner, whose son is this youth? And Abner said, As

56 thy soul liveth, O king, I cannot tell. And the king said,

57 Inquire thou whose son the stripling is. And as David returned from the slaughter of the Philistine, Abner took him, and brought him before Saul with the head of the

58 Philistine in his hand. And Saul said to him, Whose son art thou, thou young man? And David answered, I am the

18 son of thy servant Jesse the Beth-lehemite. And it came to pass, when he had made an end of speaking unto Saul, that the soul of Jonathan was knit with the soul of David,

2 and Jonathan loved him as his own soul. And Saul took him that day, and would let him go no more home

3 to his father's house. Then Jonathan and David made a covenant, because he loved him as his own soul.

4 And Jonathan stripped himself of the robe that was upon him, and gave it to David, and his apparel, even to his

5 sword, and to his bow, and to his girdle. And David

---

xvii. 55—xviii. 5. *David's (second) introduction to Saul and his advancement at court.* A further extract from the parallel narrative beginning verse 12, and, as we have seen, no part of the original text, according to which David is already a *persona grata* at court (xvi. 21). No harmonistic ingenuity has yet succeeded in reconciling the two accounts of David's introduction. It is satisfactory to know that perhaps the most striking discrepancy as to a matter of fact to be found in the historical books cannot be laid at the door of the original compiler of Samuel.

3. Jonathan and David enter into a covenant of blood-brotherhood, for which see W. R. Smith, *Rel. Sem.*[2], 314 f., and especially Trumbull, *The Blood Covenant, passim.* In xx. 8 it is called 'a covenant of Yahweh.' The mutual affection of these two, so disinterested on Jonathan's part, and so nobly requited on David's, has become for all time the type of the generous and enduring friendships of youth.

4. his apparel: rather, 'his armour,' see on xvii. 38. The commentators recall the exchange of arms between Glaucus and Diomede in the *Iliad* (vi. 230 ff.).

went out whithersoever Saul sent him, *and* behaved himself wisely : and Saul set him over the men of war, and it was good in the sight of all the people, and also in the sight of Saul's servants.

[M] And it came to pass as they came, when David 6 returned from the slaughter of the Philistine, that the women came out of all the cities of Israel, singing and dancing, to meet king Saul, with timbrels, with joy, and with instruments of music. And the women sang one to 7 another in their play, and said,

Saul·hath slain his thousands,
And David his ten thousands.

---

5. The arrangement of the clauses in Lucian's text is preferable : 'And Saul set him over the men of war, and David went out and came in (a common idiom for military duty, xxix. 6, and verses 13, 16 below), and whithersoever Saul sent him he behaved himself wisely ; and it was good,' &c.

behaved himself wisely : rather, 'was successful'; the original 'expresses not success alone, but success as the result of wise provision' (Driver).

(*e*) xviii. 6–30 *Saul becomes jealous of David's popularity, but gives him his daughter Michal in marriage.*

The relation of the incidents in this section to each other and to the foregoing is difficult to trace. But the difficulties are in great measure removed if, as in the previous chapter, we accept as the original text of Samuel the shorter form given by codex B of the LXX, which omits the following verses and parts of verses : xviii. 6ᵃ (to 'Philistine'), the first and last clauses of 8, 10, 11, 12 (all after 'David'), 17–19, 21ᵇ, 29ᵇ, 30. By the excision of these accretions a much more intelligible and psychologically consistent narrative is obtained, which may be assigned in the main to M. The sign Z (later addition) has only been inserted before the larger accretions, verses 10 f., 17 ff. (see above).

6 f. The text of B opens thus : 'And the dancing women came out,' &c. At first sight the poetical distich which follows—cited again in xxi. 11, xxix. 5—appears inappropriate, and would be more in place at a somewhat later stage of David's career, e. g. after xix. 8. On the other hand, the couplet may have been a popular mode of comparing the merits of rival leaders, and as such employed as stated in the expanded form of 6ᵃ.

K 2

8   And Saul was very wroth, and this saying displeased
him; and he said, They have ascribed unto David ten
thousands, and to me they have ascribed but thousands:
9 and what can he have more but the kingdom? And Saul
eyed David from that day and forward.

10   [Z] And it came to pass on the morrow, that an evil
spirit from God came mightily upon Saul, and he prophesied in the midst of the house: and David played
with his hand, as he did day by day: and Saul had his
11 spear in his hand.   And Saul cast the spear; for he said,
I will smite David even to the wall.   And David avoided
12 out of his presence twice.   [M] And Saul was afraid of
David, because the LORD was with him, and was departed
13 from Saul.   Therefore Saul removed him from him, and
made him his captain over a thousand; and he went out and
14 came in before the people.   And David behaved himself
15 wisely in all his ways; and the LORD was with him.   And
when Saul saw that he behaved himself very wisely, he

---

8. The premature hint as to the royal succession in the last
clause belongs to the inserted matter.

9. Saul eyed David: looked on him with envy and suspicion.

10 f. These intrusive verses place the climax of Saul's jealousy
too early (see on verse 12).

and he prophesied: rather, 'he raved,' was in a state of
frenzy; cf. x. 5.

**12 f. And Saul was afraid of David, and removed him from
him:** so the true text (B).   The psychologically accurate picture,
given by the shorter text, of the gradual growth of Saul's enmity
to David has often been noted.   Here Saul is 'afraid of David,'
in verse 15 he 'stands in awe of him,' while in verse 29 he is
'yet more afraid,' and ultimately gives orders for his assassination
(xix. 1), if this be the continuation of xviii. 29.

went out and came in: see on verse 5.   This promotion to
the command of 'a thousand' (for which see on viii. 12) is more
credible than the parallel statement of verse 5, which seems to
represent David as already commander-in-chief.   Saul's motive
was doubtless the same that we find expressed in verses 17, 21,
and 25.

stood in awe of him.   But all Israel and Judah loved 16
David ; for he went out and came in before them.

[**Z**] And Saul said to David, Behold, my elder daughter 17
Merab, her will I give thee to wife : only be thou valiant
for me, and fight the LORD's battles.   For Saul said, Let
not mine hand be upon him, but let the hand of the
Philistines be upon him.   And David said unto Saul, 18
Who am I, and what is my life, *or* my father's family in
Israel, that I should be son in law to the king ? But it 19
came to pass at the time when Merab Saul's daughter
should have been given to David, that she was given
unto Adriel the Meholathite to wife.   [**M**] And Michal 20
Saul's daughter loved David : and they told Saul, and the
thing pleased him.   And Saul said, I will give him her, 21
that she may be a snare to him, and that the hand of the

17-19. A perplexing passage, which, however, is no part of
the original text, and may be set down as an unhistorical variant
of verses 20 ff.

17. fight the LORD'S battles (also xxv. 28): the battles of
His people are Yahweh's battles, hence the title of the poetical
work cited Num. xxi. 14, 'the book of the battles of Yahweh.'
Down to the reign of David, Yahweh, as visibly represented by
the ark, frequently—at first, no doubt, invariably—took the field
with the consecrated warriors.

18. what is my life: render, as R. V. marg., 'who are my
kinsfolk,' a rare word denoting 'a group of families united by
blood-ties,' as explained by the following gloss 'my father's clan.'
Cf. 2 Sam. vii. 18.

19. Adriel the Meholathite: a native of Abel-meholah, in
the Jordan valley near Beth-shan, the native place of Elisha
(1 Kings xix. 16).   The tragic fate of the five sons of this union
is related 2 Sam. xxi. 8 ff., where for 'Michal' read, with LXX,
'Merab.'

xviii. 20-29. *Michal is given in marriage to David.*

21. that she may be a snare to him: a metaphor taken from
fowling, with no moral connotation here.   The meaning of the
reference to the Philistines, couched in the same terms as the
doublet in verse 17, is disclosed in verse 25.   The latter part of
the verse, wanting in B, is a mere harmonistic addition.

Philistines may be against him.   Wherefore Saul said to David, Thou shalt this day be my son in law a second 22 time.   And Saul commanded his servants, *saying*, Commune with David secretly, and say, Behold, the king hath delight in thee, and all his servants love thee : now 23 therefore be the king's son in law.   And Saul's servants . spake those words in the ears of David.   And David said, Seemeth it to you a light thing to be the king's son in law, 24 seeing that I am a poor man, and lightly esteemed ? And the servants of Saul told him, saying, On this manner 25 spake David.   And Saul said, Thus shall ye say to David, The king desireth not any dowry, but an hundred foreskins of the Philistines, to be avenged of the king's enemies.   Now Saul thought to make David fall by the 26 hand of the Philistines.   And when his servants told David these words, it pleased David well to be the king's 27 son in law.   And the days were not expired ; and David arose and went, he and his men, and slew of the Philistines two hundred men ; and David brought their foreskins, and they gave them in full tale to the king, that he might be the king's son in law.   And Saul gave him 28 Michal his daughter to wife.   And Saul saw and knew

23. I am a poor man: and therefore unable to pay the large dowry which would be expected for a princess.

25. dowry (Heb. *mōhar*)· the price in money, in cattle, or, as here and in the case of Jacob, in special service rendered, which according to ancient custom was paid to the bride's father as compensation for the loss to the family and tribe of a valuable member.   For a dowry (R. V. ' portion ') in the modern sense, see 1 Kings ix. 16.   The last clause discloses Saul's real motive in selecting this particular form of dowry, which, though repellent to modern sensibilities, had its analogies in contemporary Egyptian custom.

27. David spontaneously doubles the stipulated dowry.   The Greek text, however, reads ' one hundred,' which accords with David's own statement, 2 Sam. iii. 14.

28 f. The more concise and intelligible text of codex B is here

that the LORD was with David; and Michal Saul's daughter loved him.   And Saul was yet the more afraid 29 of David; [Z] and Saul was David's enemy continually.

Then the princes of the Philistines went forth: and it 30 came to pass, as often as they went forth, that David behaved himself more wisely than all the servants of Saul; so that his name was much set by.

[T] And Saul spake to Jonathan his son, and to all 19

---

generally preferred: 'And Saul saw that the LORD was with David, and that all Israel loved him, and he was yet more afraid of David.'   All that follows, to the end of the chapter, is extraneous matter.

(f) xix. 1—xx. 42. *Saul's increasing enmity compels David to flee the court. Jonathan's loyalty to David.*

The difficulties, literary and historical, raised by this section are, frankly, insuperable.   The text also is in considerable disorder, although the Greek version now resumes its normal relation to the Hebrew.   If Jonathan was personally urged by his father to compass David's death (xix. 1), how could he be ignorant of Saul's design (cf. xix. 2 with xx. 2)?   Notwithstanding Saul's determined attempt to seize David, who barely escapes with his life (xix. 11 ff.), in the following chapter the latter is still at court devising means to ascertain Saul's feelings towards him (xx. 5 ff.).   Further, in xix. 18-24, we are told of the origin of a popular saying, of which our oldest source has already given another and more credible explanation (x. 10 ff.).   This meeting of Samuel and Saul, moreover, contradicts the previous statement, xv. 35ª.   These are but a few of the difficulties which have made this period of David's life the despair of historical critics, to whose works the student is referred for further details.

On one point only is there general agreement, namely that the passage xix. 18-24 is late and unhistorical.   There is considerable agreement, also, that the main stream of the narrative in ch. xx belongs to the early source M (Budde's J), with various parts of which it shows linguistic points of contact (see notes).   Beyond this all is conjecture.   If, however, we adopt ch. xx as, in the main, M's version of this crisis in David's life, the story of Michal's stratagem (xix. 11-17) will have come from another source.   Verses 1-7 may also be a parallel version of Jonathan's part as mediator in ch. xx.   Without a doubt, such topics as Saul's jealousy on the one hand, Jonathan's friendship and Michal's

2 his servants, that they should slay David.   But Jonathan
Saul's son delighted much in David.   And Jonathan told
David, saying, Saul my father seeketh to slay thee : now
therefore, I pray thee, take heed to thyself in the morning,
3 and abide in a secret place, and hide thyself : and I will
go out and stand beside my father in the field where
thou art, and I will commune with my father of thee ;
4 and if I see aught, I will tell thee.   And Jonathan spake
good of David unto Saul his father, and said unto him,
Let not the king sin against his servant, against David ;
because he hath not sinned against thee, and because
5 his works have been to thee-ward very good : for he put
his life in his hand, and smote the Philistine, and the
LORD wrought a great victory for all Israel : thou sawest
it, and didst rejoice : wherefore then wilt thou sin against
6 innocent blood, to slay David without a cause ?   And
Saul hearkened unto the voice of Jonathan : and Saul
sware, As the LORD liveth, he shall not be put to death.

---

affection on the other, were favourite themes of the popular
traditions of a later time.   The symbol T has accordingly been
adopted for such elements of tradition as the compiler may be supposed to have incorporated in his book, as distinguished from such
post-redactional passages as xix. 18 ff., denoted throughout by Z.

The story, accordingly, as told by our oldest authority (M) may
have run somewhat as follows.   The failure of Saul's plans for
removing David (xviii. 25), and the latter's growing popularity
with the people (xviii. 28 LXX), so fanned the flame of the royal
jealousy that further successes of David against the Philistines
brought on an access of frenzy, which issued in Saul personally
attempting the life of his son-in-law (xix. 8–10).   On this David
has recourse to Jonathan, by whose connivance Saul's fixed
determination to put David to death is made so patent that David
has no alternative but to flee the court and seek the aid of the
priests at Nob (xx. 1—xxi. 1).

xix. 1–7.   *Temporary reconciliation of Saul and David.*   The fact
that the representation given in ch. xx. 1 ff. of the relations
between Saul and David on the one hand, and between David and
Jonathan on the other, seems to leave no room for this earlier

And Jonathan called David, and Jonathan shewed him 7
all those things.   And Jonathan brought David to Saul,
and he was in his presence, as beforetime.

[M] And there was war again : and David went out, 8
and fought with the Philistines, and slew them with a
great slaughter ; and they fled before him.   And an evil 9
spirit from the LORD was upon Saul, as he sat in his
house with his spear in his hand ; and David played with
his hand.   And Saul sought to smite David even to the 10
wall with the spear ; but he slipped away out of Saul's
presence, and he smote the spear into the wall : and
David fled, and escaped that night.   [T] And Saul sent 11
messengers unto David's house, to watch him, and to
slay him in the morning : and Michal David's wife told
him, saying, If thou save not thy life to-night, to-morrow
thou shalt be slain.   So Michal let David down through 12
the window : and he went, and fled, and escaped.   And 13
Michal took the teraphim, and laid it in the bed, and

---

attempt at reconciliation has led us to ascribe this passage to an
independent source.   Unless verses 2 f. are to be taken as redactional, the whole may have arisen as a variant of ch. xx (cf. xx.
19, 35).

8-10 Probably the original continuation of xviii. 29ª.   Since
the late variant xviii. 10 f. is no part of the true text, we have here
the first mention of a personal attack on David on the part of Saul.
The last two words of verse 11 'that night' belong to the next
episode (so LXX).

xix. 11-17. *Michal's stratagem enables David to escape.*   H. P.
Smith seeks to rescue this dramatic incident for our oldest source
by the conjecture that it originally followed xviii. 27.   Saul
sought to entrap David on his wedding night!   But this attribution
results in ch. xx, which undoubtedly contains ancient material (see
below), being relegated to a source by itself (H. P. Smith, *Inter.
Crit. Comm.*, p. xxv).

13. the teraphim: though plural in form, here applied to
a single object.   This is the classical passage for the conclusion
that these mysterious images were, in whole or in part, of human
form, see on xv. 23.

put a pillow of goats' *hair* at the head thereof, and covered
14 it with the clothes.   And when Saul sent messengers to
15 take David, she said, He is sick.   And Saul sent the
. messengers to see David, saying, Bring him up to me in
16 the bed, that I may slay him.   And when the messengers
came in, behold, the teraphim was in the bed, with the
17 pillow of goats' *hair* at the head thereof.   And Saul said
unto Michal, Why hast thou deceived me thus, and let
mine enemy go, that he is escaped?   And Michal answered
Saul, He said unto me, Let me go ; why should I kill
thee ?

18   [Z] Now David fled, and escaped, and came to Samuel
to Ramah, and told him all that Saul had done to him.
19 And he and Samuel went and dwelt in Naioth.   And it
was told Saul, saying, Behold, David is at Naioth in
20 Ramah.   And Saul sent messengers to take David : and
when they saw the company of the prophets prophesying,
and Samuel standing as head over them, the spirit of

---

a pillow of goats' hair : the precise meaning of the word
rendered 'pillow' is unknown.   The margin gives 'quilt' or
'network.'   The last is suggested by the etymology, and a mosquito
curtain (see Judith x. 21) of hair netting, covering and so obscuring
the features, may be intended.

xix. 18-24. *David takes refuge with Samuel at Ramah.*   In
addition to the arguments for the late date and questionable
historicity of this passage given above, it may be added (*a*) that
the portrait of Samuel as the head (verse 20) of a so-called ' school
of the prophets '—such as we find in the story of Elisha, 2 Kings
iv. 38 ff., vi. 1 ff.—is inconsistent with the historical notice of
Samuel as living and working apart from the 'prophets' of his
time (see on x. 5) ; (*b*) historical probability is in favour of David
taking refuge with his kinsfolk in the south, a step vouched for by
the narrative, xxi. 1 ff., xxii. 1.

18. in Naioth : add, with LXX, ' in Ramah,' as always in
the sequel.   The name remains a puzzle.   It may denote the
cloister in which the prophets lodged (cf. 2 Kings vi. 1 ff., and see
Driver, *Notes, in loc.*).

God came upon the messengers of Saul, and they also prophesied. And when it was told Saul, he sent other 21 messengers, and they also prophesied. And Saul sent messengers again the third time, and they also prophesied. Then went he also to Ramah, and came to the great 22 well that is in Secu: and he asked and said, Where are Samuel and David? And one said, Behold, they be at Naioth in Ramah. And he went thither to Naioth in 23 Ramah: and the spirit of God came upon him also, and he went on, and prophesied, until he came to Naioth in Ramah. And he also stripped off his clothes, and he 24 also prophesied before Samuel, and lay down naked all that day and all that night. Wherefore they say, Is Saul also among the prophets?

[M] And David fled from Naioth in Ramah, and came 20 and said before Jonathan, What have I done? what is mine iniquity? and what is my sin before thy father, that he seeketh my life? And he said unto him, God forbid; 2

22. The Greek text is more intelligible : 'And Saul was exceeding angry, and went himself also to Ramah, and came to the well of the threshing-floor which is on the height,' the usual situation of the village threshing-floor.

23. **he went thither**: the sense requires 'he went from there' (LXX).

xx. 1–42. *David and Jonathan.*
In this chapter we have one of the most effective episodes of the book, taken in the main, as has been suggested above, from the early historical work which we have designated M. In the case of so popular a story, it is to be expected that various excrescences would gather round the original stock. The opening words are of course from the hand that inserted the Ramah episode.

1. **what is mine iniquity? and what is my sin?** The two substantives are practically synonymous in ordinary usage, but the root-ideas are somewhat different. The former (Heb. '*āwōn*), from a root meaning 'to go astray,' denotes strictly 'deviation from the right track, error' (Driver), the latter (*hattāth*) 'a missing of the mark,' a failure of duty to God or man.

thou shalt not die : behold, my father doeth nothing either great or small, but that he discloseth it unto me : and why should my father hide this thing from me ? it
3 is not so. And David sware moreover, and said, Thy father knoweth well that I have found grace in thine eyes ; and he saith, Let not Jonathan know this, lest he be grieved : but truly as the LORD liveth, and as thy soul
4 liveth, there is but a step between me and death. Then said Jonathan unto David, Whatsoever thy soul desireth,
5 I will even do it for thee. And David said unto Jonathan, Behold, to-morrow is the new moon, and I should not fail to sit with the king at meat : but let me go, that I may hide myself in the field unto the third day

2. he discloseth it unto me : *lit.* 'uncovers my ear,' used of a communication between man and man as here (so verses 12 f.), as well as of a revelation from God to man (ix. 15), both chapters being, as we believe, from the same source.

3. as thy soul liveth : 'a pathetic periphrasis for the personal pronoun' (Driver), as much as 'by thy life.' Another instance of this double oath, by the life of Yahweh and the life of the person addressed, is found xxv. 26 (also M). For other forms in Samuel see on iii. 17, and cf. verse 13 below.

4. Jonathan's answer should probably take the form of a query, as in R.V. marg., to which David replies by unfolding a scheme for ascertaining Saul's intentions with regard to him.

5. to-morrow is the new moon : the day on which the new moon was first visible in Palestine was from the earliest times a religious festival of great importance. Like the Sabbath, with which it is frequently associated, it was a day of rest and worship. It was also, as we learn here, a day on which were held those religious rites by which the various sacral communities, clans and families, were bound together (verses 6, 29).

I should not fail to sit : preferable is the LXX reading, 'and I will not sit with the king at meat.' Verse 25 shows that David regularly sat, with Jonathan and Abner, at the king's table, and not merely on special occasions. The fact that the following day was new moon would give an air of plausibility to David's pretext.

unto the third day at even : read, 'until the evening.' The present ungrammatical text is due to a copyist who wished to

at even. If thy father miss me at all, then say, David 6
earnestly asked leave of me that he might run to Beth-
lehem his city : for it is the yearly sacrifice there for all the
family. If he say thus, It is well; thy servant shall have 7
peace: but if he be wroth, then know that evil is
determined by him. Therefore deal kindly with thy ser- 8
vant; for thou hast brought thy servant into a covenant
of the LORD with thee: but if there be in me iniquity,
slay me thyself; for why shouldest thou bring me to thy
father? And Jonathan said, Far be it from thee: for if I 9
should at all know that evil were determined by my father
to come upon thee, then would not I tell it thee? Then 10
said David to Jonathan, Who shall tell me if perchance
thy father answer thee roughly? [T] And Jonathan said 11
unto David, Come and let us go out into the field. And
they went out both of them into the field.

And Jonathan said unto David, The LORD, the God 12
of Israel, *be witness*; when I have sounded my father

---

make David's proposal agree with Jonathan's (verse 19; cf.
verse 12).

8. a covenant of the LORD: an expression found here only.
Yahweh was the witness and guardian of all such covenants
(verse 23). The covenant between Jonathan and David has
been previously mentioned only in the inserted passage, xviii. 3,
which shows that a later passage is not necessarily unhistorical. .

9. Far be it from me: the same expression as is rendered
'God forbid,' verse 2, xiv. 45.

xx. 11-17. *Jonathan implores the mercy of David in view of future
contingencies.*
There is a general consensus of critical opinion that these verses
are a later addition to the main narrative. (1) There is no
apparent reason for the sudden change of scene, 'into the field';
(2) the rôles of the actors are now reversed, Jonathan the powerful protector of the sections that precede and follow becoming
the humble suppliant of verses 14-16. The whole seems intended
to prepare the way for the incident of 2 Sam. ix. 1 ff. Verse 18,
it will be noted, is the natural continuation of verse 10.

about this time to-morrow, *or* the third day, behold, if
there be good toward David, shall I not then send unto
13 thee, and disclose it unto thee? The LORD do so to
Jonathan, and more also, should it please my father to
do thee evil, if I disclose it not unto thee, and send thee
away, that thou mayest go in peace: and the LORD be
14 with thee, as he hath been with my father. And thou
shalt not only while yet I live shew me the kindness of
15 the LORD, that I die not: but also thou shalt not cut
off thy kindness from my house for ever: no, not when
the LORD hath cut off the enemies of David every one
16 from the face of the earth. So Jonathan made a
covenant with the house of David, *saying*, And the LORD
17 shall require it at the hand of David's enemies. And
Jonathan caused David to swear again, for the love that

12. or the third day: a harmonistic gloss, see on verse 5.

14-16. No one can fail to be touched by the pathos of these
verses—the brave, noble-hearted Jonathan a suppliant of David's
grace, as if coming events were already casting their shadow
over his soul.   The text requires some emendation which brings
out more forcibly the earnestness and aim of Jonathan's appeal.
'Oh that while yet I live, oh that thou wouldest show me the kindness of Yahweh (see 2 Sam. ix. 2); but if I should die, oh that thou
wouldest not cut off thy kindness from my house for ever.   And
when Yahweh hath cut off the enemies of David, every one from
the face of the earth, should the name of Jonathan be destroyed
by the house of David, then may Yahweh require it of David'—
so essentially LXX, supported by the parallel in xxiv. 20 ff.   The
latter passage gives the key to the appeal before us.   Jonathan
here, like his father there, is represented as foreseeing the down-
fall of his house, and the succession of 'the house of David' to
the throne.   In view, therefore, of the barbarous oriental custom,
vouched for in 1 Kings xv. 29, xvi. 11, and elsewhere, Jonathan
prays that his 'name,' as continued in his descendants, may be
spared by David and his successors, whom otherwise God will
call to account.

17.   Read, with LXX, 'And Jonathan sware yet again to
David by his love toward him' (as R. V. marg.), i. e. he repeated
the oath of verse 13.

he had to him : for he loved him as he loved his own soul. [M] Then Jonathan said unto him, To-morrow is 18 the new moon : and thou shalt be missed, because thy seat will be empty. And when thou hast stayed three 19 days, thou shalt go down quickly, and come to the place where thou didst hide thyself when the business was in hand, and shalt remain by the stone Ezel. And I will 20 shoot three arrows on the side thereof, as though I shot at a mark. And, behold, I will send the lad, *saying*, Go, 21 find the arrows. If I say unto the lad, Behold, the arrows are on this side of thee : take them, and come ; for there is peace to thee and no hurt, as the Lord liveth. But if I say thus unto the boy, Behold, the 22 arrows are beyond thee : go thy way ; for the Lord hath sent thee away. And as touching the matter which 23 thou and I have spoken of, behold, the Lord is between thee and me for ever.

So David hid himself in the field : and when the new 24 moon was come, the king sat him down to eat meat.

---

18. We now return to the main narrative in which Jonathan elaborates a scheme of communication with David in hiding.

19. thou shalt go down quickly : the text of this verse is corrupt ; the Greek has here, 'thou wilt be greatly missed.'

when the business was in hand : *lit.* 'on the day of the deed '—probably another corruption ; at least, there is no clue in our extant record to the deed in question. The marginal reference to xix. 2 is a mere makeshift.

by the stone Ezel : read, as emended with the help of LXX, 'by yonder mound' (see on verse 41).

20. Read, 'and on the third day I will shoot with arrows at the side thereof.'

21. take them, and come : the Revisers evidently took these words as addressed to David, but the singular pronoun (note the margin) shows that Jonathan proposed to shoot a single arrow as the signal (see verses 36 f.), and we should render : 'If I say . . . the arrow is on this side of thee, fetch it, then come thou (David), for there is peace,' &c.·

xx. 24–42. *Saul's intention discovered and communicated to David.*

25 And the king sat upon his seat, as at other times, even upon the seat by the wall; and Jonathan stood up, and Abner sat by Saul's side : but David's place was empty.
26 Nevertheless Saul spake not any thing that day : for he thought, Something hath befallen him, he is not clean ;
27 surely he is not clean. And it came to pass on the morrow after the new moon, *which was* the second *day*, that David's place was empty : and Saul said unto Jonathan his son, Wherefore cometh not the son of Jesse
28 to meat, neither yesterday, nor to-day? And Jonathan answered Saul, David earnestly asked leave of me to go
29 to Beth-lehem : and he said, Let me go, I pray thee ; for our family hath a sacrifice in the city; and my brother, he hath commanded me *to be there* : and now, if I have found favour in thine eyes, let me get away, I pray thee, and see my brethren. Therefore he is not
30 come unto the king's table. Then Saul's anger was kindled against Jonathan, and he said unto him, Thou son of a perverse rebellious woman, do not I know that thou hast chosen the son of Jesse to thine own shame,

---

25. and Jonathan stood up: read, 'and Jonathan was in front' (LXX), in the seat opposite Saul. The other two places were occupied usually by the king's son-in-law, and his commander-in-chief. The more luxurious fashion of reclining at meals had not yet been introduced.

26. surely he is not clean: read, with LXX, 'for he hath not been cleansed.' Saul's modest reticence may be noted (see Lev. xv. 16; Deut. xxiii. 10). The passage is of interest as attesting the scrupulous regard, even in this early period, for ceremonial purity.

29. my brother: with LXX we should read 'my brethren,' as in the next clause. The festival was the annual reunion (verse 6) of the larger sacral community of the clan, not merely of David's immediate kinsfolk or 'father's house.'

30. son of a perverse rebellious woman: to curse a man's parents and ancestors generally is a familiar trait of the hasty Arab, but the sting of Saul's abuse lies in the insinuation that Jonathan was no son of his !

and unto the shame of thy mother's nakedness? For as 31
long as the son of Jesse liveth upon the ground, thou
shalt not be stablished, nor thy kingdom. Wherefore
now send and fetch him unto me, for he shall surely die.
And Jonathan answered Saul his father, and said unto 32
him, Wherefore should he be put to death? what hath
he done? And Saul cast his spear at him to smite him : 33
whereby Jonathan knew that it was determined of his
father to put David to death. So Jonathan arose from 34
the table in fierce anger, and did eat no meat the second
day of the month : for he was grieved for David, because
his father had done him shame.

And it came to pass in the morning, that Jonathan 35
went out into the field at the time appointed with David,
and a little lad with him. And he said unto his lad, 36
Run, find now the arrows which I shoot. And as the
lad ran, he shot an arrow beyond him. And when the 37
lad was come to the place of the arrow which Jonathan
had shot, Jonathan cried after the lad, and said, Is not
the arrow beyond thee? And Jonathan cried after the 38
lad, Make speed, haste, stay not. And Jonathan's lad
gathered up the arrows, and came to his master. But 39
the lad knew not any thing : only Jonathan and David

---

31. Saul is now seen to be haunted by the fear that David's
popularity with his countrymen would secure for him the succession to the throne. This was all the more probable since the
principle of succession by primogeniture had not yet had an
opportunity of establishing itself.

34. Since it was Jonathan himself, not David, to whom Saul
'had done shame,' it is better, with LXX (B), to omit 'for he was
grieved for David.' His father's coarse and insulting speech is
sufficient to account for Jonathan's 'fierce anger.'

37. Jonathan seems to have proceeded thus : he first shoots
a few arrows, then orders his page to run and fetch them, and
finally, while the boy is running, he shoots the signal arrow over
the boy's head (note the margin), and further than the others.

40 knew the matter. And Jonathan gave his weapons unto his lad, and said unto him, Go, carry them to the city.

41 And as soon as the lad was gone, David arose out of *a place* toward the South, and fell on his face to the ground, and bowed himself three times: and they kissed one another, and wept one with another, until David exceeded.

42 And Jonathan said to David, Go in peace, forasmuch as we have sworn both of us in the name of the LORD, saying, The LORD shall be between me and thee, and between my seed and thy seed, for ever. And he arose and departed: and Jonathan went into the city.

21 Then came David to Nob to Ahimelech the priest:

---

41. out of a place **toward the South:** a characteristic specimen of the Revisers' deference to the traditional text. We must of course read with the LXX: 'David arose from beside the mound' (see on verse 19). Verses 40-42, however, are regarded by most commentators as 'an editorial expansion, pure and simple.' For the grounds see H. P. Smith, *in loc.*

B. 1 Sam. xxi–xxvi. *David's Flight from Court and his subsequent Adventures as an Outlaw Captain in the South.*

These six chapters relate the fortunes of David from the date of his final breach with Saul until he finds himself reduced, as a last resource, to take refuge with Saul's inveterate enemies the Philistines. The story consists of a number of separate incidents, the chronological succession of which it is no longer possible to determine with accuracy. Indeed, as will appear, it is impossible to escape the conclusion that here, as elsewhere in Samuel, we have more than once duplicate accounts of the same historical incident. We may break up this subdivision into four sections: (*a*) xxi–xxii, (*b*) xxiii–xxiv, (*c*) xxv, (*d*) xxvi, the headings of which are given below.

(*a*) xxi. 1—xxii. 23 *David's reception at the sanctuary of Nob and its consequences.*

Convinced of Saul's designs upon his life, David now flees the court, and makes first for the Benjamite sanctuary to which the priestly house of Eli must have removed after the destruction of Shiloh by the Philistines (see above, p. 67). With the exception of the post-redactional passage, xxi. 10-15, these two chapters form a connected narrative from the early source, M.

1. Nob lay somewhere close to Jerusalem on the north

and Ahimelech came to meet David trembling, and
said unto him, Why art thou alone, and no man with
thee?   And David said unto Ahimelech the priest, 2
The king hath commanded me a business, and hath
said unto me, Let no man know any thing of the business whereabout I send thee, and what I have commanded thee: and I have appointed the young men to
such and such a place. Now therefore what is under 3
thine hand? give me five loaves of bread in mine hand,
or whatsoever there is present. And the priest answered 4
David, and said, There is no common bread under
mine hand, but there is holy bread; if only the young
men have kept themselves from women. And David 5
answered the priest, and said unto him, Of a truth
women have been kept from us about these three days;
when I came out, the vessels of the young men were

(Isa. x. 32), and nearer than Anathoth, which was only two
and a half miles from the capital. The head of the official
priesthood was now **Ahimelech**, the son of Ahitub (xxii. 9), and
therefore great-grandson of Eli, as we see from the genealogy,
xiv. 3.

2. On Ahimelech expressing surprise that the king's son-in-law
should travel unattended, David invents the excuse of a secret
mission, alleging that the usual escort had been given a rendezvous
elsewhere.

4. holy bread: bread hallowed (A. V.) or consecrated by being
laid before Yahweh, hence termed in Hebrew 'presence-bread'
(Exod. xxv. 30, R. V. marg.), the 'shewbread' of our English
version (verse 6). The custom of placing loaves of sweet or
unleavened bread on tables in the temples seems to have origin-
ated among the Babylonians, by whom also it was termed 'bread
of the presence' (*KAT.*³ 600). In later times the presence-bread
could only be eaten by the priests, and by them only within the
sanctuary. Such stringency does not appear in the present
narrative. It is enough that David and his men are ceremonially
clean.

5. Owing chiefly to the antique religious conceptions involved,
to the overloaded text, and to the ambiguity of the word variously
rendered **vessels** (i.e. wallets, or bags), 'weapons,' 'bodies,' &c.,

holy, though it was but a common journey ; how much
6 more then to-day shall their vessels be holy ? So the priest
gave him holy *bread* : for there was no bread there but
the shewbread, that was taken from before the LORD, to
7 put hot bread in the day when it was taken away.   Now
a certain man of the servants of Saul was there that day,
detained before the LORD ; and his name was Doeg the
Edomite, the chiefest of the herdmen that belonged to
8 Saul.   And David said unto Ahimelech, And is there
not here under thine hand spear or sword ? for I have
neither brought my sword nor my weapons with me,

the interpretation of this verse is beset with difficulties.   David's
reply may be rendered thus : ' Of a truth women have been taboo
for us as on former occasions when I went forth (i. e. on military
duty), and the wallets of the young men have been consecrated ;
how much more shall they be consecrated to-day, wallets (?) and
all.'   In justification of this interpretation it may be added : (1)
that of the various taboos which had to be observed by ' the
consecrated ones ' (see on xiii. 9) in early times, none was more
widely current than the sexual taboo, which meets us again in
the episode of Uriah (2 Sam. xi. 11 ff.) ; (2) the consecration
ceremony doubtless included the soldier's complete equipment,
although we hear only of the anointing of the shield (2 Sam. i. 21).
David, in short, asserts that by putting the consecrated bread into
the wallets of his soldiers, these would be affected by the con-
tagion of ' holiness ' in the antique sense in which this term was
then understood.   See further W. R. Smith, *Rel. Sem.*², 455 f.,
and the special discussion by Schwally, *Semitische Kriegsalter-
thumer*, 60-66.

though it was but a common journey : these words seem
to be a marginal remark of a reader pointing out that David was
prevaricating in claiming that he was then on a consecrated
military expedition.

7. detained before the LORD : a phrase from the same antique
religious terminology, and from the same root as the word above
rendered ' taboo.'   It signifies ' under a taboo ' in the sense of
' excluded from the cultus.'   Doeg had been detained overnight
in the sanctuary precincts, probably undergoing purification before
being admitted to some act of worship.

the chiefest of the herdmen : a doubtful rendering : the
LXX has ' Saul's muleherd.'

because the king's business required haste. And the 9
priest said, The sword of Goliath the Philistine, whom
thou slewest in the vale of Elah, behold, it is here
wrapped in a cloth behind the ephod: if thou wilt take
that, take it: for there is no other save that here. And
David said, There is none like that; give it me.

[Z] And David arose, and fled that day for fear of 10
Saul, and went to Achish the king of Gath. And the 11
servants of Achish said unto him, Is not this David the
king of the land? did they not sing one to another of
him in dances, saying,

> Saul hath slain his thousands,
> And David his ten thousands?

And David laid up these words in his heart, and was 12
sore afraid of Achish the king of Gath. And he changed 13
his behaviour before them, and feigned himself mad in

---

9. If the contention that 'the Philistine' of ch. xvii has been
erroneously identified with Goliath is correct (see p. 122), the
name will be here due to a glossator (also xx. 10). For the
inference to be drawn from the verse regarding the ephod, see
on ii. 28. The custom of depositing military trophies in sanctuaries also obtained among the Philistines (v. 2, xxxi. 10).

xxi. 10-15. *David flees to Achish, king of Gath.*
This curious episode is now regarded as belonging to the same
series of later additions in the style of the Midrash as xix. 18-24.
Both historically and psychologically it is an inferior duplicate of
xxvii. 1 f. (note the improbable designation of David in verse 11,
and the undignified proceedings of verse 13). The motive of this
legend was doubtless to remove the objection to David's unpatriotic action in ch. xxvii—which it was perhaps intended to
supplant—by representing him as going alone to Achish and as
quitting him as soon as possible.

11. **David the king of the land:** a curious anachronism of
a kind characteristic of the edifying but unhistorical literature
of the Midrash.

13. **feigned himself mad:** a policy frequently adopted in
similar circumstances in the East, where lunatics are held in
special dread as possessed by a powerful spirit.

their hands, and scrabbled on the doors of the gate, and
14 let his spittle fall down upon his beard.   Then said
Achish unto his servants, Lo, ye see the man is mad :
15 wherefore then have ye brought him to me? Do I lack
mad men, that ye have brought this fellow to play the
mad man in my presence? shall this fellow come into
my house?

22   [M] David therefore departed thence, and escaped to
the cave of Adullam : and when his brethren and all his
father's house heard it, they went down thither to him.
2 And every one that was in distress, and every one that
was in debt, and every one that was discontented,
gathered themselves unto him ; and he became captain
over them : and there were with him about four hundred
men.
3   And David went thence to Mizpeh of Moab : and he
said unto the king of Moab, Let my father and my
mother, I pray thee, come forth, *and be* with you, till I
4 know what God will do for me.   And he brought them
before the king of Moab : and they dwelt with him all
5 the while that David was in the hold.   And the prophet

scrabbled : rather, with LXX, ' drummed ' with his hands

xxii. 1 f., the continuation of xx. 9 ; David escapes to Adullam
and becomes the leader of a band of outlaws.   The expression
cave of Adullam, which has passed into a proverb among us, is
due to a corruption of the similar Hebrew word for ' stronghold,'
the ' hold ' of verse 4.   See also on 2 Sam. xxiii. 13 f.   Adullam,
in all probability, is the modern *Aid-el-Ma* on the edge of the
Shephelah (G. A. Smith, *Hist. Geog.* 229), about twelve miles
west by south of Beth-lehem.   That the outlaw should be joined
by his immediate relatives and the rest of his sept or **father's
house** was a natural measure of precaution.

3 ff. David places his parents in the safe keeping of the king of
Moab.   His great-grandmother was a Moabitess according to the
book which bears her name (Ruth iv. 21 f.).

Mizpeh of Moab has not been identified.

5. the prophet Gad appears again, 2 Sam. xxiv. 11, as

Gad said unto David, Abide not in the hold; depart, and get thee into the land of Judah. Then David departed, and came into the forest of Hereth.

And Saul heard that David was discovered, and the 6 men that were with him: now Saul was sitting in Gibeah, under the tamarisk tree in Ramah, with his spear in his hand, and all his servants were standing about him. And Saul said unto his servants that stood about him, 7 Hear now ye Benjamites; will the son of Jesse give every one of you fields and vineyards, will he make you all captains of thousands and captains of hundreds; that 8 all of you have conspired against me, and there is none that discloseth to me when my son maketh a league with the son of Jesse, and there is none of you that is sorry for me, or discloseth unto me that my son hath stirred up my servant against me, to lie in wait, as at this day? Then answered Doeg the Edomite, which stood by the 9 servants of Saul, and said, I saw the son of Jesse coming to Nob, to Ahimelech the son of Ahitub. And he 10

'David's seer,' and is mentioned by the Chronicler, along with Samuel and Nathan, as the author of a history of the period (1 Chron. xxix. 29).

in the hold: the Syriac reading 'in Mizpeh' is here generally preferred for the reason that 'the hold' of Adullam was itself in the land of Judah, as is plain from xxiii. 3. The **forest of Hereth** is unknown.

xxii. 6–23. *Saul takes a cruel revenge on the priests of Nob.*

6. in Ramah: read, as R. V. marg., 'on the height.' We are here introduced to Saul engaged in the administration of justice, seated like Deborah (Judges iv. 5) under a sacred tree on the moot-hill at Gibeah. **his servants** are the officers of state, the **spear in his hand** one of the insignia of royalty.

8. to lie in wait: read, with LXX, 'as an enemy'; so also verse 13.

9 f. In the opinion of the editors of the Psalter, Ps. lii commemorates this piece of tale-bearing.

10. he inquired of the LORD for him: a fact not mentioned

inquired of the LORD for him, and gave him victuals,
11 and gave him the sword of Goliath the Philistine.   Then
the king sent to call Ahimelech the priest, the son of
Ahitub, and all his father's house, the priests that were
12 in Nob: and they came all of them to the king.   And
Saul said, Hear now, thou son of Ahitub.   And he
13 answered, Here I am, my lord.   And Saul said unto
him, Why have ye conspired against me, thou and the
son of Jesse, in that thou hast given him bread, and
a sword, and hast inquired of God for him, that he
should rise against me, to lie in wait, as at this day?
14 Then Ahimelech answered the king, and said, And
who among all thy servants is so faithful as David, which
is the king's son in law, and is taken into thy council,
15 and is honourable in thine house?   Have I to-day
begun to inquire of God for him? be it far from me:
let not the king impute any thing unto his servant,
nor to all the house of my father: for thy servant
16 knoweth nothing of all this, less or more.   And the
king said, Thou shalt surely die, Ahimelech, thou, and
17 all thy father's house.   And the king said unto the
guard that stood about him, Turn, and slay the priests
of the LORD; because their hand also is with David, and
because they knew that he fled, and did not disclose it

---

in the preceding chapter, but most natural in the circumstances,
as may be seen from David's practice somewhat later (xxiii. 2 ff.;
xxx. 8; see also verse 15 below).

14. and is taken into thy council: read, with LXX and the
Targum: 'and is captain over thy bodyguard.' Ahimelech
rebuts the charge of disloyalty brought against David before
asserting the innocence of himself and his fellow priests.

17. the guard: *lit.* as marg., 'the runners,' see on viii. 11.
Saul's charge of complicity is not borne out by anything in the
previous narrative, and has just been expressly disclaimed by
Ahimelech.

to me.   But the servants of the king would not put forth
their hand to fall upon the priests of the LORD.   And 18
the king said to Doeg, Turn thou, and fall upon the
priests.   And Doeg the Edomite turned, and he fell
upon the priests, and he slew on that day fourscore and
five persons that did wear a linen ephod.   And Nob, the 19
city of the priests, smote he with the edge of the sword,
both men and women, children and sucklings, and oxen
and asses and sheep, with the edge of the sword.   And 20
one of the sons of Ahimelech the son of Ahitub, named
Abiathar, escaped, and fled after David.   And Abiathar 21
told David that Saul had slain the LORD's priests.   And 22
David said unto Abiathar, I knew on that day, when
Doeg the Edomite was there, that he would surely tell
Saul : I have occasioned *the death* of all the persons of

---

18. that did wear a linen ephod (*ephōd bad*): this, as we
know, was a distinctive item of the priestly dress (see on ii. 18).
But in this case the word for 'linen' (*bad*) is wanting in the
Greek text, and that rendered 'wear' always means 'to lift up,
carry,' &c. ; accordingly we must here render 'he slew on that
day eighty-five ephod-bearing men,' i. e. priests of full status,
each qualified to give an oracle by consulting the ephod.   This
was one of the three prerogatives of the priesthood enumerated
ii. 28, where see note on the ephod.

20. Abiathar, one of the sons of Ahimelech, who had probably
been left in charge of the sanctuary, escapes from the massacre at
Nob, carrying with him the sacred image (see xxiii. 6).   He
naturally took refuge at Adullam (see on xxiii. 2) with David,
whom he accompanied in his subsequent wanderings, and by
whom he was afterwards appointed joint custodian of the Ark.
Espousing the cause of Adonijah in the matter of the disputed
succession, he was banished by Solomon to his estate at Anathoth
(1 Kings ii. 26).   Mention may here be made of Duhm's attractive
conjecture that to Abiathar or one of his family we owe the court
and family history of David preserved in 2 Sam. ix-xx (our C),
which may carry with it the authorship of the historical document
(M) we are now following (see Introd., sect. iv).   There can be
no doubt that David's cause was greatly strengthened, now and
afterwards, by the support of the only surviving representative of
the most influential priestly family in Israel.

23 thy father's house. Abide thou with me, fear not; for he that seeketh my life seeketh thy life : for with me thou shalt be in safeguard.

23   And they told David, saying, Behold, the Philistines are fighting against Keilah, and they rob the threshing-
2 floors. Therefore David inquired of the LORD, saying, Shall I go and smite these Philistines? And the LORD said unto David, Go, and smite the Philistines, and save
3 Keilah. And David's men said unto him, Behold, we be afraid here in Judah : how much more then if we go
4 to Keilah against the armies of the Philistines? Then David inquired of the LORD yet again. And the LORD answered him and said, Arise, go down to Keilah; for I
5 will deliver the Philistines into thine hand. And David

---

23. he that seeketh my life seeketh thy life. The context requires the suffixes to be transposed ; read, ' he that seeketh thy life seeketh my life,' a sentiment which reveals the heart of one who, more than any other in Hebrew history, had the power of attaching men, in self-sacrificing devotion, to himself.

(b) xxiii–xxiv. *David relieves Keilah and spares Saul's life.* The first of David's exploits as captain of a band of freelances was his rescue of a frontier town of Judah from imminent capture by the Philistines (xxiii. 1–13). David has still his head quarters in the fort of Adullam, and the season is midsummer.

1. Keilah: the modern *Kilah*, some three miles south of Adullam. It is mentioned in the Amarna correspondence, c. 1400 B.C.

2. David inquired of the LORD: the standing formula for consulting the sacred oracle. Considerable light is thrown on the method of procedure by the narratives of this chapter and of xxx. 7 f. A succession of questions was apparently put to the oracle, each of which admitted of being answered by a simple ' yes ' or ' no ' according to the lot, Urim or Thummim, which was cast (see further the note on xiv. 41). The fact that no mention is made in this verse of the oracular ephod seems to have struck an early reader, who added in his margin the note which now stands in the text as verse 6 (but without the words 'to Keilah'). This note explains that Abiathar had brought the ephod with him when he fled to David, which he did while the latter was still at Adullam,

and his men went to Keilah, and fought with the Philistines, and brought away their cattle, and slew them with
a great slaughter. So David saved the inhabitants of
Keilah.

And it came to pass, when Abiathar the son of 6
Ahimelech fled to David to Keilah, that he came down
with an ephod in his hand. And it was told Saul that 7
David was come to Keilah. And Saul said, God hath
delivered him into mine hand; for he is shut in, by
entering into a town that hath gates and bars. And 8
Saul summoned all the people to war, to go down to
Keilah, to besiege David and his men. And David knew 9
that Saul devised mischief against him; and he said to
Abiathar the priest, Bring hither the ephod. Then said 10
David, O LORD, the God of Israel, thy servant hath
surely heard that Saul seeketh to come to Keilah, to
destroy the city for my sake. Will the men of Keilah 11
deliver me up into his hand? will Saul come down, as
thy servant hath heard? O LORD, the God of Israel, I
beseech thee, tell thy servant. And the LORD said, He
will come down. Then said David, Will the men of 12
Keilah deliver up me and my men into the hand of
Saul? And the LORD said, They will deliver thee up.
Then David and his men, which were about six hundred, 13
arose and departed out of Keilah, and went whithersoever

---

xxiii. 7-13. *Saul plans to entrap David at Keilah.*

11. In the present text the first query has inadvertently come
in from the following verse. David's first question to the oracle
was: 'Will Saul come down?' Only when this question was
answered in the affirmative was the other in place.

13. about six hundred. David's following has considerably
increased in the presumably short interval since xxii. 2. The
numbers henceforth remain stationary (xxv. 13. xxvii. 2).

and went whithersoever they could go: rather, 'they went
whithersoever they went,' a Semitic idiom 'employed where either

they could go.   And it was told Saul that David was
escaped from Keilah ; and he forbare to go forth.

14   And David abode in the wilderness in the strong holds,
and remained in the hill country in the wilderness of Ziph.
And Saul sought him every day, but God delivered him
15 not into his hand.   [T] And David saw that Saul was
come out to seek his life : and David was in the wilder-
16 ness of Ziph in the wood.   And Jonathan Saul's son
arose, and went to David into the wood, and strengthened
17 his hand in God.   And he said unto him, Fear not : for
the hand of Saul my father shall not find thee ; and thou
shalt be king over Israel, and I shall be next unto thee ;

---

the means or the desire to be more explicit does not exist'
(Driver).   Cf. 2 Sam. xv. 20 ; 1 Kings viii. 1, &c.   The phrase
aptly describes the hand-to-mouth life of the highland freebooter,
here to-day and away to-morrow.

14. A somewhat overloaded summary of David's wanderings
subsequent to the relief of Keilah.   His brush with the Philistines
had now made Adullam, which lay on their frontier, too hot for
him, a fact which throws the ingratitude of the men of Keilah
into strong relief.

xxiii. 15-18. *David and Jonathan renew their covenant of friendship*
(perhaps from the same hand as xx. 12 ff.; see below).

15. And David saw, &c. : read, by a slight change, 'And David
was afraid because Saul,' &c., as implied in verses 16 f.

the wilderness of Ziph stretched north-east of Ziph, the
modern *Tell Zif*—about four miles south by east of Hebron—
towards the Dead Sea.

in the wood : read here and verses 18 f. 'in Horesh,' as
margin, or better, 'in Horeshah,' perhaps the modern *Horeisa*
(Conder), to the south-east of Ziph.   A graphic description of this
region, in which lay ' Maon, Ziph and the Judaean Carmel, with the
farms of Nabal on which David and his men, like the Bedouin of
to-day, levied blackmail,' will be found in G. A. Smith's *Hist.
Geog.*, 306 f.

17. thou shalt be king over Israel, &c. Jonathan here gives
definite expression to the conviction which we found to underly
xx. 14 ff.   With characteristic self-sacrifice he is content to claim
the second place.   Unfortunately it is extremely doubtful if these
anticipations of David's succession can be historically substantiated.
To the critical historian they appear rather as the unconscious

and that also Saul my father knoweth. And they two 18
made a covenant before the LORD : and David abode in
the wood, and Jonathan went to his house. Then came 19
up the Ziphites to Saul to Gibeah, saying, Doth not
David hide himself with us in the strong holds in the
wood, in the hill of Hachilah, which is on the south of
the desert ? Now therefore, O king, come down, accord- 20
ing to all the desire of thy soul to come down ; and our
part shall be to deliver him up into the king's hand.
And Saul said, Blessed be ye of the LORD ; for ye have 21
had compassion on me. Go, I pray you, make yet more 22
sure, and know and see his place where his haunt is, *and*

---

creation of a later generation, which loved thus to find anticipated
the future of its favourite hero. Cf. xxiv. 20.

xxiii. 19—xxiv. 22. *David pursued by Saul, whose life he spares.*
'Perhaps in the whole O.T.,' remarks Cornill (*Einleitung*, 114),
'there is no more significant example of a doublet than xxiii. 19—
xxiv. 23 compared with xxvi, in all essential points the same story,
only in other words and with a somewhat different setting.' That
we have here two parallel versions of the same incident is the all
but unanimous verdict of modern scholars. The only question is
as to which of the two is the older and therefore presumably
the more accurate reflection of the actual facts. The balance of
probability, in the opinion of most, is in favour of ch. xxvi. The
evidence has been clearly and succinctly stated by Löhr (*Samuel*,
xlv) thus : (*a*) the precise statement as to David's companions in
xxvi. 6 compared with the indefiniteness of ' David and his men '
in xxiv. 3 f. ; (*b*) the manner in which Saul falls into David's hands
(cf. xxvi. 7 ff., with its savour of ancient heroism, with xxiv. 3) ;
(*c*) the antique religious conception of xxvi. 19, over against which
may be set the content of xxiv. 20 f. suggesting affinity with such
later passages as xx. 15 f., xxiii. 17, &c. See also on xxiv. 16 ff.
below. A list of the more striking resemblances between the two
narratives is given by Driver, *LOT.*⁶, 181. To M, therefore, we
shall assign ch. xxvi, to T the section now before us.
    19. Cf. the parallel introduction xxvi. 1. The verse seems
overloaded at the end, and probably ended with ' in Horeshah '
(R.V. ' the wood,' see verse 15). The rest has come in from
xxvi. 1, where see notes.
    22. know ... where his haunt is. A probable emendation (see

who hath seen him there : for it is told me that he dealeth

23 very subtilly.   See therefore, and take knowledge of all the lurking places where he hideth himself, and come ye again to me of a certainty, and I will go with you : and it shall come to pass, if he be in the land, that I will

24 search him out among all the thousands of Judah.   And they arose, and went to Ziph before Saul : but David and his men were in the wilderness of Maon, in the

25 Arabah on the south of the desert.   And Saul and his men went to seek him.   And they told David : wherefore he came down to the rock, and abode in the wilderness of Maon.   And when Saul heard *that*, he

26 pursued after David in the wilderness of Maon.   And Saul went on this side of the mountain, and David and his men on that side of the mountain : and David made haste to get away for fear of Saul ; for Saul and his men compassed David and his men round about to take them.

27 But there came a messenger unto Saul, saying, Haste thee, and come ; for the Philistines have made a raid upon

28 the land.   So Saul returned from pursuing after David, and went against the Philistines : therefore they called

29 that place Sela-hammahlekoth.   And David went up from thence, and dwelt in the strong holds of En-gedi.

Driver) gives the more graphic reading : 'ascertain and mark where his fleeting foot may be' (cf. margin).

24. the wilderness of Maon lies east of the modern *Ma'in* (a place a little beyond Carmel and about four miles south of Ziph), and is here described as **in the Arabah on the south of the desert**.   The Arabah is the standing designation of 'the deep valley running north and south of the Dead Sea' (Deut. i. 1, Revisers' note).

25. to the rock, and abode, &c. : read, with LXX, 'to the rock which is in the wilderness of Maon.'   David was already abiding there (verse 24).   The rock is doubtless the same that we meet with again in verse 28.

29. En-gedi : 'kid's fountain,' the well-known oasis on the

And it came to pass, when Saul was returned from 24
following the Philistines, that it was told him, saying,
Behold, David is in the wilderness of En-gedi. Then 2
Saul took three thousand chosen men out of all Israel, and
went to seek David and his men upon the rocks of the
wild goats. And he came to the sheepcotes by the way, 3
where was a cave; and Saul went in to cover his feet.
Now David and his men were abiding in the innermost
parts of the cave. And the men of David said unto him, 4
Behold, the day of which the LORD said unto thee,
Behold, I will deliver thine enemy into thine hand, and
thou shalt do to him as it shall seem good unto thee.
Then David arose, and cut off the skirt of Saul's robe
privily. And it came to pass afterward, that David's 5
heart smote him, because he had cut off Saul's skirt.
And he said unto his men, The LORD forbid that I 6
should do this thing unto my lord, the LORD's anointed,
to put forth mine hand against him, seeing he is the

---

western shore of the Dead Sea, which still bears the name (*Ain
Jidy*).

xxiv 3. 'The sheepfolds to which Saul came were possibly
caves with a rough stone wall about the entrance, such as are still
found in the Wilderness of Judah' (H. P. Smith). Into one such
cave Saul enters alone to relieve himself; the same euphemism is
found in Judges iii. 24.

4-7. There is a want of logical sequence in these verses
(note, for example, that David's asseveration in verse 6 comes too
late) which has led to a generally accepted transposition in this
order: 4^a, 6, 7^a, 4^b, 5, 7^b. So read, the passage represents
David's men as urging him, on the strength of an unrecorded
oracle, to take the persecutor's life forthwith (4^a); David is
indignant at the suggestion of such an act of sacrilege (6, 7^a); but
in order to have tangible proof that he had really had the king in
his power, he creeps stealthily forward and cuts off the skirt of his
robe (4^b). Over even this milder form of *lèse-majesté* David is
conscience-stricken (5), and Saul is quietly allowed to rejoin
his men.

6. the LORD'S anointed: see on x. 1.

7 LORD's anointed. So David checked his men with these words, and suffered them not to rise against Saul. And Saul rose up out of the cave, and went on his way.

8 David also arose afterward, and went out of the cave, and cried after Saul, saying, My lord the king. And when Saul looked behind him, David bowed with his face to

9 the earth, and did obeisance. And David said to Saul, Wherefore hearkenest thou to men's words, saying,

10 Behold, David seeketh thy hurt? Behold, this day thine eyes have seen how that the LORD had delivered thee to-day into mine hand in the cave : and some bade me kill thee : but *mine eye* spared thee ; and I said, I will not put forth mine hand against my lord ; for he

11 is the LORD's anointed. Moreover, my father, see, yea, see the skirt of thy robe in my hand : for in that I cut off the skirt of thy robe, and killed thee not, know thou and see that there is neither evil nor transgression in mine hand, and I have not sinned against thee, though

12 thou huntest after my soul to take it. The LORD judge between me and thee, and the LORD avenge me of thee :

13 but mine hand shall not be upon thee. As saith the proverb of the ancients, Out of the wicked cometh forth wickedness : but mine hand shall not be upon thee.

14 After whom is the king of Israel come out ? after whom dost thou pursue ? after a dead dog, after a flea.

---

9 ff. David protests and proves his innocence of all desire to seek the king's hurt. Nay, on the contrary, he has requited him good for evil (11, end). God Himself is Judge between them, and to Him David commits his cause.

13. the proverb of the ancients here put into David's mouth, with its suggestion that Saul's misdeeds would recoil upon his own head (cf. xxv. 39), is so utterly at variance with the fine spirit of deference and magnanimity which breathes through David's previous remarks, that it is set down by all the commentators as a marginal gloss.

The LORD therefore be judge, and give sentence between 15 me and thee, and see, and plead my cause, and deliver me out of thine hand. And it came to pass, when 16 David had made an end of speaking these words unto Saul, that Saul said, Is this thy voice, my son David? And Saul lifted up his voice, and wept. And he said to 17 David, Thou art more righteous than I : for thou hast rendered unto me good, whereas I have rendered unto thee evil. And thou hast declared this day how that 18 thou hast dealt well with me : forasmuch as when the LORD had delivered me up into thine hand, thou killedst me not. For if a man find his enemy, will he let him 19 go well away? wherefore the LORD reward thee good for that thou hast done unto me this day. And now, 20 behold, I know that thou shalt surely be king, and that the kingdom of Israel shall be established in thine hand. Swear now therefore unto me by the LORD, that thou 21

---

16. Here we have one of the most striking resemblances between the older (xxvi. 17) and younger narratives. Only in the former, however, is the query appropriate, Saul there recognizing David in the darkness by his voice. There, too, the appropriate reply is given.

17 ff. Saul is touched, even to tears, by David's magnanimous conduct, almost without a parallel in that rude age. His native generosity, which jealousy working on a mind diseased had over-laid, is evoked, and prompts him to a full acknowledgement of the higher moral ideal of David, whom he prays that God may reward. This representation, however, just because of its lofty tone, seems less original than its parallel in xxvi. 21, 25.

18. thou hast declared : read, by inserting one letter, 'this day thou hast put the crown upon thy kind dealing with me' (cf. Gen xix. 19).

20 f. Saul acknowledges David as destined to succeed him on the throne of Israel, and implores his clemency as Jonathan had done before (xx. 14 ff.). The doubtful historicity of this constant trait of our younger sources has been already commented upon (see on xxiii. 17). Its expression here certainly has the air of a later interpretation of the more indefinite parallel, xxvi. 25.

wilt not cut off my seed after me, and that thou wilt not
22 destroy my name out of my father's house.   And David
sware unto Saul.   And Saul went home ; but David and
his men gat them up unto the hold.

25   [M] And Samuel died ; and all Israel gathered themselves together, and lamented him, and buried him in his
house at Ramah.   And David arose, and went down to
the wilderness of Paran.

2   And there was a man in Maon, whose possessions
were in Carmel ; and the man was very great, and he
. had three thousand sheep, and a thousand goats : and
3 he was shearing his sheep in Carmel.   Now the name of the
man was Nabal ; and the name of his wife Abigail : and
the woman was of good understanding, and of a beautiful
countenance : but the man was churlish and evil in his
4 doings ; and he was of the house of Caleb.   And David
heard in the wilderness that Nabal did shear his sheep.
5 And David sent ten young men, and David said unto

(c) xxv. 1–44.   *David and Abigail.*
This chapter is universally regarded as an extract from our
oldest source, and as a masterpiece of Hebrew narrative.   It is
prefaced by an editorial note recording the death of Samuel (cf.
xxviii. 3), and his burial, amid universal lamentation, within the
precincts of his house in Ramah.

 1. the wilderness of Paran: read with LXX (B), and as the
context requires, 'the wilderness of Maon' (xxiii. 24 ; see also
note on xxiii. 15).   The former, the present desert of *Et-tih* and
the scene of the wanderings between Sinai and Kadesh-barnea,
lay too far to the south.

 2. Carmel: now *Kurmul*, between Ziph and Maon, about
a mile to the north of the latter (cf. xv. 12, xxx. 29, LXX).   The
sheep-shearing was from the earliest period a time of festivity and
generous hospitality (see 2 Sam. xiii. 23).   The brief but pregnant
characterization which follows—the work of a literary artist—gives
the key to the subsequent dénouement.

 3. he was of the house of Caleb: *lit.* 'a Calebite' ; the clan of
the Calebites had occupied the district of which Hebron was the
centre since the conquest (Judges i. 20).

the young men, Get you up to Carmel, and go to Nabal,
and greet him in my name : and thus shall ye say to 6
him that liveth *in prosperity*, Peace be both unto thee,
and peace be to thine house, and peace be unto all that
thou hast.   And now I have heard that thou hast 7
shearers : thy shepherds have now been with us, and we
did them no hurt, neither was there aught missing unto
them, all the while they were in Carmel.   Ask thy young 8
men, and they will tell thee : wherefore let the young
men find favour in thine eyes ; for we come in a good
day : give, I pray thee, whatsoever cometh to thine hand,
unto thy servants, and to thy son David.   And when 9
David's young men came, they spake to Nabal according
to all those words in the name of David, and ceased.
And Nabal answered David's servants, and said, Who 10
is David? and who is the son of Jesse? there be many
servants now a days that break away every man from his
master.   Shall I then take my bread, and my water, and 11
my flesh that I have killed for my shearers, and give it
unto men of whom I know not whence they be? So 12

6. The opening clause must be emended : 'and thus shall ye say
to my brother' (so Vulg., Wellh., Driver, &c.).

7 f. David contrasts the strict discipline maintained by him
with the usual licence of similar roving bands, and asks that some
acknowledgement of this should be made by the wealthy farmer.
This species of blackmail is regularly levied at the present day by
the Bedouin living on the borders of the desert and the cultivated
land.   In return they guarantee the protection of life and property
(cf. verse 21) in these notoriously insecure districts.

8. we come in a good day : a literal rendering of the Hebrew
term for 'a feast day' (Esther viii. 17, ix. 22, and the Mishna
literature *passim*).

10. Nabal shows his churlishness by insulting David and his men,
suggesting that the former is a nobody, and the latter a band of
runaway slaves.

11. my water : read, with LXX, 'my wine,' as more appropriate to a day of feasting.

David's young men turned on their way, and went back, and came and told him according to all these words.

13 And David said unto his men, Gird ye on every man his sword. And they girded on every man his sword; and David also girded on his sword: and there went up after David about four hundred men; and two hundred

14 abode by the stuff. But one of the young men told Abigail, Nabal's wife, saying, Behold, David sent messengers out of the wilderness to salute our master; and he

15 flew upon them. But the men were very good unto us, and we were not hurt, neither missed we any thing, as long as we were conversant with them, when we were in

16 the fields: they were a wall unto us both by night and by day, all the while we were with them keeping the

17 sheep. Now therefore know and consider what thou wilt do; for evil is determined against our master, and against all his house: for he is such a son of Belial, that

18 one cannot speak to him. Then Abigail made haste, and took two hundred loaves, and two bottles of wine, and five sheep ready dressed, and five measures of parched corn, and an hundred clusters of raisins, and two

19 hundred cakes of figs, and laid them on asses. And she said unto her young men, Go on before me; behold,

15 f. Nabal's shepherds testify to the excellence of David's discipline, and to the protection afforded them by his men.

17. such a son of Belial: see on i. 16. The shepherds' estimate of their master's character is confirmed by one still better qualified to judge, see verse 25.

18 ff. By her intelligent grasp of the situation, by her prompt action and generous gifts, and by her conciliatory and diplomatic address, Abigail more than justifies the author's description of her as 'a woman of good understanding' (verse 3).

five measures of parched corn: rather more than a bushel and a half, the 'measure,' in Hebrew *seah*, being the third part of the ephah or bushel (Hastings' *DB.*, iv. 910 ff.). For the **clusters of raisins**—the 'dried grapes' of Num. vi. 3—and the **cakes of figs**, see the writer's article 'Fruit,' in *EBi.*, ii. 1568, 1570.

I come after you.   But she told not her husband Nabal.
And it was so, as she rode on her ass, and came down 20
by the covert of the mountain, that, behold, David and
his men came down against her; and she met them.
Now David had said, Surely in vain have I kept all that 21
this fellow hath in the wilderness, so that nothing was
missed of all that pertained unto him: and he hath returned me evil for good.   God do so unto the enemies 22
of David, and more also, if I leave of all that pertain to
him by the morning light so much as one man child.
And when Abigail saw David, she hasted, and lighted 23
off her ass, and fell before David on her face, and bowed
herself to the ground.   And she fell at his feet, and said, 24
Upon me, my lord, upon me be the iniquity: and let
thine handmaid, I pray thee, speak in thine ears, and
hear thou the words of thine handmaid.   Let not my 25
lord, I pray thee, regard this man of Belial, even Nabal:
for as his name is, so is he; Nabal is his name, and folly
is with him: but I thine handmaid saw not the young
men of my lord, whom thou didst send.   Now therefore, 26

---

20. by the covert of the mountain: the original seems to
imply that Abigail was concealed from the view of David and his
men approaching from some neighbouring hill-top, until they all
meet suddenly at the foot.   This is in keeping with the dramatic
instincts of the narrator, who represents David as at the moment
vowing the direst vengeance on Nabal and his house.

22. Read : 'God do so unto David,' see on 2 Sam. xii. 14.

23 f. Abigail omits nothing of the punctilious courtesy of the East.
Budde calls attention to the intentional conciseness of the style at
this point, in contrast to the somewhat 'turgid eloquence' that
follows. 'Everywhere in the O. T. (he adds), women's speeches
are distinguished by this characteristic'! Cf. 2 Sam. xiv. 12 ff.

25. Fool (see R. V. marg.) **is his name, and folly is with him**
reproduces the play upon the name Nabal, although our 'fool' is
not the precise equivalent of the Hebrew term, which suggests
one who has no regard for God or man.   Cf. the definition given
in Isa. xxxii. 5 f. (note marg.), and the note on 2 Sam. xiii. 12 f.

my lord, as the LORD liveth, and as thy soul liveth,
seeing the LORD hath withholden thee from bloodguiltiness, and from avenging thyself with thine own hand, now
therefore let thine enemies, and them that seek evil to
27 my lord, be as Nabal. And now this present which thy
servant hath brought unto my lord, let it be given unto
28 the young men that follow my lord. Forgive, I pray
thee, the trespass of thine handmaid : for the LORD will
certainly make my lord a sure house, because my lord
fighteth the battles of the LORD ; and evil shall not be
29 found in thee all thy days. And though man be risen
up to pursue thee, and to seek thy soul, yet the soul of
my lord shall be bound in the bundle of life with the
LORD thy God ; and the souls of thine enemies, them
30 shall he sling out, as from the hollow of a sling. And it
shall come to pass, when the LORD shall have done to
my lord according to all the good that he hath spoken
concerning thee, and shall have appointed thee prince

---

26. let thine enemies . . . be as Nabal : this clause seems to
imply—for the author's meaning is not clear—a prevision on
Abigail's part of Nabal's impending fate (verse 38), the underlying
thought being that vengeance should be left in the hand of God.

28. a sure house : see on ii. 35 ; **the battles of the LORD :**
see on xviii. 17.

29. Since the rest of Abigail's good wishes are all for the future,
it is now usual to read : ' and should a man rise up . . . may the
life of my lord be bound in the bundle of the living (R. V. marg.)
with (i. e. under the protection of) Yahweh thy God.' This
beautiful and tender prayer has long been applied to the life
beyond the grave, and its initial letters are to-day found on almost
every Jewish tombstone. But God had not yet revealed 'the
eternal hope ' to His people, and the wish must be interpreted of
the earthly life of David, which Abigail prays may be prolonged
under the Divine protection. The figure is that of a precious jewel
carefully tied up (cf. Gen. xlii. 35) and placed in safe keeping.
The converse follows in the prayer that the lives of David's
enemies may be cast away like the stones from a sling.

over Israel; that this shall be no grief unto thee, nor 31
offence of heart unto my lord, either that thou hast shed
blood causeless, or that my lord hath avenged himself:
and when the LORD shall have dealt well with my lord,
then remember thine handmaid. And David said to 32
Abigail, Blessed be the LORD, the God of Israel, which
sent thee this day to meet me: and blessed be thy 33
wisdom, and blessed be thou, which hast kept me this
day from bloodguiltiness, and from avenging myself with
mine own hand. For in very deed, as the LORD, the 34
God of Israel, liveth, which hath withholden me from
hurting thee, except thou hadst hasted and come to meet
me, surely there had not been left unto Nabal by the
morning light so much as one man child. So David 35
received of her hand that which she had brought him:
and he said unto her, Go up in peace to thine house;
see, I have hearkened to thy voice, and have accepted
thy person. And Abigail came to Nabal; and, behold, 36
he held a feast in his house, like the feast of a king;
and Nabal's heart was merry within him, for he was very
drunken: wherefore she told him nothing, less or more,
until the morning light. And it came to pass in the 37
morning, when the wine was gone out of Nabal, that his
wife told him these things, and his heart died within him,

31. A skilful appeal to David's peace of conscience. In the
happier future David will have cause to remember Abigail and
her counsel with gratitude.

nor offence (*lit.* stumbling-block) of heart: no ground for
remorse. In the O. T. the heart is the seat of conscience,
cf. xxiv. 5.

32 ff. David acknowledges that Abigail has been a messenger of
God, sent to save him from the guilt of blood.

35. I have accepted thy person: *lit.* 'have lifted up thy face,'
here and Gen. xix. 21 equivalent to 'I have granted thy request.'

36. Abigail's silence in the circumstances is one more proof
of her discretion (verse 33, marg.).

38 and he became as a stone.   And it came to pass about
ten days after, that the LORD smote Nabal, that he died.

39 And when David heard that Nabal was dead, he said,
Blessed be the LORD, that hath pleaded the cause of my
reproach from the hand of Nabal, and hath kept back
his servant from evil: and the evil-doing of Nabal hath
the LORD returned upon his own head.   And David
sent and spake concerning Abigail, to take her to him

40 to wife.   And when the servants of David were come to
Abigail to Carmel, they spake unto her, saying, David
hath sent us unto thee, to take thee to him to wife.

41 And she arose, and bowed herself with her face to the
earth, and said, Behold, thine handmaid is a servant to

42 wash the feet of the servants of my lord.   And Abigail
hasted, and arose, and rode upon an ass, with five
damsels of hers that followed her; and she went after

43 the messengers of David, and became his wife.   David
also took Ahinoam of Jezreel; and they became both of

44 them his wives.   Now Saul had given Michal his
daughter, David's wife, to Palti the son of Laish, which
was of Gallim.

26   And the Ziphites came unto Saul to Gibeah, saying,

---

39. David sent and spake concerning Abigail: i.e. sent her
an offer of marriage, as in the Revisers' reference, Cant. viii. 8.
Such, to us unseemly, haste was not repugnant to the social code
of those days.   It is to be assumed, however, that a short interval
elapsed, as in the case of Bath-sheba (2 Sam. xi. 27).

43. Ahinoam of Jezreel, a town in the neighbourhood of
Ziph and Maon, became the mother of David's eldest son, Amnon
(2 Sam. iii. 2).

44. Palti: a shorter form of Paltiel (2 Sam. iii. 15).   A place
named **Gallim** is mentioned in the neighbourhood of Anathoth in
Benjamin (Isa. x. 30).

(d) xxvi. *An earlier version of the Ziphites' treachery and
David's magnanimity to Saul.*
The arguments for the priority of this account over that already

Doth not David hide himself in the hill of Hachilah, which is before the desert? Then Saul arose, and went 2 down to the wilderness of Ziph, having three thousand chosen men of Israel with him, to seek David in the wilderness of Ziph. And Saul pitched in the hill of 3 Hachilah, which is before the desert, by the way. But David abode in the wilderness, and he saw that Saul came after him into the wilderness. David therefore 4 sent out spies, and understood that Saul was come of a certainty. And David arose, and came to the place 5 where Saul had pitched: and David beheld the place where Saul lay, and Abner the son of Ner, the captain of his host: and Saul lay within the place of the wagons, and the people pitched round about him. Then answered 6 David and said to Ahimelech the Hittite, and to Abishai the son of Zeruiah, brother to Joab, saying, Who will go

---

given in ch. xxiv have been indicated on p. 157. No one will assert that David may not have spared Saul's life on a previous occasion, but if so, it is passing strange that there is no allusion here on the part of either Saul or David to the repetition of so remarkable an incident. In view, therefore, of the well-known methods of the Hebrew historians, the easier explanation is that adopted by almost all modern students, that in these two chapters we have duplicate versions of one and the same historical incident.

1. **the hill of Hachilah** has been identified by Conder with a ridge, *El-kolah*, six miles east of Ziph and nearly halfway to En-gedi. It is here described as 'before Jeshimon' (see marg.), that is, as overlooking the barren tract of country between the highlands of Judah and the northern half of the Dead Sea, more frequently termed the Wilderness of Judah.

4. **of a certainty**: the text is corrupt. The preposition 'unto' of the original and the context both suggest the name of a place to which Saul had come (cf. marg.).

5. **within the place of the wagons**: see on xvii. 20.

6. **Ahimelech the Hittite**: doubtless, like the more famous Uriah, a soldier of fortune belonging to the powerful race which had their principal seats at Carchemish on the Euphrates and Kadesh on the Orontes. See further Driver's *Genesis*, 228 ff.

Abishai . ... Joab: the first mention of these 'sons of

down with me to Saul to the camp?   And Abishai said,
7 I will go down with thee.   So David and Abishai came
to the people by night: and, behold, Saul lay sleeping
within the place of the wagons, with his spear stuck in
the ground at his head: and Abner and the people lay
8 round about him.   Then said Abishai to David, God
hath delivered up thine enemy into thine hand this day:
now therefore let me smite him, I pray thee, with the
spear to the earth at one stroke, and I will not smite him
9 the second time.   And David said to Abishai, Destroy
him not: for who can put forth his hand against the
10 LORD's anointed, and be guiltless?   And David said, As
the LORD liveth, the LORD shall smite him; or his day
shall come to die; or he shall go down into battle, and
11 perish.   The LORD forbid that I should put forth mine
hand against the LORD's anointed: but now take, I pray
thee, the spear that is at his head, and the cruse of water,
12 and let us go.   So David took the spear and the cruse

Zeruiah,' who with Asahel their brother figure so conspicuously
in the life of David.   Zeruiah, according to Chron. ii. 16, was
David's sister, and as David was the youngest son of a large
family, there is nothing improbable in his nephews being about
his own age.   Why these redoubtable warriors should always be
described as the sons of their mother remains a puzzle.   Their
father was probably already in his grave at Beth-lehem (2 Sam.
ii. 32).

7. At the camping-grounds of the Bedouin Arabs, a spear stuck
in the ground outside the entrance distinguishes the tent of the
sheikh.   In Saul's case also the spear seems to have been
a symbol of authority.   It is expressly mentioned as being in his
hand as he sat in state on the moot-hill at Gibeah (xxii. 6;
cf. xviii. 10, xx. 33).

8 ff. With Abishai's proposal and David's reply here compare
the parallel in xxiv. 4 ff.

10. The text of R. V. suggests three alternatives, the margin
preferably two.   In this case God will smite Saul either directly
with a sudden stroke, as in the case of Nabal, or indirectly—as
actually happened—through the hazard of battle.

of water from Saul's head; and they gat them away, and
no man saw it, nor knew it, neither did any awake : for
they were all asleep; because a deep sleep from the
LORD was fallen upon them. Then David went over 13
to the other side, and stood on the top of the mountain
afar off; a great space being between them : and David 14
cried to the people, and to Abner the son of Ner, saying,
Answerest thou not, Abner? Then Abner answered and
said, Who art thou that criest to the king? And David 15
said to Abner, Art not thou a *valiant* man? and who is
like to thee in Israel? wherefore then hast thou not kept
watch over thy lord the king? for there came one of the
people in to destroy the king thy lord. This thing is not 16
good that thou hast done. As the LORD liveth, ye are
worthy to die, because ye have not kept watch over your
lord, the LORD's anointed. And now, see, where the
king's spear is, and the cruse of water that was at his
head. And Saul knew David's voice, and said, Is this 17
thy voice, my son David? And David said, It is my
voice, my lord, O king. And he said, Wherefore doth 18
my lord pursue after his servant? for what have I done?
or what evil is in mine hand? Now therefore, I pray thee, 19
let my lord the king hear the words of his servant. If
it be the LORD that hath stirred thee up against me, let

---

17. Saul recognized David's voice, although it was still too dark
to recognize his face and figure. Here, therefore, Saul's query is
in place, see on xxiv. 16.

19 f. Verses 19 and 20 are of great interest as throwing light
upon some aspects of religious belief among the early Hebrews.
David can account for Saul's persistent enmity only by one or
other of two hypotheses. Either it is due to the direct instiga-
tion of Yahweh, in which case an offended deity can always be
placated by the smell (note marg.) of a sacrifice, an antique
conception found also in Gen. viii. 21, or it is the result of the
influence upon Saul of some slander-mongering 'children of men.'

him accept an offering: but if it be the children of men, cursed be they before the LORD; for they have driven me out this day that I should not cleave unto the inheritance of the LORD, saying, Go, serve other gods. 20 Now therefore, let not my blood fall to the earth away from the presence of the LORD: for the king of Israel is come out to seek a flea, as when one doth hunt a partridge 21 in the mountains. Then said Saul, I have sinned: return, my son David: for I will no more do thee harm, because my life was precious in thine eyes this day: behold, I 22 have played the fool, and have erred exceedingly. And David answered and said, Behold the spear, O king! let 23 then one of the young men come over and fetch it. And the LORD shall render to every man his righteousness and his faithfulness: forasmuch as the LORD delivered thee into my hand to-day, and I would not put forth 24 mine hand against the LORD's anointed. And, behold,

---

On these David invokes the curse of God, the issue of which is death. Nothing less is sufficient for men by whom David is being driven out like another Cain 'from the presence of Yahweh.' For a distinctive feature of the early Semitic religion is the belief, here so clearly illustrated, that each deity had his own land, beyond which his power and influence, and therefore his worship, did not extend. For David, Yahweh is, of course, the only legitimate object of worship within the territory of Israel, 'the inheritance of Yahweh' (1 Kings viii. 53), but the existence of other gods, as e. g. Chemosh in Moab, Milcom in Ammon, is also implied, as well as their claim upon the allegiance and worship of those who took refuge within the land of *their* 'inheritance.' See further Kautzsch on 'The Religion of Israel in the Pre-Prophetic Period' in Hastings' *DB.*, extra vol., 635.

20. away from the presence of the LORD: outside the bounds of Yahweh's land, as explained above, where David could no longer maintain communion with God by sacrifice (cf. Hos. ix. 3 ff.). The idea of dying in a land that is not Yahweh's is abhorrent to His pious worshipper.

the king . . . is come out to seek a flea: a copyist's alteration, under the influence of xxiv. 14, of the true text 'to seek my life' (LXX).

as thy life was much set by this day in mine eyes, so let
my life be much set by in the eyes of the LORD, and let
him deliver me out of all tribulation.   Then Saul said to 25
David, Blessed be thou, my son David: thou shalt both
do mightily, and shalt surely prevail.   So David went
his way, and Saul returned to his place.

And David said in his heart, I shall now perish one 27
day by the hand of Saul: there is nothing better for me
than that I should escape into the land of the Philistines;
and Saul shall despair of me, to seek me any more in all
the borders of Israel: so shall I escape out of his hand.

25. With this compare xxiv. 17 ff. A careful comparison of
the contents of the speeches in the two chapters seems to us to
show beyond any doubt on which side the greater antiquity and
originality are to be found.

C. 1 Sam. xxvii–xxxi. *David as the Vassal of the King of Gath.*
The Philistine Invasion and Death of Saul and Jonathan.

This subdivision carries forward the story of David's fortunes
from the day that he determined to put himself beyond the
jurisdiction of Saul to the tragic death of the latter upon Mount
Gilboa.   Each chapter is practically concerned with a distinct
episode, and accordingly the sections of the commentary may
follow substantially the chapter-divisions.   The compiler continues
to draw from our oldest source.   Ch. xxviii. 3 ff., which now
manifestly breaks the connexion between xxviii. 1 f. and xxix,
alone gives rise to difference of opinion as to its true position and
provenance.

(a) xxvii. 1—xxviii. 2. *David takes refuge with Achish of Gath.*
His policy as the king's vassal.

Contrary to the expectations raised by the amicable parting we
have just witnessed, we now find David compelled to take the
step from which he has just shrunk in horror (xxvi. 19 f.) and to
crave the protection of Saul's bitterest enemies, the Philistines.
The narrator shows how, in a difficult situation, David endeavoured
to steer a middle course between his duty to his protector and his
duty to his country.

1. We are given clearly to understand that David took the
extreme and unpatriotic step here recorded only as a last and
desperate resource.   That this is on every ground the more
trustworthy representation as compared with the parallel version
xxi. 10-15 is self-evident.

2 And David arose, and passed over, he and the six hundred men that were with him, unto Achish the son of
3 Maoch, king of Gath.   And David dwelt with Achish at Gath, he and his men, every man with his household, even David with his two wives, Ahinoam the Jezreelitess,
4 and Abigail the Carmelitess, Nabal's wife.   And it was told Saul that David was fled to Gath : and he sought no more again for him.

5   And David said unto Achish, If now I have found grace in thine eyes, let them give me a place in one of the cities in the country, that I may dwell there : for why should thy servant dwell in the royal city with thee ?
6 Then Achish gave him Ziklag that day : wherefore Ziklag pertaineth unto the kings of Judah unto this day.
7   And the number of the days that David dwelt in the country of the Philistines was a full year and four months.
8 And David and his men went up, and made a raid upon the Geshurites, and the Girzites, and the Amalekites :

---

5. David requests of Achish permission to retire, in modern phraseology, to one of the provincial towns.   The reason alleged seems to have been that it was too great an honour to continue in the immediate vicinity of the king, with the implication, perhaps, on David's part that he could be of more service to his suzerain as Warden of the Marches.   In reality, he must have wished to be free from the continual surveillance to which he was exposed in the capital city.   It has also been suggested that in a district of his own David would be able to observe his own religious rites as a worshipper of Yahweh.

6. Ziklag : probably *Zuheilike*, about eleven miles east by south of Gaza.   Now granted to David in fee, it afterwards became the private property of the kings of Judah.

wherefore . . . unto this day: if part of the original narrative, this clause suggests a date for the latter after the secession under Rehoboam.   Before that event there were only kings of Israel (cf. Introduction, sect. iv).

8. the Geshurites, and the Girzites : David turns his arms against several of the tribes on the marches.   The Geshurites may have been a small tribe on the frontier of Egypt (cf. Joshua xiii.

for those *nations* were the inhabitants of the land, which
were of old, as thou goest to Shur, even unto the land of
Egypt. And David smote the land, and saved neither 9
man nor woman alive, and took away the sheep, and the
oxen, and the asses, and the camels, and the apparel;
and he returned, and came to Achish. And Achish said, 10
Whither have ye made a raid to-day? And David said,
Against the South of Judah, and against the South of
the Jerahmeelites, and against the South of the Kenites.
And David saved neither man nor woman alive, to bring 11

---

2 R.V.). The better known Geshurites of the Jaulan are out of
the question here (see on 2 Sam. iii. 3). The Girzites are otherwise unknown. Another reading (see R.V. marg.) is Gizrites, the
inhabitants of Gezer. But this city lay much too far to the north.
It is possible that both Geshurites and Girzites are corrupt
duplicates of a single tribal name.

the **Amalekites**: see on xv. 2. The clause following is
obscure, and in parts corrupt. Read probably : 'for they inhabited
the land which is from Telam (cf. xv. 7) as thou goest unto Shur,'
&c. See Driver, *Notes*, &c.

9. For the ban of the second degree, of which we have here an
example, see on xv. 3. Its execution, however, was by no means
'thorough,' as is seen from the incidents of ch. xxx.

he returned, and came to Achish : from this and the similar
notice, verse 11ª, it is to be inferred that part of David's arrangement with Achish was that the latter should receive a share of the
spoils of every foray. An interesting discussion of the constitutional
position of David, as a *gēr* or outlander, will be found in Bertholet,
Die Stellung der Israeliten und der Juden zu den Fremden, 28-32.

10. **the South of Judah** : here and elsewhere it is better to
retain the geographical term of the original and render, 'the
Negeb of Judah.' The Negeb—*lit*. 'the dry, parched land'—is the
standing name of 'the southernmost of the natural divisions of
Palestine, the steppe region which forms the transition to the true
desert,' including Beer-sheba on the north, and Kadesh-barnea on
the south. See Cheyne's article 'Negeb,' *EBi.*, iii, with map.

the **Jerahmeelites** : a southern clan allied to the Calebites,
with whom they were afterwards absorbed into the tribe of Judah
(1 Chron. ii. 42). For the **Kenites** see on xv. 6. Both clans
appear again, xxx. 29.

11 f. An interesting glimpse of David's policy at this period.
By giving out that he had raided certain districts belonging to his

them to Gath, saying, Lest they should tell on us, saying,
So did David, and so hath been his manner all the while
12 he hath dwelt in the country of the Philistines.   And
Achish believed David, saying, He hath made his people
Israel utterly to abhor him; therefore he shall be my
servant for ever.

28   And it came to pass in those days, that the Philistines
gathered their hosts together for warfare, to fight with
Israel.   And Achish said unto David, Know thou as-
suredly, that thou shalt go out with me in the host, thou
2 and thy men.   And David said to Achish, Therefore
thou shalt know what thy servant will do.   And Achish
said to David, Therefore will I make thee keeper of mine
head for ever.

3   Now Samuel was dead, and all Israel had lamented

---

own tribe and its allies he succeeded in lulling the suspicions that
were bound to arise as to his complete loyalty to his suzerain (cf.
xxix. 3, 6).

xxviii. **1.** continues the preceding narrative.   The Philistines
collect their forces for the last campaign of that 'sore war' (xiv.
52) which lasted 'all the days of Saul.'   This gives Achish occasion
to remind his vassal of his duty to fight under his lord's banner.

2. Therefore thou shalt know: for 'thou' read with LXX
'now,' and render: 'good and well, now shalt thou know,' &c.
The ambiguity is intentional.   At this stage David declines to
commit himself; Achish, however, assumes that David will
accompany him.

keeper of mine head: captain of the royal bodyguard, as
rendered by LXX (for the Greek term see Deissmann, *Bible
Studies*, 98).   David soon afterwards followed this precedent by
appointing a bodyguard of foreign mercenaries.

(b) xxviii. **3-25.** *Saul's visit to the necromancer at En-dor.*
This section, as has been already noted, breaks the main thread
of the narrative, which is found again at xxix. 1 ff.   Thus we hear
of the Philistine call to arms in xxviii. 1; in xxix. 1 the place of
meeting is given as Aphek, which lay in the plain of Sharon (see
on iv. 1).   From Aphek the Philistines advance, through one of
the passes connecting Sharon with Esdraelon, to Jezreel where the
Israelite army lay encamped (xxix. 1, 11).   But in xxviii. 4 the

him, and buried him in Ramah, even in his own city.
And Saul had put away those that had familiar spirits,
and the wizards, out of the land.   And the Philistines 4
gathered themselves together, and came and pitched in
Shunem : and Saul gathered all Israel together, and they

---

former are still further north at Shunem, while the latter have
evidently retired before the Philistine advance to the mountain
ridge of Gilboa.   Again, Saul's visit to En-dor is represented as
taking place on the night before the battle (xxviii. 19).   Chronologically, therefore, the place of the section now before us is
immediately in front of ch. xxxi.   That it actually stood there in
the historical document (M) to which, by universal consent, the
rest of these chapters (xxvii–xxxi) belong is, we believe, the more
probable view (so Budde and others), although by the majority of
critics it is assigned to the same source as ch. xv (the younger and
less historical S).   The main argument for the latter attribution is
drawn from verses 17 f., which are a recapitulation of the contents
of ch. xv.   But the verses in question are better taken as a later
addition to the true text (see notes below).   Budde, further, has
made the plausible suggestion that the present dislocation is due
to the fact that this account of Saul's resort to necromancy was
omitted by the Deuteronomic compiler of Samuel as unworthy of
one who was the LORD's anointed, just as it is probable that the
great section 2 Sam. ix–xx was omitted as containing so much
that reflected on the character of David.   The later and more
liberal-minded editor who gave our Book of Samuel its present
form restored both the omitted sections, but inadvertently inserted
xxviii. 3 ff. somewhat too early in the narrative (see further,
Introduction, sects. v, vi).

3. The first half of this verse has already appeared in the
redactional note, xxv. 1.

those that had familiar spirits, and the wizards : the
precise meaning of the words so rendered and the distinction
between them, if there be a distinction, are still matters of dispute.
Budde has a very full note here, see also Driver on the classical
passage, Deut. xviii. 10 f., and Davies' article 'Divination' in
EBi., i. 1120 f.   There is a peculiar pathos in this picture of Saul,
once so jealous of the honour of Yahweh, reduced to having
recourse to those dishonouring forms of superstition which he had
done his best to suppress.

4. See introductory note above.   The two armies are facing
each other across the eastern end of the plain of Esdraelon.
Shunem, now *Sulem* or *Solam*, lies on its northern edge, at
the foot of *Jebel Dahi*, or Little Hermon, **Gilboa,** now *Jebel Fakua*,

5 pitched in Gilboa.   And when Saul saw the host of the
   Philistines, he was afraid, and his heart trembled greatly.
6 And when Saul inquired of the LORD, the LORD answered
   him not, neither by dreams, nor by Urim, nor by prophets.
7 Then said Saul unto his servants, Seek me a woman that
   hath a familiar spirit, that I may go to her, and inquire
   of her.   And his servants said to him, Behold, there is
8 a woman that hath a familiar spirit at En-dor.   And
   Saul disguised himself, and put on other raiment, and
   went, he and two men with him, and they came to the
   woman by night: and he said, Divine unto me, I pray
   thee, by the familiar spirit, and bring me up whomsoever
9 I shall name unto thee.   And the woman said unto him,
   Behold, thou knowest what Saul hath done, how he hath
   cut off those that have familiar spirits, and the wizards,
   out of the land: wherefore then layest thou a snare for
10 my life, to cause me to die?   And Saul sware to her by
   the LORD, saying, As the LORD liveth, there shall no
11 punishment happen to thee for this thing.   Then said the
   woman, Whom shall I bring up unto thee?   And he said,
12 Bring me up Samuel.   And when the woman saw Samuel,
   she cried with a loud voice: and the woman spake to

---

is the ridge running south-east along the southern side of the
valley of Jezreel.

   6. By none of the recognized channels of Divine communication
—dreams, the sacred lot (see on xiv. 41), prophets—does God
vouchsafe an answer to Saul's inquiry as to the issue of the
impending engagement.

   7. a woman that hath a familiar spirit: in modern phrase,
'a woman that is a necromancer'; so in verse 8: 'divine unto me
by necromancy.'

   En-dor: the modern *Endûr*, on the north side of Little
Hermon, opposite Mount Tabor.

   12. The want of logical connexion between the two halves of
this verse has long been felt.   Why should the sight of Samuel,
whom of course she was expecting to see, have had such an effect

Saul, saying, Why hast thou deceived me? for thou art
Saul. And the king said unto her, Be-not afraid: for 13
what seest thou? And the woman said unto Saul, I see
a god coming up out of the earth. And he said unto 14
her, What form is he of? And she said, An old man
cometh up; and he is covered with a robe. And Saul
perceived that it was Samuel, and he bowed with his face
to the ground, and did obeisance. And Samuel said to 15
Saul, Why hast thou disquieted me, to bring me up?
And Saul answered, I am sore distressed; for the Philistines make war against me, and God is departed from
me, and answereth me no more, neither by prophets, nor
by dreams: therefore I have called thee, that thou mayest
make known unto me what I shall do. And Samuel 16
said, Wherefore then dost thou ask of me, seeing the
LORD is departed from thee, and is become thine adversary? And the LORD hath wrought for himself, as he 17

---

upon this professional necromancer, and how did it cause her to
recognize Saul in his disguise? Perles, followed by Budde and
Nowack, proposes to read 'Saul' for 'Samuel': 'when the
woman looked at Saul, she cried,' &c. The connexion is now
clear. The mention of Samuel's name (verse 11), coupled with
her knowledge that Saul was in the neighbourhood, led to her
recognition of Saul, and the conviction that she had been caught
in a trap which the king had set for her. Hence her abject fear,
which is quieted by Saul in verse 13. It appears, further, that
Saul was the first to recognize Samuel in the ascending spirit,
which verse 14 shows to have been visible to the woman, but
invisible to Saul.

15. to bring me up: i. e. from Sheol, the abode of the dead;
see on ii. 6.

16. and is become thine adversary: a doubtful reading and
rendering. The original may have been: 'and is on the side of
thine adversaries,' the Philistines. The LXX reading in R.V.
marg. seems to betray the influence of verse 17.

xxviii. 17-19ᵈ (to Philistines). These verses have been recognized as a later insertion based on ch. xv (especially verse 28) even
by some who regard the chapter before us as the natural sequel

spake by me: and the LORD hath rent the kingdom out of thine hand, and given it to thy neighbour, even to
18 David. Because thou obeyedst not the voice of the LORD, and didst not execute his fierce wrath upon Amalek, therefore hath the LORD done this thing unto
19 thee this day. Moreover the LORD will deliver Israel also with thee into the hand of the Philistines: and to-morrow shalt thou and thy sons be with me: the LORD shall deliver the host of Israel also into the hand of the
20 Philistines. Then Saul fell straightway his full length upon the earth, and was sore afraid, because of the words of Samuel: and there was no strength in him; for he
21 had eaten no bread all the day, nor all the night. And the woman came unto Saul, and saw that he was sore troubled, and said unto him, Behold, thine handmaid hath hearkened unto thy voice, and I have put my life in my hand, and have hearkened unto thy words which
22 thou spakest unto me. Now therefore, I pray thee, hearken thou also unto the voice of thine handmaid, and let me set a morsel of bread before thee; and eat, that thou mayest have strength, when thou goest on thy way.
23 But he refused, and said, I will not eat. But his servants, together with the woman, constrained him; and he

to the account there given of Saul's rejection. That they are foreign to the original context is best seen from the double reference, in identical terms, to the Philistines in verse 19. Verse 16, therefore, should be continued thus: 'and to-morrow shalt thou,' &c. For the bearing of this on the literary affinity of the chapter, and ultimately on the historicity of the episode, see introductory note above.

17. **the LORD hath wrought for himself**: read. with LXX (see marg.): 'and the LORD hath done unto thee as he spake by me.' Cf. the original passage xv. 28.

19. **to-morrow shalt thou and thy sons be with me**: the original will scarcely bear this rendering; read, with LXX and most editors: 'to-morrow shalt thou and thy sons with thee be fallen.'

hearkened unto their voice. So he arose from the earth, and sat upon the bed. And the woman had a fatted 24 calf in the house; and she hasted, and killed it; and she took flour, and kneaded it, and did bake unleavened bread thereof: and she brought it before Saul, and before 25 his servants; and they did eat. Then they rose up, and went away that night.

Now the Philistines gathered together all their hosts **29** to Aphek: and the Israelites pitched by the fountain which is in Jezreel. And the lords of the Philistines 2 passed on by hundreds, and by thousands: and David and his men passed on in the rearward with Achish. Then said the princes of the Philistines, What *do* these 3 Hebrews *here*? And Achish said unto the princes of the Philistines, Is not this David, the servant of Saul the king of Israel, which hath been with me these days or these years, and I have found no fault in him since he fell away *unto me* unto this day? But the princes of the 4 Philistines were wroth with him; and the princes of the Philistines said unto him, Make the man return, that he may go back to his place where thou hast appointed him, and let him not go down with us to battle, lest in the battle he become an adversary to us: for wherewith

---

(c) xxix. *David is dismissed by the lords of the Philistines.*
This chapter and the following continue the narrative of xxviii. 1 f. As on a former occasion (iv. 1), the Philistines muster their forces at Aphek, while the Israelites encamp **by the fountain which is in Jezreel**, generally identified with the copious spring *Ain Jalud* at the foot of Gilboa. in Judges vii. 1 called 'the spring of Harod.'

3 ff. Achish justifies David's presence on the twofold ground (1) that he had every reason to take arms against Saul, and (2) that he had shown himself thoroughly loyal during his period of vassalage. The arguments of the Philistine princes are unanswerable (cf. the incident, xiv. 21).

4. lest ... he become an adversary to us: Heb. *sātān*. as

should this *fellow* reconcile himself unto his lord? should
5 it not be with the heads of these men? Is not this David,
of whom they sang one to another in dances, saying,

Saul hath slain his thousands,
And David his ten thousands?

6 Then Achish called David, and said unto him, As the
LORD liveth, thou hast been upright, and thy going out
and thy coming in with me in the host is good in my
sight: for I have not found evil in thee since the day of
thy coming unto me unto this day: nevertheless the lords
7 favour thee not. Wherefore now return, and go in peace,
8 that thou displease not the lords of the Philistines. And
David said unto Achish, But what have I done? and
what hast thou found in thy servant so long as I have
been before thee unto this day, that I may not go and
9 fight against the enemies of my lord the king? And
Achish answered and said to David, I know that thou art
good in my sight, as an angel of God: notwithstanding
the princes of the Philistines have said, He shall not go
10 up with us to the battle. Wherefore now rise up early
in the morning with the servants of thy lord that are
come with thee: and as soon as ye be up early in the

2 Sam. xix. 22 and elsewhere of a human antagonist. Only in later
literature does the word become the name of the great adversary
of mankind (Zech. iii. 1 f., 1 Chron. xxi. 1, and the opening
chapters of Job).

8. David affects to regard Achish's polite expression of the
princes' order as casting suspicion on his loyalty. The narrator does
not disclose the real mind of David on the subject (cf. xxviii. 2).

9. as an angel of God: blamelessness seems here the point of
comparison. Otherwise 2 Sam. xiv. 17, xix. 27, which see.

10. The following has been dropped from the end of this verse:
'depart and go to the place where I have stationed you [viz.
Ziklag], and put no wicked design in thy heart, for thou art good
in my sight' (LXX). 'It is assumed by Achish that the high-
spirited warrior will feel insulted, and be tempted to take revenge'
(H. P. Smith).

morning, and have light, depart. So David rose up early, 11 he and his men, to depart in the morning, to return into the land of the Philistines. And the Philistines went up to Jezreel.

And it came to pass, when David and his men were 30 come to Ziklag on the third day, that the Amalekites had made a raid upon the South, and upon Ziklag, and had smitten Ziklag, and burned it with fire; and had taken 2 captive the women *and all* that were therein, both small and great: they slew not any, but carried them off, and went their way. And when David and his men came 3 to the city, behold, it was burned with fire; and their wives, and their sons, and their daughters, were taken captives. Then David and the people that were with 4 him lifted up their voice and wept, until they had no more power to weep. And David's two wives were taken 5 captives, Ahinoam the Jezreelitess, and Abigail the wife of Nabal the Carmelite. And David was greatly dis- 6 tressed; for the people spake of stoning him, because the soul of all the people was grieved, every man for his sons and for his daughters: but David strengthened himself in the LORD his God.

---

11. The Philistines advance from Aphek to **Jezreel**, the important city, now *Zerin*, at the head of the valley of Jezreel.

(*d*) xxx. *The Amalekite raid on Ziklag, and its sequel.*
On the third day after leaving Aphek, David and his men arrive at Ziklag to find it raided and burned. The absence of the fighting men afforded these wild Bedouin an excellent opportunity of revenging David's treatment of their tribe (xxviii. 7).

2. The intention of the raiders was apparently to sell their captives in the Egyptian slave-market.

6. David was greatly distressed: rather, 'was in great straits,' the reference being not to inward emotion, but to his personal danger, as explained in the next clause. But David's courage did not fail. for 'the rock of his strength and his refuge were in God' (Ps. lxii. 7).

7 And David said to Abiathar the priest, the son of Ahimelech, I pray thee, bring me hither the ephod. And Abiathar brought thither the ephod to David.
8 And David inquired of the LORD, saying, If I pursue after this troop, shall I overtake them? And he answered him, Pursue: for thou shalt surely overtake *them*, and
9 shalt without fail recover *all*. So David went, he and the six hundred men that were with him, and came to the brook Besor, where those that were left behind
10 stayed. But David pursued, he and four hundred men: for two hundred stayed behind, which were so faint that
11 they could not go over the brook Besor: and they found an Egyptian in the field, and brought him to David, and gave him bread, and he did eat; and they gave him
12 water to drink: and they gave him a piece of a cake of figs, and two clusters of raisins; and when he had eaten, his spirit came again to him: for he had eaten no bread,
13 nor drunk any water, three days and three nights. And David said unto him, To whom belongest thou? and whence art thou? And he said, I am a young man of Egypt, servant to an Amalekite; and my master left me,
14 because three days agone I fell sick. We made a raid upon the South of the Cherethites, and upon that which

7 f. David proceeds to ascertain the will of Yahweh by the customary means, the oracle of the ephod (see on xiv. 41, and xxiii. 2). Although only two questions are given in the text, we see from the answers that three were put in succession, each of which received an affirmative answer.

9. the brook Besor: probably, if the Amalekites were making for Egypt, the modern *Wadi-esh-Sheriah*, a branch of the *Wadi Ghuzeeh*.

10. One-third of David's force is found to be too exhausted for further pursuit, a condition by no means surprising, if they had just covered the eighty miles or thereby from Aphek to Ziklag in three days (verse 1).

12. a cake of figs, &c.: see on xxv. 18.

14. the South of the Cherethites: the Cherethite Negeb (see

belongeth to Judah, and upon the South of Caleb ; and
we burned Ziklag with fire. And David said to him, 15
Wilt thou bring me down to this troop ? And he said,
Swear unto me by God, that thou wilt neither kill me,
nor deliver me up into the hands of my master, and I
will bring thee down to this troop. And when he had 16
brought him down, behold, they were spread abroad over
all the ground, eating and drinking, and feasting, because
of all the great spoil that they had taken out of the land
of the Philistines, and out of the land of Judah. And 17
David smote them from the twilight even unto the
evening of the next day : and there escaped not a man
of them, save four hundred young men, which rode upon
camels and fled. And David recovered all that the 18
Amalekites had taken : and David rescued his two wives.
And there was nothing lacking to them, neither small 19
nor great, neither sons nor daughters, neither spoil, nor
any thing that they had taken to them : David brought
back all. And David took all the flocks and the herds, 20
which they drave before those *other* cattle, and said, This

---

on xxvii. 10), that portion of Southern Palestine occupied by the
Cherethites, a clan closely allied to the Philistines, with whom
they are associated by Zephaniah (ii. 5) and Ezekiel (xxv. 16).
See also on 2 Sam. viii. 18.

the South of Caleb : the Calebite Negeb, the country round
Maon, Carmel, and Ziph occupied by the clan of Caleb. For the
five Negebs. see reference on xxvii. 10.

17. of the next day : the original is here corrupt : read, with
Wellh., Budde. and others. 'to put them to the ban.' The rout
will thus have extended only over the period before and after
sunset.

20. A corrupt and unintelligible text is responsible for what
appears in our version as a selfish abuse of authority on David's
part. The original probably told that, besides recovering their
own property, David and his men captured an enormous loot, the
destination of which we hear of later (verses 26 ff.).

21 is David's spoil. And David came to the two hundred men, which were so faint that they could not follow David, whom also they had made to abide at the brook Besor : and they went forth to meet David, and to meet the people that were with him : and when David came
22 near to the people, he saluted them. Then answered all the wicked men and men of Belial, of those that went with David, and said, Because they went not with us, we will not give them aught of the spoil that we have recovered, save to every man his wife and his children,
23 that they may lead them away, and depart. Then said David, Ye shall not do so, my brethren, with that which the LORD hath given unto us, who hath preserved us, and delivered the troop that came against us into our
24 hand. And who will hearken unto you in this matter ? for as his share is that goeth down to the battle, so shall his share be that tarrieth by the stuff : they shall share

---

21. The last clause should read : 'and they came near to the people (the returning troop) and saluted them.'

xxx. 22-25. An interesting illustration of the creation of a precedent in Hebrew law, regulating the equitable division of booty captured in war.

23. with that which the LORD hath given unto us, who, &c. : this cannot fairly be got from the received text. Read, as suggested by LXX : 'after that the LORD hath wrought for (or helped) us, and hath preserved us,' &c. 'In any case we have a warning against ingratitude to God ; everywhere gratitude manifests itself in kindness to others, cf. xi. 13' (Budde).

24 f. The equitable distribution here formulated became a **statute and an ordinance for Israel** from this time forward. Notwithstanding the explicit account given of the origin of this statute, its introduction in the course of time was ascribed to Moses by one of those legal fictions characteristic of all ancient systems of jurisprudence. see Num. xxxi. 27 ff., with Gray's *Commentary* (Intern. Crit. Series), where numerous parallels from other systems are given. The light which is thereby thrown upon the growth of the 'Mosaic' legislation is ably discussed by W. R. Smith in *OTJC.*[2] 386 f,

alike. And it was so from that day forward, that he 25
made it a statute and an ordinance for Israel, unto this
day.

And when David came to Ziklag, he sent of the spoil 26
unto the elders of Judah, even to his friends, saying,
Behold a present for you of the spoil of the enemies of
the LORD; to them which were in Beth-el, and to them 27
which were in Ramoth of the South, and to them which
were in Jattir; and to them which were in Aroer, and to 28
them which were in Siphmoth, and to them which were in
Eshtemoa; and to them which were in Racal, and to 29
them which were in the cities of the Jerahmeelites, and
to them which were in the cities of the Kenites; and to 30
them which were in Hormah, and to them which were
in Cor-ashan, and to them which were in Athach; and 31
to them which were in Hebron, and to all the places
where David himself and his men were wont to haunt.

---

xxx. 26-31. *David's politic disposal of his share of the spoil.*

26. a present: *lit.* 'a blessing' (R. V. marg.), in the secondary
sense of this word. the gift that accompanied the message of good-
will, as x. 27.

27 ff. Beth-el, not the well-known Benjamite city, but a town
in Southern Judah, named, under a slightly different form, in
1 Chron. iv. 30 along with Hormah and Ziklag. **Ramoth,** better
Ramah (LXX), lay in the territory of Simeon (Joshua xix. 8). **Jattir**
and **Eshtemoa,** also Joshua xv. 48, xxi. 14. **Aroer,** the modern
Ararah in the wady of that name, south-east of Beer-sheba. For
Racal read, with LXX, Carmel. The **Jerahmeelites** and the
Kenites have been already met with as clans of the Negeb (xxvii.
10). **Hormah,** not yet identified, is frequently mentioned elsewhere
among the towns of the extreme south. **Cor-ashan,** better, as
margin, Bor-ashan. is a corruption of Beer-sheba (LXX. B), which
would scarcely have been omitted. **Hebron,** the chief city of
Judah. and soon to be David's first capital. **Siphmoth** and **Athach**
have not been identified.

In this distribution of the loot among **all the places where
David himself and his men were wont to haunt,** David showed
his talent for diplomacy, as well as his gratitude to those who had

31 Now the Philistines fought against Israel : and the
    men of Israel fled from before the Philistines, and fell
2 down slain in mount Gilboa.   And the Philistines
    followed hard upon Saul and upon his sons ; and the
    Philistines slew Jonathan, and Abinadab, and Malchi-
3 shua, the sons of Saul.   And the battle went sore against
    Saul, and the archers overtook him ; and he was greatly
4 distressed by reason of the archers.   Then said Saul to
    his armourbearer, Draw thy sword, and thrust me through
    therewith ; lest these uncircumcised come and thrust me
    through, and abuse me.   But his armourbearer would

___

befriended him in the past. His temporary alliance with the
Philistines was no doubt much criticized, and it was wise, in view
of future contingencies, to take the first opportunity of removing
all suspicion of his loyalty to his own tribe of Judah, at least, and
the allied clans.

(e) xxxi. *The death of Saul and Jonathan on Mount Gilboa.*
In the original sequence of M. the story of Saul's visit to En-dor
now followed as the prelude to ch. xxxi (see above). The account
here given of Saul's tragic end—the relation of which to the
contents of 2 Sam. i. 6 ff. will be discussed later—is also found
with slight variations, representing in some cases a purer text, in
1 Chron. x. 1–12.

2. Abinadab is identified by the Revisers (note marg.) with
Ishvi of xiv. 49, but the latter was there shown to be a variant
for Ish-baal (Ish-bosheth), who does not appear to have been
present on Gilboa.

3. and he was greatly distressed, &c.: the words of the
original seem to denote mental distress, as if the once courageous
king were paralysed with fear, but the text is open to question.
The A. V. rendering 'and he was sore wounded of the archers,'
though supported by the LXX, cannot be got from the received
text, yet this or something similar is implied by the appeal of
verse 4.

4. thrust me through, and abuse me: this can only mean
that Saul dreaded insult to his dead body by mutilation or otherwise. But this contingency could not be evaded by his being
slain by a Hebrew rather than by a Philistine. Hence the
preference is generally given to the reading of 1 Chron. x. 4,
which omits the first clause. This makes the wounded king dread
the possibility of being taken alive to be made a mock or sport of,

not; for he was sore afraid. Therefore Saul took his sword, and fell upon it. And when his armourbearer 5 saw that Saul was dead, he likewise fell upon his sword, and died with him. So Saul died, and his three sons, 6 and his armourbearer, and all his men, that same day together. And when the men of Israel that were on 7 the other side of the valley, and they that were beyond Jordan, saw that the men of Israel fled, and that Saul and his sons were dead, they forsook the cities, and fled; and the Philistines came and dwelt in them.

And it came to pass on the morrow, when the Philis- 8 tines came to strip the slain, that they found Saul and his three sons fallen in mount Gilboa. And they cut off 9 his head, and stripped off his armour, and sent into the land of the Philistines round about, to carry the tidings unto the house of their idols, and to the people. And 10 they put his armour in the house of the Ashtaroth : and they fastened his body to the wall of Beth-shan. And 11

---

like Samson, by the Philistines. Cases of suicide are remarkably rare in Scripture, cf. 2 Sam xvii. 23 (Ahithophel), 1 Kings xvi. 18 (Zimri), Matt. xxvii. 5 (Judas Iscariot). The later views on the subject of suicide will be found in Josephus, *Wars of the Jews*, III. viii. 5.

7. on the other side of the valley : the country to the north of the valley of Jezreel (cf. Hos. i. 5). The next clause is wanting in Chronicles (which see), and should be dropped here, as it is extremely improbable that the Philistines occupied (see end of verse) any part of the trans-Jordanic territory.

9. unto the house of their idols : the original and more expressive reading is that of Chronicles and the LXX, which omits 'the house of.'

10. the house of the Ashtaroth : rather, 'the temple of Astarte,' probably at Ashkelon (Herod. i. 105). The Chronicler records that 'they fastened his skull to the house of Dagon,' but this appears to be merely a false reading of the latter half of this verse.

Beth-shan : the modern *Beisān*, an important centre commanding the Jordan valley and the valley of Jezreel. The spot selected was probably above the principal gate, opening on the

when the inhabitants of Jabesh-gilead heard concerning him that which the Philistines had done to Saul,
12 all the valiant men arose, and went all night, and
took the body of Saul and the bodies of his sons from
the wall of Beth-shan ; and they came to Jabesh, and
13 burnt them there. And they took their bones, and
buried them under the tamarisk tree in Jabesh, and
fasted seven days.

---

sūk, or market-place, *outside* the walls. Hence the practicability
of the exploit recorded 2 Sam. xxi. 12 (which see).

11 ff. These verses tell of the gratitude of the men of Jabesh-
gilead, who had not forgotten what they owed to Saul (xi. 1 ff.).

12. and burnt them there : it is impossible that this can be the
true reading. The idea of burning dead bodies was altogether
abhorrent to the eschatological thought of the time (Amos ii. 1).
Read, with Klostermann, Budde, and others, by a slight change :
'and made lamentation for them there,' the invariable prelude to
burial (xxv. 1, xxviii. 3). This involves reading 'and they took
their bodies' in verse 13. After the corrupt reading 'burnt them'
had crept in, the substitution of 'bones' for 'bodies' will have
been made more easy by the note in 2 Sam. xxi. 12, where the
mention of 'the bones of Saul and Jonathan' is quite in place.

13. and fasted seven days : for fasting as an expression of
mourning, cf. 2 Sam. i. 12, iii. 35, and xii. 16.

THE

SECOND BOOK OF SAMUEL

[M] AND it came to pass after the death of Saul, when **1**
David was returned from the slaughter of the Amalekites,

D. 2 Sam. i–viii. *David installed as King, first of Judah,*
then of all Israel.

The first and more detailed portion of this subdivision tells the
story of seven eventful years in the life of David.   The authority
is still in the main the early document which forms, as we have
seen, the groundwork of the whole of the second division of the
Books of Samuel.   After recording David's elevation to the throne
of the reunited kingdom, the compiler contents himself with giving
a number of historical extracts somewhat loosely joined together,
and finally brings his book to a close with a summary record of
David's wars and of the chief officials of his court (see Introduction,
sects. iv and v).   Ch. vii is of an entirely different cast from the
rest, and, as will appear, comes from a source apart.   The whole
falls naturally into five sections, the extent and contents of which
are given below.

(*a*) Ch. i.   *How David received the tidings of Saul's death, with his*
lament over Saul and Jonathan.
In the first part of this chapter we have an account of the
manner of Saul's death, which in several points contradicts that
given in the preceding chapter (see the notes).   The explanation
that first occurs to one is that the Amalekite youth, prowling on
the battlefield in search of loot, came upon the body of Saul *after*
the events of 1 Sam. xxxi. 4 f., but *before* the Philistines had
arrived 'on the morrow to strip the slain' (*ibid.* 8).   Taking the
crown and the armlet from the person of the dead king, he carried
these in all haste to David, for whose benefit, in the hope of
a substantial reward (see iv. 10), *he concocted the story of the text.*
A closer examination, however, throws grave doubts upon this,
in itself plausible, relation of the two accounts—the one, fact, the
other, falsehood.   (1) Nothing in the narrative gives the slightest
indication that the messenger was romancing ; (2) the trustworthy
passage, iv. 9 ff.—from the same source as ch. xxxi—which com-
pares the deserts of this Amalekite with those of the murderers of
Ish-bosheth, does not represent the former as claiming to have

2 and David had abode two days in Ziklag; it came even
to pass on the third day, that, behold, a man came out
of the camp from Saul with his clothes rent, and earth
upon his head: and so it was, when he came to David,
3 that he fell to the earth, and did obeisance.   And David
said unto him, From whence comest thou?   And he said
4 unto him, Out of the camp of Israel am I escaped.   And
David said unto him, How went the matter?   I pray thee,
tell me.   And he answered, The people are fled from the
battle, and many of the people also are fallen and dead;
5 and Saul and Jonathan his son are dead also.   And David
said unto the young man that told him, How knowest thou
6 that Saul and Jonathan his son be dead?   [T] And the
young man that told him said, As I happened by chance
upon mount Gilboa, behold, Saul leaned upon his spear;
and, lo, the chariots and the horsemen followed hard after
7 him.   And when he looked behind him, he saw me, and

killed Saul, which would have made the comparison still more
apposite.   Indeed the words of iv. 11, 'how much more,' seem to
exclude this possibility, and in the previous verse David claims to
have slain the Amalekite with his own hand (contrast i. 15).   On
the whole, therefore, it is better with almost all recent critics to
regard verses 6-10, 13-16, at least, as representing a variant
tradition regarding the last moments of the unfortunate king, and
David's reception of the messenger.   Verse 5 will then form the
editorial joining of the two sources, M and T, while 1-4, 11, 12,
17 ff. will represent a fairly continuous narrative, in which Jonathan
is throughout associated with Saul, and from which the Amalekite
has disappeared.

 2. a man came out of the camp: presumably a Hebrew
soldier.   Cf. the identical description of the messenger in 1 Sam.
iv. 12, and note the similar artistic form of the messages, *ibid.* 17
and verse 4 below.   In both cases the reply leads up to a climax,
there the capture of the Ark, here the death of Saul and Jonathan.

 6 ff. The tradition here inserted gives quite a different picture
of Saul's condition at the close of the battle from that found in
1 Sam. xxxi. 3 ff. (1) The chariots and the horsemen take the
place of the archers of the older narrative; (2) there Saul is
undoubtedly represented as wounded (see note on xxxi. 3), here

called unto me.   And I answered, Here am I.   And he 8
said unto me, Who art thou?   And I answered him, I am
an Amalekite.   And he said unto me, Stand, I pray thee, 9
beside me, and slay me, for anguish hath taken hold of
me; because my life is yet whole in me.   So I stood 10
beside him, and slew him, because I was sure that he
could not live after that he was fallen: and I took the
crown that was upon his head, and the bracelet that was
on his arm, and have brought them hither unto my lord.
[M] Then David took hold on his clothes, and rent them; 11
and likewise all the men that were with him: and they 12
mourned, and wept, and fasted until even, for Saul, and
for Jonathan his son, and for the people of the LORD,
and for the house of Israel; because they were fallen by
the sword.   [T] And David said unto the young man that 13
told him, Whence art thou?   And he answered, I am the
son of a stranger, an Amalekite.   And David said unto 14

---

as standing leaning on his spear apparently unhurt (verse 9 end),
but seized with giddiness or cramp.

9. The meaning of the word rendered **anguish** is quite uncertain; 'cramp,' and 'dizziness' or 'giddiness' (R.V. marg.)
have been proposed.   The last clause appears, as we have seen,
to indicate that Saul was otherwise uninjured.

10. after that he was fallen: apparently as the result of the
giddiness, even as he talked with the Amalekite.

the bracelet: rather, 'armlet,' an ornament worn on the
upper part of the arm.   The armlet and the diadem are again
named together as insignia of royalty in the true text of 2 Kings
xi. 12, see Skinner's Commentary (Century Bible).

12. the people of the LORD must here, if the text is correct,
denote the army, the LORD's 'consecrated ones' (see on 1 Sam.
xiii. 9), but probably, in view of the following clause, we should
read with LXX, 'the people of Judah.'

13. I am the son of a stranger (Heb. *gēr*): the technical term
for a non-Israelite admitted to a modified civil status with corresponding rights.   See 'Stranger and Sojourner,' *EBi.* iv, and
Bertholet's standard treatise, *Die Stellung der Israeliten zu den
Fremden*, 29 ff., where this passage is fully discussed.

O

him, How wast thou not afraid to put forth thine hand to
15 destroy the LORD's anointed? And David called one of
the young men, and said, Go near, and fall upon him.
16 And he smote him that he died. And David said unto
him, Thy blood be upon thy head; for thy mouth hath
testified against thee, saying, I have slain the LORD's
anointed.

17   [M] And David lamented with this lamentation over
18 Saul and over Jonathan his son: and he bade them

---

15 f. The older tradition in iv. 9 f. represents David as personally inflicting the death penalty upon the 'man' (verse 2) for
presuming that David would rejoice in his country's loss and for
hinting, perhaps, at a suitable reward.

i. 17-27.   *David's lament over Saul and Jonathan.*

That David was in truth the author of this noble elegy, as of
the shorter lament for Abner (iii. 3 f.), is allowed by all save a few
recent critics of the extremer sort. Next to the Song of Deborah
in Judges v, it is the oldest surviving specimen of early Hebrew
poetry of moderate extent. At first transmitted orally, we may
suppose, it found a place in the national collection of poetry,
which bore the title of the Book of Jashar (see on verse 18), from
which it was probably extracted by the author of M. Unfortunately
the text in many places is corrupt beyond hope of recovery. Only
a few of the more probable of the emendations suggested by
recent scholars can find a place in the brief notes that follow.
With all this uncertainty in points of detail, the poem stands out
as the genuine outpouring of a noble heart, a heart too great to
harbour one selfish thought in this dark hour of his country's
humiliation. This Hebrew *In Memoriam* falls easily into two
parts. In the first (verses 19-22), the poet gives expression
to the thought of the death of Saul and Jonathan as a crowning
misfortune to the nation of Israel. In the second (23-27), the
personal virtues of the fallen heroes are commemorated, the poem
reaching its most personal and most passionate note in David's
immortal tribute to the love of his 'brother,' Jonathan.

17. David lamented with this lamentation: better, 'chanted
this lament,' in Hebrew 'this ḳinā'—the technical term for the
lament for the dead chanted by professional mourners (2 Chron.
xxxv. 25), usually women (Jer. ix. 7).

18. By inserting the words 'the song of' before 'the bow,' the
Revisers have sought to make sense of an unintelligible text,
perpetuating an unfounded conjecture that the poem was known

teach the children of Judah *the song of* the bow : behold,
it is written in the book of Jashar.

> Thy glory, O Israel, is slain upon thy high places !   19
> How are the mighty fallen !
> Tell it not in Gath;   20
> Publish it not in the streets of Ashkelon ;
> Lest the daughters of the Philistines rejoice,
> Lest the daughters of the uncircumcised triumph.
> Ye mountains of Gilboa,   21

---

as ' the song of the bow ' from the incidental reference in verse 22.
Three points are now generally conceded : (1) the two halves of
the verse have been transposed, the second half belonging rather
to the preceding verse ; (2) the verb ' and he said ' (R.V. wrongly :
'and he bade them') must refer to and introduce the lament itself,
as in iii. 33 ; (3) the words that follow this verb are a corruption of
the first line or lines of the elegy (see below).

the book of Jashar : R.V. marg. 'the book of The Upright.'
No completely satisfactory explanation of the name has yet been
found.   From the other two extracts from the same source,
Joshua x. 12-14 and 1 Kings viii. 12 f. according to the true text
(for which see Skinner's Commentary in this series), it was
evidently a collection of national poetry, compiled in or soon after
the reign of Solomon.   The clause, as has just been said, properly
forms the conclusion of verse 17.

19. The opening line or *stichos* is almost certainly to be found
in the first half of the preceding verse.   The poem appears to run
in quatrains, and Klostermann's emendation has been generally
approved, thus : ' And he said (cf. iii. 33ᵃ) :

> Hear, O Judah, hard things,
> Be grieved, O Israel.
> Upon thy heights (lie) the slain ;
> How are the mighty fallen ! '

The changes in the received text required to give this excellent
sense do not extend beyond one or two consonants.

20. The second quatrain anticipates the receipt of the evil
tidings in the cities of the Philistines, and the songs of the women
at the victors' home-coming (cf. 1 Sam. xviii. 6).   The two
distichs of which it is composed afford an excellent illustration of
the parallelism, or repetition of the same thought in a somewhat
different form, which is the outstanding characteristic of Hebrew
poetry.

Let there be no dew nor rain upon you, neither
   fields of offerings :
For there the shield of the mighty was vilely cast
   away,
The shield of Saul, not anointed with oil.

22   From the blood of the slain, from the fat of the
   mighty,
The bow of Jonathan turned not back,
And the sword of Saul returned not empty.

23   Saul and Jonathan were lovely and pleasant in their
   lives,
And in their death they were not divided ;
They were swifter than eagles,
They were stronger than lions.

24   Ye daughters of Israel, weep over Saul,
Who clothed you in scarlet delicately,

---

21. In the third quatrain a curse is pronounced upon the. scene
of the disaster.

fields of offerings : a doubtful reading, and moreover most
inappropriate to the rock-strewn ridge of Gilboa. 'Mountains of
death' (Lucian and Old Lat.), or 'fields of death' (H. P. Smith),
would be more in place.

not anointed with oil : i.e. to keep the leather in good
condition, a trivial thought ! Perhaps, with Budde, we should
omit 'not,' and read : 'the shield of Saul, (once) anointed with
oil,' referring to the formal consecration of the warrior and his
weapons at the opening of a campaign (Isa. xxi. 5 ; see on I Sam.
xxi. 5).

22. The brave deeds of Saul and Jonathan are now commemorated. The first line of R. V. should be printed in two lines, as
the parallelism and the four-line (quatrain) measure require.

23 ff. The second part is devoted to the personal characteristics
of the two heroes, first together, then Saul and Jonathan indi-
vidually. The first distich should be rendered :

Saul and Jonathan, the loved and the lovely,
(As) in life, so in death, they were not divided.

The points of comparison in the second distich are the swiftness
and irresistibleness of the heroes' attack.

24. The public lamentation for the dead was the special busi-

Who put ornaments of gold upon your apparel.

How are the mighty fallen in the midst of the battle ! 25
Jonathan is slain upon thy high places.

I am distressed for thee, my brother Jonathan: ·26
Very pleasant hast thou been unto me:
Thy love to me was wonderful,
Passing the love,of women.

How are the mighty fallen,   27
And the weapons of war perished !

And it came to pass after this, that David inquired of 2

---

ness of the women, who are here reminded of their share in the spoil which Saul had assigned them.

25. The first distich leads up to the climax of the elegy, the passionate outburst of grief over the untimely fate of Jonathan. The second is now so mutilated as to occupy but a single line, and can only be conjecturally restored. The reference to verse 19 generally found in the words **is slain upon thy high places** is too remote. The same consonants yield 'by thy death (Lucian, Budde) is pierced'; hence we read tentatively:

How are the mighty fallen
In the midst of the battle !
Jonathan, my heart (?) by thy death
Is pierced through.

This preserves the alternation of three and two beats characteristic of the Hebrew elegiac verse.

26. The text, as elsewhere, is not free from difficulty. **Jonathan**, in the first line, exceeds the measure and is not required.

27. The lament ends with a couplet repeating the main theme. The parallelism suggests that in **the weapons of war** we have a figure for Saul and Jonathan.

As has frequently been pointed out, the poem is marked by an entire absence of religious feeling. 'The feeling expressed by it is purely human' (Driver), and in this characteristic we have the best guarantee of its genuineness. No later poet, writing when the character of David had begun to be idealized—as was soon the case—would have put into David's mouth sentiments which, exquisitely tender as they are, are so entirely secular.

(*b*) ii—iv. *David, King of Judah in Hebron, and the story of the Civil War.*

The fragmentary nature of the record which the compiler of

the LORD, saying, Shall I go up into any of the cities of
Judah? And the LORD said unto him, Go up. And
David said, Whither shall I go up? And he said, Unto
2 Hebron.   So David went up thither, and his two wives
also, Ahinoam the Jezreelitess, and Abigail the wife of
3 Nabal the Carmelite.   And his men that were with him
did David bring up, every man with his household : and
4 they dwelt in the cities of Hebron.   And the men of
Judah came, and there they anointed David king over
the house of Judah.

And they told David, saying, The men of Jabesh-gilead
5 were they that buried Saul.   And David sent messengers
unto the men of Jabesh-gilead, and said unto them,

Samuel has here preserved for us renders it no longer possible to
construct a thoroughly consistent account of the events of the
critical period during which David made himself master of the
united tribes of Israel.   Especially difficult is the question of his
relations with the victorious Philistines.   These, we may be sure,
did not stand aside in complacent indifference while David fought
his way to the throne.   Rather, we must suppose that at first
David continued as before in a position of dependence, as king by
the grace of the Philistines, and that only when he had strengthened his position by war and diplomacy did he break with his
powerful suzerains.

ii. 1-4ᵃ. *David anointed in Hebron as king over the house of
Judah.*

1. David now, as always before taking any important step in
his career, seeks to ascertain the Divine will by means of the
ephod-oracle.   Note the series of questions as in 1 Sam. xxiii. 2 ff.,
9 ff., xxx. 7 f., where see notes.

Hebron, now *El-Khalil* (the friend)—a contraction for 'the
city of the friend of God,' viz. Abraham—about twenty miles by road
from Jerusalem, was the chief city of Judah, and, as the name
implies, the centre of the league or confederation of the clans of
Judah, Caleb, &c.

4. His own clansmen, as we should expect, were the first to
recognize in David the man whom the time required.   For the
significance of the rite of anointing, see on 1 Sam. x. 1.

ii. 4ᵇ-7 *David's message of thanks to the men of Jabesh-gilead*
(cf. 1 Sam. xxxi. 11 ff. with the notes).

Blessed be ye of the LORD, that ye have shewed this
kindness unto your lord, even unto Saul, and have buried
him.   And now the LORD shew kindness and truth unto 6
you : and I also will requite you this kindness, because
ye have done this thing. · Now therefore let your hands 7
be strong, and be ye valiant : for Saul your lord is dead,
and also the house of Judah have anointed me king over
them.

Now Abner the son of Ner, captain of Saul's host, had 8
taken Ish-bosheth the son of Saul, and brought him over
to Mahanaim ; and he made him king over Gilead, and 9
over the Ashurites, and over Jezreel, and over Ephraim,
and over Benjamin, and over all Israel.   (Ish-bosheth 10
Saul's son was forty years old when he began to reign

5. this kindness : better, 'this pious act '; the proper burial of
the dead was regarded by the Semites, as by other ancient peoples,
as a true act of piety.

7. In sending this royal message David was doubtless actuated
by motives of policy as well as by gratitude.   Here, for the first
time, he claims to be Saul's legitimate successor, and hopes for the
loyal support of the men of Gilead.

ii. 8-11. *Abner sets up a rival king.*

8. Ish-bosheth : 'man of shame,' a disguised and disfigured form
of the name Ish-baal (see 1 Chron. viii. 33, ix. 39).   In early times
the title *ba'al* (lord) was quite innocently applied to Yahweh, but
on account of the associations of the title with the Canaanite deities
and their worship (see on 1 Sam. vii. 4) this application was
afterwards discontinued.   To mark their abhorrence of the name
later editors substituted in this and other proper names the word
for 'shame.'   Cf. Mephibosheth (iv. 4), which shows a double
disguise.

Mahanaim lay to the north of the Jabbok (Gen. xxxii. 2), but
the exact site is still in dispute.   *Mahneh* and *Ajlun* have the
best claims (see the dictionaries).   In Solomon's day it was still,
as here, the capital of Gilead (1 Kings iv. 14).

9. over the Ashurites : read, 'the Asherites' (Judges i. 32),
the men of Asher, the dominant tribe north of the great plain.
The 'Geshurites' of R. V. marg. are excluded by the fact that
they had their own king (iii. 3).

10 f. The part within parentheses so manifestly breaks the

over Israel, and he reigned two years.) , But the house
11 of Judah followed David.   And the time that David was
king in Hebron over the house of Judah was seven years
and six months.

12   And Abner the son of Ner, and the servants of
Ish-bosheth the son of Saul, went out from Mahanaim
13 to Gibeon.· And Joab the son of Zeruiah, and the
servants of David, went out, and met them by the pool
of Gibeon; and they sat down, the one on the one side
of the pool, and the other on the other side of the pool.
14 And Abner·said to Joab, Let the young men, I pray thee,
arise and play before us.   And Joab said, Let them arise.
15 Then they arose and went over by number; twelve for
Benjamin, and for Ish-bosheth the son of Saul, and
16 twelve of the servants of David.   And they caught every
one his fellow by the head, and *thrust* his sword in his

---

connexion between 9 and 10[b], that it must be taken along with
the similar note in verse 11 as an editorial insertion (cf. v. 4 f.).
It is very doubtful if Saul could have had a younger son of such
mature age.   In any case his reign must have more nearly coin-
cided with that of David in Hebron than is here stated.

ii. 12-32. *The first battle of the Civil War and the death of Asahel.*

12. Gibeon: now *El-Jib,* in Benjamin, about six miles north-
west of Jerusalem.   Probably Ish-bosheth had come to an understanding with the Philistines by which, under their suzerainty,
he was acknowledged as king over North Israel. By playing off
the two vassal-kings of the north and the south against each
other, the Philistines no doubt hoped to maintain their hold over
the country.

13. Joab the son of Zeruiah, David's nephew (see on 1 Sam.
xxvi. 6)—the first appearance on the scene of David's masterful
but devoted general, who plays so prominent a part in the whole
after history of the time.

14 f. Abner proposes a display of mimic warfare. Such, rather
than a proposal to settle the dispute by a serious combat, seems
the meaning of the words used. Unfortunately the mimic display
turned to stern reality.

16. The two parties, apparently, were to contend in pairs,
a man from either side. But at the first onset each combatant

fellow's side; so they fell down together: wherefore that place was called Helkath-hazzurim, which is in Gibeon. And the battle was very sore that day; and Abner was 17 beaten, and the men of Israel, before the servants of David. And the three sons of Zeruiah were there, Joab, 18 and Abishai, and Asahel: and Asahel was as light of foot as a wild roe. And Asahel pursued after Abner; 19 and in going he turned not to the right hand nor to the left from following Abner. Then Abner looked behind 20 him, and said, Is it thou, Asahel? And he answered, It is I. And Abner said to him, Turn thee aside to thy 21 right hand or to thy left, and lay thee hold on one of the young men, and take ·thee his armour. But Asahel would not turn aside from following of him. And Abner 22 said again to Asahel, Turn thee aside from following me: wherefore should I smite thee to the ground? how then should I hold up my face to Joab thy brother? Howbeit 23 he refused to turn aside: wherefore Abner with the hinder end of the spear smote him in the belly, that the spear came out behind him; and he fell down there, and died

treacherously 'caught his opponent by the head with his hand' (so LXX), and plunged his sword into his side, the whole twenty-four falling together.

Helkath-hazzurim: 'the field of sword-edges' (Driver; cf. R. V. marg. and Ps. lxxxix. 43). The LXX read Helkath-hazzodim 'the field of the plotters,' which is more appropriate.

17. On seeing the tragic issue of the 'play,' the main body of troops on either side at once joined battle. The narrator's interest, however, is centred in an incident that followed, out of which were to develop important results for the future.

21 ff. Asahel rejects the advice of the older and more experienced swordsman to be content with a lesser prey, and falls a victim to his rashness.

23. with the hinder end of the spear: read, by a slight change, 'Abner smote him with a backward stroke,' &c. (Klostermann). Without slackening his pace, Abner delivers a powerful thrust backwards with his long sharp-pointed spear, piercing his pursuer through and through.

in the same place : and it came to pass, that as many as
came to the place where Asahel fell down and died stood
24 still. · But Joab and Abishai pursued after Abner : and
the sun went down when they were come to the hill of
Ammah, that lieth before Giah by the way of the wilder-
25 ness of Gibeon.   And the children of Benjamin gathered
themselves together after Abner, and became one band,
26 and stood on the top of an hill.   Then Abner called to
Joab, and said, Shall the sword devour for ever? knowest thou not that it will be bitterness in the latter end?
how long shall it be then, ere thou bid the people return
27 from following their brethren? And Joab said, As God
liveth, if thou hadst not spoken, surely then in the
morning the people had gone away, nor followed every
28 one his brother.   So Joab blew the trumpet, and all the
people stood still, and pursued after Israel no more,
29 neither fought they any more.   And Abner and his men
went all that night through the Arabah ; and they passed
over Jordan, and went through all Bithron, and came to
30 Mahanaim.   And Joab returned from following Abner :
and when he had gathered all the people together, there
lacked of David's servants nineteen men and Asahel.

24. The topography is obscured by the uncertainty of the text.
Neither **the hill of Ammah** nor **Giah** is mentioned elsewhere.

25. on the top of an hill: read, ' on the top of the hill of
Ammah.'

26. Abner appeals to Joab to stay the pursuit and so prevent
further bloodshed.   The Revisers, by their marginal reference to
Abner's proposal in verse 14, interpret Joab's answer as throwing
the blame for the day's work on the former.   The context, however, shows that ' Joab, though ruthless, is not altogether without
conscience,' since he declares that, but for Abner's intervention
now, he would have continued the pursuit until next morning.

29. through (i. e. along) **the Arabah** or Jordan valley (see on
1 Sam. xxiii. 24).   Crossing the Jordan they followed the course
of the **Bithron** (*lit.* 'ravine'), probably a narrow valley at the
head of which stood Mahanaim (cf. verse 8 above).

But the servants of David had smitten of Benjamin, and 31
of Abner's men, *so that* three hundred and threescore
men died.   And they took up Asahel, and buried him 32
in the sepulchre of his father, which was in Beth-lehem.
And Joab and his men went all night, and the day brake
upon them at Hebron.

[R] Now there was long war between the house of Saul 3
and the house of David: and David waxed stronger and
stronger, but the house of Saul waxed weaker and weaker.
And unto David were sons born in Hebron: and his 2
firstborn was Amnon, of Ahinoam the Jezreelitess; and 3
his second, Chileab, of Abigail the wife of Nabal the
Carmelite; and the third, Absalom the son of Maacah
the daughter of Talmai king of Geshur; and the fourth, 4
Adonijah the son of Abital; and the fifth, Shephatiah
the son of Abital; and the sixth, Ithream, of Eglah 5
David's wife.   These were born to David in Hebron.

[M] And it came to pass, while there was war between 6
the house of Saul and the house of David, that Abner

---

iii. **1.** A statement, probably from the pen of the compiler,
summarizing the fuller record of the Civil War which lay before
him in his source (M).

2-5. A family register (1 Chron. iii. 1-4) similar to that given
v. 13-16, both owing their present form, in all probability, to the
compiler (R).   In addition to the two wives whom he had at the
date of his installation (ii. 2), David took to himself other four,
each of the six bearing him one son.   The eldest was **Amnon**,
whom we shall meet later (xiii. 1 ff.); **Chileab** has the same
consonants as Caleb, recalling the fact that his mother was of the
clan of the Calebites (1 Sam. xxv. 3).   **Adonijah** became in the
course of events Solomon's rival for the throne (1 Kings i. 4 ff.).

3. Geshur: a petty kingdom in the district now known as the
Jaulān, N. E. of the Sea of Galilee (cf. on x. 6).

iii. **6-16.** *Abner's quarrel with Ish-baal and its consequences.*

6. Abner made himself strong in the house of Saul: the
precise meaning is doubtful; either, as R. V. marg.. he was

7 made himself strong in the house of Saul.   Now Saul had
a concubine, whose name was Rizpah, the daughter of
Aiah : and *Ish-bosheth* said to Abner, Wherefore hast thou
8 gone in unto my father's concubine?   Then was Abner
very wroth for the words of Ish-bosheth, and said, Am I
a dog's head that belongeth to Judah?   This day do I
shew kindness unto the house of Saul thy father, to his
brethren, and to his friends, and have not delivered thee
into the hand of David, and yet thou chargest me this
9 day with a fault concerning this woman.   God do so to
Abner, and more also, if, as the Lord hath sworn to
10 David, I do not even so to him; to translate the
kingdom from the house of Saul, and to set up the
throne of David over Israel and over Judah, from Dan
11 even to Beer-sheba.   And he could not answer Abner
another word, because he feared him.

---

a tower of strength in defence of the house of Saul, a sense
which the verb has in x. 12 ('let us play the man for '), or showed
himself powerful, overbearing in connexion with the house or
party of Saul.   The latter gives a better introduction to the
particular case of arrogance about to be related.

7 f. Rizpah, the daughter of Aiah : the heroine of the tragedy
of ch. xxi.   Ish-baal's remonstrance was no doubt based on other
than moral grounds (see note on xii. 8), although it suited Abner
to affect to regard it as a trifling affair of morals, which should
never have been brought up against a man of his position and
merits.

8. that belongeth to Judah : wanting in LXX, and generally
regarded as an addition here by a scribe who read *keleb* (dog) as
kāleb—the old Hebrew text had no vowels —i. e. Caleb, the clan
afterwards incorporated with the tribe of Judah.

concerning this woman : better, with LXX, 'concerning
a woman,' a mere peccadillo, as explained above.

9 f. as the LORD hath sworn to David : no trace of the
promise here referred to (cf. verse 18, v. 2) is now found in this
document (M).   Budde would connect it with the unrecorded
oracle given by Ahimelech, see 1 Sam. xxii. 10, 13, 15.

11. A brief but significant illustration of the character and
position of this *roi fainéant*.

And Abner sent messengers to David on his behalf, 12 saying, Whose is the land? saying *also*, Make thy league with me, and, behold, my hand shall be with thee, to bring about all Israel unto thee. And he said, Well; I 13 will make a league with thee: but one thing I require of thee, that is, thou shalt not see my face, except thou first bring Michal Saul's daughter, when thou comest to see my face. And David sent messengers to Ish-bosheth 14 Saul's son, saying, Deliver me my wife Michal, whom I betrothed to me for an hundred foreskins of the Philistines. And Ish-bosheth sent, and took her from her 15 husband, even from Paltiel the son of Laish. And her 16 husband went with her, weeping as he went, and followed her to Bahurim. Then said Abner unto him, Go, return: and he returned.

And Abner had communication with the elders of 17 Israel, saying, In times past ye sought for David to be king over you: now then do it: for the LORD hath spoken of 18 David, saying, By the hand of my servant David I will save my people Israel out of the hand of the Philistines,

---

12. Smarting under the insult of his puppet-king, Abner opens communications with David. With Klostermann and Budde we should probably read thus: 'And Abner sent messengers to David, saying, Under my hand (a slight emendation of **on his behalf**) is the land to give it to whom I please.' This forms an admirable introduction to what follows, and is in keeping with Abner's estimate of himself in the preceding verses.

13. David makes the restoration of Michal the indispensable preliminary to further negotiations. Apart from the question of legal rights, this demand was a matter of sound policy as strengthening his claim to be recognized as Saul's successor.

15. Paltiel the son of Laish: see on 1 Sam. xxv. 44.

16. A masterly miniature with its inimitable contrast between the meek, broken-hearted husband and the curt, unsympathetic soldier. For **Bahurim** see on xvi 5, xvii. 20.

iii. 17-27. *The progress of the negotiations, ending in the treacherous murder of Abner by Joab.*

19 and out of the hand of all their enemies. And Abner
also spake in the ears of Benjamin : and Abner went also
to speak in the ears of David in Hebron all that seemed
20 good to Israel, and to the whole house of Benjamin. So
Abner came to David to Hebron, and twenty men with
him. And David made Abner and the men that were
21 with him a feast. And Abner said unto David, I will
arise and go, and will gather all Israel unto my lord the
king, that they may make a covenant with thee, and that
thou mayest reign over all that thy soul desireth. And
22 David sent Abner away ; and he went in peace. And,
behold, the servants of David and Joab came from a
foray, and brought in a great spoil with them : but Abner
was not with David in Hebron; for he had sent him
23 away, and he was gone in peace. When Joab and all
the host that was with him were come, they told Joab,
saying, Abner the son of Ner came to the king, and he
24 hath sent him away, and he is gone in peace. Then
Joab came to the king, and said, What hast thou done?
behold, Abner came unto thee; why is it that thou hast
25 sent him away, and he is quite gone? Thou knowest
Abner the son of Ner, that he came to deceive thee, and
to know thy going out and thy coming in, and to know
26 all that thou doest. And when Joab was come out from
David, he sent messengers after Abner, and they brought

19. Saul's tribe of Benjamin is specially mentioned, as the
quarter from which opposition to Abner's proposals was most to
be expected.

24 f. The first of several occasions on which Joab's masterful
spirit asserts itself in an inexcusable freedom of speech and
action in relation to his sovereign. There was no ground, so far
as is now known, for this charge of *mala fides* on Abner's part.
It is by no means improbable that David, knowing Joab's jealous
and vindictive character, had purposely arranged that he should
be absent on the occasion of Abner's visit.

him back from the well of Sirah: but David knew it not. And when Abner was returned to Hebron, Joab took 27 him aside into the midst of the gate to speak with him quietly, and smote him there in the belly, that he died, for the blood of Asahel his brother. And afterward 28 when David heard it, he said, I and my kingdom are guiltless before the LORD for ever from the blood of Abner the son of Ner: let it fall upon the head of Joab, 29 and upon all his father's house; and let there not fail from the house of Joab one that hath an issue, or that is a leper, or that leaneth on a staff, or that falleth by the sword, or that lacketh bread. So Joab and Abishai his 30 brother slew Abner, because he had killed their brother Asahel at Gibeon in the battle.

And David said to Joab, and to all the people that 31

---

27. into the midst of the gate: the most public spot in the city is not the place for a 'quiet word' with any one. Read, with LXX, 'to the side of the gate,' into a retired corner. The only motive for this act of treachery given by the narrator is that of blood revenge (for which see on xiv. 7), but we can scarcely leave jealousy out of account, nor—to be perfectly just to one who with all his faults was passionately devoted to David's cause—a mistaken zeal for what he considered the best interests of his king (see verse 25).

iii. 28-39. *David protests his innocence and gives Abner honourable burial.*

David follows up his solemn denial of complicity in the murder of Abner by an exhaustive curse on the murderer and all his kin. The reference to his 'kingdom' shows, further, that he was alive to the misconstruction which might be put upon his apparent breach of faith by public opinion generally, and especially by the northern tribes.

29. that leaneth on a staff: rather, 'that holdeth a spindle.' There is an evident appropriateness in the wish that the descendants of the stern soldier may be womanish and effeminate. Loathsome disease, effeminacy, bloodshed, and poverty compose the elements of this terrible imprecation.

30 interrupts the narrative, contradicts verse 27. and is therefore regarded on all hands as an interpolation.

were with him, Rend your clothes, and gird you with
sackcloth, and mourn before Abner.   And king David
32 followed the bier.   And they buried Abner in Hebron :
and the king lifted up his voice, and wept at the grave of
33 Abner ; and all the people wept.   And the king lamented
for Abner, and said,

> Should Abner die as a fool dieth ?
>
> 34   Thy· hands were not bound, nor thy feet put into
>   fetters :
>
> As a man falleth before the children of iniquity, so
>   didst thou fall.

35 And all the people wept again over him.   And all the
people came to cause David to eat bread while it was yet
day ; but David sware, saying, God do so to me, and
more also, if I taste bread, or aught else, till the sun be
36 down.   And all the people took notice of it, and it
pleased them : as whatsoever the king did pleased all the
37 people.   So all the people and all Israel understood that
day that it was not of the king to slay Abner the son of
38 Ner.   And the king said unto his servants, Know ye not
that there is a prince and a great man fallen this day in

---

33 f. The lament is in the form of a quatrain (see on i. 17 ff.).
Instead of the usual parallelism of successive lines, the first line
here corresponds to the fourth, the second to the third, the first
line of verse 34 in R. V. being really the second and third of the
quatrain.

Should Abner die, &c. : rather, 'had Abner to die as dies the
fool,' that is, in dishonour, in contrast to the honourable death of
the warrior.   Abner's death was murder, and the pity of it was
increased by the treachery which prevented him raising a hand
in self-defence, although both hands and feet were unfettered.

38 f. The narrator is at pains to show that David succeeded in
clearing himself of all suspicion of complicity in the murder, not
only in the eyes of his own people, but also in the eyes of 'all Israel.'

38 f. After a generous tribute to the worth of Abner, David—
in a verse the first part of which has been variously interpreted
—excuses his inability to secure the punishment of Joab.   This

Israel? And I am this day weak, though anointed king; 39 and these men the sons of Zeruiah be too hard for me : the LORD reward the wicked doer according to his wickedness.

And when *Ish-bosheth*, Saul's son, heard that Abner 4 was dead in Hebron, his hands became feeble, and all the Israelites were troubled. And *Ish-bosheth*, Saul's son, 2 *had* two men that were captains of bands : the name of the one was Baanah, and the name of the other Rechab, the sons of Rimmon the Beerothite, of the children of Benjamin : (for Beeroth also is reckoned to Benjamin : and the Beerothites fled to Gittaim, and have been 3 sojourners there until this day.)

Now Jonathan, Saul's son, had a son that was lame of 4 his feet. He was five years old when the tidings came of Saul and Jonathan out of Jezreel, and his nurse took

---

he has perforce to leave in the hand of God, whom he prays to 'requite the doer of evil according to his evil.'

iv. 1–12. *The assassination of Ish-baal (Ish-bosheth).*
On hearing of the murder of Abner, Ish-baal and his supporters realize that their cause is lost. The unfortunate prince is subsequently assassinated by two of his officers, who bring his head to David in the hope of a reward, but are treated as common criminals.

2. Beeroth: usually identified with *El-bireh*, on the great north road, a short distance south-east of Beth-el. The purpose of the parenthesis is to explain how the Canaanite inhabitants of Beeroth, which was originally a member of the Gibeonite league (Josh. ix. 17) and an *enclave* within Benjamin, had been compelled for some reason to flee to **Gittaim**, an unknown locality, where they long enjoyed the rights of hospitality as sojourners (see on i. 13). Some would bring this incident into connexion with Saul's cruel treatment of the Gibeonites as recorded in xxi. 1 ff., and see in the murder of Ish-baal by Baanah and Rechab an act of vengeance.

4. Mephibosheth: really either Merib-baal, 'the lord (i. e. Yahweh) contends,' as 1 Chron. viii. 34; ix. 40[d], or more probably Meri-baal, 'the lord's (Yahweh's) hero,' as in the Hebrew text of 1 Chron. ix. 40[b]. For the motive of the double disguise see on ii. 8, and for Meri-baal's subsequent history, ix. 1 ff.

him up, and fled : and it came to pass, as she made haste
to flee, that he fell, and became lame.   And his name
was Mephibosheth.

5   And the sons of Rimmon the Beerothite, Rechab and
Baanah, went, and came about the heat of the day to the
6 house of Ish-bosheth, as he took his rest at noon.   And
they came thither into the midst of the house, as though
they would have fetched wheat ; and they smote him in
the belly : and Rechab and Baanah his brother escaped.
7 Now when they came into the house, as he lay on his bed
in his bedchamber, they smote him, and slew him, and
beheaded him, and took his head, and went by the way
8 of the Arabah all night.   And they brought the head of
Ish-bosheth unto David to Hebron, and said to the king.
Behold the head of Ish-bosheth the son of Saul thine
enemy, which sought thy life ; and the LORD hath avenged
9 my lord the king this day of Saul, and of his seed.   And
David answered Rechab and Baanah his brother, the sons
of Rimmon the Beerothite, and said unto them, As the
LORD liveth, who hath redeemed my soul out of all

---

iv. 5-7 give details of the assassination.   The Hebrew text of
verse 6 is very corrupt, that of the Greek Version being now
universally preferred.   As given in the marg. of R. V. it runs :
'And, behold, the woman that kept the door of the house was
winnowing [rather, 'was cleaning'] wheat, and she slumbered and
slept ; and the brethren, Rechab and Baanah, went privily into the
house, as he lay,' &c., as in verse 7.   This picturesque description
throws an interesting light on the low estate to which his Majesty,
King Ish-baal, had fallen.

7. by the way of the Arabah: in the opposite direction to the
line of Abner's retreat, see ii. 29.

8. the LORD hath avenged my lord the king, &c.: 'the
apparent hypocrisy which made Yahweh a partner in their bloody
crime called forth the indignation of the older expositors.   But
such language is second nature to an Oriental' (H. P. Smith).

9. The second half of this verse shows how even our oldest
extant Hebrew literature is suffused with true religious feeling.

adversity, when one told me, saying, Behold, Saul is dead, 10
thinking to have brought good tidings, I took hold of him,
and slew him in Ziklag, which was the reward I gave him
for his tidings. How much more, when wicked men 11
have slain a righteous person in his own house upon his
bed, shall I not now require his blood of your hand, and
take you away from the earth? And David commanded 12
his young men, and they slew them, and cut off their
hands and their feet, and hanged them up beside the
pool in Hebron. But they took the head of Ish-bosheth,
and buried it in the grave of Abner in Hebron.

Then came all the tribes of Israel to David unto 5
Hebron, and spake, saying, Behold, we are thy bone and

---

10 f. David serves the murderers of Ish-baal as he had served
the messenger from the field of Gilboa. The latter—who must
not be confused with the Amalekite of i. 6 ff. (see the introductory
note to that chapter)—paid with his life for what after all was
little more than an error of judgement, 'how much more' (verse
11) had these confessed assassins incurred the penalty of death.

(c) v. 1—vi. 23. *David, now king over all Israel, captures
Jerusalem to which he removes the Ark of God.*

In these chapters we have a record from our oldest source of
two historical events, the importance of which for the future
political and religious development of Israel can scarcely be
exaggerated. Chapter v is evidently of the nature of a compilation
from more detailed accounts of this critical period of Hebrew
history. As a consequence, the chronological relation of the
different entries is extremely uncertain (see especially on verses
17 ff.). The student is referred to the standard histories and to
Budde's *Kurzer Handcommentar* 218 for further examination of
the historical problems.

v. 1–3. *David anointed king over Israel in Hebron* (cf. ii. 4).

Accepting the arrangement of the text adopted by the compiler,
we find the northern tribes, here designated 'the tribes of Israel'
as distinguished from the tribe of Judah, repairing to Hebron to
offer David, through their representatives 'the elders,' or heads
of the clans, the crown now vacant through the murder of Ish-baal.

1. we are thy bone and thy flesh: for this idea of the
solidarity of Judah and the northern tribes, cf. ii. 26, 'their
brethren,' xix. 41, 'our brethren the men of Judah.'

2 thy flesh.   In times past, when Saul was king over us, it was thou that leddest out and broughtest in Israel : and the LORD said to thee, Thou shalt feed my people Israel,
3 and thou shalt be prince over Israel.   So all the elders of Israel came to the king to Hebron ; and king David made a covenant with them in Hebron before the LORD : and they anointed David king over Israel.

4   [R] David was thirty years old when he began to reign,
5 and he reigned forty years.   In Hebron he reigned over Judah seven years and six months : and in Jerusalem he reigned thirty and three years over all Israel and
6 Judah.   [M] And the king and his men went to Jerusalem

---

2. The reference in the first half of the verse is to David's military leadership under Saul, in the second half probably to the same oracle as was referred to in iii. 9. The Chronicler (1 Chron. xi. 3) naturally understood the words as referring to the later passage, 1 Sam. xvi. 1 ff.

Thou shalt feed my people Israel: the earliest instance of this metaphor, the king the shepherd of his people ; it became a favourite figure from Jeremiah onwards.

3. David made a covenant with them (cf. iii. 21): embodying the mutual rights and duties of ruler and ruled, the ' manner of the kingdom ' (see on 1 Sam. viii. 9).

4 f. A chronological note by the Deuteronomic editor of the same tenor as that in 1 Kings ii. 11 (cf. ii. 11 above). Its accuracy is guaranteed by general considerations (see Introduction, sect. ix), and by the precision of the text 'seven years and six months.'

v. 6-10. *The capture of Jerusalem* (cf. 1 Chron. xi. 4-9).

This famous fortress had remained since the conquest in the possession of the Canaanite tribe of the Jebusites (Judges i. 21). The fragmentary character of the extracts in this chapter render it impossible to say with certainty at what precise point in David's reign this epoch-making event took place (see above). The compiler at least represents it as the first notable event of David's reign over all Israel. See further on verse 17 below and on vi. 1.

6. Jerusalem: the first historical mention of this famous city is found in the Tell-el-Amarna correspondence, *circa* 1400 B.C., where it appears as *U-ru-sa-lim* with a native ruler under the suzerainty of Egypt. For the meaning of the name, its situation and history, reference must be made to the standard dictionaries.

against the Jebusites, the inhabitants of the land: which spake unto David, saying, Except thou take away the blind and the lame, thou shalt not come in hither: thinking, David cannot come in hither. Nevertheless 7 David took the strong hold of Zion; the same is the city of David. And David said on that day, Whosoever 8 smiteth the Jebusites, let him get up to the watercourse, and *smite* the lame and the blind, that are hated of David's soul. Wherefore they say, There are the blind and

---

the Jebusites, the inhabitants of the land: one of, the seven races which, according to O. T. writers, occupied the land of Canaan before the Hebrew conquest (see Driver's *Deuteronomy*, 97 ff.). In Judges xix. 10, 1 Chron. xi. 4 f. their capital is called Jebus, probably a mistaken inference from the name of its inhabitants. The Jebusites' taunt is explained by the narrator as referring to the impregnable position of the fortress. This idea is more clearly brought out by the marginal rendering: 'thou shalt not come in hither, but the blind and the lame shall turn thee away.' The walls, they meant, were so strong that it was sufficient to man them with the blind and the lame to secure the safety of the city.

7. the strong hold of Zion: Zion is now identified with the more easterly of the two hills on which the modern city is built. The fortress must have stood on its southern portion, doubtless in close proximity to the only perennial spring in the neighbourhood, the Virgin's Fountain. With later writers, the poets especially, Zion became a synonym for Jerusalem as a whole. There is nothing in the text, which represents Zion as the citadel of Jerusalem, to negative the supposition that part at least of the western hill—often falsely supposed to be Zion—was already built upon.

the same is the city of David: a marginal gloss anticipating verse 9.

8. The first half of this verse is so corrupt as to have been long the despair of textual critics. No purpose would be served by a recital of the bewildering variety of conjectures that have been put forward. The second half has all the appearance of a late and mistaken gloss to be rendered as in the margin: 'the blind and the lame shall not come into the house,' that is, the temple, as expressly stated in the LXX rendering. There is here probably a reference to Lev. xxi. 18. According to the Chronicler (1 Chron.

9 the lame; he cannot come into the house.　And David dwelt in the strong hold, and called it the city of David. And David built round about from Millo and inward.
10 And David waxed greater and greater; for the LORD, the God of hosts, was with him.
11 　And Hiram king of Tyre sent messengers to David, and cedar trees, and carpenters, and masons: and they
12 built David an house.　And David perceived that the LORD had established him king over Israel, and that he had exalted his kingdom for his people Israel's sake.

---

xi. 6), Joab's prowess on this occasion procured for him the position of commander-in-chief of David's forces.

9. And David dwelt in the strong hold: in these few and commonplace words we have all that is recorded of the momentous step taken by David in removing his capital from Hebron to Jerusalem.　That it was a wise and politic move on David's part none can doubt.　By its almost impregnable position, and by its geographical situation on the dividing line between Judah and Israel, Jerusalem was marked out as the natural capital of the united kingdom.　The removal of the royal residence from the Judahite city of Hebron, moreover, was a step likely to conciliate the tribes of the north, while the fact that Jerusalem was a new conquest, in which the men of Judah had played an honourable part, would go far to mitigate the regrets of the south at this desertion of their ancient city (but see on xv. 7 ff.).

the city of David: rather, as the context requires, 'the fortress of David' or 'David's burg'; so vi. 12, &c.

Millo was evidently an important part of the fortress, although meaning and situation are both unknown.　See Skinner's note on 1 Kings ix. 15 (Century Bible).

10. Cf. note on iv. 9 above.

11 ff. Hiram king of Tyre: Hiram I, the friend and contemporary of Solomon, whose reign is given by ancient and modern authorities as 968-935, B.C. (see Menander's list in *KAT*.[3] 129).　If this date is correct, we must suppose that the name of Hiram has been inadvertently inserted here for that of his father Abibaal.　The extreme condensation of the narrative has probably brought together what should be kept apart.　The ambassadors of Hiram were no doubt those usually sent with friendly greetings at the beginning of a new reign (see x. 1 f.).　By them, we may suppose, David sent a request for materials for his palace and for the necessary craftsmen.

[R] And David took him more concubines and wives 13
out of Jerusalem, after he was come from Hebron : and
there were yet sons and daughters born to David.   And 14
these be the names of those that were born unto him in
Jerusalem ; Shammua, and Shobab, and Nathan, and
Solomon, and Ibhar, and Elishua ; and Nepheg, and 15
Japhia ; and Elishama, and Eliada, and Eliphelet.   16

[M] And when the Philistines heard that they had 17
anointed David king over Israel, all the Philistines went up
to seek David ; and David heard of it, and went down

---

v. 13-16.   *A list of David's sons born in Jerusalem.*
The list is repeated with some variations (for which see the
tabular lists in Driver, *Notes* 201) in 1 Chron. iii. 5-8, xiv. 4-7, and,
in all probability, originally formed, as in Chronicles, the continuation of iii. 2-5.   Of the names given, we may note only
Solomon, the circumstances of whose birth are fully related below
(xi. f.), and **Eliada**, whose true name was Baal-iada (1 Chron.
xiv. 7).   The motive for the change has been explained in the note
on ii. 8.

v. 17-25.   *David and the Philistines.*
It is altogether probable, as we have seen (p. 198), that David
while at Hebron continued to acknowledge the Philistine suzerainty over Judah, one trace of which we may perhaps find in the
presence, at the date of the section before us, of a Philistine
resident (or garrison, or both) at Beth-lehem (xxiii. 14).   But
David as the head of a united Israel was many times more
dangerous than as the king of Judah alone.   His installation, therefore, at Hebron recorded in the opening verses of this chapter
seems to have changed the attitude of the Philistines from one
of watchful tolerance to one of active hostility.   The reason for
believing that David had not yet achieved the conquest of Jerusalem, and consequently that v. 4-10 and v. 17—vi. 1 have changed
places, will appear presently.
17. David . . . went down to the hold : David's place of
retreat cannot, as the present context suggests, be 'the strong
hold of Zion.'   One always 'went up,' one never 'went down,' to
Jerusalem, and besides David was already settled 'in the strong
hold' (verse 9).   The solution of the difficulty is to be found in
the episode preserved in the appendix to Samuel, xxiii. 11ff.   The
scene of the exploit there recorded is the same as that of the

18 to the hold.   Now the Philistines had come and spread
19 themselves in the valley of Rephaim.   And David inquired
   of the LORD, saying, Shall I go up against the Philistines? wilt thou deliver them into mine hand? And the
   LORD said unto David, Go up: for I will certainly deliver
20 the Philistines into thine hand.   And David came to
   Baal-perazim, and David smote them there; and he said,
   The LORD hath broken mine enemies before me, like the
   breach of waters.   Therefore he called the name of that
21 place Baal-perazim.   And they left their images there,
   and David and his men took them away.
22   And the Philistines came up yet again, and spread
23 themselves in the valley of Rephaim.   And when David
   inquired of the LORD, he said, Thou shalt not go up:
   make a circuit behind them, and come upon them over

section before us, 'the valley of Rephaim,' David being then in
'the hold of Adullam' (xxiii. 13—for this rendering in place of the
erroneous 'cave' see on 1 Sam xxii. 1).   David, then, retired from
Hebron, not Jerusalem, to his old fortress of Adullam.

18. the valley of Rephaim lay to the south of Jerusalem
towards Beth-lehem (Josh. xv. 8; cf. xxiii. 13 ff. below).

20. Baal-perazim: 'Baal (or lord) of breaches,' as explained
in the second half of the verse.   This shows once more that Baal
was at this period an unobjectionable title of Yahweh.   The
locality has not been identified.

21. David carries off the 'gods' of the Philistines, which the
latter had taken into battle with them, as the Hebrews took the
Ark at Eben-ezer (1 Sam. iv. 5 ff.).   The reading 'gods' for
images is attested by the LXX and by 1 Chron. xiv. 12.   The
form which this verse has assumed in Chronicles is instructive.
The Chronicler has taken offence at the idea of the man after
God's heart carrying off, as trophies of war, a set of heathen gods,
and has made David give commandment (cf. Deut. vii. 5, 25), 'and
they were burned with fire'! This is one of many illustrations of
the manner in which the pious historians of a later age dealt with
certain passages of the older literature.   An illustration of an
Assyrian warrior with a captured idol in his hand will be found
EBi. ii. col. 1918.

22. The scene of this second encounter is again the valley of
Rephaim.

against the mulberry trees. And it shall be, when thou 24
hearest the sound of marching in the tops of the mulberry
trees, that then thou shalt bestir thyself: for then is the
LORD gone out before thee to smite the host of the
Philistines. And David did so, as the LORD com- 25
manded him; and smote the Philistines from Geba until
thou come to Gezer.

And David again gathered together all the chosen men 6

---

23 f. mulberry trees: R. V. marg. 'balsam trees'; better than
either would be 'baka trees,' keeping the original form of the word,
since the authorities are not agreed as to the tree in question.
The belief in trees as the abodes of divine beings, and as media
of divination and revelation, was deeply rooted in early Semitic
thought (W. R. Smith, *Rel. Sem.*[2] 195 ff.).

25. from Geba until thou come to Gezer: the LXX and the
Chronicler (note R. V. marg.) read 'Gibeon' for Geba here. For
the former see on ii. 12, for the latter, 1 Sam. xiii. 2. But this part
of Palestine was full of Gebas, Gibeahs and Gibeons—all practically
synonymous—and some place nearer Jerusalem and the valley of
Rephaim than either Geba or Gibeon may be intended. The site
of the ancient Canaanite city of **Gezer** is represented by *Tell Jezer*
—otherwise *Tell ej-Jesari*—near the modern village of Abu
Shusheh, south-east of Ramleh. It first appears in the Amarna
correspondence, *circa* 1400 B. C. More than four centuries later it
was presented by the then king of Egypt as a dowry to his
daughter, the wife of Solomon (1 Kings ix. 16). It is now (1904)
being excavated by the Palestine Exploration Society. The
history of Jezer has been fully treated by Clermont Ganneau in
his *Archaeological Researches in Palestine*, ii. 224-275; a *résumé* by
Macalister will be found in the *Quarterly Statement* of the above
Society for 1902, pp. 227 ff.

vi. 1-19. *The transference of the Ark from Kiriath-jearim to the
city of David.*
If the selection of Jerusalem as the capital of the united
kingdom of Israel was, as is universally admitted, a conspicuous
proof of David's statesmanship, it is evident that the decision to
convey thither, and to house within its citadel, the sacred Ark of
God is equally a proof of his political sagacity and religious zeal.
The possession of the ancient palladium of the tribes of Israel
gave the new metropolis the necessary religious sanction, and
gradually secured for it a pre-eminence among the sanctuaries of
the land which in due time paved the way for the Deuteronomic

2 of Israel, thirty thousand.   And David arose, and went

---

centralization of the cultus, with all the far-reaching results that flowed therefrom. ˙ It is all the more to be regretted that our extant records throw so little light upon the inexplicable neglect of the Ark during the long lifetime of Samuel and the reign of Saul. That this precious shrine, whose presence was as the presence of Yahweh, and whose loss was the passing of the glory from Israel (1 Sam. iv. 21), should have played no-part in the revival of national and religious life which culminated in the institution of the monarchy, is surely to be explained only by the hypothesis that the Ark was inaccessible to the leaders we have named, and to all who rallied round them.   Of this inaccessibility no other explanation seems possible than the further supposition, that during all these years the Ark in some way or other continued to be jealously retained within the jurisdiction, though not within the actual territory, of the Philistines.   Its ultimate recovery, we cannot doubt, stands in close connexion with David's repeated victories over the latter.   *Only when their power had been completely broken was it possible for Israel to regain possession of the Ark.* The subject is too complex to admit of adequate treatment in a note, and its fuller discussion must be relegated to the Appendix to this commentary.

The parallel account of the removal of the Ark in 1 Chron. xiii. 5 ff. should be compared with that given here.   'The variations between the two narratives are here remarkably striking and instructive' (Driver).

1. In his recent commentary, Budde still adheres to the opinion expressed in his earlier works on Samuel that this verse was originally followed by v. 6 ff., the account of the conquest of Jerusalem, and that v. 12 gives the justification of and introduction to vi. 2 ff.   This mainly on the ground that an army of thirty thousand men 'does not suggest a festival procession, but a serious warlike undertaking.'   As will be shown more fully in the Appendix, we consider Budde's premise correct, but his conclusion false.   Both the form (note the words '*again* gathered together') and the contents of this verse clearly suggest another military expedition against the Philistines, while the fresh start made in verse 2 equally suggests that something has fallen out between these verses.   This we take to have been an account of the success of the expedition, which put an end to the Philistine suzerainty over the cities of the Gibeonite league, including Kiriath-jearim, and thereby opened the way for the recovery of the Ark.   This account the compiler will have suppressed under the misapprehension that the Ark, because of its location on nominally Hebrew territory, had all along been under Hebrew control.

with all the people that were with him, from Baale Judah,
to bring up from thence the ark of God, which is called
by the Name, even the name of the LORD of hosts that
sitteth upon the cherubim.   And they set the ark of God 3
upon a new cart, and brought it out of the house of
Abinadab that was in the hill : and Uzzah and Ahio, the
sons of Abinadab, drave the new cart.   And they brought 4
it out of the house of Abinadab, which was in the hill,
with the ark of God : and Ahio went before the ark.
And David and all the house of Israel played before the 5
LORD with all manner of *instruments made of* fir wood,
and with harps, and with psalteries, and with timbrels,
and with castanets, and with cymbals.   And when they 6
came to the threshing-floor of Nacon, Uzzah put forth
his hand to the ark of God, and took hold of it ; for the
oxen stumbled.   And the anger of the LORD was kindled 7
against Uzzah ; and God smote him there for his error ;

---

2. from Baale Judah : read, 'to Baalah of Judah to bring up
from thence,' &c. ; cf. 1 Chron. xiii. 6, 'to Baalah, *that is* Kiriath-
jearim,' the name which the place bears in 1 Sam. vi. 21 f.

which is called by the Name, &c. : render more literally,
'over which is called the name of Yahweh Sebaoth,' reading 'the
name' once only as in LXX.   The phrase denotes ownership
(see on xii. 28).   For the expanded title, which has been added
later, see the Appendix.

3 f. The awkwardness of the style shows that the text of these
two verses is in some confusion, cf. 1 Chron. xiii. 7.

5. with all manner . . . of fir wood (the words omitted are, as
the italics show, no part of the text) : an interesting example of
textual corruption involving only slight deviations from the
original text, which ran : 'with all (their) might and with songs.'
as 1 Chron. xiii. 8.   For the instruments employed see the Bible
dictionaries.

6. the oxen stumbled : the meaning of the original, as the
margin shows, is uncertain.

7. for his error : R. V. marg. 'for his rashness,' but the text
is palpably corrupt, and probably a mutilated fragment of what
the Chronicler read in his copy : 'because he put forth his hand
to the Ark. and he died before God' (1 Chron. xiii. 10).   The last

8 and there he died by the ark of God. And David was displeased, because the LORD had broken forth upon Uzzah : and he called that place Perez-uzzah, unto this 9 day. And David was afraid of the LORD that day ; and he said, How shall the ark of the LORD come unto me ? 10 So David would not remove the ark of the LORD unto him into the city of David ; but David carried it aside 11 into the house of Obed-edom the Gittite. And the ark of the LORD remained in the house of Obed-edom the Gittite three months : and the LORD blessed Obed-edom, 12 and all his house. And it was told king David, saying, The LORD hath blessed the house of Obed-edom, and all that pertaineth unto him, because of the ark of God.

---

clause in the form just given is also more likely to represent the original, reading, however, 'the LORD' (Yahweh) for 'God.' The Ark is here, as in 1 Sam. iv–vi, identified with Yahweh. To this a late copyist took exception, and substituted the present reading.

This incident with its, to us, excessive punishment of an action, whose motive was the perfectly legitimate and laudable one of preventing an accident to the Ark, must be judged from the religious standpoint of this early narrator (M). For him and his contemporaries it was not a question of moral transgression and its punishment (see on 1 Sam. xiv. 43, for the as yet imperfect conception of sin), but rather a question of the sacrosanct character of the Ark, whose 'holiness' was contagious and therefore a source of danger and even of death to ordinary 'unsanctified' persons (see on 1 Sam. vii. 1). Many modern scholars, however, regard this incident of Uzzah's death as a legendary accretion to the historical narrative, which has grown out of the *older* place-name **Perez-uzzah,** 'the breach of Uzzah.'

10. Obed-edom the Gittite : i. e. native of Gath, who must, however, have been a *gēr* (see on i. 13), admitted to certain civil and religious privileges, including admission to the worship of Yahweh. Later ecclesiastical tradition enrolled him among the Levites from motives that are readily apparent (1 Chron. xv. 18, 24). His house must have been in or near Jerusalem.

11 f. By the blessing bestowed upon Obed-edom, the nature of which is not specified, David recognizes that the anger of Yahweh has passed away, and resolves to make another and more cautious attempt to transfer the Ark to his new citadel.

And David went and brought up the ark of God from the house of Obed-edom into the city of David with joy. And it was so, that when they that bare the ark of the 13 LORD had gone six paces, he sacrificed an ox and a fatling. And David danced before the LORD with all 14 his might; and David was girded with a linen ephod. So David and all the house of Israel brought up the ark 15 of the LORD with shouting, and with the sound of the trumpet. And it was so, as the ark of the LORD came 16 into the city of David, that Michal the daughter of Saul looked out at the window, and saw king David leaping and dancing before the LORD; and she despised him in her heart. And they brought in the ark of the LORD, 17 and set it in its place, in the midst of the tent that David had pitched for it: and David offered burnt offerings and peace offerings before the LORD. And when David had 18 made an end of offering the burnt offering and the peace offerings, he blessed the people in the name of the LORD

---

13. The Ark on this occasion is reverently carried, not driven (cf. xv. 24, 29). After a few moments of anxious suspense, it is seen that Yahweh is graciously pleased to go with David, who thereupon offers a sacrifice of thanksgiving. The instructive parallel in 1 Chron. xv should be compared, in which the ecclesiastical arrangements of the third century before Christ are transferred to the tenth.

14. David danced before the LORD: *lit.* 'whirled,' as do the modern dervishes in their devotional dances. Note here, and in verse 7 above (restored text), the practical identification of Yahweh with the Ark, as in the narrative 1 Sam. iv-vi.

girded with a linen ephod: see on 1 Sam. ii. 18. The whirling movement of the dance caused the indecent exposure of which we hear in verse 20, and against which the later legislation took precautions (Exod. xxviii. 42, Lev. vi. 10).

16. Michal is deeply offended at what she considers the unkingly behaviour of her husband—note the emphasis on '*king* David.'

18. he blessed the people in the name of the LORD of hosts: rather, 'with the name'; the preposition denotes the means or

19 of hosts.   And he dealt among all the people, even
among the whole multitude of Israel, both to men and
women, to every one a cake of bread, and a portion *of
flesh*, and a cake of raisins.   So all the people departed
20 every one to his house.   Then David returned to bless
his household.   And Michal the daughter of Saul came
out to meet David, and said, How glorious was the king
of Israel to-day, who uncovered himself to-day in the eyes
of the handmaids of his servants, as one of the vain
21 fellows shamelessly uncovereth himself !   And David said
unto Michal, *It was* before the LORD, which chose me
above thy father, and above all his house, to appoint me

---

instrument, the solemn invocation of the Name being the channel
of the Divine blessing.   David ' put the Name of Yahweh upon the
children of Israel' (Num. vi. 27, where verses 24–26 give the
later form of the priestly benediction ; see Kautzsch in Hastings'
DB., extra vol. 640 f., for the full significance of the 'name of
Yahweh' in the earlier literature, and cf. on vii. 13 below).   To
pronounce the benediction is reckoned as the third of the peculiar
prerogatives of the priesthood in Deut. x. 8 (cf. Num. vi. 23,
Lev. ix. 22).   Here, however, David, in virtue of his prerogative
as 'the anointed of Yahweh,' combines priestly with royal functions,
not merely wearing the priestly dress, but himself offering sacrifice
and blessing the people at the close of the service.   So too
Solomon, 1 Kings viii. 14, 55, which clearly shows that these
functions were not yet limited to a special class.   See further on
viii. 18.

19. a portion of flesh : to the meaning of the single word in
the original we have no clue.   The margin gives 'a portion of
wine,' an alternative quite in keeping with the festive occasion,
and suggesting that we may have to do with a corruption of
shēkār, perhaps in its original sense of 'date-wine.'.   The corresponding *shikaru* is repeatedly associated with gifts of food, oil,
&c., in the Palestinian correspondence of the Amarna period.
See the writer's article 'Wine and Strong Drink,' *EBi.* iv.
col. 5310.

21 f. The opening words of David's reply should read (cf. LXX) :
' Before Yahweh was I dancing, who chose me,' &c.   The last
clause belongs to verse 22.   The answer, though little calculated
to appease the queen's anger, shows both David's native humility
and his recognition of the true source of his royal dignity.

prince over the people of the LORD, over Israel : therefore will I play before the LORD. And I will be yet 22
more vile than thus, and will be base in mine own sight :
but of the handmaids which thou hast spoken of, of them
shall I be had in honour. And Michal the daughter of 23
Saul had no child unto the day of her death.

[D] And it came to pass, when the king dwelt in his 7
house, and the LORD had given him rest from all his
enemies round about, that the king said unto Nathan 2
the prophet, See now, I dwell in an house of cedar, but
the ark of God dwelleth within curtains. And Nathan 3

---

23. Michal's childlessness has usually been regarded as a
Divine judgement upon her conduct. The narrator, however,
seems to regard it as the result of a permanent estrangement, Michal
being henceforth treated like the members of the royal harem mentioned in xx. 3.

(*d*) vii. *The Divine guarantee of the permanence of David's
dynasty.*

The true significance of this chapter has been obscured by the
insertion, either by the compiler or by a later reader, of verse 13
(see note). The point of the prophetic message is, in brief, that
it is not David who shall build a 'house,' that is, a temple *for
Yahweh, but Yahweh who shall build a 'house,'* that is, a dynasty,
for David. In the text, apart from the intrusive verse 13, there
is no mention of the building of Solomon's temple, but rather the
contrary. The chapter forms a literary unit by itself. Its
general style connects it with the literary products of the
Deuteronomic school, and its contents suggest a date in the latter
part of the reign of Josiah, or the period immediately succeeding,
circa 610-600 B.C., while the dynasty of David was still upon the
throne (so Wellhausen and others). The fundamental importance
of this chapter for the study of the growth of the Messianic hope
in Israel is rightly emphasized by all writers on this great
subject. The parallel passage, 1 Chron. xvii, should be compared throughout.

1. the LORD had given him rest, &c. : a favourite Deuteronomistic expression, Deut. xii. 10, xxv. 19; 1 Kings v. 4, &c.

2. Nathan the prophet: the standing designation of the seer
who figures so prominently in the story of Uriah and in the
matter of the succession (1 Kings i. 1 ff.).

dwelleth within curtains: i. e. in a tent, the curtains being

said to the king, Go, do all that is in thine heart; for
4 the LORD is with thee.   And it came to pass the same
night, that the word of the LORD came unto Nathan,
5 saying, Go and tell my servant David, Thus saith the
LORD, Shalt thou build me an house for me to dwell in?
6 for I have not dwelt in an house since the day that I
brought up the children of Israel out of Egypt, even to
this day, but have walked in a tent and in a tabernacle.
7 In all places wherein I have walked with all the children
of Israel, spake I a word with any of the tribes of Israel,
whom I commanded to feed my people Israel, saying,
8 Why have ye not built me an house of cedar? Now
therefore thus shalt thou say unto my servant David,
Thus saith the LORD of hosts, I took thee from the
sheepcote, from following the sheep, that thou shouldest

the breadths of goats' hair cloth of which the tent was made.   The
house of cedar refers back to v. 11.

3 f. Nathan at first approves of David's proposal, but in the
following night is divinely informed that it is contrary to the
good pleasure of Yahweh, who prefers, as heretofore, the shelter
of a simple tent.   With this reason for David's abstaining from
the erection of a temple in Jerusalem, cf. 1 Kings v. 3 with
Skinner's note (Century Bible).

6. The author of this chapter can scarcely have known the
narrative of 1 Sam. i-iii with its temple at Shiloh.

have walked in a tent and in a tabernacle: the idea is
more fully expressed in 1 Chron. xvii. 5 : 'I have gone from tent
to tent, and from dwelling to dwelling.'   Yahweh, as represented
by the Ark, was not tied to any one spot, or to any one form of
shelter.   In xi. 11 we hear of the Ark being housed in a 'booth.'
How far removed all this is from the gorgeous tabernacle of the
Priests' Code is self-evident.

7. with any of the tribes : a corruption of 'with any of the
judges,' see margin of R.V.

8 ff. Nathan's special message contains three elements : (1) a
reminder of God's gracious dealings with David in the past (8, 9ⁿ);
(2) an assurance of the continuance of the same to David and to
Israel in the future (9ᵇ-11ᵃ); (3) the crowning promise of the
permanence of David's seed upon the throne of Israel (11ᵇ, 12,
14-16).

be prince over my people, over Israel : and I have been 9
with thee whithersoever thou wentest, and have cut off
all thine enemies from before thee ; and I will make thee
a great name, like unto the name of the great ones that
are in the earth.   And I will appoint a place for my 10
people Israel, and will plant them, that they may dwell
in their own place, and be moved no more ; neither shall
the children of wickedness afflict them any more, as at
the first, and *as* from the day that I commanded judges to 11
be over my people Israel ; and I will cause thee to rest
from all thine enemies.   Moreover the LORD telleth thee
that the LORD will make thee an house.   When thy days 12
be fulfilled, and thou shalt sleep with thy fathers, I will
set up thy seed after thee, which shall proceed out of thy
bowels, and I will establish his kingdom.   He shall build 13

---

10 f. As the punctuation of R. V. shows, 11ᵃ must be taken
with 10.   Render 'as at the first, even from the day that,' &c.
The troublous times of the Judges shall recur no more, and
Israel shall abide in peaceful and permanent possession of the
land of promise.   Evidently this was written before the Exile.

and I will cause thee to rest: this goes with the preceding
clause, and should be read : ' I will cause them [my people Israel]
to rest from all their enemies.'

the LORD will make thee an house: read, with LXX here
and 1 Chron. xvii. 10, 'will build thee an house,' as in verse 27.
This, as was indicated above, gives the key-note of the chapter.
For the figure see on 1 Sam. ii. 35, where we have the com-
plement to the passage before us.   There we had the promise
of the permanence of the Zadokite priesthood, here the permanence of the Davidic dynasty is assured, as is stated more
explicitly in verse 16.

12 repeats and expounds the promise of 11ᵇ.   Note that the
pronoun in 'his kingdom' refers back to David's seed or posterity,
and so in verses 14 ff.   That the Davidic dynasty as a whole, not
any individual member of it, is the burden of the prophecy must
be kept in mind throughout.   Cf. the summary of this passage
given by the Deuteronomic compiler of Kings (1 Kings ii. 4).

13. Wellhausen's contention that this verse has been interpolated is approved by almost all recent writers.   It requires

an house for my name, and I will establish the throne of
14 his kingdom for ever.   I will be his father, and he shall
be my son : if he commit iniquity, I will chasten him
with the rod of men, and with the stripes of the children
15 of men ; but my mercy shall not depart from him, as I

---

us to limit the 'seed' of verse 12 to Solomon, and by introducing
a thought alien to the rest of the chapter robs Nathan's message
of its point. David, moreover, in his subsequent thanksgiving,
makes no reference to this postponement of his cherished plan.
The interpolation, however, must have taken place at an early
date, as it was already known to the Deuteronomic editor or
editors of Kings (see Skinner (Century Bible) on 1 Kings v. 5,
vi. 18 ff., viii. 14 ff., especially p. 145), by whom the whole prophecy is definitely referred to Solomon by the substitution of 'son'
for 'seed,' the individual for the dynasty.

an house for my name : this association of Yahweh's 'name'
with the temple is characteristic of, and almost peculiar to,
Deuteronomy (xii. 5, 11, 21, and elsewhere), and the Deuteronomic
school of editors (1 Kings v. 17, 19, &c.), by whom Yahweh is
said to 'set his name' or 'cause his name to dwell' in the temple.
For this school God's true dwelling-place is heaven, but in the
sanctuary is His Name, the special manifestation of the Deity
vouchsafed to the worshippers by whom His name was invoked.
For this important theological conception, see Davidson, *Theology of
the O. T.*, 36 ff., 'The Idea of the Divine Name'; Schultz, *O. T.
Theology*, ii. 123 f.; Cheyne's article 'Name,' *EBi.* iii. 3268;
Skinner's *Kings* (Century Bible), p. 147; and Kautzsch, as cited
on vi. 18 above.

14. I will be his father, and he shall be my son (cf. Ps. lxxxix.
26 f.) : the rules of Hebrew grammar require us to apply this
verse and the following to the successive members of David's
dynasty, although the Chronicler has limited their reference to
Solomon (1 Chron. xxii. 10, xxviii. 6). Even Israel as a whole
had already been called Yahweh's son (Exod. iv. 22, Hos. xi. 1),
and the relation between Yahweh and the Messianic King is
expressed in similar terms in Ps. ii. 7.

with the rod of men : 'i. e. with punishments such as all
men incur when they sin, and from which the seed of David will
not be exempted. Cf. the poetical paraphrase, Ps. lxxxix. 30-51'
(Driver).

15. For cogent reasons the text of Chronicles is generally
preferred : 'and I will not take my mercy away from him [still
the dynasty], as I took it from him that was before thee'
(1 Chron. xvii. 13).

took it from Saul, whom I put away before' thee. And 16
thine house and thy kingdom shall be made sure for ever
before thee : thy throne shall be established for ever.
According to all these words, and according to all this 17
vision, so did Nathan speak unto David.

Then David the king went in, and sat before the LORD ; 18
and he said, Who am I, O Lord GOD, and what is my
house, that thou hast brought me thus far ? And this 19
was yet a small thing in thine eyes, O Lord GOD ; but
thou hast spoken also of thy servant's house for a great
while to come ; and this *too* after the manner of men, O
Lord GOD ! And what can David say more unto thee ? 20
for thou knowest thy servant, O Lord GOD. For thy 21
word's sake, and according to thine own heart, hast thou
wrought all this greatness, to make thy servant know it.

---

16. A concluding summary of the prophet's message. For the
idea of permanence conveyed by the term 'sure' see on 1 Sam. ii.
35. The thought of David's everlasting kingdom (cf. 1 Kings ii.
45, Ps. lxxxix. 4, 29, 36) contributed an essential element to the
Messianic eschatology.

vii. 18–29. *David's thanksgiving prayer.*
18. David . . . went in and sat before the LORD : namely,
in the tent in which the Ark was housed in the city, or rather
citadel, of David (vi. 12, 17). The attitude of devotion which he
assumed is not mentioned elsewhere in the O. T. It probably
consisted of 'raising his head and body and sinking backward
upon his heels,' which is one of the prescribed attitudes of
Mohammedan worship (Hughes, *Dictionary of Islam*, 467, with
illustrations).
19. The last clause is now unintelligible, and was already
corrupt by the third century B. C. (Chron. and LXX). It probably
continued the thought of the preceding clause : 'and thou wilt let
me see the generations of men for evermore' (so Budde basing
on Ewald and Wellhausen). David hopes to live in his descendants. For this thought see A. B. Davidson's *Theology*, p. 407.
21. The text is again in disorder, as a comparison with LXX
and Chronicles shows. H. P. Smith and Budde read : 'To glorify
thy servant hast thou promised, and according to thine own heart
hast thou wrought in making thy servant know all this greatness.'

22 Wherefore thou art great, O Lord God: for there is
none like thee, neither is there any God beside thee,
23 according to all that we have heard with our ears. And
what one nation in the earth is like thy people, even like
Israel, whom God went to redeem unto himself for a
people, and to make him a name, and to do great things
for you, and terrible things for thy land, before thy
people, which thou redeemedst to thee out of Egypt,
24 *from* the nations and their gods? And thou didst
establish to thyself thy people Israel to be a people unto
thee for ever; and thou, Lord, becamest their God.
25 And now, O Lord God, the word that thou hast spoken
concerning thy servant, and concerning his house, con-
26 firm thou it for ever, and do as thou hast spoken. And
let thy name be magnified for ever, saying, The Lord of
hosts is God over Israel: and the house of thy servant
27 David shall be established before thee. For thou, O
Lord of hosts, the God of Israel, hast revealed to thy
servant, saying, I will build thee an house: therefore hath
thy servant found in his heart to pray this prayer unto
28 thee. And now, O Lord God, thou art God, and thy
words are truth, and thou hast promised this good thing

23. This verse affords an interesting example of an early text
intentionally altered for dogmatic reasons (cf. on v. 21). Originally
it ran somewhat as follows: 'And what other nation in the earth
is like thy people Israel, whom [referring to 'other nation'] a god
has ever gone to redeem for himself as a people to make himself
a name, and to do for them great and terrible things, in driving
out before his people a nation and its gods?' The theological
particularism, which involved, though only as an hypothesis, the
existence and working in history of other gods, was offensive to
the monotheistic thought of a later age and led to the present
confused text. (So Geiger, followed by most recent commentators.)
For the ideas expressed see Deut. iv. 7, 34.
24. The familiar covenant relation between Yahweh and
Israel—Yahweh the God of Israel, Israel the people of Yahweh.

unto thy servant: now therefore let it please thee to 29
bless the house of thy servant, that it may continue for
ever before thee : for thou, O Lord GOD, hast spoken it:
and with thy blessing let the house of thy servant be
blessed for ever.

[R] And after this it came to pass, that David smote 8
the Philistines, and subdued them : and David took the
bridle of the mother city out of the hand of the Philistines.
And he smote Moab, and measured them with the line, 2
making them to lie down on the ground; and he
measured two lines to put to death, and one full line to
keep alive. And the Moabites became servants to

(c) viii. *A summary of David's wars with a list of his principal
officers of state.*
The summary character of the contents shows that this chapter
was compiled with a view to form the conclusion to David's reign,
and, in all probability, to what may be called 'the first edition' of
the Book of Samuel (p. 26). It has its counterpart in the briefer
summary which forms the provisional close of the reign of Saul,
1 Sam. xiv. 47-51. Both summaries may be assigned to the Deuteronomic compiler or redactor (R). The materials are of course
much older; in the case of some of the campaigns, indeed, we have
the older record itself preserved in later chapters. Wellhausen
and others are of opinion that the lists now found in iii. 2-5 and
v. 13-16 originally formed part of this chapter. Here, again, the
parallel in 1 Chron. (xviii. 1 ff.) should be compared.
1. **the bridle of the mother city** : by this the Revisers no
doubt mean the power (or possession) of the Philistine metropolis.
But this is exceedingly doubtful. The A. V. and R. V. marg. take
the words as a proper name, Metheg-ammah. In reality the text
is corrupt. The Chronicler read or guessed : 'Gath and her
daughters,' i. e. dependent villages (1 Chron. xviii. 1).
2. The reasons for the changed relations with Moab (see 1 Sam.
xxii. 3f.) are unknown, as this campaign is not elsewhere referred to.
Two-thirds of the (male ?) inhabitants David put to the ban. This
mode of conducting warfare, though quite in accord with the
spirit of David's age, offended the moral sense of a later day, as
we see from the Chronicler's omission of the middle portion of the
verse (1 Chron. xviii. 2).

3 David, and brought presents.   David smote also
  Hadadezer the son of Rehob, king of Zobah, as he went
4 to recover his dominion at the River.   And David took
  from him a thousand and seven hundred horsemen, and
  twenty thousand footmen : and David houghed all the
  chariot horses, but reserved of them for an hundred
5 chariots.   And when the Syrians of Damascus came to
  succour Hadadezer king of Zobah, David smote of the
6 Syrians two and twenty thousand men.   Then David
  put garrisons in Syria of Damascus : and the Syrians became servants to David and brought presents.   And the
7 LORD gave victory to David whithersoever he went.   And
  David took the shields of gold that were on the servants
8 of Hadadezer, and brought them to Jerusalem.   And from
  Betah and from Berothai, cities of Hadadezer, king

---

3 ff. The compiler here gives a longer summary of a campaign
against the king of Zobah and his allies, of which the original
account, apparently, may still be read in x. 6 ff. (which see).

king of Zobah : a small Aramaean kingdom somewhere in
or near the modern district of the *Jaulān* (see on x. 6).   The
text of the last clause is doubtful (see margin) ; probably we should
read as in Chronicles : 'as he went to stablish his dominion by
the river Euphrates.'

4. The uncertainty of the numbers in the received text of O. T.
is well illustrated by a comparison of this verse with x. 18, with
1 Chron. xviii. 4, and with the Greek readings in all three
passages.

chariot horses . . . chariots : the same word is used in the
original in both places ; we should therefore render : 'and he
reserved of them a hundred chariot horses.'

5. the Syrians of Damascus here take the place of 'the
Syrians beyond the Euphrates' of x. 16.   In any case it is
exceedingly doubtful if David's kingdom included the ancient
and powerful city of Damascus.

6. garrisons : or 'officers,' political residents, see on 1 Sam.
x. 5, and cf. 1 Kings vii. 7.

8. Betah and . . . Berothai : the accuracy of these names, and
therefore their position, is doubtful, see 1 Chron. xviii. 8, and the
margin here.

David took exceeding much brass.   And when Toi king 9
of Hamath heard that David had smitten all the host of
Hadadezer, then Toi sent Joram his son unto king David, 10
to salute him, and to bless him, because he had fought
against Hadadezer and smitten him : for Hadadezer had
wars with Toi.   And *Joram* brought with him vessels of
silver, and vessels of gold, and vessels of brass : these also 11
did king David dedicate unto the Lord, with the silver
and gold that he dedicated of all the nations which he
subdued ; of Syria, and of Moab, and of the children of 12
Ammon, and of the Philistines, and of Amalek, and of
the spoil of Hadadezer, son of Rehob, king of Zobah.
And David gat him a name when he returned from 13
smiting of the Syrians in the Valley of Salt, even eighteen
thousand men.   And he put garrisons in Edom ; through- 14
out all Edom put he garrisons, and all the Edomites

---

9 f. David receives an embassy from Toi, or Tou (see Chron.),
king of Hamath on the Orontes.   Budde considers that these two
verses may originally have stood after x. 19.

Joram: in Chron. more correctly 'Hadoram,' which is
probably a corruption of Hadad-ram.   The last contains, like
Hadad-ezer and Ben-hadad, the name of the Syrian thunder god,
who was identified with the Assyrian Rammānu (Rimmon).

13. the Valley of Salt : probably the modern wady of the
same name, the *Wadi el-Milh*, a continuation of the *Wadi es-Seba*
beside Beer-sheba.   This is the last place where we should expect
to find the **Syrians.**   Read therefore, with other slight emendations : 'and when he had returned from smiting the Syrians, he
smote Edom (Chron., LXX) in the Valley of Salt.'   Aram (Syria)
and Edom closely resemble each other in the Hebrew character [1],
and are frequently confused.   See also R. V. marg. and verse 14.
The Valley of Salt was also the scene of a later victory over the
Edomites (2 Kings xiv. 7).   The particular victory of our text is
ascribed to Joab in the heading of Ps. lx, and to Abishai in
1 Chron. xviii. 12, but the latter is manifestly a mistaken reading
of the word rendered 'had returned' in the emended text as
given above.

---

[1] אדם, ארם.

became servants to David. And the LORD gave victory
to David whithersoever he went.

15 And David reigned over all Israel; and David executed
16 judgement and justice unto all his people. And Joab the
son of Zeruiah was over the host; and Jehoshaphat the
17 son of Ahilud was recorder: and Zadok the son of Ahitub,
and Ahimelech the son of Abiathar, were priests; and
18 Seraiah was scribe; and Benaiah the son of Jehoiada

---

viii. 15-18. *David's principal officers of state.*

The greater part of this paragraph, verses 16-18, is repeated
with some deviations in xx. 23-26. In the latter passage the
order is more logical, first the chiefs of the army, then the heads
of the civil administration, and finally the chief priests. To the
first category belong **Joab**, the commander-in-chief of David's
military forces, consisting for the most part of militia, and
Benaiah, who
     was over **the Cherethites and the Pelethites** (see the
marginal note): these were a company of foreign mercenaries
forming the royal bodyguard. The former, in Hebrew *Krēthi*,
had their home in the Negeb (1 Sam. xxx. 14), and were akin to
the Philistines. Their name has usually been understood as
implying that their original home was the island of Crete. The
latter, in Hebrew *Plēthi*, are assumed to have been Philistines,
the name *Pelishti* having become *Plēthi* through assimilation to
Krēthi, from which *Plēthi* is never found dissociated (xv. 18, xx. 7,
23, &c.).

The heads of the civil administration were **Jehoshaphat**, the
recorder (Heb. *mazkir*), and **Seraiah**, the **scribe**. The *mazkir*
is generally supposed to have been the official annalist or
chronicler (so R. V. marg.), but etymologically the term signifies
'one who reminds' another (cf. Isa. xlii. 26, lxii. 6, 'the LORD's
remembrancers,' R. V.). In this sense the English official designation, 'the king's remembrancer,' is the exact equivalent. The duty
of the remembrancer was probably to keep the king informed of
the business of the state, and to advise him thereon, like the
grand vizir of an oriental court. To the **scribe** or secretary
(R. V. marg.) was doubtless committed the drafting and custody
of official documents, perhaps also the task of recording the outstanding events of the reign. Curiously the name of David's
scribe, here Seraiah, appears at every mention in a different
disguise. In 1 Kings iv. 3 his name is given as Shisha. Cf. below
xx. 25, and the parallels in Chronicles and LXX.

was over the Cherethites and the Pelethites; and David's
sons were priests.

[C] And David said, Is there yet any that is left of 9

In the third category we find David's priests, chief of whom
were **Zadok** and **Abiathar** (see xx. 25). To these was committed
in particular the custody of the Ark of God (see on xv. 24 f.). By
a dislocation of the text, two errors have crept in, so that Zadok
is now falsely represented as a descendant of Eli, and Abiathar is
displaced by his father, who fell a victim to his loyalty to David
(1 Sam. xx. 16 ff.). Read accordingly: 'and Abiathar the son
of Ahimelech, the son of Ahitub, and Zadok were priests.' The
latter, here mentioned for the first time, became sole priest on
Abiathar's deposition by Solomon on his accession (1 Kings ii.
27), and thus the progenitor of the Jerusalem priesthood of later
days. The most notable item remains.

and David's sons were priests: this statement must be
taken literally, not as the Chronicler, writing at a time when the
priesthood had become the exclusive right of the descendants of
Aaron, interpreted the words, 'chief about the king' (1 Chron.
xviii. 17), nor yet as 'chief ministers,' as the Revisers strangely
suggest in their margin. See the notes on vi. 17 f. and on xx. 26.

Third Division. 2 SAMUEL IX—XX.

AT THE COURT OF DAVID.

These twelve chapters of the Book of Samuel form the longest
continuous section of historical narrative from a single source to
be found in the Old Testament. With their continuation in
1 Kings i–ii, they have been extracted from an early document
which is universally regarded, on many grounds, as one of the
finest extant examples of Hebrew prose literature (p. 24). As
distinguished from the immediately preceding chapters, which
deal with matters of public interest, the capture of Jerusalem, the
wars with Israel's neighbours and the like, chapters ix–xx are
concerned primarily with the court and family life of David in
Jerusalem. Hence we propose to indicate this source by the
symbol C, and the nature of its contents by the heading—'At the
Court of David.' The identity of this document with the other
early source, M, which has supplied the great mass of the
narrative since 1 Sam. ix, must be left an open question.

One receives the impression from 'the abundance and particu-
larity of detail,' and from the freshness and vividness of the
narrative, that the author of C stands nearer to the incidents
recorded than is the case with M. But this impression may be

the house of Saul, that I may shew him kindness for
2 Jonathan's sake? And there was of the house of Saul
a servant whose name was Ziba, and they called him
unto David; and the king said unto him, Art thou Ziba?
3 And he said, Thy servant is he. And the king said, Is
there not yet any of the house of Saul, that I may shew
the kindness of God unto him? And Ziba said unto the
king, Jonathan hath yet a son, which is lame on his feet.
4 And the king said unto him, Where is he? And Ziba
said unto the king, Behold, he is in the house of Machir
5 the son of Ammiel, in Lo-debar. Then king David sent,
and fetched him out of the house of Machir the son of
6 Ammiel, from Lo-debar. And Mephibosheth, the son
of Jonathan, the son of Saul, came unto David, and

---

delusive (see further, Introduction, p. 21, note where also mention
is made of two interesting suggestions as to the ultimate source
of C). The contents of the division may be arranged in five subdivisions as given in section ii of the Introduction.

       A.   2 Sam. ix.   *David's Kindness to Meri-baal.*

The abrupt manner in which the chapter opens shows it to be
the continuation of something that went before. Klostermann and
more recent writers have accordingly suggested that our chapter
was originally preceded by ch. xxi, with its account of the tragedy
which befell the seven descendants of Saul. There are difficulties
in the way of accepting this suggestion, but it must be admitted
that the peculiar form of David's inquiry (verses 1, 3) requires
some preceding explanation of the disappearance from public
view of 'the house of Saul.' The insinuations conveyed in a
later part of this document (see xvi. 7 f. xix. 28) also point in
the same direction.

     3. the kindness of God: cf. the terms of David's oath to
Jonathan, 1 Sam. xx. 14 f. The cause of Meri-baal's lameness
was explained above, iv. 4, where see for the name Mephibosheth
= Meri-baal or Merib-baal.

     4. Machir the son of Ammiel: a prominent member of the
Manassite clan of the same name (Num. xxvi. 29 ff.) settled east
of the Jordan. His friendly relations with David appear later,
see xvii. 27, a passage which shows that **Lo-debar** was not far
from Mahanaim, the former residence of Meri-baal's uncle, Ish-baal.

fell on his face, and did obeisance. And David said,
Mephibosheth. And he answered, Behold thy servant!
And David said unto him, Fear not: for I will surely 7
shew thee kindness for Jonathan thy father's sake, and
will restore thee all the land of Saul thy father; and thou
shalt eat bread at my table continually. ·And he did 8
obeisance, and said, What is thy servant, that thou
shouldest look upon such a dead dog as I am? Then 9
the king called to Ziba, Saul's servant, and said unto
him, All that pertained to Saul and to all his house have
I given unto thy master's son. And thou shalt till the 10
land for him, thou, and thy sons, and thy servants; and
thou shalt bring in *the fruits*, that thy master's son may
have bread to eat: but Mephibosheth thy master's son
shall eat bread alway at my table. Now Ziba had fifteen
sons and twenty servants. Then said Ziba unto the king, 11
According to all that my lord the king commandeth his
servant, so shall thy servant do. As for Mephibosheth,
said the king, he shall eat at my table, as one of the king's

---

7. Fear not: Meri-baal's fear was by no means groundless in
view of the 'thorough' policy then, and still in the East, adopted
by the founder of a new dynasty towards possible rivals from the
old. The tragedy of Gibeah (ch. xxi) was also fresh in his mind.
In addition to the restitution of the family property, Meri-baal
receives a place at the royal table. In this decision motives of
policy perhaps had a place, as well as loyalty to the memory of
Jonathan.

10. Although 'eating continually at the king's table' (verse 13),
Meri-baal would naturally have a house and establishment of his
own to maintain in the capital. The means for their maintenance
was supplied by the restored estates of Saul, of which Ziba
was appointed resident administrator.

11. By the insertion of the words in italics, the second half of
this verse is put, against the grammar, into David's mouth,
thereby repeating 10[b]. The Greek form of the text is preferable:
'So Meri-baal ate at David's table as one of the king's sons.'
Cf. R. V. marg.

12 sons. And Mephibosheth had a young son, whose name was Mica. And all that dwelt in the house of Ziba were
13 servants unto Mephibosheth. So Mephibosheth dwelt in Jerusalem: for he did eat continually at the king's table; and he was lame on both his feet.

·10 And it came to pass after this, that the king of the children of Ammon died, and Hanun his son reigned in
2 his stead. And David said, I will shew kindness unto Hanun the son of Nahash, as his father shewed kindness unto me. So David sent by the hand of his servants to comfort him concerning his father. And David's serv-
3 ants came into the land of the children of Ammon. But

---

12. Since the reception of Meri-baal must be placed comparatively early in David's reign at Jerusalem, the mention of Mica must be given by anticipation, if Meri-baal was only five years old at his father's death (iv. 4). Through Mica the house of Saul was continued for several centuries according to 1 Chron. viii. 35 ff.

B. 2 Sam. x–xii. *David's War with the Ammonites, including the Affair of Bath-sheba.*

The narrator's main interest centres in the episode of David's criminal relations with Bath-sheba, which issued ultimately in the birth of Solomon, with whose accession to the throne this document C concludes (see above). This episode is given its proper historical setting by the account of the campaigns against the Ammonites and their Syrian allies. The Chronicler, it may be noted, omits from his life of David this dark stain on his hero's character, retaining only 2 Sam. x, xi. 1 and xii. 26, 30 f. See 1 Chron. xix. 1—xx. 3. The narrative falls into the following sections, the contents of which are indicated below: (a) x. 1—xi. 1, (b) xi. 2-27, (c) xii. 1-25, (d) xii. 26-31.

(a) x. 1—xi. 1. *David makes war on Ammon to avenge an insult to his ambassadors.*

1 f. the king of the children of Ammon: this was the Nahash (verse 2) who gave Saul the opportunity of winning his spurs by the relief of Jabesh-gilead (1 Sam. xi. 1 ff.). The occasion on which Nahash 'shewed kindness' to David is not recorded. His sympathies were doubtless with the latter in the 'long war between the house of Saul and the house of David' (iii. 1).

the princes of the children of Ammon said unto Hanun their lord, Thinkest thou that David doth honour thy father, that he hath sent comforters unto thee? hath not David sent his servants unto thee to search the city, and to spy it out, and to overthrow it? So Hanun took David's 4 servants, and shaved off the one half of their beards, and cut off their garments in the middle, even to their buttocks, and sent them away.   When they told it unto 5 David, he sent to meet them; for the men were greatly ashamed.   And the king said, Tarry at Jericho until your beards be grown, and then return.   And when the 6 children of Ammon saw that they were become odious to David, the children of Ammon sent and hired the Syrians of Beth-rehob, and the Syrians of Zobah, twenty

---

3. to search the city: this, we may assume, was Rabbah of Ammon, the capital of the kingdom, see on xi. 1.

4 f. Note the threefold indignity involved (1) in laying hands on the inviolate persons of ambassadors: (2) in shaving any part of the beard, the oriental symbol of manhood; and (3) in making the victims the objects of further ridicule by their having only one half of the beard removed.   In addition to all this, these dignified and sacrosanct ambassadors had to submit to an indecent exposure. No wonder that 'the men were greatly ashamed.'

6-14 relate the first campaign against the Ammonites, who, in anticipation of David's action, engage a number of the neighbouring petty states of Syria to come to their assistance—for a consideration of a thousand talents of silver, according to 1 Chron. xix. 6.

6. the Syrians of Beth-rehob: a city at the foot of Hermon, near Dan (Num. xiii. 21, Judges xviii. 28).   The other principalities here named, **Zobah, Maacah, Tob**, to which Geshur (xv. 8) may be added as a fifth, seem all to have lain between Mount Hermon and the Jabbok, the northern boundary of Gilead. This region is now known as the *Jaulān*.   See the Bible dictionaries for more precise details.   Winckler would identify Maacah with Geshur, thus reducing the principalities to four (*KAT*.[3] 291). Absalom's mother, it will be remembered, the daughter of the king of Geshur, was named Maacah (iii. 3).   The smallness of the Maacah contingent compared with those of its neighbours has roused suspicion, but is likely to be nearer the actual numbers sent by these petty states than the traditional figures.

thousand footmen, and the king of Maacah with a thousand men, and the men of Tob twelve thousand men.
7 And when David heard of it, he sent Joab, and all the
8 host of the mighty men. And the children of Ammon came out, and put the battle in array, at the entering in of the gate: and the Syrians of Zobah, and of Rehob, and the men of Tob and Maacah, were by themselves
9 in the field. Now when Joab saw that the battle was set against him before and behind, he chose of all the choice men of Israel, and put them in array against the
10 Syrians: and the rest of the people he committed into the hand of Abishai his brother, and he put them in
11 array against the children of Ammon. And he said, If the Syrians be too strong for me, then thou shalt help me: but if the children of Ammon be too strong for
12 thee, then I will come and help thee. Be of good courage, and let us play the men for our people, and for

7. and all the host of the mighty men: *lit.* 'and all the host, (even) the mighty men'; but elsewhere 'the mighty men' (*gibbôrim*) figure as a corps of veterans, probably the survivors and successors of the six hundred that accompanied David in his outlaw period. We should therefore read here: 'all the host and the mighty men,' i. e. the militia specially levied for the occasion and this nucleus of a standing army. Cf. xx. 7 where the corps of the *gibbôrim* is distinguished both from the royal bodyguard, the 'Krethi and Plethi' (see on viii. 18), and from the main body of the militia under Amasa.

8-12 give a lucid account of Joab's tactics. The Ammonite troops are drawn up a short distance from the principal gate of Rabbah, their capital, on which they can fall back in case of defeat. The Syrian contingents take up their position so as to place the Hebrew army between two fires, so to say. The Syrians are regarded by Joab as the more formidable opponents, and accordingly he decides to engage them in person with a body of picked men, leaving his brother Abishai with the rest of the militia to deal with the Ammonites. Should either division of the Hebrew army show signs of distress, the other is to advance to its assistance.

12. and for the cities of our God: a unique and difficult ex-the cities of our God: and the LORD do that which seemeth him good.   So Joab and the people that were 13 with him drew nigh unto the battle against the Syrians: and they fled before him.   And when the children of 14 Ammon saw that the Syrians were fled, they likewise fled before Abishai, and entered into the city.   Then Joab returned from the children of Ammon, and came to Jerusalem.   [R] And when the Syrians saw that they 15 were put to the worse before Israel, they gathered themselves together.   And Hadarezer sent, and brought out 16 the Syrians that were beyond the River: and they came to Helam, with Shobach the captain of the host of Hadarezer at their head.   And it was told David; and 17 he gathered all Israel together, and passed over Jordan,

---

pression; read, with Klostermann and Budde, 'let us play the men for our people and for the Ark of God.'   Since the Ark accompanied the army in the second Ammonite campaign in the following year (xi. 11), there is every reason to assume its presence on this occasion.   Joab's devout expression of resignation is identical with that used by Eli (1 Sam. iii. 18).

14. On the flight of the Syrians, the Ammonites retire behind the shelter of their city walls.   As it was now probably too late in the year for a formal siege, Joab returns to Jerusalem.

x. 15-19.   *David reduces several Syrian principalities.*
We have here a doublet of viii. 3-8, the source of which is not clear.   If it originally belonged to C. at least its position here is due to the compiler, as it cannot well be fitted into the latter's narrative, for in xi. 1 we find Joab resuming warlike operations against Ammon as soon as the season allowed.   Here, moreover, David appears in command to the exclusion of Joab, while the position of Hadadezer is at variance with that implied in verse 6 (see on 19 below), all pointing to a source distinct from C.

15. The logic of this verse leaves something to be desired. The first half, to 'Israel,' may be part of C's narrative, the continuation of which is now found at the end of verse 19.   The connexion of thought is then perfect.

16. Hadarezer: in the best Hebrew MSS. Hadadezer, as viii. 3.   The 'River' here—as always when so printed in R. V.— is the Euphrates, and implies that Hadadezer's authority extended into Mesopotamia.   The position of **Helam** is unknown.

and came to Helam.   And the Syrians set themselves in
18 array against David, and fought with him.   And the
Syrians fled before Israel ; and David slew of the Syrians
the men of seven hundred chariots, and forty thousand
horsemen, and smote Shobach the captain of their host,
19 that he died there.   And when all the kings that were
servants to Hadarezer saw that they were put to the
worse before Israel, they made peace with Israel, and
served them.   So the Syrians feared to help the children
of Ammon any more.

11 [C] And it came to pass, at the return of the year, at
the time when kings go out *to battle*, that David sent
Joab, and his servants with him, and all Israel ; and they
destroyed the children of Ammon, and besieged Rabbah.
But David tarried at Jerusalem.

2   And it came to pass at eventide, that David arose

---

18. The divergent details of David's victory which are found
here, in viii. 4, and in 1 Chron. xix. 18, are the despair alike of
the textual and of the historical critic.

19. This representation of Hadadezer as the head of a number
of subject kings conflicts both with viii. 3, where he is merely
king of Zobah, and with x. 6, where Zobah is one of four co-
ordinate states.   The inference has been already drawn.   There
is no reason, however, for questioning the fact that David
succeeded in establishing a suzerainty over these principalities
of the Jaulan.   The date may have been after the close of the
Ammonite war.

xi. **1. at the return of the year:** in the following spring, after
the rains had ceased about the beginning of May.   This was the
usual time, as the narrator informs us, for resuming warlike
operations (cf. 1 Kings xx. 22, 26).   The second campaign opened
with the siege of **Rabbah**, the Ammonite capital, which stood
some twenty miles, as the crow flies, east of the Jordan at the
head of the *Wadi Ammān*.   Under the name of Philadelphia it
had an honourable history from the time of Ptolemy Philadelphus
to the third century A. D.   Its modern name is *Ammān*.

(*b*) xi. **2-27.** *David and Bath-sheba.*
2. David's new palace on the eastern ridge (vi. 11) would over-

from off his bed, and walked upon the roof of the king's house: and from the roof he saw a woman bathing; and the woman was very beautiful to look upon.   And David 3 sent and inquired after the woman.   And one said, Is not this Bath-sheba, the daughter of Eliam, the wife of Uriah the Hittite?   And David sent messengers, and took 4 her; and she came in unto him, and he lay with her; (for she was purified from her uncleanness;) and she returned unto her house.   And the woman conceived; 5 and she sent and told David, and said, I am with child. And David sent to Joab, *saying*, Send me Uriah the 6 Hittite.   And Joab sent Uriah to David.   And when 7 Uriah was come unto him, David asked of him how Joab did, and how the people fared, and how the war prospered.   And David said to Uriah, Go down to thy 8 house, and wash thy feet.   And Uriah departed out of

---

look the houses on at least three sides.   The time was late after-noon, when David had finished his siesta (cf. iv. 5).   The motive of the bath is suggested by the parenthesis in verse 4 (see Lev. xv. 19 ff.).

3. Bath-sheba: in 1 Chron. iii. 5 'Bath-shua' by a mistaken pointing for 'Bath-sheva,' a variant pronunciation merely.   Her husband **Uriah** and her father **Eliam** are both enrolled in David's second order of knighthood (xxiii. 34, 39).   The latter was the son of the famous Ahithophel (cf. on xv. 12).

Uriah the Hittite.   The name Uriah, probably 'Yahweh is light' or 'fire,' shows either that his father had been a Yahweh-worshipper before him. or that Uriah had taken this name when admitted as a *gēr* to the cultus of his patron.   We learn further from this passage that in those early days non-Hebrew *gērim* or outlanders enjoyed the *connubium*—the right of intermarriage— in contrast to the rigid exclusiveness of a later period.

6 ff. To conceal his crime David devises a scheme which is frustrated by the husband's religious scruples as a 'consecrated' soldier.   For the sexual taboo enforced in war-time, see on 1 Sam. xxi. 5 (p. 148).

7. did, ... fared, ... prospered: variant renderings of the idiomatic Hebrew phrase 'to ask after the welfare (*lit.* peace)' of some one.

R

the king's house, and there followed him a mess *of meat*
9 from the king.   But Uriah slept at the door of the king's
house with all the servants of his lord, and went not
10 down to his house.   And when they had told David,
saying, Uriah went not down unto his house, David said
unto Uriah, Art thou not come from a journey? where-
11 fore didst thou not go down unto thine house?   And
Uriah said unto David, The ark, and Israel, and Judah,
abide in booths; and my lord Joab, and the servants of
my lord, are encamped in the open field; shall I then
go into mine house, to eat and to drink, and to lie with my
wife? as thou livest, and as thy soul liveth, I will not do
12 this thing.   And David said to Uriah, Tarry here to-day
also, and to-morrow I will let thee depart.   So Uriah
13 abode in Jerusalem that day, and the morrow.   And
when David had called him, he did eat and drink before
him; and he made him drunk: and at even he went out
to lie on his bed with the servants of his lord, but went
14 not down to his house.   And it came to pass in the
morning, that David wrote a letter to Joab, and sent it
15 by the hand of Uriah.   And he wrote in the letter,
saying, Set ye Uriah in the forefront of the hottest battle,

---

8. a mess of meat from the king: *lit.* 'a portion' or 'gift
from the king.'   Such a gift was a special mark of favour from
a superior (see Gen. xliii. 34).

11. The presence of the Ark, as the visible representative of
the deity, with the army on active service, which this passage
attests, is a significant fact in early Hebrew religion.   See the
Appendix, and cf. on x 12, xv. 24.

as thou livest: read, to obviate the tautology, 'as Yahweh
liveth' (Wellhausen).   See on 1 Sam. xx. 3.

13 ff. The narrator continues unsparingly to unfold a second
and still more discreditable attempt to break down Uriah's self-
restraint.   Finally, in despair of overcoming the soldier's scruples,
David resolves upon his death.   Verse 13 should begin thus:
'And on the morrow when David,' &c., as in the margin.

and retire ye from him, that he may be smitten, and die. And it came to pass, when Joab kept watch upon the 16 city, that he assigned Uriah unto the place where he knew that valiant men were. And the men of the city 17 went out, and fought with Joab: and there fell some of the people, even of the servants of David; and Uriah the Hittite died also. Then Joab sent and told David 18 all the things concerning the war; and he charged the 19 messenger, saying, When thou hast made an end of telling all the things concerning the war unto the king, it shall be that, if the king's wrath arise, and he say unto 20 thee, Wherefore went ye so nigh unto the city to fight? knew ye not that they would shoot from the wall? who 21 smote Abimelech the son of Jerubbesheth? did not a woman cast an upper millstone upon him from the wall, that he died at Thebez? why went ye so nigh the wall? then shalt thou say, Thy servant Uriah the Hittite is dead also. So the messenger went, and came and 22 shewed David all that Joab had sent him for. And the 23

---

xi. 16-25. *Joab carries out his master's order and Uriah falls in battle.*

18 ff. Joab sends a messenger to report verbally to David on the sortie and the loss of life it had entailed. Anticipating that the latter would censure his rashness, Joab instructs the reporter to inform David that Uriah was among the slain. The narrator evidently wishes us to understand that Joab had grasped the situation, and confidently counted upon the effect of the last item of news upon the king.

21. Abimelech the son of Jerubbesheth: a disguised form of Jerub-baal (see on ii. 18). The incident is told in Judges ix. 50 ff. **Thebez** is generally identified with the modern *Tubas*, about halfway between Shechem and Beth-shan.

22. At the end of this verse the Hebrew text has dropped a few lines preserved in the Greek version, which proceeds thus: 'even all the things concerning the war' (as in verse 18). 'And David was angry with Joab, and he said to the messenger, Wherefore went ye so nigh unto the city to fight?'—and so on, repeating

messenger said unto David, The men prevailed against
us, and came out unto us into the field, and we were
24 upon them even unto the entering of the gate.   And the
shooters shot at thy servants from off the wall ; and some
of the king's servants be dead, and thy servant Uriah
25 the Hittite is dead also.   Then David said unto the
messenger, Thus shalt thou say unto Joab, Let not this
thing displease thee, for the sword devoureth one as well
as another : make thy battle more strong against the city,
26 and overthrow it : and encourage thou him.   And when
the wife of Uriah heard that Uriah her husband was
27 dead, she made lamentation for her husband.   And
when the mourning was past, David sent and took her
home to his house, and she became his wife, and bare
him a son.   But the thing that David had done displeased
the LORD.

12   And the LORD sent Nathan unto David.   And he

with slight variations the words of verses 20 f., to ' why went ye
so nigh the wall ? '   To these questions the messenger replies in
verse 23.

25. The result is precisely as Joab anticipated.   Instead of
being censured, he is encouraged to persevere with the siege.

26 f. After a short period of mourning, Bath-sheba is taken
into the royal harem.   The last clause of verse 27 is the introduction to the third act of this domestic tragedy (xii. 15ᵇ–23).

(c) xii. 1–25.   *David rebuked by Nathan : the death of Bath-sheba's
child and the birth of Solomon.*

The objective character of the rest of this history of David's
family life, and the fact that in the further development of the
tragedy no reference is made to Nathan's interposition, while
verse 15ᵇ, as has just been pointed out, forms an excellent
sequence to xi. 27, have led several recent scholars to regard
Nathan's appearance and rebuke as an addition by the compiler
from another source.   It is true that the oldest Hebrew writers—
and C is the earliest we have (see the Introduction pp. 8, 21)—were
content as a rule to allow their story to point its own moral.   In
the present instance, for example, the author of C may have been
content with allowing his readers to see that the death of the child
was sufficient evidence of David's sin and the Divine displeasure.

came unto him, and said unto him, There were two men in one city; the one rich, and the other poor. The rich 2 man had exceeding many flocks and herds: but the poor 3 man had nothing, save one little ewe lamb, which he had bought and nourished up: and it grew up together with him, and with his children; it did eat of his own morsel, and drank of his own cup, and lay in his bosom, and was unto him as a daughter. And there came a traveller 4 unto the rich man, and he spared to take of his own flock and of his own herd, to dress for the wayfaring man that was come unto him, but took the poor man's lamb, and dressed it for the man that was come to him. And 5 David's anger was greatly kindled against the man; and he said to Nathan, As the LORD liveth, the man that hath done this is worthy to die: and he shall restore the lamb 6 fourfold, because he did this thing, and because he had no pity.

And Nathan said to David, Thou art the man. Thus 7 saith the LORD, the God of Israel, I anointed thee king over Israel, and I delivered thee out of the hand of Saul; and I gave thee thy master's house, and thy master's 8

On the other hand, it may be sufficient with Wellhausen, Kittel, and others to regard verses 10-12 as having been inserted by the compiler into the older narrative for the purpose of 'underscoring the moral of the history,' and heightening the colour of the prophetic rebuke, and to leave the rest of the chapter to C.

1. Nathan approaches David ostensibly to ask his decision in a case of high-handed oppression of a poor man by a wealthy neighbour. In reality he tells the parable of the ewe lamb, one of the few examples in the O. T. of this species of composition.

6. fourfold: read, with LXX, 'sevenfold.' The proverbial expression of the Greek text is more likely to be the original. A later copyist corrected this to 'fourfold' in order to harmonize with the law of Exod. xxii. 1.

7 ff. David is convicted out of his own mouth, and is, moreover, accused of base ingratitude to the Author of all his good fortune.

8. thy master's wives. The reference is to the ancient custom

wives into thy bosom, and gave thee the house of Israel and of Judah; and if that had been too little, I would

9 have added unto thee such and such things. Wherefore hast thou despised the word of the LORD, to do that which is evil in his sight? thou hast smitten Uriah the Hittite with the sword, and hast taken his wife to be thy wife, and hast slain him with the sword of the children

10 of Ammon. [R] Now therefore, the sword shall never depart from thine house; because thou hast despised me, and hast taken the wife of Uriah the Hittite to be thy wife.

11 Thus saith the LORD, Behold, I will raise up evil against thee out of thine own house, and I will take thy wives before thine eyes, and give them unto thy neighbour, and he shall lie with thy wives in the sight of this sun.

12 For thou didst it secretly: but I will do this thing before

13 all Israel, and before the sun. [C] And David said unto Nathan, I have sinned against the LORD. And Nathan said unto David, The LORD also hath put away thy sin;

14 thou shalt not die. Howbeit, because by this deed thou

---

by which a sovereign's harem passed with the crown to his successor. For an illustration see xvi. 21 f., and cf. 1 Kings ii. 17 ff. with Skinner's notes (Century Bible).

10-12. The nature of these three verses has been pointed out in the introductory note above. It can scarcely be doubted that they are a *vaticinium post eventum* inserted by the compiler or another into the original text of 1-15. According to the latter David's crime is to find its punishment solely in the death of his child (verse 14). The opening words (verse 10) are a reflection of the family feuds which brought about the deaths of Amnon, Absalom, and Adonijah, while verse 11 clearly alludes to the unfilial conduct of the latter as related below (xvi. 21 f.).

13 continues verse 9, and gives David's confession of his sin which calls forth the assurance that Yahweh had caused his sin to pass away (so literally). 'The sin rested upon David and would (if not taken away) work death for him. Yahweh took it away. that he should not die, but it wrought the death of the child' (H. P. Smith).

14. Read: 'Howbeit, because thou hast despised Yahweh in hast given great occasion to the enemies of the LORD to blaspheme, the child also that is born unto thee shall surely die. And Nathan departed unto his house. 15

And the LORD struck the child that Uriah's wife bare unto David, and it was very sick. David therefore be- 16 sought God for the child; and David fasted, and went in, and lay all night upon the earth. And the elders of 17 his house arose, *and stood* beside him, to raise him up from the earth: but he would not, neither did he eat bread with them. And it came to pass on the seventh 18 day, that the child died. And the servants of David feared to tell him that the child was dead: for they said, Behold, while the child was yet alive, we spake unto him, and he hearkened not unto our voice: how will he then vex himself, if we tell him that the child is dead? But 19 when David saw that his servants whispered together, David perceived that the child was dead: and David said unto his servants, Is the child dead? And they said, He is dead. Then David arose from the earth, and washed, 20 and anointed himself, and changed his apparel; and he came into the house of the LORD, and worshipped: then

---

this thing.' The verb rendered 'give occasion to blaspheme' nowhere bears this meaning, but always denotes 'to scorn, despise,' with Yahweh, the name of Yahweh, &c., as object. A copyist who took offence at the strong language of the original inserted 'enemies of,' as in a similar case, 1 Sam. xxv. 22.

xii. 15^b-23. *The death of Bath-sheba's child.*

16. The tenses of the original are frequentative, showing that David renewed his intercession every day of the seven (verse 18). The place to which David **went in** is not specified. The context suggests an inner room in the palace rather than, as in vii. 18, the sacred tent (see on verse 20).

17. the elders of his house: the senior officers of his household.

18. The R.V. marginal rendering of the latter half of the verse is closer to the Hebrew idiom.

20. came into the house of the LORD: the tent which he had pitched for the Ark in the citadel (vi. 17; cf. 1 Kings i. 39, ii. 28).

he came to his own house; and when he required they
21 set bread before him, and he did eat. Then said his
servants unto him, What thing is this that thou hast
done? thou didst fast and weep for the child, while it
was alive; but when the child was dead, thou didst rise
22 and eat·bread. And he said, While the child was yet
alive, I fasted and wept: for I said, Who knoweth
whether the LORD will not be gracious to me, that the
23 child may live? But now he is dead, wherefore should I
fast? can I bring him back again? I shall go to him,
24 but he shall not return to me. And David comforted
Bath-sheba his wife, and went in unto her, and lay with
her: and she bare a son, and he called his name
25 Solomon. And the LORD loved him; and he sent by
the hand of Nathan the prophet, and he called his name
Jedidiah, for the LORD's sake.
26   Now Joab fought against Rabbah of the children of

23. David consoles himself with the thought that the child lives
—though it was but a shadowy existence—in Sheol, 'the house of
meeting for all living' (Job xxx. 23 R.V. marg.). There by and
by he will rejoin his child, as Jacob hoped to go to Joseph (Gen.
xxxvii. 35). This thought of a continued existence of a sort in
Sheol is reflected in the frequent O. T. phrase, 'he was gathered
to his fathers.' On the early Hebrew conceptions of the after-
world, see A. B. Davidson, *The Theology of the O. T.*, 425 ff.;
Charles, *Eschatology*, 33 ff.; Driver, *Sermons on the O. T.*, 72 ff.

24 f. *Birth of Solomon.* The easiest construction of the somewhat difficult text is to take the last clause of verse 24 with the
following verse: 'And Yahweh loved him, and sent by the hand
of Nathan the prophet, and called his name Yedidyah (the beloved
of Yahweh).'

The following words, **for the LORD'S sake**, have been added
by a reader who misunderstood the construction of the sentence.
It should be added, however, that some scholars would read:
'and he (David) committed him to the charge (*lit.* hand) of
Nathan.' That Nathan acted as Solomon's tutor would be an
interesting biographical detail could it be substantiated.

(*d*) xii. 26-31.   *The capture of Rabbah.*
Our author now resumes the thread of the narrative which was

Ammon, and took the royal city. And Joab sent mes- 27
sengers to David, and said, I have fought against Rabbah,
yea, I have taken the city of waters. Now therefore gather 28
the rest of the people together, and encamp against the
city, and take it: lest I take the city, and it be called
after my name. And David gathered all the people 29
together, and went to Rabbah, and fought against it, and
took it. And he took the crown of their king from off 30
his head; and the weight thereof was a talent of gold,
and *in it were* precious stones; and it was set on David's
head. And he brought forth the spoil of the city, exceeding much. And he brought forth the people that 31

dropped after xi. 1, although he has already advanced considerably
beyond the date of this section, since the capture of Rabbah was
evidently the result of Joab's second summer campaign.

26 f. and took the royal city. This reading, which stultifies
Joab's message, is clearly a copyist's slip for **the city of waters.**
Here, as in v. 7, 9, the word rendered 'city' has its original
meaning of 'fortress'; hence we should render 'the Water Fort,'
the work defending the water supply. An interesting parallel
is furnished by Polybius (v. 71) in his account of the siege of
Rabbath-Ammon by Antiochus Epiphanes. The latter succeeded
in stopping the water supply, when the garrison surrendered
(218 B.C.). The city proper was built on the high ground above.

28. and it be called after my name: literally and more
expressively, 'and my name be called over it' (cf. R. V. marg.),
in token of possession. So David renamed the Jebusite citadel
'David's burg' (v. 7, 9). Joab's self-abnegation in this case
should not be forgotten in our estimate of the character of this
truculent but loyal subject.

30. he took the crown of their king, &c. If the weight of the
crown in question is correctly given as a talent—54 lb. avoirdupois at the lowest computation (see Hastings' *DB.* iii. 419,
iv. 903)—it is impossible that it could have been worn either by
Hanun or by David. But the same consonants as yield 'their
king' may be read 'Milcom,' the national deity of the Ammonites
(note margin); and this, the reading of most Greek MSS., is undoubtedly original. In the sequel we should read: 'and in it
(the crown of Milcom) was a precious stone, which was set upon
David's head.'

31. The old controversy as to whether the Ammonites were

were therein, and put them under saws, and under
harrows of iron, and under axes of iron, and made them
pass through the brickkiln : and thus did he unto all the
cities of the children of Ammon.   And David and all
the people returned unto Jerusalem.

13   And it came to pass after this, that Absalom the son
of David had a fair sister, whose name was Tamar ; and
2 Amnon the son of David loved her.   And Amnon was
so vexed that he fell sick because of his sister Tamar ;

---

savagely done to death by means of certain instruments of torture
here enumerated, or whether they were merely set to various
forms of hard labour, is reflected in the alternative renderings of
the text and margin of R. V.   The text advocates torture, the
margin hard labour.   The latter is supported by the grammar and
the lexicon, and is the view now generally adopted.   Render
somewhat as follows : 'and he set them to saws and iron picks
and iron axes and made them labour at the brick-moulds.'   For
a full discussion of the difficulties see Driver's *Notes* in loc.

C. 2 Sam. xiii–xiv.   *Amnon and Absalom.*

From this point to the end of ch. xx, this history of David's court
is continued in precise chronological sequence.   The incidents
and episodes are almost all mutually related as cause and effect.
Thus, to take only the most outstanding, Amnon's lust leads to
Absalom's revenge, the sequel of which is banishment to a heathen
land.   As he broods in exile over his fancied wrongs, the
prince's character deteriorates, and this deterioration in due course
issues in his ambitious attempt to seize the throne and all that
flowed therefrom.   The progress of the narrative is marked by
three stages, (*a*) xiii. 1-22, (*b*) xiii. 23-39, (*c*) xiv.

(*a*) xiii. 1-22.   *Amnon deforces Tamar, the sister of Absalom.*
1. Absalom the son of David.   The narrator introduces us at
once to the young prince who is the central figure in the tragic
events to be disclosed in the following chapters.   Absalom and
Tamar were full brother and sister, children of Maacah, daughter
of the king of Geshur (iii. 3).   Amnon was David's first-born,
the son of Ahinoam the Jezreelitess (iii. 2), and therefore Tamar's
half-brother.   The case of Abraham and Sarah shows that
marriage between the children of the same father by different
mothers was sanctioned by early Hebrew custom (cf. verse 13,
end), though forbidden by the later legislation (Lev. xviii. 9).
2. An excellent illustration both of the strong emotions and of

for she was a virgin; and it seemed hard to Amnon to do any thing unto her. But Amnon had a friend, whose 3 name was Jonadab, the son of Shimeah David's brother: and Jonadab was a very subtil man. And he said unto 4 him, Why, O son of the king, art thou thus lean from day to day? wilt thou not tell me? And Amnon said unto him, I love Tamar, my brother Absalom's sister. And Jonadab said unto him, Lay thee down on thy bed, 5 and feign thyself sick: and when thy father cometh to see thee, say unto him, Let my sister Tamar come, I pray thee, and give me bread to eat, and dress the food in my sight, that I may see it, and eat it at her hand. So Amnon lay down, and feigned himself sick: and when 6 the king was come to see him, Amnon said unto the king, Let my sister Tamar come, I pray thee, and make me a couple of cakes in my sight, that I may eat at her hand. Then David sent home to Tamar, saying, Go 7 now to thy brother Amnon's house, and dress him food. So Tamar went to her brother Amnon's house; and he 8 was laid down. And she took dough, and kneaded it, and made cakes in his sight, and did bake the cakes. And she took the pan, and poured them out before him; 9 but he refused to eat. And Amnon said, Have out all men from me. And they went out every man from him.

---

the social customs of the East. Amnon was literally 'sick of love' (Cant. ii. 5, v. 8, and the Arabian Nights *passim*), and had few opportunities of seeing the unmarried members of the royal harem, and probably none of seeing Tamar alone.

3 introduces Amnon's **subtil** cousin and Mephistopheles.

7. David sent home to Tamar: rather, 'sent (a message) to the palace to Tamar.' Amnon, as the king's eldest son, evidently had a separate establishment.

9 f. The sequence of the action in these two verses is difficult to follow. We should probably read with Klostermann, by a slight change: 'And she called the attendant (cf. verse 17), and he poured them out before him.' The untasted cakes, we

10 And Amnon said unto Tamar, Bring the food into the chamber, that I may eat of thine hand. And Tamar took the cakes which she had made, and brought them
11 into the chamber to Amnon her brother. And when she had brought them near unto him to eat, he took hold of her, and said unto her, Come lie with me, my sister.
12 And she answered him, Nay, my brother, do not force me; for no such thing ought to be done in Israel: do
13 not thou this folly. And I, whither shall I carry my shame? and as for thee, thou shalt be as one of the fools in Israel. Now therefore, I pray thee, speak unto the
14 king; for he will not withhold me from thee. Howbeit he would not hearken unto her voice: but being stronger
15 than she, he forced her, and lay with her. Then Amnon hated her with exceeding great hatred; for the hatred wherewith he hated her was greater than the love where-with he had loved her. And Amnon said unto her,
16 Arise, be gone. And she said unto him, Not so, because this great wrong in putting me forth is *worse* than the other that thou didst unto me. But he would not hearken

---

must suppose, the attendant brought back to Tamar, who had till then modestly refrained from entering the bed-chamber.

12 f. Tamar's touching appeal to her brother's conscience, setting clearly before him the sinfulness of his desire and the consequences both to herself and to him, while frankly assuring him of her willingness to enter into lawful wedlock with him.

do not thou this folly: a standing expression in the O. T. for acts of immorality, hence rather 'this villany,' as the word is rendered in Isa. xxxii. 6; 'profligates' and 'profligacy' are nearer the mark than the weaker terms 'fools' (verse 13) and 'folly.' Morality, it will be observed, finds its sanction in custom, not in a written code (cf. Kautzsch in Hastings' *DB.*, extra vol., 624[a]).

15. Amnon's heartless treatment of the victim of his lust betrays the hardened profligate.

16. Read: 'Not so, my brother, for greater is this wrong (to send me away) than the other that thou didst unto me,' for which see Driver, *Notes* in loc.

unto her. Then he called his servant that ministered 17
unto him, and said, Put now this woman out from me,
and bolt the door after her. And she had a garment of 18
divers colours upon her: for with such robes were the
king's daughters that were virgins apparelled. Then his
servant brought her out, and bolted the door after her.
And Tamar put ashes on her head, and rent her garment 19
of divers colours that was on her; and she laid her hand
on her head, and went her way, crying aloud as she went.
And Absalom her brother said unto her, Hath Amnon 20
thy brother been with thee? but now hold thy peace,
my sister: he is thy brother; take not this thing to heart.
So Tamar remained desolate in her brother Absalom's
house. But when king David heard of all these things, 21
he was very wroth. And Absalom spake unto Amnon 22
neither good nor bad: for Absalom hated Amnon, because he had forced his sister Tamar.

And it came to pass after two full years, that Absalom 23

---

18 f. The greater part of verse 18 was originally a marginal
gloss upon **her garment of divers colours** in verse 19. This
rendering represents the Alexandrian tradition regarding this
garment, which is mentioned only here and Gen. xxxvii. 3 ff.
Modern authorities give 'a tunic of palms and soles' (*lit.* 'of
extremities'), i. e. a tunic reaching to and covering hands and feet.
It was evidently a mark of distinction compared with the ordinary
short tunic which had no sleeves.

19. she laid her hand on her head: an attitude of grief
frequently represented on the Egyptian monuments.

21. Add, with LXX, 'yet did he not pain the spirit of Amnon
his son, for he loved him because he was his first-born.' David,
alas! took no measures against his profligate son. The same
expression is used by our author of David's remissness in the up-
bringing of Adonijah (1 Kings i. 6). This weakness on David's
part is perhaps the most conspicuous defect in his character.
To it, as the historian clearly perceived, the greatest sorrows of
his life were due.

(*b*) xiii. 23-29. *Absalom's revenge and flight.*
After the lapse of two years Absalom embraces the occasion of

had sheepshearers in Baal-hazor, which is beside Ephraim :
24 and Absalom invited all the king's sons.   And Absalom
came to the king, and said, Behold now, thy servant hath
sheepshearers ; let the king, I pray thee, and his servants
25 go with thy servant.   And the king said to Absalom,
Nay, my son, let us not all go, lest we be burdensome
unto thee.   And he pressed him : howbeit he would not
26 go, but blessed him.   Then said Absalom, If not, I pray
thee, let my brother Amnon go with us.   And the king
27 said unto him, Why should he go with thee?   But
Absalom pressed him, that he let Amnon and all the
28 king's sons go with him.   And Absalom commanded his
servants, saying, Mark ye now, when Amnon's heart is
. merry with wine ; and when I say unto you, Smite
Amnon, then kill him, fear not : have not I commanded
29 you ? be courageous, and be valiant.   And the servants
of Absalom did unto Amnon as Absalom had com-

the annual sheep-shearing to invite all the king's sons to the
accompanying festivities (see on 1 Sam. xxv. 2 ff.).   When the
merry-making is at its height, Amnon is murdered by Absalom's
order, whereupon the latter flees to the court of his grandfather,
the king of Geshur.

23. Baal-hazor, which is beside Ephraim. Both places have
been identified with sites near Beth-el, where Absalom's estate
must have lain.

26. In default of the king, Absalom doubtless gave out that he
would be honoured by the presence of the heir-apparent.

27. The Greek text shows that a line has fallen out at the end
of the Hebrew.   The last two lines of the MS. each ended in the
word for ' king,' and the copyist's eye passed inadvertently from
the one to the other (*homoeoteleuton* as in verse 34, cf. 1 Sam. x. 1).
Read : ' and Absalom made a feast like the feast of a king.'

29. Amnon's assassination causes a panic among the royal
guests.   The mule is here mentioned for the first time (but see
on 1 Sam. xxi. 7).   In this reign it seems to have supplanted the
ass as the mount of royalty (1 Kings i. 33) and of the royal family.
The horse was used only for the war-chariots (see on viii. 4).
The breeding of mules and other hybrids was forbidden by the
later legislation (Lev. xix. 19).   .

manded. Then all the king's sons arose, and every man
gat him up upon his mule, and fled. And it came to 30
pass, while they were in the way, that the tidings came to
David, saying, Absalom hath slain all the king's sons,
and there is not one of them left. Then the king arose, 31
and rent his garments, and lay on the earth; and all his
servants stood by with their clothes rent. And Jonadab, 32
the son of Shimeah David's brother, answered and said,
Let not my lord suppose that they have killed all the
young men the king's sons; for Amnon only is dead:
for by the appointment of Absalom this hath been determined from the day that he forced his sister Tamar.
Now therefore let not my lord the king take the thing to 33
his heart, to think that all the king's sons are dead: for
Amnon only is dead. But Absalom fled. And the 34
young man that kept the watch lifted up his eyes, and
looked, and, behold, there came much people by the way

32. for by the appointment (*lit.* mouth) **of Absalom,** &c. The
sentence is obscure in the original; it is now usual to read, 'for
upon the mouth' (better perhaps 'the face') 'of Absalom there
hath been a scowl since the day,' &c. (so Ewald, *History of Israel*,
iii 172; cf. Driver, *Notes* in loc.), a graphic touch worthy of our
court historian (C).

34. But Absalom fled. The threefold repetition of this statement (verses 34, 37, 38) is suspicious. Here we have probably
a corruption of the last words of Jonadab's speech: 'and the
rest of his brethren are safe' (Klost., Budde). On this follows
an incident of which the scene in xviii. 25 ff. affords a close
parallel. The LXX (slightly emended by Wellhausen) has preserved the full text of the original, reading in the second half of
the verse: 'and behold there came much people by the **way** of
the two Beth-horons, on the descent; and the watchman came
and told the king, saying, I see men coming from the **way** of
the two Beth-horons on the hill-side.' The scribe of the Hebrew
MS. passed from the one **way** to the other, omitting the two lines
between. The curious expression **behind him** in the text is now
seen to be a corruption of *Ḥōrōnaim*, the two Beth-horons, upper
and lower (Josh. xvi. 3, 5), halfway between Jerusalem and
Lydda.

35 of the hill side behind him.   And Jonadab said unto the
king, Behold, the king's sons are come: as thy servant
36 said, so it is.   And it came to pass, as soon as he had
made an end of speaking, that, behold, the king's sons
came, and lifted up their voice, and wept: and the king
37 also and all his servants wept very sore.   But Absalom
fled, and went to Talmai the son of Ammihur, king of
Geshur.   And *David* mourned for his son every day.
38   So Absalom fled, and went to Geshur, and was there
39 three years.   And *the soul of* king David longed to go
forth unto Absalom: for he was comforted concerning
Amnon, seeing he was dead.

14   Now Joab the son of Zeruiah perceived that the
2 king's heart was toward Absalom.   And Joab sent to

37–39. The text of these verses is clearly overloaded (cf. 38ᵃ =
37ᵃ).   Three points are emphasized by the historian, Absalom's
flight, David's mourning for his first-born, and finally the growth
of an intense longing on David's part for the absent Absalom.

37. Talmai the son of Ammihur, king of Geshur: read,
with R. V. marg., 'Ammihud' (Num. i. 10, &c.).   He was the
father of Absalom's mother Maacah.   For **Geshur** see on iii. 3 and
x. 6.   Here Absalom remained three years, so that this chapter
covers the space of five years (see verse 23).   When the chapter
opens David had already been twenty years, more or less, on the
united throne, since the sons born in Hebron are now grown up.

39. The Hebrew text is unintelligible.   The italics of R. V.
have been supplied from LXX (L).   The sense, if not the text, is:
'and David's spirit was consumed with a longing for Absalom.'
The historian thus prepares his readers for the next chapter of
this closely articulated story.

(c) xiv.   *Joab by a ruse secures Absalom's return and ultimate
pardon.*

Absalom's full forgiveness is brought about by two stages.   In
the first, Joab obtains David's permission to bring the prince back
to Jerusalem.   Here he continues for two years in partial disgrace
until Joab is again persuaded to intervene, when a full reconciliation of father and son is brought about.   The whole is
a striking testimony at once to Joab's affection for his sovereign
(note verse 1) and to the unique position which he occupied at
David's court.

Tekoa, and fetched thence a wise woman, and said unto her, I pray thee, feign thyself to be a mourner, and put on mourning apparel, I pray thee, and anoint not thyself with oil, but be as a woman that had a long time mourned for the dead: and go in to the king, and speak on this 3 manner unto him. So Joab put the words in her mouth. And when the woman of Tekoa spake to the king, she 4 fell on her face to the ground, and did obeisance, and said, Help, O king. And the king said unto her, What 5 aileth thee? And she answered, Of a truth I am a widow woman, and mine husband is dead. And thy handmaid 6 had two sons, and they two strove together in the field, and there was none to part them, but the one smote the other, and killed him. And, behold, the whole family 7 is risen against thine handmaid, and they said, Deliver him that smote his brother, that we may kill him for the life of his brother whom he slew, and so destroy the heir also: thus shall they quench my coal which is left, and

---

2. Tekoa: the birthplace of Amos, about six miles south of Beth-lehem.

4. spake to the king: read, with some Hebrew MSS. and all Versions, 'came to the king,' as the ultimate court of appeal in matters of justice.

7. The whole clan to which the brothers belonged took upon themselves, according to tribal law and custom, the duty of blood-revenge, that is, of securing the death of the murderer as punishment for the life he had taken. The task of finding and slaying the murderer was delegated by the clan to one of their number, the *góel* or 'avenger of blood' (verse 11). For details of this ancient institution of blood-revenge see the articles 'Goel' in *EBi.* (Driver) and Hastings' *DB.* (Kennedy). The incident before us is instructive as showing how under the monarchy the central authority had already begun to exercise a salutary control over the excesses of tribal zeal.

and so destroy the heir also: a clever insinuation that the desire to secure the survivor's property was also an element in the case.

quench my coal which is left: a pathetic figure for the extinction of one's family as explained in the following clause.

shall leave to my husband neither name nor remainder
8 upon the face of the earth.   And the king said unto the
woman, Go to thine house, and I will give charge
9 concerning thee.   And the woman of Tekoa said unto
the king, My lord, O king, the iniquity be on me, and
on my father's house : and the king and his throne be
10 guiltless.   And the king said, Whosoever saith aught
unto thee, bring him to me, and he shall not touch thee
11 any more.   Then said she, I pray thee, let the king
remember the LORD thy God, that the avenger of blood
destroy not any more, lest they destroy my son.   And he
said, As the LORD liveth, there shall not one hair of thy
12 son fall to the earth.   Then the woman said, Let thine
handmaid, I pray thee, speak a word unto my lord the
13 king.·   And he said, Say on.   And the woman said,
Wherefore then hast thou devised such a thing against
the people of God ? for in speaking this word the king
is as one which is guilty, in that the king doth not fetch

---

9 ff. 'These verses,' says Budde, 'furnish an exquisite picture
of female loquacity and insistence and of royal forbearance' (cf.
this distinguished commentator's criticism of Abigail, p. 165 above).
Instead, however, of regarding this 'picture from the life' as
showing how careful a Hebrew king had to be in dealing with
his free subjects (Budde), we would rather see in it a reflection
of two excellent traits in David's character—his sympathy with
his subjects, and his desire to deal out even-handed justice
to all.

11. the avenger of blood: see on verse 7.   The king, as
requested, swears 'by the life of Yahweh' that the avenger's
hand shall be stayed.

12 ff. The woman has gained her case and now proceeds to
apply her parable. ·Verse 13 consists of three sentences, of which
the last, in that the king, &c., is explanatory of such a thing in
the first sentence, while the second is merely a parenthesis.   The
sense of the whole is that the king stands self-convicted of acting
like the avenger of blood who sought to slay the woman's son
and heir, for by keeping Absalom in exile David is depriving the
people of God of the heir to their throne.

home again his banished one.   For we must needs die, 14
and are as water spilt on the ground, which cannot be
gathered up again ; neither doth God take away life, but
deviseth means, that he that is banished be not an
outcast from him.   Now therefore seeing that I am come 15
to speak this word unto my lord the king, it is because
the people have made me afraid : and thy handmaid
said, I will now speak unto the king ; it may be that the
king will perform the request of his servant.   For the 16
king will hear, to deliver his servant out of the hand of
the man that would destroy me and my son together
out of the inheritance of God.   Then thine handmaid 17
said, Let, I pray thee, the word of my lord the king be
comfortable : for as an angel of God, so is my lord the

---

14. A difficult verse, the second half being particularly obscure.
Two things are clear, (1) that he that is banished must here, as in
verse 13, represent Absalom, and therefore (2) that the latter half of
the verse cannot, as in our R. V. rendering, be a general statement
of God's long-suffering mercy to sinners.   Ewald's simple emendation, now generally accepted, gives the following : ' but God will
not take away the life of him who deviseth[1] means whereby one
that is banished may not remain banished from Him.'   In the first
half of the verse, accordingly, the wise woman suggests that at
any moment it may be too late to show kindness to Absalom, so
uncertain and irrevocable are human life and opportunity ; in the
second half she conveys to David an assurance of long life and
Divine favour should he now bring back his son, for in so doing
he would restore to Yahweh and His worship one who, in being
banished from the soil of Canaan, was *ipso facto* banished from the
more immediate presence of Yahweh.   For this thought see on
1 Sam. xxvi. 19.

15-17. With verse 14 the woman has clearly reached the end
of her commission, which verse 18 shows that David now understood.   It is surprising, therefore, to find her in these verses
reverting to her original suit, and there is much to be said for the
view that verses 15-17 originally stood between verses 7 and 8
(Cook, *Amer. Journ. of Sem. Languages*, 1900, Budde in loc.).

17. as an angel of God: the woman ascribes to David a more

---

[1] Reading חושב for וחשב.

king to discern good and bad: and the LORD thy God
18 be with thee.   Then the king answered and said unto
the woman, Hide not from me, I pray thee, aught that
I shall ask thee.   And the woman said, Let my lord the
19 king now speak.   And the king said, Is the hand of
Joab with thee in all this?   And the woman answered and
said, As thy soul liveth, my lord the king, none can turn
to the right hand or to the left from aught that my lord
the king hath spoken: for thy servant Joab, he bade me,
and he put all these words in the mouth of thine
20 handmaid: to change the face of the matter hath thy
servant Joab done this thing: and my lord is wise,
according to the wisdom of an angel of God, to know all
21 things that are in the earth.   And the king said unto
Joab, Behold now, I have done this thing: go therefore,
22 bring the young man Absalom again.   And Joab fell to
the ground on his face, and did obeisance, and blessed
the king: and Joab said, To-day thy servant knoweth
that I have found grace in thy sight, my lord, O king, in
that the king hath performed the request of his servant.
23 So Joab arose and went to Geshur, and brought Absalom
24 to Jerusalem.   And the king said, Let him turn to his
own house, but let him not see my face.   So Absalom
turned to his own house, and saw not the king's face.

than human clearness of perception to discern the right; cf. verse
20, xix. 27.
   19. The woman's reply begins with 'an admiring testimony to
the king's shrewdness.'
   24. David's vacillating treatment of his sons has already been
characterized as a serious blemish in his character (see on xiii. 21).
When he ought to have exercised discipline he was inexcusably
indulgent.   Now when he might be expected to be indulgent and
forgiving, he is unnecessarily harsh.   Humanly speaking, David
might have escaped the crowning sorrow of his life, had he now
fully forgiven his impulsive and ambitious son instead of leaving
him to brood longer in solitude, exposed to the deterioration of

[Z] Now in all Israel there was none to be so much 25 praised as Absalom for his beauty : from the sole of his foot even to the crown of his head there was no blemish in him. And when he polled his head, (now it was at 26 every year's end that he polled it : because *the hair* was heavy on him, therefore he polled it :) he weighed the hair of his head at two hundred shekels, after the king's weight. And unto Absalom there were born three sons, 27 and one daughter, whose name was Tamar : she was a woman of a fair countenance.

[C] And Absalom dwelt two full years in Jerusalem ; 28 and he saw not the king's face. Then Absalom sent for 29 Joab, to send him to the king ; but he would not come to him : and he sent again a second time, but he would not come. Therefore he said unto his servants, See, 30 Joab's field is near mine, and he hath barley there ; go and set it on fire. And Absalom's servants set the field on fire. Then Joab arose, and came to Absalom unto 31 his house, and said unto him, Wherefore have thy

---

character which such unexpected treatment would inevitably produce.

25-27. A paragraph of later date eulogizing Absalom's personal beauty, and giving information regarding his family which can scarcely be reconciled with the data of the older narrative (xviii. 18).

26. two hundred shekels, after the king's weight. This unique expression seems to be modelled on the legends on Assyrian weights, and is now generally regarded as an indication of the origin of the paragraph in the post-exilic period, the **king** in question being the Persian over-lord. The weight here given has been estimated by the present writer at 3⅝ lb. avoirdupois (Hastings' *DB.* iv. 904ᵃ).

27. With the statements of this verse cf. xviii. 18 (which see) and 1 Kings xv. 2.

xiv. 28-33. *The final reconciliation of David and Absalom.*

29. Joab's refusal to obey the prince's summons shows that his intervention two years before was due to consideration for the father, and not to a desire to stand well with the son.

32 servants set my field on fire? And Absalom answered Joab, Behold, I sent unto thee, saying, Come hither, that I may send thee to the king, to say, Wherefore am I come from Geshur? it were better for me to be there still: now therefore let me see the king's face; and if
33 there be iniquity in me, let him kill me. So Joab came to the king, and told him: and when he had called for Absalom, he came to the king, and bowed himself on his face to the ground before the king: and the king kissed Absalom.

15 And it came to pass after this, that Absalom prepared him a chariot and horses, and fifty men to run before
2 him. And Absalom rose up early, and stood beside the way of the gate: and it was so, that when any man had a suit which should come to the king for judgement, then Absalom called unto him, and said, Of what city art thou? And he said, Thy servant is of one of the

---

33. Absalom's desperate plan for securing an interview with the all-powerful minister is successful. So, too, is his crave for a full pardon, of which his father's kiss is the token and pledge.

D. 2 Sam. xv–xix. *The Story of Absalom's Rebellion.*

Five well-marked stages are traceable in this narrative of Absalom's ill-fated attempt to usurp the throne, viz. (*a*) xv. 1–12, the antecedents and outbreak of the revolt; (*b*) xv. 13—xvi. 14, David retires from the capital to the east of the Jordan; (*c*) xvi. 15—xvii. 19, Absalom's occupation of Jerusalem and other incidents; (*d*) xviii. 1—xix. 8ᵃ, Absalom's death and David's grief; (*e*) xix. 8ᵇ–43, David's return to Jerusalem.

(*a*) xv. 1–12. *The antecedents and outbreak of the revolt.*

1. Some time after his restoration to favour—how long after is not stated—Absalom assumes the state belonging to the successor to the throne. A chariot, horses, and runners were marks of royalty (1 Sam. viii. 11). Cf. Adonijah's similar pretensions, 1 Kings i. 5.

2-7. Absalom next lays himself out to curry favour with the people by employing the usual arts of the popularity-hunter and demagogue.

tribes of Israel.   And Absalom said unto him, See, thy 3
matters are good and right; but there is no man deputed
of the king to hear thee.   Absalom said moreover, Oh 4
that I were made judge in the land, that every man
which hath any suit or cause might come unto me, and
I would do him justice!   And it was so, that when any 5
man came nigh to do him obeisance, he put forth his
hand, and took hold of him, and kissed him.   And on 6
this manner did Absalom to all Israel that came to the
king for judgement : so Absalom stole the hearts of the
men of Israel.

And it came to pass at the end of forty years, that 7
Absalom said unto the king, I pray thee, let me go and
pay my vow, which I have vowed unto the LORD, in
Hebron.   For thy servant vowed a vow while I abode 8
at Geshur in Syria, saying, If the LORD shall indeed
bring me again to Jerusalem, then I will serve the LORD.
And the king said unto him, Go in peace.   So he arose, 9
and went to Hebron.   But Absalom sent spies through- 10

---

6. stole the hearts of the men of Israel. This expression
does not mean that Absalom captivated the affections of his
father's subjects, but that he duped or befooled them as Jacob
duped Laban (Gen. xxxi. 20, 26, where the same expression is
used).   The heart in Hebrew psychology was the seat of intellect
and conscience rather than of feeling.

7 ff. Absalom raises the standard of revolt at Hebron, whither
he had gone under pretext of a vow made while he was in exile.
In reality he had probably discovered that the ancient city of
Hebron still bore David a grudge for removing the seat of government to Jerusalem, and that the allied clans of the Negeb, through
whose good offices David had first mounted the throne, were
jealous of the power and influence with the king of the northern
tribes, now 'the predominant partner' in the united kingdom.

forty years: a clerical error for 'four' (Lucian, &c.), to be
reckoned probably from the date of the final reconciliation.

10. sent spies: rather, 'sent secret messengers.'   A good deal
must be read between the lines here.   The seeds of disaffection

out all the tribes of Israel, saying, As soon as ye hear
the sound of the trumpet, then ye shall say, Absalom is
11 king in Hebron.   And with Absalom went two hundred
men out of Jerusalem, that were invited, and went in
12 their simplicity ; and they knew not any thing.   And
Absalom sent for Ahithophel the Gilonite, David's
counsellor, from his city, even from Giloh, while he
offered the sacrifices.   And the conspiracy was strong ;
for the people increased continually with Absalom.
13   And there came a messenger to David, saying, The
14 hearts of the men of Israel are after Absalom.   And
David said unto all his servants that were with him at
Jerusalem, Arise, and let us flee ; for else none of us

---

had been sedulously sown by Absalom in the preceding four
years, and now he hoped to reap the crop.

12. Ahithophel the Gilonite : or native of **Giloh**, probably *Jala*,
six or seven miles north-west of Hebron.   Ahithophel was the
grandfather of Bath-sheba (see on xi. 3), and his espousal of
Absalom's cause is usually attributed to a desire to avenge the
disgrace in which David had involved his family, as well as the
murder of Uriah.

while he offered the sacrifices, which accompanied the
coronation ceremony (1 Sam. xi. 15).   By whom Absalom was
anointed (see xix. 10) is not stated.

(b) xv. 13—xvi. 14.   *David retires from the capital to the east of the
Jordan.*

David is evidently taken completely by surprise.   The reasons
for his hasty resolution to leave his fortified capital are not clear
from the narrative before us.   Had he grounds for suspecting the
loyalty of the population, perhaps still predominantly Jebusite ?
Of no single day in the whole course of the recorded history
of the Hebrews have we so detailed a record as we have of the
day on which David fled before his undutiful son.   From the time
when, in the morning hours, he passed in haste through the
eastern gate until, before the next day had dawned (xvii. 22), he
and all his following had safely crossed the Jordan, every hour is
crowded with life and incident, and every line of the narrative is
instinct with the emotions and impulses, good and bad, that mould
the lives of men.

14. all his servants : here, and elsewhere in this narrative, the
chief officers of the court.

shall escape from Absalom : make speed to depart, lest
he overtake us quickly, and bring down evil upon us,
and smite the city with the edge of the sword. And the 15
king's servants said unto the king, Behold, thy servants
are ready to do whatsoever my lord the king shall choose.
And the king went forth, and all his household after him. 16
And the king left ten women, which were concubines, to
keep the house. And the king went forth, and all the 17
people after him; and they tarried in Beth-merhak.
And all his servants passed on beside him; and all the 18
Cherethites, and all the Pelethites, and all the Gittites,
six hundred men which came after him from Gath,
passed on before the king. Then said the king to Ittai 19
the Gittite, Wherefore goest thou also with us? return,
and abide with the king : for thou art a stranger, and
also an exile; *return* to thine own place. Whereas thou 20

---

17 ff. The difficulties of these verses have been solved in large
measure by Wellhausen (*Text der Bücher Samuelis*) with the help
of the LXX. (1) The words **all the people** of verse 17 and **all
his servants** of verse 18 must change places (so LXX); (2) for
in Beth-merhak (*lit.* 'the house of distance,' hence R. V. marg. 'at
the Far House') read 'at the last house,' viz. on the eastern face of
the ridge of Zion, above the Kidron (verse 23). In verse 17,
therefore, David and his suite pass out first and halt at the last
house above the Kidron. In verse 18 'all the people' (transferred
from verse 17), i. e. the rank and file of the loyal troops, camp-
followers, &c., march past the king, followed by the royal bodyguard, now strengthened by six hundred men from Gath. For
and all the Gittites, &c., we should probably read : 'and the men
of Ittai the Gittite [of whom verse 19 leads us to expect some
mention here], six hundred men,' &c.

19. The fidelity of this foreign soldier to David stands in vivid
contrast to the treachery of David's son. He may have been an
exile for political reasons from his native Gath, or merely a soldier
of fortune. His military capacity is shown by his being put in
command of a division of David's army (xviii. 2).

abide with the king: Absalom is of course intended.

an exile ... to thine own place: a copyist's slip for 'an
exile from thine own place' (LXX).

camest but yesterday, should I this day make thee go up
and down with us, seeing I go whither I may? return
thou, and take back thy brethren; mercy and truth be
21 with thee.   And Ittai answered the king, and said, As
the Lord liveth, and as my lord the king liveth, surely
in what place my lord the king shall be, whether for
death or for life, even there also will thy servant be.
22 And David said to Ittai, Go and pass over.   And Ittai
the Gittite passed over, and all his men, and all the little
23 ones that were with him.   And all the country wept
with a loud voice, and all the people passed over: the
king also himself passed over the brook Kidron, and all
the people passed over, toward the way of the wilderness.
24 And, lo, Zadok also *came*, and all the Levites with him,

---

20. Render: 'Yesterday was thy coming, and to-day shall I
make thee,' &c.   At the end three words have been dropped from
the Hebrew text.   Read, with LXX: 'return thou and take
back thy brethren with thee, and Yahweh shew unto thee mercy
and truth.'

21. Ittai's reply, which is not unworthy to stand beside
Ruth i. 16 f., is not only honourable to himself, but is also a striking
illustration of the magnetism which David still exercised over those
that came into contact with him.   Ittai's name will ever remain
a synonym for gratitude to a personal benefactor, and for unselfish devotion to a losing cause, for such David's cause must
have seemed at this critical juncture.

xv. 23-29.   *David refuses to take the Ark with him.*

23. The text is once more in disorder.   Following Wellhausen
and most recent critics, we get: 'and all the land wept with
a loud voice as they passed over; but the king (still) stood in the
valley of the Kidron, while all the people passed over before him
in the direction of the olive-tree which is in the wilderness' (so
Lucian).   The route lay across the Kidron, up the face of the Mount
of Olives (verse 30), and over its summit (verse 32) by the then
usual road to the Jordan, which must have passed a conspicuous
tree near the spot where the uncultivated land began.

24. The narrator now supplements his former general statement in verse 17 (emended text), that David and his chief officers
halted at the Far House beside the Kidron, by the fact that

bearing the ark of the covenant of God; and they set down the ark of God, and Abiathar went up, until all the people had done passing out of the city. And the king said unto Zadok, Carry back the ark of God into the city: if I shall find favour in the eyes of the LORD, he will bring me again, and shew me both it, and his habitation: but if he say thus, I have no delight in thee; behold, here am I, let him do to me as seemeth good unto him. The king said also unto Zadok the priest, Art thou *not* a seer? return into the city in peace,

25

26

27

---

among these officers, as we should expect (see the entry xx. 25), were Zadok and Abiathar, the two priests with the Ark of God. The text has been tampered with by later editors, in the interests of Zadok, the founder of the later priestly caste. The introduction of the Levites also is an anachronism in the Books of Samuel (see on 1 Sam. vi. 15). Read somewhat as follows: 'And with him were Zadok and Abiathar bearing the Ark of God, and they set down the Ark of God until all the people,' &c. That the Ark should accompany the king and his troops was regarded by its custodians as a matter of course, for its presence was the presence of Yahweh and the pledge of victory (cf. 1 Sam. iv. 3 ff.).

25 f. It is almost certain that in the original text both priests were addressed throughout (note the plurals in 27b, 28). The decision taken by David to restore the Ark 'to its place'—so expressly Lucian here—has been well characterized by Cheyne as 'probably a turning-point in Israel's, as well as in David's, religious development' (*EBi.* i. col. 305). This decision was due to scruples of conscience on the king's part, lest by taking the Ark with him he might appear as presuming to force the hand of Yahweh and so provoke the Divine anger. It may be, so David argues, that he has proved himself unworthy of the great trust which God had committed to him, in which case he leaves himself with splendid resignation in the hand of God (verse 26). Whereas, should this crisis prove but a passing trial, God will send him aid from **his habitation** on Mount Zion as effectively as if He were present in the Ark on the field of battle (see further, the note in the Appendix).

27. Art thou not a seer? But a priest is never called a seer, and the introduction of 'not' cannot be justified. Render, with R.V. marg., 'seest thou,' or better still, taking the words as addressed to both priests, as the LXX reads and the sequel demands: 'See now, return ye to the city in peace.'

and your two sons with you, Ahimaaz thy son, and
28 Jonathan the son of Abiathar.   See, I will tarry at the
fords of the wilderness, until there come word from you
29 to certify me.   Zadok therefore and Abiathar carried the
ark of God again to Jerusalem : and they abode there.
30   And David went up by the ascent of the *mount of
Olives*, and wept as he went up ; and he had his head
covered, and went barefoot : and all the people that were
with him covered every man his head, and they went up,
31 weeping as they went up.   And one told David, saying,
Ahithophel is among the conspirators with Absalom.
And David said, O LORD, I pray thee, turn the counsel
32 of Ahithophel into foolishness.   And it came to pass, that
when David was come to the top *of the ascent*, where God
was worshipped, behold, Hushai the Archite came to
meet him with his coat rent, and earth upon his head :
33 and David said unto him, If thou passest on with me,

---

28. at the fords of the wilderness : these in all probability
are the two fords, *Maḥaḍat el-Ḥajlah* and *Maḥaḍat el-Henu*, four
and three miles respectively from the mouth of the Jordan.

xv. 30-37.   *Hushai is engaged by David to oppose the counsel of
Ahithophel.*

30. The entire cavalcade having now passed the king, the
latter follows by the road described above, with covered head
(Jer. xiv. 3) and bare feet (Ezek. xxiv. 17) in token of mourning.

32. the top . . . where God was worshipped. On the summit
of the Mount of Olives stood the usual sanctuary or high place (see
on 1 Sam. ix. 12).   In N. T. times the road to Jericho and the
Jordan valley passed over the southern shoulder of the hill by
way of Bethany.

Hushai the Archite: 'the border of the Archites' lay between
Beth-el and Ataroth (Joshua xvi. 2, R.V.).   The LXX adds
'David's friend,' which is to be expected here where Hushai is
first introduced (cf. verse 37, and note on xvi. 16 f.).

33 ff. David unfolds a scheme by which Hushai may counteract
the influence of Ahithophel, and at the same time keep the king
informed of what passes in the capital.   Hushai returns in time
to welcome the arrival of Absalom.

then thou shalt be a burden unto me : but if thou return 34
to the city, and say unto Absalom, I will be thy servant,
O king ; as I have been thy father's servant in time past,
so will I now be thy servant : then shalt thou defeat for
me the counsel of Ahithophel.   And hast thou not there 35
with thee Zadok and Abiathar the priests ? therefore it
shall be, that what thing soever thou shalt hear out of
the king's house, thou shalt tell it to Zadok and Abiathar
the priests.   Behold, they have there with them their 36
two sons, Ahimaaz Zadok's son, and Jonathan Abiathar's
son ;   and by them ye shall send unto me every thing
that ye shall hear.   So Hushai David's friend came into 37
the city ; and Absalom came into Jerusalem.

And when David was a little past the top *of the ascent*, 16
behold, Ziba the servant of Mephibosheth met him,
with a couple of asses saddled, and: upon them two
hundred loaves of bread, and an hundred clusters of
raisins, and an hundred of summer fruits, and a bottle of
wine.   And the king said unto Ziba, What meanest thou 2
by these ? And Ziba said, The asses be for the king's
household to ride on ; and the bread and summer fruit
for the young men to eat ; and the wine, that such as
be faint in the wilderness may drink.   And the king said, 3
And where is thy master's son ? And Ziba said unto the
king, Behold, he abideth at Jerusalem : for he said, To-
day shall the house of Israel restore me the kingdom of

---

xvi. 1–4.   David and the crafty Ziba (ix. 2 ff.), another of those
personal interviews which are the feature of this section.
   1. Cf. Abigail's present. 1 Sam. xxv. 18.   There the figs were
dried and pressed, here they are brought in their fresh state as
summer fruits (Amos viii. 1), showing that the season was early
summer, probably the month of June.
   3. An *ex-parte* statement, almost certainly false in view of the
greater verisimilitude of xix. 25 ff.

4 my father.   Then said the king to Ziba, Behold, thine is
all that pertaineth unto Mephibosheth.   And Ziba said,
I do obeisance; let me find favour in thy sight, my lord,
O king.   :

5   And when king David came to Bahurim, behold, there
came out thence a man of the family of the house of
Saul, whose name was Shimei, the son of Gera : he came
6 out, and cursed still as he came.   And he cast stones at
David, and at all the servants of king David : and all the
people and all the mighty men were on his right hand
7 and on his left.   And thus said Shimei when he cursed,
Begone,. begone, thou man of blood, and man of Belial :
8 the LORD hath returned upon thee all the blood of the
house of Saul, in whose stead thou hast reigned ; and
the LORD hath delivered the kingdom into the hand of
Absalom thy son : and, behold, thou art *taken* in thine
9 own mischief, because thou art a man of blood.   Then
said Abishai the son of Zeruiah unto the king, Why
should this dead dog curse my lord the king? let me go
10 over, I pray thee, and take off his head.   And the king
said, What have I to do with you, ye sons of Zeruiah ?
Because he curseth, and because the LORD hath said

---

xvi. 5-14.   *Shimei curses his king*.

5. Bahurim lay, as we learn here, on the road leading to the
fords of the Jordan (see on xvii. 20), within the territory of
Benjamin.   Shimei's hostility to David was doubtless of ancient
date, since he belonged to the same Benjamite clan as did the
family of Saul.

7 f. thou man of blood . . . all the blood of the house of Saul.
This sweeping charge need not be confined to the tragedy of
ch. xxi, which comes from a different source ; it is better explained
by a reference to iii. 1.

9. let me go over, &c. For a similar request on the part of this
Hebrew Hotspur, see 1 Sam. xxvi. 8.

10. Because he curseth, &c. Read as in 11[b]: 'Let him
curse ; if the LORD hath said,' &c. (so most moderns, cf. margin).

unto him, Curse David; who then shall say, Wherefore
hast thou done so? And David said to Abishai, and to 11
all his servants, Behold, my son, which came forth of my
bowels, seeketh my life: how much more *may* this
Benjamite now *do it?* let him alone, and let him curse;
for the LORD hath bidden him. It may be that the 12
LORD will look on the wrong done unto me, and that the
LORD will requite me good for *his* cursing of me this
day. So David and his men went by the way: and 13
Shimei went along on the hill side over against him, and
cursed as he went, and threw stones at him, and cast
dust. And the king, and all the people that were with 14
him, came weary; and he refreshed himself there.

· And Absalom, and all the people the men of Israel, 15
came to Jerusalem, and Ahithophel with him. And it 16
came to pass, when Hushai the Archite, David's friend,

---

12. the LORD will look on the wrong done unto me. Read
with the Versions and margin: 'the LORD will look on mine
affliction' (1 Sam. i. 11, ix. 16). David's mood is still that of
resignation to the Divine will (see on xv. 25 ff.).

13. on the hill side over against him: rather, 'on the hill
side parallel with him,' of course higher up the hill.

14. The name of the place to which the company **came weary**
has fallen out. The Hebrew word for 'weary' is put in the
margin as a proper name, 'to Ayephim,' which is very improbable.
Lucian has 'to the Jordan,' which may be right (see on xvii. 16).

(*c*) xvi. 15—xvii. 29. *Absalom occupies Jerusalem: Ahithophel
and Hushai*, &c.

The historian now turns to the duel between the two counsellors,
starting from the usurper's arrival in Jerusalem, which has already
been mentioned by anticipation (xv. 37).

15. Absalom and all the men of Israel: so read with LXX
(B), **the people** having come in from the preceding verse.
'Throughout the narrative "all the people" are with David, "all
the men of Israel" are with Absalom' (Driver).

16 f. Absalom's play upon the word **friend** suggests that the
designation **David's friend** was not first given to Hushai by the
historian, but was a court title. The 'king's friend' is a title

was come unto Absalom, that Hushai said unto Ab-
17 salom, God save the king, God save the king. And
Absalom said to Hushai, Is this thy kindness to thy
18 friend? why wentest thou not with thy friend? And
Hushai said unto Absalom, Nay; but whom the LORD,
and this people, and all the men of Israel have chosen,
19 his will I be, and with him will I abide. And again,
whom should I serve? *should I* not *serve* in the presence
of his son? as I have served in thy father's presence, so
20 will I be in thy presence.   Then said Absalom to
21 Ahithophel, Give your counsel what we shall do.   And
Ahithophel said unto Absalom, Go in unto thy father's
concubines, which he hath left to keep the house; and
all Israel shall hear that thou art abhorred of thy father:
then shall the hands of all that are with thee be strong.
22 So they spread Absalom a tent upon the top of the house;
and Absalom went in unto his father's concubines in the
23 sight of all Israel.   And the counsel of Ahithophel,
which he counselled in those days, was as if a man
inquired at the oracle of God: so was all the counsel of
Ahithophel both with David and with Absalom.

---

found at the court of Egypt from an early period, as later among
the Ptolemies (Deissmann, *Bible Studies*, 167 ff.) and the Seleucids
(1 Macc. ii. 18, x. 65).   Similarly, Zabud the son of Nathan was
'the king's friend' at the court of Solomon (1 Kings iv. 5).

18 f. Hushai argues (1) that the *vox Dei* and the *vox populi* have
united in the choice of Absalom, and (2) that after all he is merely
transferring his allegiance from the father to the son. The
narrator leaves us to infer that Hushai was thereupon admitted
into the inner circle of the new court.

20-23. On Ahithophel's advice Absalom takes over part of his
father's harem. The crafty adviser urges this step on grounds of
public policy. It would be a proof to **all Israel** that the breach
between father and son was now beyond hope of healing.
Absalom's friends would thereby be strengthened in their allegiance
(verse 21, end), and the waverers brought over to his side. At
the same time it would be evidence to all and sundry that Absalom

Moreover Ahithophel said unto Absalom, Let me now 17
choose out twelve thousand men, and I will arise and
pursue after David this night: and I will come upon him 2
while he is weary and weak handed, and will make him
afraid: and all the people that are with him shall flee;
and I will smite the king only: and I will bring back all 3
the people unto thee: the man whom thou seekest is as
if all returned: *so* all the people shall be in peace. And 4
the saying pleased Absalom well, and all the elders of
Israel.

Then said Absalom, Call now Hushai the Archite also, 5
and let us hear likewise what he saith. And when 6
Hushai was come to Absalom, Absalom spake unto him,
saying, Ahithophel hath spoken after this manner: shall
we do *after* his saying? if not, speak thou. And Hushai 7
said unto Absalom, The counsel that Ahithophel hath

---

was *de facto* king, and was exercising his rights as David's successor
(see on xii. 8).

xvii. 1-14. *The duel between the counsellors.*
1. Ahithophel begs to be allowed to set out immediately in
pursuit of David, arguing that the death of the latter is all that
is required to secure the undivided allegiance of the people to
Absalom and the re-establishment of peace.
   this night: the night following the eventful day into which
so much has been already crowded (cf. verse 16).
3. The present unintelligible text has arisen from the accidental
omission of four words still preserved in the LXX: 'and I will
bring back all the people unto thee as a bride returneth to her
husband; thou seekest but the life of one man, and all the people
shall be in peace.'
4. **And the saying pleased Absalom well:** nothing could better
illustrate the depth of moral callousness to which the misguided
prince had fallen than his approval of this cold-blooded proposal
to take his father's life.
5-14 give us the contrary counsel of Hushai. This life-like
picture of the *divan* of the sheikhs—to give the council of the
elders (verse 4) its oriental designation—with its highly meta-
phorical and somewhat bombastic rhetoric, is painted in the true
colours of the Semitic orient.

T

8 given this time is not · good.   Hushai said moreover,
Thou knowest thy father and his men, that they be
mighty men, and they be. chafed in their minds, as a
bear robbed of her whelps in the field : and thy father is
a man of war, and will not lodge with the people.
9 Behold, he is hid now in some pit, or in some *other*
place : and it will come to pass, when some of them be
fallen at the first, that whosoever heareth it will say,
There is a slaughter among the people that follow
10 Absalom.   And even he that is valiant, whose heart is
as the heart of a lion, shall utterly melt : for all Israel
knoweth that thy father is a mighty man, and they which
11 be with him are valiant men.   But I counsel that all
Israel be gathered together unto thee, from Dan even to
Beer-sheba, as the sand that is by the sea for multitude ;
12 and that thou go to battle in thine own person.   So
shall we come upon him in some place where he shall

---

8. will not lodge with the people : an obscure phrase.   If
the text is right, it may mean that, as a precaution against surprise, David would camp apart from the rank and file, surrounded
by his faithful bodyguard.·

9. The second half of the verse describes what will happen
when the two sides engage.   Read probably : ' when he (David)
falleth upon the people (R. V. marg.), and some of them fall at
the first attack ' (Budde).

10. A panic · among Absalom's untrained levies would be the
result of a formal engagement with David's veterans—a very
plausible forecast.

11. The two points of Hushai's counter-proposal are (1) that
a much larger force was needed than Absalom as yet had at his
command, and (2) that the new king's presence with his troops
was indispensable (contrast verse 1).   This latter argument was
an adroit appeal to the usurper's personal vanity.   The speaker's
real object was, of course, to gain time for David to mature his
plan of campaign, and to collect the necessary troops.

to battle : read with the Versions, ' in their midst '—' with
thy Majesty [*lit.* ' thy presence,· see R. V. marg.] marching in the
midst of them ' (H. P. Smith).

be found, and we will light upon him as the dew falleth
on the ground : and of him and of all the men that are
with him we will not leave so much as one.   Moreover, 13
if he be gotten into a city, then shall all Israel bring
ropes to that city, and we will draw it into the river, until
there be not one small stone found there.   And Absalom 14
and all the men of Israel said, The counsel of Hushai
the Archite is better than the counsel of Ahithophel.   For
the LORD had ordained to defeat the good counsel of
Ahithophel, to the intent that the LORD might bring evil
upon Absalom.

Then said Hushai unto Zadok and to Abiathar the 15
priests, Thus and thus did Ahithophel counsel Absalom
and the elders of Israel ; and thus and thus have I
counselled.   Now therefore send quickly, and tell David, 16
saying, Lodge not this night at the fords of the wilderness,
but in any wise pass over ; lest the king be swallowed
up, and all the people that are with him.   Now Jonathan 17

---

13. Render, as in the margin : 'if he withdraw himself into
a (fortified) city'; the whole is a fine specimen of rhetorical
exaggeration.

14 b. The historian's comment on the result of the duel, forming
the Hebrew counterpart and illustration of the familiar maxim,
Quem vult perdere Deus prius dementat.

xvii. 15-21.   *Hushai communicates with David as arranged.*
The reason for such urgency as Hushai recommends, which
seems unnecessary in the altered circumstances, was doubtless
his fear that Absalom might after all revert to Ahithophel's proposal (cf. verse 21 end).   Hushai's policy, like that of the Bruce's
friend Kirkpatrick, was to 'mak siccar.'

17. As compared with A. V. and R. V. marg., the text of R. V.
alone does justice to the frequentative tenses of the original.
These imply that regular communication between David and
Hushai was kept up for some time through the priests' sons as
intermediaries.   The latter, again, were kept in touch with
Hushai by a slave-girl as go-between.   Such was the situation
while David and Absalom were respectively collecting their forces

and Ahimaaz stayed by En-rogel; and a maidservant
used to go and tell them; and they went and told king
David: for they might not be seen to come into the
18 city.   But a lad saw them, and told Absalom: and they
went both of them away quickly, and came to the house
of a man in Bahurim, who had a well in his court; and
19 they went down thither.   And the woman took and
spread the covering over the well's mouth, and strewed
20 bruised corn thereon; and nothing was known.   And
Absalom's servants came to the woman to the house; and
they said, Where are Ahimaaz and Jonathan? And the
woman said unto them, They be gone over the brook of
water.   And when they had sought and could not find
21 them, they returned to Jerusalem.   And it came to pass,
after they were departed, that they came up out of the
well, and went and told king David; and they said unto
David, Arise ye, and pass quickly over the water: for
22 thus hath Ahithophel counselled against you.   Then
David arose, and all the people that were with him,
and they passed over Jordan: by the morning light
there lacked not one of them that was not gone over
23 Jordan.   And when Ahithophel saw that his counsel was
not followed, he saddled his ass, and arose, and gat him

---

on either side of the Jordan. Verses 18 ff. tell of a particular
incident of the situation sketched above.
    stayed by En-rogel: 'the fuller's spring,' now usually
identified with the modern *Bir Eyyûb* (Job's well), at the south-
east of Jerusalem, where the valley of Hinnom joins the valley of
the Kidron.
    20. the brook of water: the first word is extremely doubtful
(see Driver, in loc.). Budde would read: 'they be gone hur-
riedly (so Vulgate, *festinanter*) over the water,' i.e. the Jordan, as
in verse 21. This helps us to locate **Bahurim** as at no great distance from the river, probably in the neighbourhood of Beth-hoglah
(see on xix. 15 f.).
    23. Deeply chagrined at the failure of his scheme, in which

home, unto his city, and set his house in order, and hanged himself; and he died, and was buried in the sepulchre of his father.

Then David came to Mahanaim. And Absalom passed 24 over Jordan, he and all the men of Israel with him. And Absalom set Amasa over the host instead of Joab. 25 Now Amasa was the son of a man, whose name was Ithra the Israelite, that went in to Abigal the daughter of Nahash, sister to Zeruiah Joab's mother. And Israel 26 and Absalom pitched in the land of Gilead.

And it came to pass, when David was come to 27 Mahanaim, that Shobi the son of Nahash of Rabbah of the children of Ammon, and Machir the son of Ammiel of Lo-debar, and Barzillai the Gileadite of Rogelim, brought beds, and basons, and earthen vessels, and 28 wheat, and barley, and meal, and parched *corn*, and beans, and lentils, and parched *pulse*, and honey, and 29

---

private revenge doubtless played a leading motive (see on xv. 12), and at being superseded in Absalom's confidence by his rival, Ahithophel dies by his own hand, a victim of wounded pride and disappointed ambition.

24 ff. David proceeds to **Mahanaim** (see on ii. 8), which he makes his head quarters. Absalom follows in due course with Amasa in command of his levies. The latter is now curiously described as the son of **Ithra the Israelite.** Since only foreigners like Uriah and Ittai are designated in this way by their nationality, the Chronicler's reading is to be preferred (see margin), viz.: 'the son of Jether the Ishmaelite.' Through his mother **Abigail** (so read) he was a full cousin of Absalom and Joab, and, like the latter, a nephew of David (see 1 Chron. ii. 15 ff.).

27. Shobi the son of Nahash: now apparently governor of the Ammonites, in room of his brother Hanun, the late king. For **Machir** see on ix. 4.

Barzillai the Gileadite of Rogelim is more fully described xix. 32 f. His home has not been identified, but his name shows that it must have lain in the Aramaic-speaking tract to the north-east.

28. parched pulse: an unheard-of food-stuff, and another of the too numerous illustrations of the Revisers' bondage to the

butter, and sheep, and cheese of kine, for David, and for
the people that were with him, to eat: for they said,
The people is hungry, and weary, and thirsty, in the
wilderness.

18 And David numbered the people that were with him,
and set captains of thousands and captains of hundreds
2 over them. And David sent forth the people, a third
part under the hand of Joab, and a third part under the
hand of Abishai the son of Zeruiah, Joab's brother, and a
third part under the hand of Ittai the Gittite. And the
king said unto the people, I will surely go forth with you
3 myself also. But the people said, Thou shalt not go
forth: for if we flee away, they will not care for us;
neither if half of us die, will they care for us: but thou
art worth ten thousand of us: therefore now it is better
4 that thou be ready to succour us out of the city. And
the king said unto them, What seemeth you best I will
do. And the king stood by the gate side, and all the
5 people went out by hundreds and by thousands. And
the king commanded Joab and Abishai and Ittai, saying,
Deal gently for my sake with the young man, even with

received text. The word means only 'parched corn' (1 Sam.
xvii 17), and has simply crept in from the line above.
29. cheese of kine: a doubtful rendering of a doubtful text.
Probably 'dried curds' is meant (see the writer's article 'Milk,'
EBi. iii. 3091); the text may originally have read 'and sheep'—
or rather 'flocks,' for the word includes goats as well—'and cattle
and dried curds.'

(*d*) xviii. 1—xix. 8. *Absalom's death and David's grief.*

2. And David sent forth the people: read with Lucian:
'and David divided the people (i. e. his forces, see Driver as
quoted on xvi. 15) into three parts.' The tactics are the same as
those employed by Saul against the Ammonites (1 Sam. xi. 11),
with the addition of a body of reserves in Mahanaim under the
king's personal command (verse 3 end).

4. A 'march past' in more hopeful circumstances than on
a former occasion, xv. 17 ff.

Absalom. And all the people heard when the king gave all the captains charge concerning Absalom. So the 6 people went out into the field against Israel: and the battle was in the forest of Ephraim. And the people of 7 Israel were smitten there before the servants of David, and there was a great slaughter there that day of twenty thousand men. For the battle was there spread over 8 the face of all the country: and the forest devoured more people that day than the sword devoured. And 9 Absalom chanced to meet the servants of David. And Absalom rode upon his mule, and the mule went under the thick boughs of a great oak, and his head caught hold of the oak, and he was taken up between the heaven and the earth; and the mule that was under him went on. And a certain man saw it, and told Joab, and 10

---

5. Deal gently for my sake . . . with Absalom. It is pathetic to observe how, throughout this day in which the gravest interests were at stake, David has not only no thought for himself—this we could excuse—but none for his loyal troops or for the future of his country (see xix. 5 ff.), but only for the son, 'the lad Absalom' (verses 5, 12, 29, 32), who had cast every vestige of filial affection to the winds (cf. on xvii. 4).

6. the forest of Ephraim : rather, 'the jungle of Ephraim,' an unknown locality in Gilead. Cf. G. A. Smith, *Hist. Geog.* 335 note.

8. and the forest devoured, &c.: the sense is uncertain. Probably the district over which the rout extended presented a rocky surface—'a sea of rocks' is Wetzstein's phrase—covered with jungle growth which concealed the clefts between the rocks into which the fugitives dropped and perished.

xviii. 9-18. *The fate of Absalom.*

9. his head caught hold of the oak, &c.: rather, 'was caught fast in the oak, and he was suspended,' &c. The popular idea that Absalom owed his death to the long hair (xiv. 26), of which he is supposed to have been unduly proud, may suit the requirements of poetic justice, but finds no support in the narrative before us. Rather we must suppose that, as he rode at full speed upon his mule, his head got wedged into the fork of a branch and was there held fast 'in the heart of the oak' (verse 14).

11 said, Behold, I saw Absalom hanging in an oak.   And
   Joab said unto the man that told him, And, behold, thou
   sawest it, and why didst thou not smite him there to the
   ground? and I would have given thee ten *pieces of* silver,
12 and a girdle.   And the man said unto Joab, Though I
   should receive a thousand *pieces of* silver in mine hand,
   yet would I not put forth mine hand against the king's
   son: for in our hearing·the king charged thee and
   Abishai and Ittai, saying, Beware that none touch the
13 young man Absalom.   Otherwise if I had dealt falsely
   against his life, (and there is no matter hid from the
   king,) then thou thyself wouldest have stood aloof.
14 Then said Joab, I may not tarry thus with thee.   And
   he took three darts in his hand, and thrust them through
   the heart of Absalom, while he was yet alive in the midst
15 of the oak.   And ten young men that bare Joab's armour
   compassed about and smote Absalom, and slew him.
16 And Joab blew the trumpet, and the people returned
   from pursuing after Israel: for Joab held back the
17 people.   And they took Absalom, and cast him into the

---

   11. ten pieces **of silver:** ten shekels (see on 1 Sam. ix. 8), as
in A V., which is here needlessly altered.

   12. Beware, &c.   A better rendering of the difficult original
is that of the margin, but we should probably read with the
Versions: 'Have a care for my sake (as in verse 5) of the young
man, even of Absalom.'

   13 f. thou wouldest have stood aloof.   Joab, the soldier says,
would not have lifted a finger to save him from David's wrath.
Joab refuses to argue the matter, and with his own hand stabs
Absalom through the heart.

   15.   A somewhat better connexion is got by taking the last
clause of verse 14 with this verse (so Vulgate): 'and while he
was yet alive . . . ten young men,' &c.   However richly
Absalom deserved his fate, nothing can free Joab from the charge
of flagrant disobedience of his king's express command, of which,
the narrator takes pains to assure us, he was thoroughly informed
(see verses 5, 12).

great pit in the forest, and raised over him a very great
heap of stones: and all Israel fled every one to his tent.
Now Absalom in his life time had taken and reared up 18
for himself the pillar, which is in the king's dale: for he
said, I have no son to keep my name in remembrance:
and he called the pillar after his own name: and it is
called Absalom's monument, unto this day.

Then said Ahimaaz the son of Zadok, Let me now 19
run, and bear the king tidings, how that the LORD hath
avenged him of his enemies. And Joab said unto him, 20
Thou shalt not be the bearer of tidings this day, but thou
shalt bear tidings another day: but this day thou shalt
bear no tidings, because the king's son is dead. Then 21
said Joab to the Cushite, Go tell the king what thou hast
seen. And the Cushite bowed himself unto Joab, and
ran. Then said Ahimaaz the son of Zadok yet again to 22

18. Absalom being without male offspring, according to this
early writer (see another account xiv. 27), had provided for the
perpetuation of his name by the erection of a memorial **pillar in
the king's dale,** a locality mentioned only here and Gen. xiv. 17,
and not yet identified. According to Josephus it was two stadia
from Jerusalem (*Antiquities,* VIII. x. 3).

xviii. 19-32. *How the tidings were conveyed to David.*
Ahimaaz, the son of Zadok the priest, already known to us
(xv. 27, xvii. 17), and a certain Ethiopian unnamed, vie with each
other in the race to Mahanaim.

19. hath avenged him of his enemies: *lit.* as marg., 'hath
judged him from the hand of his enemies,' where 'judged' is used,
as in 1 Sam. xxiv. 15 end, in the sense of 'delivered.' So 'the
Judges' who give their name to the book were the deliverers or
liberators of their tribes.

20 f. Joab at first refuses to expose Ahimaaz to the danger involved in being the bearer of evil tidings to the king (see iv. 10),
and seems to play upon the double meaning of the original as
expressing both good and bad tidings. In place of Ahimaaz Joab
sends a **Cushite** or Ethiopian, perhaps a slave, the risk of violent
treatment being of less account in his case.

22. Ahimaaz succeeds on a second appeal, expressing himself
as ready to take the risk at which Joab had hinted.

Joab, But come what may, let me, I pray thee, also run
after the Cushite.   And Joab said, Wherefore wilt thou
run, my son, seeing that thou wilt have no reward for the
23 tidings?   But come what may, *said he*, I will run.   And
he said unto him, Run.   Then Ahimaaz ran by the way
of the Plain, and overran the Cushite.

24   Now David sat between the two gates : and the watchman went up to the roof of the gate unto the wall, and
lifted up his eyes, and looked, and, behold, a man
25 running alone.   And the watchman cried, and told the
king.   And the king said, If he be alone, there is tidings
26 in his mouth.   And he came apace, and drew near.   And
the watchman saw another man running : and the watchman called unto the porter, and said, Behold, *another* man
running alone.   And the king said, He also bringeth
27 tidings.   And the watchman said, Me thinketh the
running of the foremost is like the running of Ahimaaz
the son of Zadok.   And the king said, He is a good

23. by the way of the Plain of the Jordan (Gen. xiii. 10 f.,
1 Kings vii. 46).   While the Ethiopian probably took a bee-line
across the difficult country to Mahanaim, his rival, who knew the
route well (see on xvii. 17), made a detour to reach the high road
running up the *Wadi Ajlun* from the Jordan.   Though the longer,
it was the easier and quicker route.

24 ff. For a companion to this graphic watch-tower scene, see
2 Kings ix. 17 ff.

David sat between the two gates : the gates, or rather gate-
houses, of an Eastern city may be described as extensions outwards
and inwards of the city wall, with an outer and inner gateway.
The space between these was lined with stone benches, on which
the elders sat 'in the gate,' as did David now and later (xix. 8).
This particular gate-house had an upper story (verse 33), the
roof of which was apparently on a level with the wall (verse 24).

25. If he be alone : then the runner is a courier from the battlefield ; were it a case of defeat and a rout, he would be accompanied by other fugitives.

26. called unto the porter : read, with a slight change, 'and
the watchman upon the gate called out and said ' (cf. Lucian's
Greek text).

man, and cometh with good tidings. And Ahimaaz 28
called, and said unto the king, All is well. And he
bowed himself before the king with his face to the earth,
and said, Blessed be the LORD thy God, which hath
delivered up the men that lifted up their hand against
my lord the king. And the king said, Is it well with the 29
young man Absalom? And Ahimaaz answered, When
Joab sent the king's servant, even me thy servant, I saw
a great tumult, but I knew not what it was. And the 30
king said, Turn aside, and stand here. And he turned
aside, and stood still. And, behold, the Cushite came; 31
and the Cushite said, Tidings for my lord the king: for
the LORD hath avenged thee this day of all them that
rose up against thee. And the king said unto the 32
Cushite, Is it well with the young man Absalom? And
the Cushite answered, The enemies of my lord the king,
and all that rise up against thee to do thee hurt, be as
that young man is. And the king was much moved, and 33
went up to the chamber over the gate, and wept: and as
he went, thus he said, O my son Absalom, my son, my
son Absalom! would God I had died for thee, O
Absalom, my son, my son!

---

28. All is well: an unfortunate rendering. As the margin
shows, Ahimaaz merely gives a shortened form of the universal
greeting, 'Peace be upon thee.' It seems as if the youth's courage
failed him when face to face with the king, for he finally takes
refuge in a falsehood.

29. Read simply: 'When Joab sent thy servant, I saw,' &c.
(Wellhausen, Budde). The rest is ungrammatical and unnecessary.

32. The negro is more courageous, and succeeds in conveying
the fact of Absalom's death without naming him.

xviii. 33—xix. 8ᵃ. *David's grief and Joab's rebuke.*

33. and as he went: read with Lucian and most moderns:
'and as he wept,' a little touch which adds to the poignancy of
David's grief.

19 And it was told Joab, Behold, the king weepeth and
2 mourneth for Absalom.   And the victory that day was
turned into mourning unto all the people: for the people
3 heard say that day, The king grieveth for his son.   And
the people gat them by stealth that day into the city, as
people that are ashamed steal away when they flee in
4 battle.   And the king covered his face, and the king
cried with a loud voice, O my son Absalom, O Absalom,
5 my son, my son! And Joab came into the house to the
king, and said, Thou hast shamed this day the faces of
all thy servants, which this day have saved thy life, and
the lives of thy sons and of thy daughters, and the lives of
6 thy wives, and the lives of thy concubines; in that thou
lovest them that hate thee, and hatest them that love
thee.   For thou hast declared this day, that princes and
servants are nought unto thee: for this day I perceive,
that if Absalom had lived, and all we had died this day,
7 then it had pleased thee well.   Now therefore arise, go
forth, and speak comfortably unto thy servants: for I

---

xix. 2 f. These two verses are among the most perfect specimens
of literary art in the O. T.   With a few master-strokes the writer
paints the sudden revulsion of feeling from the joy and pride of
victory to the sorrow that is born of perfect sympathy with
another's grief.   Then follows the inimitable picture of the victorious veterans 'getting them by stealth that day into the city,'
like the conscience-smitten cowards that sneak away when the
day is lost, or like the thief that creeps on tip-toe to his home
before the dawn.   But what a man must this David have been to
have so endeared himself to his men, that his personal grief
became so completely theirs! Joab, the incarnation of state policy
('die verkörperte Staatsraison') as Budde elsewhere calls him,
fears as sudden a revulsion of feeling in the opposite direction.
(5 ff.).   No one can gainsay the truth of his statements or the force
of his arguments, and yet who can suppress a feeling of sympathy
with the broken-hearted king?

6.   The soldier's indignation here leads him into an excusable
exaggeration.

7. speak comfortably unto: *lit.* 'speak to the heart of thy

swear by the LORD, if thou go not forth, there will not
tarry a man with thee this night: and that will be worse
unto thee than all the evil that hath befallen thee from
thy youth until now.   Then the king arose, and sat in 8
the gate.   And they told unto all the people, saying,
Behold, the king doth sit in the gate: and all the people
came before the king.

Now Israel had fled every man to his tent.   And all 9
the people were at strife throughout all the tribes of Israel,
saying, The king delivered us out of the hand of our
enemies, and he saved us out of the hand of the Philistines; and now he is fled out of the land from Absalom.
And Absalom, whom we anointed over us, is dead in 10
battle.   Now therefore why speak ye not a word of
bringing the king back?

And king David sent to Zadok and to Abiathar the 11
priests, saying, Speak unto the elders of Judah, saying,

---

servants' (cf. Isa. xl. 1).   The history of popular movements
in the East has proved, times without number, the accuracy of
Joab's diagnosis of the oriental character.

(e) xix. 8ᵇ-43. *David's return to Jerusalem.*
In his account of what followed, as of what preceded the crisis
of the rebellion (chaps. xv, xvi), the historian has cast the bulk of his
narrative into the form of personal interviews with the king.

8. every man to his tent: not to be taken literally, but as
equivalent to 'to his home.'   This archaism is a survival from the
nomadic period of Hebrew history, and is frequently found in the
historical books (1 Sam. iv. 10, xiii. 2, &c.).

9 f. The common sense of the nation once more asserts itself.
The people recall the benefits which David had conferred, and
chide their leaders for the delay in bringing back their rightful
king.   The original continuation of verse 10 must be restored
from 11ᵇ: 'and the speech of all Israel came to (the ears of) the
king' (so the Versions and most moderns).

xix. 11-15. *David's secret overtures to the tribe of Judah.*
Himself a member of the tribe whose ancient sanctuary had been
the focus of the rebellion, David, with his statesman's eye, saw in
the new situation a favourable opportunity of binding the southern

Why are ye the last to bring the king back to his house?
seeing the speech of all Israel is come to the king, *to*
12 *bring him* to his house. Ye are my brethren, ye are my
bone and my flesh: wherefore then are ye the last to
13 bring back the king? And say ye to Amasa, Art thou
not my bone and my flesh? God do so to me, and more
also, if thou be not captain of the host before me
14 continually in the room of Joab. And he bowed the
heart of all the men of Judah, even as *the heart of* one
man; so that they sent unto the king, *saying*, Return
15 thou, and all thy servants. So the king returned, and
came to Jordan. And Judah came to Gilgal, to go to
meet the king, to bring the king over Jordan.
16 And Shimei the son of Gera, the Benjamite, which
was of Bahurim, hasted and came down with the men

---

clans anew to his person. Accordingly he opens negotiations with
the sheikhs through his faithful allies, Zadok and Abiathar. In
thus playing off the South against the North, David was doubtless
aware of the risk he ran of increasing the jealousy, already of
long standing, between them, but in the circumstances David can
scarcely be blamed for seeing in his southern kinsfolk, in the men
who, as he says, were his bone and his flesh (verse 12), the natural
support of his dynasty.

11. **to bring the king back to his house**: the plea of kinship
put forward in the following verse favours the rendering 'to bring
the king home again,' a significant addition to the northmen's
phrase in verse 10. The reason why the sheikhs of Judah held
back is evident enough (see note above), and is all to their credit.

13. Amasa, David's nephew, is offered the post of commander-
in-chief, Joab having forfeited his sovereign's confidence by his
flagrant disobedience of orders in the matter of Absalom. He
who would command must first learn to obey.

15. The representatives of Judah go to meet David at the
entrance to their own territory, in all probability at the ford of
El-Hajla, which preserves the name of Beth-hoglah, in the neighbourhood of Gilgal (Josh. xv. 6 f.).

16 ff. The first of the personal interviews to which reference
was made above is that between David and Shimei. The
introduction of Ziba (17[b], 18[a]) is a parenthesis which should be

of Judah to meet king David. And there were a 17
thousand men of Benjamin with him, and Ziba the
servant of the house of Saul, and his fifteen sons and his
twenty servants with him ; and they went through Jordan
in the presence of the king. And there went over a 18
ferry boat to bring over the king's household, and to do
what he thought good. And Shimei the son of Gera
fell down before the king, when he was come over
Jordan. And he said unto the king, Let not my lord 19
impute iniquity unto me, neither do thou remember that
which thy servant did perversely the day that my lord
the king went out of Jerusalem, that the king should
take it to his heart. For thy servant doth know that I 20
have sinned : therefore, behold, I am come this day the
first of all the house of Joseph to go down to meet my
lord the king. But Abishai the son of Zeruiah answered 21
and said, Shall not Shimei be put to death for this,
because he cursed the LORD's anointed ? And David 22

rendered thus : 'Now Ziba . . . with him, had dashed through the
Jordan in the presence of the king and kept crossing (and
recrossing) the ford '—the word rendered 'ferry boat' in the text
of R. V.—'to bring over the king's household.' Ziba's fifteen
sons and twenty servants carried the women and children and
some perhaps of the dainty courtiers through the ford. Foreseeing
the day of reckoning, the crafty Ziba hastens to render David a
service, and thus, like the unjust steward, secure at least one
entry to his credit. At the end of verse 18 render with the
margin : 'when he would go over Jordan,' the king being still on
the eastern bank.

20. It is noteworthy that Shimei, a member of the tribe of
Benjamin, claims to belong to the house of Joseph. Cf. Judges
i. 22, and for the conclusions that have been drawn from this and
from the name Benjamin ('men of the south') as to the historical
origin of the tribe, see Hope Hogg's article 'Benjamin' in *EBi.*

21. Abishai, impulsive and bloodthirsty as ever (see on xvi. 9),
intervenes with the reminder that Shimei had been guilty of
blasphemy. Only here, in this narrative (C), is the expression
'the LORD's anointed' applied to David.

22 f. David asserts his royal prerogative of mercy in face of the

said, What have I to do with you, ye sons of Zeruiah,
that ye should this day be adversaries unto me? shall
there any man be put to death this day in Israel? for do
23 not I know that I am this day king over Israel? And
the king said unto Shimei, Thou shalt not die.   And the
king sware unto him.

24   And Mephibosheth the son of Saul came down to meet
the king; and he had neither dressed his feet, nor
trimmed his beard, nor washed his clothes, from the day
the king departed until the day he came home in peace.
25 And it came to pass, when he was come to Jerusalem to
meet the king, that the king said unto him, Wherefore
26 wentest not thou with me, Mephibosheth? And he
answered, My lord, O king, my servant deceived me:
for thy servant said, I will saddle me an ass, that I may
ride thereon, and go with the king; because thy servant
27 is lame.   And he hath slandered thy servant unto my
lord the king; but my lord the king is as an angel of
28 God: do therefore what is good in thine eyes.   For all
my father's house were but dead men before my lord the

masterful and unforgiving sons of Zeruiah, refusing to mar the joy
of so auspicious a day by further bloodshed.   For the ultimate
fate of Shimei and the difficult questions raised by it, see Skinner
on 1 Kings ii in this series (Century Bible).

24 ff. The second interview—David and Meri-baal (Mephibosheth), here described loosely as **the son of Saul** (cf. ix. 7,
'Saul thy father').   During the whole period of David's absence
from Jerusalem he had lived as a mourner.

neither dressed his feet: render, as in the original text of
LXX, 'neither trimmed his toe-nails'—Lucian adds 'nor his
finger-nails'—'nor his beard,' &c.   The verb is the same for both
operations (*lit.* 'to do'); cf. Deut. xxi. 12, where it is rendered
'to pare (the nails),' and has reference, as here, to the intermission
of the care of the person during the period of mourning.   In the
next verse read, of course, 'when he was come *from* Jerusalem.'

27. as an angel of God: the embodiment of wisdom to discern
the right, as xiv. 17, 20.   The last clause, 'do therefore' &c.,
belongs to the next verse.

king : yet didst thou set thy servant among them that did eat at thine own table. What right therefore have I yet that I should cry any more unto the king? And the 29 king said unto him, Why speakest thou any more of thy matters? I say, Thou and Ziba divide the land. And 30 Mephibosheth said unto the king, Yea, let him take all, forasmuch as my lord the king is come in peace unto his own house.

And Barzillai the Gileadite came down from Rogelim ; 31 and he went over Jordan with the king, to conduct him over Jordan. Now Barzillai was a very aged man, even 32 fourscore years old : and he had provided the king with sustenance while he lay at Mahanaim ; for he was a very great man. And the king said unto Barzillai, Come 33 thou over with me, and I will sustain thee with me in Jerusalem. And Barzillai said unto the king, How 34 many are the days of the years of my life, that I should go up with the king unto Jerusalem? I am this day 35 fourscore years old : can I discern between good and bad ? can thy servant taste what I eat or what I drink ?

---

29. The king's impatience is more forcibly brought out by Lucian's text, 'why wilt thou further multiply words.'

30. Yea, let him take all : from Western lips this would be set down as the sarcasm of a disappointed man, but in reality it has a fine flavour of oriental etiquette.

31 ff. The third interview—David and Barzillai. The latter had been David's host at Mahanaim, and has now escorted his guest as far as the Jordan. The narrative has become obscured through the ambiguity of the verb ' to pass over, cross,' which also means ' to pass on,' &c. Read here : ' and Barzillai . . . passed on with the king to conduct him to the Jordan.' The text has suffered in the same way in verses 36, 40. '

34 ff. Barzillai's two reasons for declining the king's invitation. (1) The tree was too old to bear transplanting ; (2) age had dulled both his senses and his faculties so that he could hope neither to appreciate the dainties of the royal table nor to enjoy the refinements of court life.

can I hear any more the voice of singing men and
singing women? wherefore then should thy servant be
36 yet a burden unto my lord the king? Thy servant would
but just go over Jordan with the king: and why should
37 the king recompense it me with such a reward? Let thy
servant, I pray thee, turn back again, that I may die in
mine own city, by the grave of my father and my mother.
But behold, thy servant Chimham; let him go over with
my lord the king; and do to him what shall seem good
38 unto thee.   And the king answered, Chimham shall go
over with me, and I will do to him that which shall seem
good unto thee: and whatsoever thou shalt require of
39 me, that will I do for thee.   And all the people went over
Jordan, and the king went over: and the king kissed
Barzillai, and blessed him; and he returned unto his
own place.

40   So the king went over to Gilgal, and Chimham went
over with him: and all the people of Judah brought the
41 king over, and also half the people of Israel.   And,
behold, all the men of Israel came to the king, and said

---

35. the voice of singing men and singing women : David's
interest in music is also attested by our oldest literary prophet,
Amos vi. 5.

36. Render : 'Thy servant would pass on with (or, accompany)
the king but a little way,' deleting **Jordan**, which has come in
through a scribe taking the verb in the more usual sense of passing
over, see above.

39. the king went over : this is premature (see below), and
we must read with Lucian, 'but the king stood still' (Smith,
Budde).   As in xv. 23, where the same error has crept in, the
troops march past the king, who is stationed with Barzillai on the
east bank of the Jordan.

40. Now, at last, David crosses the river to find the men of
Judah waiting to welcome and escort him (see verse 15).   Render
however : 'and all the people of Judah passed on with the king,
and also half the people of Israel.'

41. The northern representatives complain to the king that
their southern fellow subjects had stolen a march upon them—for

unto the king, Why have our brethren the men of Judah
stolen thee away, and brought the king, and his household, over Jordan, and all David's men with him? And 42
all the men of Judah answered the men of Israel, Because
the king is near of kin to us: wherefore then be ye
angry for this matter? have we eaten at all of the king's
cost? or hath he given us any gift? And the men of 43
Israel answered the men of Judah, and said, We have ten
parts in the king, and we have also more *right* in David
than ye: why then did ye despise us, that our advice
should not be first had in bringing back our king? And
the words of the men of Judah were fiercer than the
words of the men of Israel.

And there happened to be there a man of Belial, 20

---

the true explanation see pp. 285 ff.—and were present in their
full strength to welcome the king, while only a fraction apparently
(note 'half the people of Israel,' verse 40) of the north men had
had time to assemble. The last clause should perhaps be read,
with the slightest possible change, 'and *all* David's men are his
people' (Smith, Budde), i.e. are all equally loyal and therefore
entitled to equal treatment.

42. The men of Judah intervene in their own defence, claiming
that theirs is the first place in the king's favour by right of kinship
and of disinterested service. They protest that they had derived
no advantage from their tribal connexion with David. For the
difficulty of text and rendering here, see Driver's *Notes* in loc.

43. The men of Israel retort with the argument of numbers.
For the **ten parts** cf. 1 Kings xi. 31 f. with Skinner's note
(Century Bible).

we have also more right **in David than ye**: an attempt to
translate a corrupt text. Read with LXX and all modern critics:
'and I am also the firstborn rather than thou,' on which 1 Chron.
v. 1 f. is the best commentary.

that our advice ... king: rather (see R.V. marg.), 'and
was not I the first to speak of bringing back my king?' (verse 10).
The historian adds that the reply of the men of Judah was still
more vigorous and heated, but he forbears to give it.

E. 2 Sam. xx. *The Revolt of Sheba.*
The mutual recriminations of north and south culminated, even

whose name was Sheba, the son of Bichri, a Benjamite :
and he blew the trumpet, and said, We have no portion
in David, neither have we inheritance in the son of

2 Jesse : every man to his tents, O Israel.   So all the men
of Israel went up from following David, and followed
Sheba the son of Bichri : but the men of Judah clave
unto their king, from Jordan even to Jerusalem.

3   And David came to his house at Jerusalem ; and the
king took the ten women his concubines, whom he had
left to keep the house, and put them in ward, and
provided them with sustenance, but went not in unto
them.   So they were shut up unto the day of their
death, living in widowhood.

4   Then said the king to Amasa, Call me the men of
Judah together within three days, and be thou here

5 present.   So Amasa went to call *the men of* Judah
together : but he tarried longer than the set time which

6 he had appointed him.   And David said to Abishai,
Now shall Sheba the son of Bichri do us more harm than
did Absalom : take thou thy lord's servants, and pursue
after him, lest he get him fenced cities, and escape out

7 of our sight.   And there went out after him Joab's men,
and the Cherethites and the Pelethites, and all the
mighty men : and they went out of Jerusalem, to pursue

---

before the king had left the Jordan valley, in one of the northern
representatives, a Benjamite noble named Sheba, renouncing his
allegiance to David, and summoning the tribes of Israel to his
standard.   The text is unfortunately in many places uncertain.

1. Sheba's war-cry reappears at a later crisis in the relations
of north and south, 1 Kings xii. 16.

3. David's first public act on his return, necessitated by the
incident recorded xvi. 21 f.

4. Amasa's commission implies that David had kept the promise
of xix. 13.

7. Here we should probably read, with Graetz and later scholars :
'and there went out after Abishai, Joab and the Cherethites,'

after Sheba the son of Bichri. When they were at the 8
great stone which is in Gibeon, Amasa came to meet
them. And Joab was girded with his apparel of war
that he had put on, and thereon was a girdle with a
sword fastened upon his loins in the sheath thereof; and
as he went forth it fell out. And Joab said to Amasa, 9
Is it well with thee, my brother? And Joab took Amasa
by the beard with his right hand to kiss him. But 10
Amasa took no heed to the sword that was in Joab's
hand: so he smote him therewith in the belly, and shed
out his bowels to the ground, and struck him not again;
and he died. And Joab and Abishai his brother pursued
after Sheba the son of Bichri. And there stood by him 11
one of Joab's young men, and said, He that favoureth
Joab, and he that is for David, let him follow Joab.
And Amasa lay wallowing in his blood in the midst of 12
the high way. And when the man saw that all the
people stood still, he carried Amasa out of the high way
into the field, and cast a garment over him, when he saw
that every one that came by him stood still. When he 13

&c. For the last see on viii. 18, and for **the mighty men** see on
x. 7.

8. Amasa came to meet them: Abishai and his command had
only reached Gibeon, about six miles from Jerusalem, when they
met Amasa on his way to the capital with the levies he had
raised. The rest of the verse 'is involved and obscure, though
the fact is effectively concealed in the free rendering of R. V.'
Thus Driver (*Notes* in loc.) who adopts the emendation of Klostermann and reads: 'and as for Joab a sword was in his hand
underneath his warrior's dress (cf. Judges iii. 16), and upon it (i.e.
outside) he was girt with a sword fastened,' &c. In addition to the
usual sword, which slipped from its sheath, Joab like Ehud carried
another in his left hand (verse 10), concealed beneath his military
cloak, and with this he stabbed Amasa.

10. Joab and Abishai his brother: from this point, by his
force of character and experience, Joab becomes the real leader of
the expedition.

was removed out of the high way, all the people went on
after Joab, to pursue after Sheba the son of Bichri.
14 And he went through all the tribes of Israel unto Abel,
and to Beth-maacah, and all the Berites : and they were
15 gathered together, and went also after him.   And they
came and besieged him in Abel of Beth-maacah, and
they cast up a mount against the city, and it stood
against the rampart : and all the people that were with
16 Joab battered the wall, to throw it down.   Then cried
a wise woman out of the city, Hear, hear ; say, I pray
you, unto Joab, Come near hither, that I may speak

---

14. This verse describes the progress of Sheba, not of Joab.
The text, however, is in disorder, and may have originally run
somewhat as follows : 'Now he (Sheba) had gone through all the
tribes of Israel, but they treated him with contempt (so the con-
sonantal text), and he came to Abel-beth-maacah, and all the
Bichrites went after him.'

unto Abel and to Beth-maacah : to be read as one word as
above (cf. next verse), and to be identified with the modern *Abil*
on a strong site about five miles west of Dan (*Tell-el-Ḳādi*) and
the same distance from the sharp bend of the Litany river.

and all the Berites : read as above, 'and all the Bichrites,'
the clan to which Sheba belonged (verse 1).   His following seems
to have been almost confined to his own kinsfolk.

15 f. David's anticipation in verse 6 (end) was fulfilled.   The
details of the siege are obscured by the uncertainty of the text.

they cast up a mount : i. e. a mound of earth (cf. 2 Kings
xix. 32) on which the battering-rams and other engines were
mounted.

and it stood against the rampart (*ḥêl*): ancient cities were
defended, as a rule, by two walls, the city-wall proper, and a
lower wall at a short distance in advance of the other, termed in
Hebrew the *ḥêl* or rampart.   The received text represents Joab
as pressing forward his mound until it reached this first wall, but
for various reasons, textual and other, it is necessary after 'the
city' in the preceding clause to read : 'and there came a wise
woman out of the city and stood upon the rampart, while all the
people that were with Joab were devising means to throw down
the wall, and she said, Hear, hear,' &c.   This assumes that two
lines of the Hebrew MS. have been transposed (Klostermann and
others).

with thee.   And he came near unto her; and the woman 17
said, Art thou Joab? And he answered, I am.   Then
she said unto him, Hear the words of thine handmaid.
And he answered, I do hear.   Then she spake, saying, 18
They were wont to speak in old time, saying, They shall
surely ask *counsel* at Abel: and so they ended *the matter*.
I am of them that are peaceable and faithful in Israel: 19
thou seekest to destroy a city and a mother in Israel: why
wilt thou swallow up the inheritance of the LORD? And 20
Joab answered and said, Far be it, far be it from me,
that I should swallow up or destroy.   The matter is not 21
so: but a man of the hill country of Ephraim, Sheba the
son of Bichri by name, hath lifted up his hand against
the king, even against David: deliver him only, and I
will depart from the city.   And the woman said unto
Joab, Behold, his head shall be thrown to thee over the
wall.   Then the woman went unto all the people in her 22
wisdom.   And they cut off the head of Sheba the son of

---

18 f. Here again the text has suffered. By inserting the words
'counsel' and 'matter' the Revisers get a fair sense, which, however, has little bearing on the situation and leaves 19ᵃ in its
obscurity.. Since Ewald (*Hist. of Israel*, iii. 195), scholars have
given the preference to the Greek text, which runs : 'They were
wont to quote a proverb in old time, saying, Ask in Abel and in
Dan whether anything has ever fallen into disuse which the faithful of Israel had once ordained; but thou seekest to destroy,' &c.
The woman, in other words, reproaches Joab with seeking to
destroy a city which was famed as one of the two most faithful
conservators of Hebrew manners and customs in the country.

a mother in Israel: an important and venerable city with
dependent villages, which in the Hebrew idiom were called its
'daughters' (Num. xxi. 25, 32, and oftener). The phrase 'a
mother in Israel' is elsewhere applied only to Deborah (Judges
v. 7).

20. Joab indignantly repels the woman's impeachment. Only
Sheba the traitor is the object of his quest; if he is given up the
siege will be raised.

22. Read: 'Then the woman went into the city and spake
unto all the people in her wisdom' (cf. LXX).

Bichri, and threw it out to Joab.   And he blew the trumpet, and they were dispersed from the city, every man to his tent.   And Joab returned to Jerusalem unto the king.

23   [R] Now Joab was over all the host of Israel: and Benaiah the son of Jehoiada was over the Cherethites and 24 over the Pelethites: and Adoram was over the tribute: and Jehoshaphat the son of Ahilud was the recorder: 25 and Sheva was scribe: and Zadok and Abiathar were 26 priests: and Ira also the Jairite was priest unto David.

21   [Z] And there was a famine in the days of David

---

xx. 23-6. *A duplicate list of David's chief officers of state.*
This list is a repetition, with some variations in order and contents, of that already given in viii. 16-18.   Its presence here is best explained by Budde's suggestion that the editor who restored chs. ix–xx, which were probably wanting in the first edition of Samuel (see Introduction, sect. v), reproduced the list as an appropriate close to his book.   The arrangement of the various offices is more logical than in ch. viii, as was noted there.

24. Adoram was over the tribute: rather, 'the labour-gangs' or levies (R. V. marg.) raised under the system of corvée or forced labour, an item omitted from the previous list.   Adoram or Adoniram held this office until the reign of Rehoboam (1 Kings iv. 6, xii. 18).

26. Ira .. the Jairite, a member of the Gileadite family of Jair (Num. xxxii. 41), here takes the place of David's sons in viii. 18.

Fourth Division.   2 SAMUEL XXI–XXIV.

AN APPENDIX OF VARIOUS CONTENTS.

These four chapters are universally recognized as a later appendix to the original Book (or Books) of Samuel.   They interrupt the main current of the early narrative in chs. ix–xx, which is now continued in the first two chapters of the Book of Kings.   The contents are of varied character, comprising two additional narratives, two poems, and two lists of David's heroes and their achievements, six sections in all.   The gradual literary process by which the appendix probably assumed its present form has been indicated in the Introduction (p. 23).

three years, year after year; and David sought the face of the LORD. And the LORD said, It is for Saul, and for his bloody house, because he put to death the Gibeonites. And the king called the Gibeonites, and 2 said unto them; (now the Gibeonites were not of the children of Israel, but of the remnant of the Amorites; and the children of Israel had sworn unto them: and Saul sought to slay them in his zeal for the children of Israel and Judah:) and David said unto the Gibeonites, 3 What shall I do for you? and wherewith shall I make

---

(a) xxi. 1–14. *The famine and its consequences for the house of Saul.*

The first and last sections of the appendix are closely related (see on xxiv. 1), and may with comparative certainty be referred to the same source. That this source, though undoubtedly old, was the early document which has just given us the court and family history of David cannot for various reasons be entertained (see below). We propose therefore to group the contents of the appendix with the later additions to the book (e. g. 1 Sam. ii. 1–10) under the symbol Z, without implying that there is any connexion whatever between the very different sections thus indicated.

1. A three years' famine is attributed by a Divine oracle to the fact that Saul had violated the sanctity of a covenant between Israel and the Gibeonites, a crime of sacrilege which could only be expiated by the blood of the house of Saul. 'Few sections of the O. T. show more clearly the religious ideas of the time. We see how Yahweh as the avenger of a broken covenant requires from the children of the offender the blood that has been shed' (H. P. Smith).

It is for Saul and for his bloody house: read by dividing the text differently, 'upon Saul and upon his house (rests) blood,' i. e. as LXX explains, the guilt of blood (cf. Deut. xix. 10 and above xvi. 8). The original narrator gave no explanation of the crime referred to, nor was this required in his day, but a marginal note was appended later and now occupies the greater part of verse 2.

2. This treaty with Gibeon is now recorded in Joshua ix. Another hint of Saul's attempt to exterminate the members of the Gibeonite league has been found by some in an earlier chapter (iv. 2 f.), where perhaps the same annotator has left his mark.

atonement, that ye may bless the inheritance of the
4 LORD? And the Gibeonites said unto him, It is no
matter of silver or gold between us and Saul, or his
·house; neither is it for us to put any man to death in
Israel.   And he said, What ye shall say, that will I do
5 for you.   And they said unto the king, The man that
consumed us, and that devised against us, *that* we should
be destroyed from remaining in any of the borders of
6 Israel, let seven men of his sons be delivered unto us,
and we will hang them up unto the LORD in Gibeah of
Saul, the chosen of the LORD.   And the king said, I
7 will give them.   But the king spared Mephibosheth, the
son of Jonathan the son of Saul, because of the LORD's
oath that was between them, between David and
8 Jonathan the son of Saul.   But the king took the two
sons of Rizpah the daughter of Aiah, whom she bare

---

3. the inheritance of the LORD: the people of Israel as
xiv. 16, xx. 19; 1 Sam. x. 1; xxvi. 19, where see note.

4. The Gibeonites reply (1) that there can be no question of
blood-money as compensation for the blood that Saul had shed (for
the *wergild* among the early Hebrews, see Driver, *Deut.* 234);
(2) that, as Amorites, they have no *locus standi* entitling them
to execute blood-revenge against the Israelite house of Saul.
Therefore, they hint, the king as the supreme justiciar must
intervene.   David understood the hint, and in verse 5 the Gibeonites formulate their demand.

6. we will hang them up unto the LORD: the precise form
of execution denoted by the obscure verb of the original is unknown.   It was certainly not death by strangulation as in xvii. 3.
Probably some form of impalement is intended. See further on
verse 9, also Gray on Num. xxv. 4 (Intern. Crit. Comm.) the only
other occurrence of the word in question.

in Gibeah of Saul, the chosen of the LORD: read, 'in Gibeon
(LXX), in the hill of Yahweh,' the consonants of which greatly
resemble those of the received text.   The site of the execution
was beside 'the great high place' (1 Kings iii. 4) of Gibeon. ·

7. If not a gloss (so Budde) this verse points to a different
source for ch. xxi from that of ch. ix (C).   Cf. on verse 12.

8. Rizpah has been already introduced iii. 7.

unto Saul, Armoni and Mephibosheth ; and the five sons
of Michal the daughter of Saul, whom she bare to Adriel
the son of Barzillai the Meholathite : and he delivered 9
them into the hands of the Gibeonites, and they hanged
them in the mountain before the LORD, and they fell *all*
seven together : and they were put to death in the days
of harvest, in the first days, at the beginning of barley
harvest.   And Rizpah the daughter of Aiah took sack- 10
cloth, and spread it for her upon the rock, from the
beginning of harvest until water was poured upon them
from heaven ; and she suffered neither the birds of the
air to rest on them by day, nor the beasts of the field by
night.   And it was told David what Rizpah the daughter 11
of Aiah, the concubine of Saul, had done.   And David 12
went and took the bones of Saul and the bones of
Jonathan his son from the men of Jabesh-gilead, which
had stolen them from the street of Beth-shan, where the
Philistines had hanged them, in the day that the
Philistines slew Saul in Gilboa : and he brought up from 13

Michal: a slip for 'Merab' (so Lucian and the Syriac version),
see on 1 Sam. xviii. 19.

9. they fell all seven together: in the sense of 'they
perished' with the implication, as always, of a violent death
(*BDB.*, *Heb. Lex.* 657ᵃ). W. R. Smith, taking the words in
a literal sense, has suggested that the seven were hurled from
a precipice (*Rel. Sem.*², 419), but for this a different expression
from that in verse 6 is used in 2 Chron. xxv. 12.   The time of
year was about the latter half of April, so that for six weary
months Rizpah watched by her dead until the October rains
began to fall, showing that Yahweh had accepted the expiation
and was once more gracious to His land (verse 14).   By her
devotion, which artist and poet have vied in commemorating,
she was able to obtain burial for her sons, without which they
would have been debarred from the life—such as it was—in
Sheol.

12. from the street of Beth-shan: if this is not a variant
tradition the expression is to be explained as on 1 Sam. xxxi. 12.

thence the bones of Saul and the bones of Jonathan his
son; and they gathered the bones of them that were
14 hanged.   And they buried the bones of Saul and
Jonathan his son in the country of Benjamin in Zela, in
the sepulchre of Kish his father: and they performed all
that the king commanded.   And after that God was
intreated for the land.
15   And the Philistines had war again with Israel; and
David went down, and his servants with him, and fought
16 against the Philistines: and David waxed faint.   And
Ishbi-benob, which was of the sons of the giant, the
weight of whose spear was three hundred *shekels* of brass
in weight, he being girded with a new *sword*, thought to
17 have slain David.   But Abishai the son of Zeruiah
succoured him, and smote the Philistine, and killed him.

---

14. Zela, also Joshua viii. 28, has not been identified.   The
family burying-place was not in Gibeah.

(*b*) xxi. 15-22.   *A series of exploits against the Philistines.*
This section is entirely of a piece with xxiii. 8 ff., from which it
is now separated by the two poems that follow.   Both sections
may originally have stood in some connexion with the two brief
accounts of David's early struggles with the Philistines, which
now stand in v. 17-25.
15-17. David's narrow escape at Gob.   His head quarters were
still presumably at Hebron: see on v. 17.
and David waxed faint.   And Ishbi-benob, &c.: the text
shows deep-seated corruption (see Driver and H. P. Smith).   The
original may have run as follows: 'and David went down and his
servants with him and dwelt in Gob (an unknown locality), and
they fought with the Philistines.   Then arose —— (a name no longer
recoverable), who was of the sons of the giants,' &c.
16. the sons of the giant (Heb. 'the Raphah,' as margin):
or 'of the giants,' taking the singular in a collective sense.   For
the Rephaim, the remains of a prehistoric population of abnormal
stature, see the Bible dictionaries.
the weight of whose spear: read, 'of whose helmet' (so
Klostermann, Budde) as 1 Sam. xvii. 5.
three hundred shekels of brass: about 13 lbs. avoir., see on
1 Sam. *loc. cit.*   Delete **in weight,** a corruption of 'shekel.'

Then the men of David sware unto him, saying, Thou shalt go no more out with us to battle, that thou quench not the lamp of Israel.

And it came to pass after this, that there was again 18 war with the Philistines at Gob: then Sibbecai the Hushathite slew Saph, which was of the sons of the giant. And there was again war with the Philistines at Gob; 19 and Elhanan the son of Jaare-oregim the Beth-lehemite slew Goliath the Gittite, the staff of whose spear was like a weaver's beam. And there was again war at Gath, 20 where was a man of great stature, that had on every hand

---

18. Another exploit at Gob, for which the Chronicler has Gezer (1 Chron. xx. 4), the Greek and Syrian versions Gath.

Sibbecai the Hushathite: a member of a Beth-lehemite clan (1 Chron. iv. 4).

19. This verse has attracted much attention on account of the variant tradition which it contains regarding the slayer of Goliath. No unbiassed textual critic can escape the conclusion that the true reading here is: 'and Elhanan the son of Jair, the Beth-lehemite, slew Goliath the Gittite.' **Jaare-oregim,** 'woods of weavers,' is frankly nonsense; 'weavers' has come in from the line below, and 'Jaare' is of course a corruption of Jair who appears in the parallel passage 1 Chron. xx. 5. There we read that 'Elhanan the son of Jair slew Lahmi [a corruption of Beth-*lehemite*], the brother of Goliath the Gittite'—an evident endeavour to get rid of the discrepancy between our passage and the received text of 1 Sam. xvii (where see notes for the conjecture that there originally the Philistine giant was anonymous). An appeal to the historical critic, further, gives the result that a statement standing in a fragment of an early narrative—for though the section before us was inserted later into the Book of Samuel it contains ancient material—attributing a certain exploit to an obscure individual, is more likely to represent the actual facts of the case than a statement elsewhere describing the same exploit as the youthful adventure of the most popular hero of his time. (See Cheyne's detailed treatment in *Aids to the devout Study of Criticism*, 80 ff., 125 f.) The present writer's solution of the difficulty has been indicated above, and more fully in the notes on the earlier chapter.

a weaver's beam: see on 1 Sam. xvii. 7.

20 f. A fourth adventure, the scene of which was Gath. For the variant forms of the name **Shimei** see the margin. **Jonathan**

six fingers, and on every foot six toes, four and twenty in
21 number; and he also was born to the giant.   And when
he defied Israel, Jonathan the son of Shimei David's
22 brother slew him.   These four were born to the giant in
Gath; and they fell by the hand of David, and by the
hand of his servants.

22   And David spake unto the LORD the words of this
song in the day that the LORD delivered him out of the
hand of all his enemies, and out of the hand of Saul:
2 and he said,

> The LORD is my rock, and my fortress, and my
>   deliverer, even mine;

3   The God of my rock, in him will I trust;

> My shield, and the horn of my salvation, my high
>   tower, and my refuge;

> My saviour, thou savest me from violence.

4   I will call upon the LORD, who is worthy to be
>   praised:

> So shall I be saved from mine enemies.

---

is apparently the 'brother's son' whose wisdom is noted in 1 Chron.
xxvii. 32 (R. V. marg.).

(c) xxii.   *David's Thanksgiving Hymn.*
More favoured than the Song of Hannah (1 Sam. ii. 1 ff.),
which we found to differ in no respect from a typical psalm, this
great religious poem was received into the earliest of the three
collections of 'sacred songs' which compose the Book of Psalms.
There it now appears, with some unimportant variations, as
Ps. xviii.   Following the precedent of Driver, Smith, and Budde
in their commentaries on Samuel, we propose to refer the student
to the excellent notes by Professor Davison in his commentary
on the Psalms in this series (the Century Bible).   The present
writer, however, does not feel able to go so far as this scholar in
the direction of a 'probable Davidic authorship' (Ps. xcviii),
holding that the Davidic element—if such there be—has now been
so overlaid by the thoughts of a later poet or poets as to be no
longer distinguishable from them.   This being so, it remains
doubtful whether it would not be more scientific frankly to assign
the whole poem to a later age.

For the waves of death compassed me,   5
The floods of ungodliness made me afraid.
The cords of Sheol were round about me: 6
The snares of death came upon me.
In my distress I called upon the LORD,   7
Yea, I called unto my God:
And he heard my voice out of his temple,
And my cry *came* into his ears.
Then the earth shook and trembled,   8
The foundations of heaven moved
And were shaken, because he was wroth.
There went up a smoke out of his nostrils,   9
And fire out of his mouth devoured:
Coals were kindled by it.
He bowed the heavens also, and came down;   10
And thick darkness was under his feet.
And he rode upon a cherub, and did fly: 11
Yea, he was seen upon the wings of the wind.
And he made darkness pavilions round about him,   12
Gathering of waters, thick clouds of the skies.
At the brightness before him   13
Coals of fire were kindled.
The LORD thundered from heaven,   14
And the Most High uttered his voice.
And he sent out arrows, and scattered them;   15
Lightning, and discomfited them.
Then the channels of the sea appeared,   16
The foundations of the world were laid bare,
By the rebuke of the LORD,
At the blast of the breath of his nostrils.
He sent from on high, he took me;   17
He drew me out of many waters;
He delivered me from my strong enemy,   18

From them that hated me ; for they were too mighty
for me.

19   They came upon me in the day of my calamity :
But the LORD was my stay.

20   He brought me forth also into a large place :
He delivered me, because he delighted in me.

21   The LORD rewarded me according to my righteousness :
According to the cleanness of my hands hath he
recompensed me.

22   For I have kept the ways of the LORD,
And have not wickedly departed from my God.

23   For all his judgements were before me :
And as for his statutes, I did not depart from them.

24   I was also perfect toward him,
And I kept myself from mine iniquity.

25   Therefore hath the LORD recompensed me according to my righteousness ;
According to my cleanness in his eyesight.

26   With the merciful thou wilt shew thyself merciful,
With the perfect man thou wilt shew thyself perfect ;

27   With the pure thou wilt shew thyself pure ;
And with the perverse thou wilt shew thyself froward.

28   And the afflicted people thou wilt save :
But thine eyes are upon the haughty, that thou
mayest bring them down.

29   For thou art my lamp, O LORD :
And the LORD will lighten my darkness.

30   For by thee I run upon a troop :
By my God do I leap over a wall.

31   As for God, his way is perfect :
The word of the LORD is tried ;
He is a shield unto all them that trust in him.

For who is God, save the LORD?   32
And who is a rock, save our God?
God is my strong fortress: 33
And he guideth the perfect in his way.
He maketh his feet like hinds' *feet*:   34
And setteth me upon my high places.
He teacheth my hands to war;   35
So that mine arms do bend a bow of brass.
Thou hast also given me the shield of thy salvation: 36
And thy gentleness hath made me great.
Thou hast enlarged my steps under me,   37
And my feet have not slipped.
I have pursued mine enemies, and destroyed them; 38
Neither did I turn again till they were consumed
And I have consumed them, and smitten them 39
    through, that they cannot arise:
Yea, they are fallen under my feet.
For thou hast girded me with strength unto the 40
    battle:
Thou hast subdued under me those that rose up
    against me.
Thou hast also made mine enemies turn their backs 41
    unto me,
That I might cut off them that hate me.
They looked, but there was none to save;   42
Even unto the LORD, but he answered them not.
Then did I beat them small as the dust of the earth, 43
I did stamp them as the mire of the streets, and did
    spread them abroad.
Thou also hast delivered me from the strivings of 44
    my people;
Thou hast kept me to be the head of the nations:
A people whom I have not known shall serve me.

45   The strangers shall submit themselves unto me:
    As soon as they hear of me, they shall obey me.

46   The strangers shall fade away,
    And shall come trembling out of their close places.

47   The LORD liveth; and blessed be my rock;
    And exalted be the God of the rock of my salvation:

48   Even the God that executeth vengeance for me,
    And bringeth down peoples under me,

49   And that bringeth me forth from mine enemies:
    Yea, thou liftest me up above them that rise up
      against me:
    Thou deliverest me from the violent man.

50   Therefore I will give thanks unto thee, O LORD,
      among the nations,
    And will sing praises unto thy name.

51   Great deliverance giveth he to his king:
    And sheweth lovingkindness to his anointed,
    To David and to his seed, for evermore.

23   Now these be the last words of David.

(d) xxiii. 1–7. *David's 'Last Words.'*
The second of the poetical insertions in this appendix is of the nature of a testament, such as Hebrew poets, down to the fall of the Jewish state, loved to put into the mouth of the dying heroes of the past. The so-called blessings of Jacob (Gen. xlix) and Moses (Deut. xxxiii) at once suggest themselves as models from the earlier, the 'Testaments' of the Twelve Patriarchs as illustrations from the later, period of Hebrew literature. Of Davidic authorship there can be no question in this case. The text has suffered greatly in transmission, especially towards the end. The Versions give little help, since ' they differ extraordinarily in their understanding of the Psalm, and their apprehension is usually misapprehension' (H. P. Smith). The first two stanzas or quatrains are of an introductory character.

    1. Now these . . . David: an introduction in prose by the editor who inserted the poem, which begins:
      Oracle of David the son of Jesse,
      Oracle of the man set on high.

David the son of Jesse saith,
And the man who was raised on high saith,
The anointed of the God of Jacob,
And the sweet psalmist of Israel:
The spirit of the LORD spake by me,   2
And his word was upon my tongue.
The God of Israel said,   3
The Rock of Israel spake to me:
One that ruleth over men righteously,
That ruleth in the fear of God,
He shall be as the light of the morning, when the 4
   sun riseth,
A morning without clouds;
When the tender grass *springeth* out of the earth,
Through clear shining after rain.

For similar openings see Num. xxiv. 3, 15, two 'oracles' of Balaam, and Prov. xxxi. The second distich expands the thought conveyed by 'set on high.' David has been greatly honoured both by God and man, for he is

> The anointed of Jacob's God,
> The darling of Israel's songs.

the sweet psalmist of Israel: a rendering open to grave suspicion (see, however, BDB., *Heb. Lex.* 654ª). There seems no reason for departing from the usual connotation of the crucial word in the line (note R.V. marg.), which in i. 23 and Cant. i. 16 is used as a synonym of 'beloved'—the 'beloved' or 'the darling of the songs (or melodies) of Israel'—a rendering altogether more suitable to the parallelism.

2, 3ª. A second quatrain in which David is represented as claiming the inspiration of a prophet as the mouthpiece of Yahweh (cf. Exod. iv. 16, vii. 1).

3ᵇ, 4. A five-line stanza giving the kernel of the oracle in praise of the ideal ruler.

4. Render:

> Like the morning light shall he rise,
> (Like) the sun of a cloudless morn,
> Making the grass to spring (?) from the earth (after rain ?).

The rendering of the last line, which in the original has a word

5 Verily my house is not so with God;
Yet he hath made with me an everlasting covenant,
Ordered in all things, and sure:
For it is all my salvation, and all *my* desire,
Although he maketh it not to grow.

6 But the ungodly shall be all of them as thorns to be
thrust away,
For they cannot be taken with the hand:

7 But the man that toucheth them
Must be armed with iron and the staff of a spear;
And they shall be utterly burned with fire in *their*
place.

8 These be the names of the mighty men whom David

too many for the metre, is quite uncertain. For the probable thought see Ps. lxxii. 6, where the ideal ruler is compared to 'showers that water the earth.'

5. A quatrain in which David recalls the Divine promise of the permanence of his dynasty (vii. 11 ff., 16). The margin shows the straits to which the Revisers were reduced with the traditional text, the first and fourth lines, in particular, being no longer intelligible in their present form. The first should probably read: 'Established is my house with God' (Nestle), for which see vii. 16, 26. For the fourth line we may adopt Smith's conjecture: 'For all my delight is in him.' The closing words of the received text will then belong to the following stanza as in codex B of the LXX.

6 f. Here the original becomes still more corrupt. The student is referred to Driver's *Notes*, and the larger commentaries for more or less plausible emendations.

(e) xxiii. 8-39. *The members of David's two orders of knighthood.*
The remainder of this chapter is occupied with a list of the members of two orders *pour le mérite*, the order of the Three, and the order of the Thirty. The honour of admission to these orders, especially to the order of the Three, seems, like our own Victoria Cross, to have been gained by conspicuous bravery in the face of the enemy. Owing to the similarity of the Hebrew words for 'three' and 'thirty,' and to the ignorance of copyists as to the true significance of the lists, these are now in some confusion, and the names both of persons and of places are frequently corrupt. The list as a whole is repeated in 1 Chron. xi. 11-41,

had: Josheb-basshebeth a Tahchemonite, chief of the
captains; the same was Adino the Eznite, against eight
hundred slain at one time. And after him was Eleazar 9
the son of Dodai the son of an Ahohite, one of the three
mighty men with David, when they defied the Philistines
that were there gathered together to battle, and the men
of Israel were gone away: he arose, and smote the 10
Philistines until his hand was weary, and his hand clave
unto the sword: and the LORD wrought a great victory
that day; and the people returned after him only to

---

and in part in 1 Chron. xxvii. 2-15 (see Driver's arrangement in
parallel columns, *Notes* 278 f.).

xxiii. 8-12. *The Order of the Three.*
To this, the higher order, belonged Ish-baal, the 'chief of the
Three,' Eleazar and Shammah. Joab is conspicuous by his absence.
8. Josheb-basshebeth a Tahchemonite: these names are not
'probably,' as the margin has it, but most certainly corrupt. The
first is a disfigured form of Ish-bosheth (so the LXX), itself a disguise for Ish-baal (see on ii. 8); the second should be read 'the
Hachmonite' (cf. 1 Chron. xi. 11, xxvii. 32).
chief of the captains: the last word is very uncertain.
Lucian read 'chief of the Three,' which gives an excellent sense.
In other words, Ish-baal was the commander of the order.
the same was Adino the Eznite: a curious corruption either
of 'he lifted up,' or rather 'he wielded his spear,' as in the parallel
text of Chronicles (cf. verse 18 below), or of 'he wielded his axe
(Marquardt, Budde, which is nearer the received text) against
eight hundred,' &c. This remarkable feat of arms procured
Ish-baal his admission into the order.
9. The second member of the Three was **Eleazar, the son of
Dodai** (or Dodo, see on 1 Sam. xvi. 13) the **Ahohite**—so read
with Chronicles.
with David when they defied, &c.: read, with Chron., 'he
was with David at Pas-dammim, when the Philistines were
gathered together there to battle.' The place is called Ephes-
dammim in 1 Sam. xvii. 17. The last clause belongs to the next
verse.
10. Read: 'And when the men of Israel ... he arose,' &c.
H. P. Smith cites, from Doughty's *Arabia Deserta*, ii. 28, an
interesting modern parallel to this feat.

11 spoil.   And after him was Shammah the son of Agee
   a Hararite.   And the Philistines were gathered together
   into a 'troop, where was a plot of ground full of lentils;
12 and the people fled from the Philistines.   But he stood
   in the midst of the plot, and defended it, and slew the
13 Philistines : and the LORD wrought a great victory.   And
   three of the thirty chief went down, and came to David
   in the harvest time unto the cave of Adullam ; and the
   troop of the Philistines were encamped in the valley
14 of Rephaim.   And David was then in the hold, and the
15 garrison of the Philistines was then in Beth-lehem.   And
   David longed, and said, Oh that one would give me
   water to drink of the well of Beth-lehem, which is by the
16 gate !   And the three mighty men brake through the

---

11. The third member was **Shammah the son of Agee,** the
scene of whose adventure was 'at Lehi' (Judges xv. 9)—so read
for **into a troop.**

xxiii. 13-17ᵃ.   *An act of devotion of three of the Thirty to David.*
The famous episode of the water from the well of Beth-lehem,
loosely connected with what precedes and follows, owes its
place here apparently to the opinion of an editor that the three
paladins of the well were the three heroes above commemorated.
Its proper place is after the Thirty have been enumerated,

13. The word 'chief' is wanting in the best texts of LXX, and
is unnecessary.   **In the harvest time** is an attempt to render
two words of which the first is 'unto' and the second something
which the Chronicler read as 'the rock.'   For **unto the cave** read
'to the hold,' or fortress of Adullam (see on 1 Sam. xxii. 1, and
2 Sam. v. 18).

15 ff. The adventure that follows has in all ages appealed to
the generous instincts of humanity.   David longs for a draught
from the well of his boyhood!   Through the Philistine army
encamped in the valley of Rephaim (see on v. 18) the three
heroes cut their way into the town of Beth-lehem, and having
drawn the water return as they went.   But the self-sacrifice of
'the dauntless three,' who took their life in their hand for love of
their king, had in his eyes changed the water into blood.   As blood
it belonged to God, and so was poured out as an offering to the
King of kings.

host of the Philistines, and drew water out of the well of Beth-lehem, that was by the gate, and took it, and brought it to David: but he would not drink thereof, but poured it out unto the LORD. And he said, Be 17 it far from me, O LORD, that I should do this: *shall I drink* the blood of the men that went in jeopardy of their lives? therefore he would not drink it. These things did the three mighty men. And Abishai, the 18 brother of Joab, the son of Zeruiah, was chief of the three. And he lifted up his spear against three hundred and slew them, and had a name among the three. Was 19 he not most honourable of the three? therefore he was made their captain: howbeit he attained not unto the *first* three. And Benaiah the son of Jehoiada, the son 20 of a valiant man of Kabzeel, who had done mighty deeds,

---

17. The last sentence is rather the conclusion of the narrative of the achievements of the three in verses 8-12, another indication that 13-17ᵃ has got displaced.

xxiii. 18-23. *The achievements of Abishai and Benaiah.*
Between the story of the Three and the list of the Thirty of whom no special deeds of heroism are recorded the author inserts an eulogium of Abishai, the chief or commander of the order of the Thirty, and of Benaiah the most distinguished ordinary member of that body.

18. chief of the three: read, 'chief of the Thirty,' with the Syriac and all moderns. Abishai's achievement was considerably below that of the real chief of the Three (verse 8).

and had a name among the three: the author cannot have thus contradicted himself (see verse 19 end). We should read, with Smith and Budde, 'so he gat himself a name like that of the three.'

19. Read: 'behold, he was more honourable than the Thirty (so 1 Chron. xi. 25 R. V.), and became their captain, but unto the Three did he not attain.'

20. The text of the description of Benaiah is very uncertain. Read, perhaps, 'a man of valour, and a man of many achievements, a native of Kabzeel.' This last was a southern town on the border of Edom (Josh. xv. 21).

he slew the two *sons of* Ariel of Moab: he went down
also and slew a lion in the midst of a pit in time of snow:
21 and he slew an Egyptian, a goodly man: and the Egyptian had a spear in his hand; but he went down to him
with a staff, and plucked the spear out of the Egyptian's
22 hand, and slew him with his own spear. These things
did Benaiah the son of Jehoiada, and had a name
23 among the three mighty men. He was more honourable
than the thirty, but he attained not to the *first* three.
And David set him over his guard.

24   Asahel the brother of Joab was one of the thirty;

---

he slew the two sons of Ariel of Moab: the Revisers have
adopted the Greek text, the Hebrew lacking the word for 'sons
of' (cf. A. V. 'two lion-like men of Moab'). Of the various attempts to recover the original form of the sentence, Klostermann's
has at least the merit of simplicity. Starting from the Greek text,
as above, he obtains by a slight emendation: 'he slew the two
young lions (*lit.* sons of the lion) in their lair, after he had gone
down and slain the lion (himself) in the midst of a pit,' &c. The
mention of the **time of snow** suggests the means by which the
lions were tracked.

21. a goodly man: read, a man of great stature,' with the
Chronicler (1 Chron. xi. 23), who adds the popular comparison of
the Egyptian's spear to 'a weaver's beam' (see 1 Sam. xvii. 7,
2 Sam. xxi. 19).

22 f. This eulogy of Benaiah has to be emended as in verses 18 f.
It has been suggested that these two heroes, Abishai and Benaiah,
were in modern phrase gazetted for promotion to the order of the
Three when a vacancy should occur.

23. over his guard: the royal bodyguard, composed of the
foreign mercenaries, the Cherethites and the Pelethites (viii. 18,
xx. 23).

xxiii. 24-39. *The members of the Order of the Thirty.*
The fact that the first on the list is the youngest of the three
sons of Zeruiah, who was slain by Abner (ii. 18 ff.) while David
was still in Hebron, shows that these orders were instituted very
early in David's reign. It also suggests that the vacancies were
filled up from time to time by other candidates, which is probably
the explanation of the fact that considerably over thirty names are
given in the list that follows. Few of these knights are mentioned
elsewhere.

Elhanan the son of Dodo of Beth-lehem; Shammah the 25
Harodite, Elika the Harodite; Helez the Paltite, Ira the 26
son of Ikkesh the Tekoite; Abiezer the Anathothite, 27
Mebunnai the Hushathite; Zalmon the Ahohite, Maharai 28
the Netophathite; Heleb the son of Baanah the Neto- 29
phathite, Ittai the son of Ribai of Gibeah of the children
of Benjamin; Benaiah a Pirathonite, Hiddai of the 30
brooks of Gaash; Abi-albon the Arbathite, Azmaveth 31
the Barhumite; Eliahba the Shaalbonite, the sons of 32
Jashen, Jonathan; Shammah the Hararite, Ahiam the 33
son of Sharar the Ararite; Eliphelet the son of Ahasbai, 34
the son of the Maacathite, Eliam the son of Ahithophel
the Gilonite; Hezro the Carmelite, Paarai the Arbite; 35
Igal the son of Nathan of Zobah, Bani the Gadite; 36
Zelek the Ammonite, Naharai the Beerothite, armour- 37
bearers to Joab the son of Zeruiah; Ira the Ithrite, 38
Gareb the Ithrite; Uriah the Hittite: thirty and seven 39
in all.

And again the anger of the LORD was kindled against 24

(*f*) xxiv. *David's census and its consequences.*

The last entry in the appendix to Samuel consists of a document which may be described as the charter of the most famous of the world's holy places. By the theophany here recorded the threshing-floor of Araunah the Jebusite received a consecration which has made it holy ground not only for Judaism and Christianity, but for Islam as well. Upon this spot, we can scarcely doubt, stood the great altar of Solomon's temple. To-day, as all the world knows, the site is covered by the magnificent mosque, the *Kubbet es-sahra*, or Dome of the Rock, the most sacred of Mohammedan shrines after those of Mecca and Medina. In contents and style the narrative before us shows a marked affinity with that of chap. xxi. Both tell the tale of man's trespass and the judgement that followed, and how the anger of the Deity was finally appeased, and 'God was intreated for the land' (xxi. 14, xxiv. 25). The incidents of both are probably to be referred to the beginning of David's reign over all Israel. This chapter has been carefully edited by the Chronicler in his characteristic manner. Indeed, the variations are so numerous that Budde is of

Israel, and he moved David against them, saying, Go,
2 number Israel and Judah. And the king said to Joab
the captain of the host, which was with him, Go now to
and fro through all the tribes of Israel, from Dan even
to Beer-sheba, and number ye the people, that I may
3 know the sum of the people. And Joab said unto the
king, Now the LORD thy God add unto the people, how
many soever they be, an hundredfold, and may the eyes
of my lord the king see it: but why doth my lord the
4 king delight in this thing? Notwithstanding the king's
word prevailed against Joab, and against the captains

---

opinion that the narrative in Chronicles (1 Chron. xxi) may rest
on a different recension of the text from that to which we now
proceed.

1. The opening words, **And again,** are best taken as referring
to the incidents of xxi. 1-14, of which this chapter is probably the
continuation.

　and he moved David against them: namely, Israel (for the
verb in a similar connexion see 1 Sam. xxvi. 19, R.V., 'stirred
up'). The conception of the Deity in the author's mind seems
a reflection of the idea, not yet obsolete, of an oriental ruler to
whose absolutism there are no bounds. Yahweh is incensed
against Israel—it is not for His subjects to ask the why or the
wherefore—and David is made the instrument of His anger. Of
surpassing interest for the study of the progressiveness of
revelation in the O. T. period is the form which the Chronicler
has given to this verse. To his more developed religious sense
the idea was abhorrent that God could be subject to moods, and
incite men to a course of action for which He afterwards calls
them to account. Accordingly he writes: 'And *Satan* stood up
against Israel, and moved David to number Israel' (1 Chron. xxi.
1). Wherein the sinfulness of the numbering consisted our
narrator does not say. Probably in the popular thought of the
time it was regarded as a sinful ambition on the part of the
creature to possess a secret which the Creator intended should be
His alone.

　2. Joab the captain of the host: read, as required by verse
4, 'Joab and the captains of the host who were with him.' The
object of the census, we may gather from this, was the preparation of a register of all the males capable of bearing arms
(cf. verse 9).

of the host. And Joab and the captains of the host went out from the presence of the king, to number the people of Israel. And they passed over Jordan, and 5 pitched in Aroer, on the right side of the city that is in the middle of the valley of Gad, and unto Jazer: then they came to Gilead, and to the land of Tahtim- 6 hodshi; and they came to Dan-jaan, and round about to Zidon, and came to the strong hold of Tyre, and to all 7 the cities of the Hivites, and of the Canaanites: and they went out to the south of Judah, at Beer-sheba. So when they had gone to and fro through all the land, 8 they came to Jerusalem at the end of nine months and twenty days. And Joab gave up the sum of the number- 9 ing of the people unto the king: and there were in Israel eight hundred thousand valiant men that drew the sword;

---

5. and pitched in Aroer: read with LXX (L): 'and they began from Aroer, and from the city which is in the midst of the valley (wady) towards the Gadites, and on to Jazer,' the first part *verbatim* as in Deut. ii. 36. Aroer, the modern *Arâir*, lay on the north bank of the Arnon, now the *Wadi Mojib*, which formed the southern boundary of Israelitish territory on the east of the Jordan.

Jazer was the frontier town towards Ammon (Num. xxi. 24, LXX). The enumerators thus began work at the extreme south, and worked their way northwards to the Jabbok.

6. Then followed the district of **Gilead**, between the Jabbok and the Yarmuk.

and to the land of Tahtim-hodshi: an evident corruption for which we must either substitute Lucian's text, 'to the land of the Hittites towards Kadesh,' the Hittite capital on the left bank of the Orontes, or adopt one or other of the more recent conjectures, for which see *EBi.* iv. col. 4888 f.

Dan-jaan: read either, 'and they came to Dan (the modern *Tel-el-Kâdi* at the base of Hermon), and from Dan they went round towards Zidon' (Wellh., Driver), or 'they came to Dan and Ijon (see 1 Kings xv. 20), and went round,' &c. (Klost., Budde). The enumerators now proceed to take a census of Western Palestine from Dan in the north to Beer-sheba, the modern *Bir-es-Seba*, in the south.

9. The numbers, as usual, have not been consistently handed down (cf. Chron. and Lucian), and may safely be regarded, even

and the men of Judah were five hundred thousand men.

10 And David's heart smote him after that he had numbered the people. And David said unto the LORD, I have sinned greatly in that I have done: but now, O LORD, put away, I beseech thee, the iniquity of thy

11 servant; for I have done very foolishly. And when David rose up in the morning, the word of the LORD

12 came unto the prophet Gad, David's seer, saying, Go and speak unto David, Thus saith the LORD, I offer thee three things; choose thee one of them, that I may

13 do it unto thee. So Gad came to David, and told him, and said unto him, Shall seven years of famine come unto thee in thy land? or wilt thou flee three months before thy foes while they pursue thee? or shall there be three days' pestilence in thy land? now advise thee, and consider what answer I shall return to him that sent

14 me. And David said unto Gad, I am in a great strait: let us fall now into the hand of the LORD; for his mercies are great: and let me not fall into the hand of

15 man. So the LORD sent a pestilence upon Israel from

---

at the lowest figure in any of the texts, as considerably exaggerated.

10. After the census had been concluded, David, conscience-stricken, makes humble confession of his sin.

11. The prophet **Gad** has been already introduced, 1 Sam. xxii. 5.

12. I offer thee : literally and more graphically, 'I hold over thee' (cf. R. V. marg.).

13. seven years : read with the Chronicler, 'three years,' which makes the duration of the offered judgements three years, three months, and three days respectively.

14. David chooses the plague—'the sword of Yahweh,' as it is termed in 1 Chrón. xxi. 12—for God is more merciful than man.

15. The Greek text is here preferred by recent scholars : 'So David chose the pestilence ; and it was the days of the wheat harvest when the pestilence began among the people, and there

the morning even to the time appointed: and there died of the people from Dan even to Beer-sheba seventy thousand men. And when the angel stretched out his 16 hand toward Jerusalem to destroy it, the LORD repented him of the evil, and said to the angel that destroyed the people, It is enough; now stay thine hand. And the angel of the LORD was by the threshing-floor of Araunah the Jebusite. And David spake unto the LORD when 17 he saw the angel that smote the people, and said, Lo, I have sinned, and I have done perversely: but these sheep, what have they done? let thine hand, I pray thee, be against me, and against my father's house.

And Gad came that day to David, and said unto him, 18 Go up, rear an altar unto the LORD in the threshing-floor of Araunah the Jebusite. And David went up 19 according to the saying of Gad, as the LORD commanded. And Araunah looked forth, and saw the king and his 20 servants coming on toward him: and Araunah went out, and bowed himself before the king with his face to the

---

died,' &c. 'The circumstantiality and force' of this form of the narrative—seventy thousand victims though the plague had only just begun—'constitute a presumption in favour of its originality, as against the more colourless and ordinary narrative of the Hebrew text' (Driver, *Notes*, in loc.).

16. Reading this as the sequel of the emended text in the preceding verse, we have a striking justification of David's confidence in the Divine mercy (verse 14), for the plague, as we have seen, had but begun when Yahweh stayed the hand of the destroying angel. Jerusalem, in particular, was still spared.

Araunah: in Chron. Ornan, in LXX, Ornah (see R.V. marg.), one of the original Jebusite inhabitants of the city.

17. Compare the more circumstantial account, 1 Chron. xxi. 16.

18 ff. The spot where the angel's hand was stayed is to be consecrated for all future ages by the erection of an altar to Yahweh.

20. The Chronicler adds the information that 'Araunah was threshing wheat,' cf. the restored text of verse 15.

21 ground.   And Araunah said, Wherefore is my lord the
king come to his servant?   And David said, To buy the
threshing-floor of thee, to build an altar unto the LORD,
22 that the plague may be stayed from the people.   And
Araunah said unto David, Let my lord the king take
and offer up what seemeth good unto him : behold, the
oxen for the burnt offering, and the threshing instruments
23 and the furniture of the oxen for the wood : all this, O
king, doth Araunah give unto the king.   And Araunah
said unto the king, The LORD thy God accept thee.
24 And the king said unto Araunah, Nay ; but I will verily
buy it of thee at a price : neither will I offer burnt offerings unto the LORD my God which cost me nothing.
So David bought the threshing-floor and the oxen for
25 fifty shekels of silver.   And David built there an altar

22 f. Araunah asserts that there is no need for David to *buy*
the threshing-floor, everything is at his sovereign's disposal for
the contemplated sacrifice ; but see on verse 23.

the threshing instruments and the furniture of the oxen :
the former are the wooden sledges still in use in Syria.   They
are driven over the corn, the ears of which are stripped from the
stalk by the sharp flints with which the under surface of the
sledge is set (see illustration *EBi.* i. col. 83).   The **furniture**
consisted of the wooden yokes by which the oxen were harnessed
to the sledges (1 Kings xix. 21).   Cf. the proceedings 1 Sam.
vi. 14.

23. Read : 'the whole doth the servant of my lord the king
give unto the king' (see Driver, *Notes*).   This offer must not be
taken seriously.   Like the similar offer of Ephron the Hittite
(Gen. xxiii. 11), it is merely a part of the conventional courtesy
which still regulates buying and selling in the Nearer East.

24. The fine thought to which David here gives utterance
underlies all true sacrifice.   In the older Hebrew religion this
principle may have had its limitations (cf. Mic. vi. 6 ff.), in the
religion and ethics of Christianity it has none.

fifty shekels of silver :   under £7 sterling, valued as bullion,
but of course of immensely greater purchasing power.   The price
is small compared with that paid for the cave of Machpelah
(400 shekels, Gen xxiii. 16).   The Chronicler raises the price to

unto the LORD, and offered burnt offerings and peace offerings.   So the LORD was intreated for the land, and the plague was stayed from Israel.

6oo shekels of gold, *circa* £1200.   For the values see the writer's article 'Money' in Hastings' *DB*. iii. 420.

25. That the site of David's altar corresponded with that of Solomon's altar of burnt-offering, and that both are now occupied by the Dome of the Rock, are points on which there is a general agreement among scholars (see Skinner's *Kings* in this series, Appendix, note 1).

APPENDIX

Note A. The Ark in the Books of Samuel [1]

The importance of the Ark in the religious history of the Hebrews, and the prominent place which it occupies in the earliest sources of Samuel, demand a slightly more extended study of this unique object of the Hebrew cultus than was possible in the notes. The term 'Ark,' from the Latin *arca*, a chest, is the rendering (since Wiclif, 1380) suggested by the Vulgate of the Hebrew *'ārōn*, a chest, as the word is rendered 2 Kings xii. 10 f. Either alone or in the combination 'Ark of the Covenant,' to be presently explained, the Ark has become the usual designation among us of the sacred chest in which were deposited, according to the *latest* form of the ecclesiastical tradition, 'a golden pot holding the manna, and Aaron's rod that budded, and the tables of the covenant' (Heb. ix. 4). It is instructive, however, to note the different names or titles of the Ark in the different strata of Hebrew literature.

(a) *The Titles of the Ark in the O.T.* In the O.T. the Ark is mentioned close on 200 times, and by at least twenty-two different designations. But if the simplest name of all 'the Ark' (fifty-four times) is set aside as scarcely a title, these many designations are found to fall into three groups. (1) In our oldest extant sources, which are precisely those of Samuel (A, M, and C), followed by the prophetic source JE of the Hexateuch [2], we find 'the Ark of Yahweh—by every token the earliest designation of all—alternating with 'the Ark of God,' which, however, appears in several instances to have been substituted for the other. (2) In Deuteronomy and the writings of the Deuteronomic school (see pp. 10 ff.) the favourite designation of the decalogue is the *běrîth*, in our versions rendered covenant, but in this connexion properly 'law' or even 'decalogue,' as is evident from Deut. ix.

---

[1] This Note may be regarded as supplementing, and to some extent correcting, the writer's article 'Ark' in Hastings' *DB*. vol. i, to which the reader is referred for points not touched upon here.

[2] It is remarkable that in the Pentateuch the Ark is mentioned in this source *only three times*, namely, Num. x. 33, 35 f., xiv. 44, and afterwards in the early chapters of Joshua (iii, iv and vi).

9, 11, 15, 'the tables of the *bĕrîth*' or decalogue, which Moses placed in the Ark (x. 5). From this circumstance the Ark bears, in Deuteronomic writers, the title 'Ark of the *bĕrîth*' (R. V. covenant), that is, 'the chest containing the decalogue.' The *seventh century* author of Deuteronomy, it should be noted, is the first in our extant literature to associate the Ark with the tables of the law, or *even with contents of any sort* (see below). The last-cited title, however, although so familiar to us as 'the Ark of the covenant,' occurs but a few times, and that exclusively in the Deuteronomistic parts of Joshua. The more usual form is 'the Ark of the law (*bĕrîth*) of Yahweh,' rarely varied by 'the Ark of the law of God.' In some half-dozen passages of pre-Deuteronomic writings it is evident on grammatical and other grounds that the word *bĕrîth* has been inserted in one or other of the older titles (so in Joshua iii. 11, 14, 17; 1 Sam iv. 3, 4, 5). (3) In the Priests' Code (P), and here only, is found the designation 'the Ark of the testimony' (thirteen times), again equivalent to 'the chest containing the decalogue,' P's favourite term for which is 'the testimony.'

Turning now to the Books of Samuel, we find the Ark mentioned no fewer than sixty-one times[1], under seven separate designations, viz. 'the Ark of God' (twenty-four), 'the Ark of Yahweh' (twenty), for which is substituted in the mouth of the Philistines 'the Ark of the God of Israel' (seven times, 1 Sam. v. 7 ff., vi. 3), 'the Ark' simply, four times. In four other passages we have the composite forms 'the Ark [of the covenant] of Yahweh,' or 'of God' (iv. 3, 4, 5[2]; xv. 24, a gloss). The two references that remain (1 Sam. iv. 4; 2 Sam. vi. 2, see note on the latter) show greatly expanded titles, the most distinctive parts of which contain the formula 'the LORD of hosts, which sitteth upon the cherubim.' As regards the first part, the Divine name, Yahweh Ṣebaoth, has already been explained (p. 37) as denoting Yahweh as 'the God of the armies (or hosts) of Israel' (1 Sam. xvii 45). The qualifying epithet unites two streams of influence, the one the primitive conception of the cherubim as the storm-clouds, the visible manifestation in nature of Yahweh (2 Sam. xxii. 11), the other the later conception of the cherubim as the guardians of the Ark, in the temple of Solomon. In the cases before us, therefore, the phrase

---

[1] Of these the two occurrences, 1 Sam. xiv. 18, should be deleted as glosses (see the notes), also the post-redactional gloss, 2 Sam. xv. 24. On the other hand, an original mention in 2 Sam. xii. 12 should be restored (see note).

[2] These, it will be observed, are the *first three* references out of twenty-seven in the document A, but even in these the LXX has preserved the older and original forms.

'that sits enthroned upon the cherubim' is a late expansion of
the original titles, suggesting the Ark as the earthly throne of
Yahweh (cf. Davison's *Psalms* (*Cent. Bible*), i. 361 f.).

(*b*) *The special significance of the Ark in Samuel.* In almost
every reference in the oldest pre-Deuteronomic sources, above
specified, to the Ark—which must be thought of as a simple chest,
very different from the gold-covered shrine of the Priests' Code
(Exod. xxv. 10 ff.) with its mercy-seat and over-arching cherubim
—*it is associated with war and the national militia of Israel* (Num.
xiv. 42 ff. ; Joshua vi. 6 ff. ; 1 Sam. iv. 3 ff. ; 2 Sam. xi. 11, xii. 12,
emended text). Its presence with the host on the battlefield is
the guarantee of victory (1 Sam. iv. 3), its absence the cause of
defeat, as at Eben-ezer, and as on an earlier occasion at Hormah
(Num. xiv. 44 f.). War was a religious exercise, begun with
sacrifices and prayer; the warriors were 'the consecrated ones'
(see on 1 Sam. xiii. 9) ; the battles of His people were Yahweh's
battles (xviii. 17), and Yahweh Himself bears the name of Yahweh
Sebaoth, 'the God of the armies of Israel' (xvii. 45).

The earliest of all the extant references to the Ark connects it
with the fact of war. In the ancient poetical fragment, Num. x.
35 f., which may well have been taken from the collection entitled
'the book of the wars of Yahweh' (Num. xxi. 14), is preserved
the prayer with which the Ark was sent forth to battle :

'Arise, O Yahweh, and let thine enemies be scattered,
   Let them that hate thee flee before thee.'

Also that with which its return was welcomed :

'Return, O Yahweh, unto the myriad clans of Israel.'

In these, it will be noted, *the Ark is addressed directly as Yahweh.*
The same identification of the Ark with Yahweh meets us in the
early source A of Samuel. 'Let us fetch the Ark of Yahweh,' is
the resolution of the Hebrew sheikhs after the defeat at Eben-ezer,
'that He (not 'it' as in R.V.) may come unto us and save us' (1
Sam. iv. 3 ; cf. the Philistines' comment in verses 7 f.). Its capture
is described in the striking words, 'the Glory has departed (lit. 'has
gone into captivity') from Israel' (verse 21 f.) ; where 'the Glory'
is a synonym for Yahweh. This identification is so complete that,
on the return of the Ark, the men of Beth-shemesh exclaim, 'who
is able to stand before this holy God' (vi. 20). At a later time
David played and danced, even as he sacrificed, 'before Yahweh,'
inasmuch as these acts were done before the Ark (2 Sam. vi. 5 ff. ;
cf. Joshua vii 6 ff.).

In all these early passages, then, it is clear that the Ark is
identified with the presence of Yahweh. It is not, as is generally held, a mere symbol of that presence. This must not be

understood in a crass, material sense, as if the Ark were a fetish, or contained one or more fetishes in the shape of meteoric stones or stones from the original abode of Yahweh on Horeb, as is the almost universal opinion of German scholars, of Cheyne in this country (*EBi.* i. 307), and Moore in America (*EBi* ii. 2155). The key to the problem is to be sought elsewhere [1].

In the tangled skein of traditions respecting the wilderness wanderings of the children of Israel and the guides provided for them through the desert, now found in scattered fragments of our Pentateuch sources, we find, in addition to Jethro (Num. x. 29 ff., compared with Judges i. 16) and the Ark (Num. x. 33), mention made of 'the angel of Yahweh' (Exod. xxiii. 20 ff.), the pillar of cloud and of fire (*passim*), and finally the mysterious 'Face' or 'Presence (*pānim*) of Yahweh' (Exod. xxxiii. 6 f.)[2]. Now these three last mentioned are, in the conception of the writers, varying degrees of the personal manifestation of Yahweh to His people. In the angel this 'temporary descent to visibility' on the part of Yahweh assumes human form, the cloud is the visible representation of the 'Glory of Yahweh' (for which see Kautzsch in Hastings' *DB.*, extra vol. 639 f.), while *the ark is the supreme embodiment of the 'Presence of Yahweh.'* Thus when Moses expresses himself as dissatisfied with the promise of the 'angel of Yahweh' to go before the tribes on their march to Canaan (Exod. xxxii. 34, xxxiii. 2), he obtains the further promise of what is evidently a fuller manifestation in the shape of 'the Presence,' which is even identified with Yahweh. 'My presence shall go with thee, and I will give thee rest' (xxxiii. 14 f.). This fundamental passage is the original both of Deut. iv. 37, 'he brought them out by his presence,' and of Isa. lxiii. 9, which must be read: 'neither a messenger nor an angel, but his presence delivered them.'

Had we only the good fortune to have access to one or other of the prophetic sources, J and E, we are convinced that the Ark would have been explicitly brought into connexion with the mysterious *pānim*, the Face, or Presence, of Yahweh. Higher than the temporary visibility of the angel, and than the more lasting but still transitory 'glory' of the cloud, the Ark remained as a permanent possession, at once the highest embodiment of Yahweh's presence and the substitute for that still more complete presence of Yahweh in person, which no man could see and live (xxxiii. 20).

We are here in a region of primitive conceptions where it is

---

[1] When the writer first expounded the following explanation in public (1903), a subsequent speaker remarked that 'the Ark had been at once emptied and glorified'!

[2] For this difficult *theologoumenon*, see now Kautzsch in Hastings' *DB.*, extra vol. 639; Lagrange, *Rev. Biblique*, 1903, 215 ff.

difficult for us moderns to feel at home. But the expression of Yahweh's 'face' or 'presence,' as a synonym for Yahweh's 'self,' had its origin in Hebrew usage, by which the person of royalty was described as the king's 'face,' or 'presence,' a usage indeed not unknown among ourselves. Thus, to take an illustration from the Book of Samuel, Hushai urges the advantage to Absalom's army of 'thy Presence (='your Majesty') marching in the midst of them' (2 Sam. xvii. 11 ; cf. R. V. marg. and the notes). Similarly Absalom a few years earlier 'saw not the king's face' (xiv. 24, 28), i. e. he was not admitted to 'the royal presence.' The writer hopes elsewhere to show that even in the earlier parts of the O. T. the Ark originally was explicitly identified with the 'Presence' of Yahweh. The further discussion of the question here would require citation of the Hebrew texts, and is therefore unsuitable for this already too extended note.

(c) *The stay of the Ark at Kiriath-jearim* (cf. pp. 217 f. above). Another problem of great difficulty, raised by the fortunes of the Ark in Samuel, is the unaccountable neglect of this guarantee of the 'presence of Yahweh' during the period covered by the narrative from 1 Sam. vii to 2 Sam. vi. This neglect has been described with truth as 'one of the most singular circumstances of a singular age' (*Oxf. Hexateuch*, i. 81). The merit of having first recognized and grappled with the problem belongs to the late Professor Kosters of Leiden, who propounded the view that the account of the voluntary restitution of the Ark by the Philistines, now given in 1 Sam. vi, is unhistorical (*Theol. Tijdschrift*, 1893, 361 ff.). The Ark, according to Kosters, remained in the safe custody of the Philistines at Gath in the house of Obed-edom until forcibly retaken by David in the course of his Philistine campaigns, to which a brief allusion is made in 2 Sam. xxi. 20 ff. David took the precious relic first to Kiriath-jearim pending the preparation of proper quarters in Jerusalem, or even the capture of the fortress itself.

The antiquity and general credibility of the early source A is fatal to Koster's theory. But some explanation of the long continued inaccessibility of the Ark is urgently required. The following is put forward as a probable theory, developing a suggestion by Karl Budde, to account for the facts as known to us from the present fragmentary record. During the period in question Kiriath-jearim, which we know to have been a member of the Gibeonite league (Joshua ix. 17), and therefore a predominantly Amorite or Canaanite city, was under Philistine suzerainty, although not situated in Philistine territory. The Philistines, it is true, sent the dangerous representative of the God of Israel (vi. 3) forth from the confines of Philistia, but it still remained within the sphere of their political jurisdiction, and so was inaccessible to the Hebrew authorities. It may even be conjectured that Saul's mysterious 'zeal' against the Gibeonites and other members of the league (cf. 2 Sam. xxi. 2, with note on iv. 2 f.) was not unconnected with an attempt on his part to recover the ancient palladium of the Hebrew tribes. At Kiriath-jearim the Ark remained until David's victory, in the campaign initiated in 2 Sam. vi. 1, rescued the city from the Philistine power, and with it the Ark of Yahweh (see note on vi 1, p. 218) [1].

NOTE B.   BIBLIOGRAPHY OF SAMUEL

THE following are the most important recent works for the study of Samuel, in addition to the standard histories of Ewald, Stade, Kittel (whose work, *The History of the Hebrews* (2 vols.), now translated, is of great value for the study of the sources), Wellhausen, and H. P. Smith, and the elaborate articles on the Books of Samuel by Stade and Stenning in *EBi.* and Hastings' *DB.* respectively.

(*a*) *Commentaries.*

H. P SMITH *A Critical and Exegetical Commentary on the Books of Samuel*, 1899.

A. KLOSTERMANN. *Die Bücher Samuelis und Könige*, 1887.

O. THENIUS. *Die Bücher Samuelis erklärt*, 3rd edition by Dr. Max Löhr, 1898 (with a valuable parallel synopsis and criticism of the analysis of the sources).

K. BUDDE. *Die Bücher Samuelis erklärt*, 1902.

W. NOWACK. *Die Bücher Samuelis übersetzt und erklärt*, 1902.

(*b*) *Aids for literary and textual criticism.*

S. R. DRIVER. *The Literature of the Old Testament.*

——*Notes on the Hebrew Text of the Books of Samuel.*

K. BUDDE. *Die Bücher Richter und Samuel.*

—— *The Books of Samuel. A Critical Edition of the Hebrew Text* (in Haupt's *Sacred Books of the Old Testament*).

J. WELLHAUSEN. *Die Composition des Hexateuchs und der historischen Bücher des A. T.*

—— *Der Text der Bücher Samuelis.*

A. KUENEN. *Historisch-kritisch Onderzoek, etc.*

C. H. CORNILL. *Einleitung in das A. T.*

W. H. BENNETT and W. F. ADENEY. *A Biblical Introduction.*

N. PETERS. *Beiträge zur Text- und Literarkritik der Bücher Samuel* (conservative).

(*c*) *To these may be added:*

G. A. SMITH. *Historical Geography of Palestine.*

F. BUHL. *Geographie des alten Palästina.*

---

[1] For the probable ultimate fate of the Ark, see Hastings' *DB.* i. 150.

INDEX

omissions and alterations, *passim*; *see Homoeoteleuton*.

Theocracy, theocratic ideal, ruler, &c., 16 f., 24, 28, 67, 71 ff., 94 f., 99.

Thirty, Order of the, 308, 310, 312 f.

Thousand, technical sense of, 75, 124, 132, 151, 158, 278.

Three, the Order of the, 308 ff.

Threshing-floor of Araunah, 313, 317 f.

Tithes, 76.

Tob, 237 f.

Toi, king of Hamath, 231.

Torture, punishment by, 249 f.

Tribute (= forced labour, corvée), 296.

Trophies, military, in sanctuaries, 61, 149.

Tumours, 62 ff., 66.

Tyre, 214, 315.

Uriah, the Hittite, 241 ff., 264, 313.

Urim and Thummim, 106 f., 154, 178.

Uzzah, 219 f.

Vow, 39, 41, 263.

Wagons, place of the, 124, 169 f.

War, consecration for, *see* Consecration.

War-taboos, 99, 147 f., 241 f.; cf. Taboos.

Watches (night), 90.

Water in ritual, 70; cf. 310.

Weaning, age of child, 41.

Weaver's beam explained, 123.

Witch, witchcraft, wizard, 113 f., 176 ff.

Women in the cultus, 38.

Worship, 36 ff., 38 f., 140 f.; *see* 'Detained,' Sacrifice.

Yahweh, form and significance of the name, 36 f.; not put into the mouth of non-Israelites, 58; the national God of Israel, as Chemosh of Moab, &c., 171 f., 228; *see* further under 'Lord,' also, Covenant, Israel; replaced by Satan in Chronicles, 314; *see* also Oath.

Zadok, 51, 232 f., 266 ff., 285 f., 296.

Zadokite priesthood, 51 f., 225, 267.

Zeruiah, sons of, 170, 209; *see* Abishai, Joab

Ziba, 234 ff., 269 f., 287 ff.

Zidon, 315.

Ziklag, 174, 182 ff., 211.

Zion, 213 f., 265, 267.

Ziph, Ziphites, 156 ff., 168 ff.

Zobah, 108, 230 f., 237 f.

Zuph, Zuphite, 35 f., 78.